Irish Catholicism and Science

From 'Godless Colleges' to the
'Celtic Tiger'

IRISH CATHOLICISM AND SCIENCE
From 'Godless Colleges' to the
'Celtic Tiger'

DON O'LEARY

First published in 2012 by
Cork University Press
Youngline Industrial Estate
Pouladuff Road, Togher
Cork, Ireland

British Library Cataloguing in Publication Data
A CIP catalogue record for this book is available from the British Library.

ISBN-978-185918-497-4
Printed in Spain by Grafo
Typeset by Tower Books, Ballincollig, Co. Cork
www.corkuniversitypress.com

*For Kate
and for Karen, Kevin,
Sarah, and Claire*

Contents

Acknowledgements

I am indebted to the two anonymous readers for their very helpful comments on an earlier draft of this work. I am grateful to Fr Fergus O'Donoghue (S.J.), Archivist, Society of Jesus (Dublin), for access to the Edward J. Coyne (S.J.) papers; to the Board of Management, Blackrock College (Dublin), for access to the Alfred O'Rahilly papers; and to the Board of Trinity College Dublin for access to the John Joly papers. Information from documents in the papers of Thomas Larcom and William Monsell is published in this book with the permission of the Board of the National Library of Ireland.

Don O'Leary,
University College Cork, 1 November 2011.

Introduction

In the nineteenth century advances in the historical and natural sciences demonstrated that some Biblical narratives were not literally true. Geology, for example, undermined literal interpretations of some verses in the first chapter of Genesis. Chapters six, seven, and eight of Genesis, giving an account of the Flood, had lost credibility – at least if interpreted in a literal sense – due to progress in the zoological, geological and geographical sciences.[1] The impact of historical criticism was even greater than that of the natural sciences. The 'higher criticism' of the Bible was pioneered in Germany and spread outwards from there. In England it provoked widespread controversy with the publication of *Essays and Reviews* (1860) by a number of liberal Anglicans. The tempestuous debates provoked by *Essays and Reviews* overshadowed the controversy which followed the publication of *The Origin of Species* by Charles Darwin (1809–1882) in the previous year.[2]

Although progress in the disciplines of history and science converged to create difficulties for sustaining belief in the veracity of scriptural narratives, especially as understood in a literal sense, and weakened the influence of religion to some extent, it did not send religious belief into an irreversible downward spiral. Most people were not able to evaluate the truth or falsity of complex scientific theories on a philosophical or a scientific basis and they tended to regard their religious beliefs as far more important than science.[3] Generally, Catholics trusted their church to decide the meaning of scripture. Therefore, when scientific theories seemed to contradict church teaching, science was rejected rather than religion. It was religion rather than science that informed their thinking. Science was not a major concern for most Catholics.[4] This was particularly true of Catholic Ireland in the 1860s when Darwin's theory was hotly debated, especially in Western Europe and North America. In the first decade after the publication of the *The Origin of Species*, discussions about evolution made little impact. There was also a lack of interest in evolution amongst Irish Protestants in the 1860s.[5] According to L. Perry Curtis, *The Origin of Species* stimulated 'only a few ripples in Ireland, and most of those barely reached the outer perimeter of the Anglo-Irish Pale.'[6]

All of the above may suggest that, at least for the mid-nineteenth century, there is little to discuss about the relationship between Irish Catholicism and science, beyond an attitude of mutual indifference. This would be true if Irish Catholicism could be understood entirely within the parameters of theology and devotional practices. There would be little to explore if the practice of science was a purely objective study of nature, free of external influences. But of course scientific research, and the dissemination of scientific knowledge, does not occur in a cultural vacuum. Social, economic, and political circumstances have to be taken into account.[7] The history of science is, and has to be, studied in an international context, but historians have for quite some time realised that there are also regional and national dimensions to be considered. The same points apply to the history of religion. It cannot be understood within the narrow confines of theology and devotional practices without taking cognisance of the wider cultural milieu in which it is embedded. It too has its regional, national and international dimensions. Varied responses to developments in modern science occurred within, as well as between, Christian denominations. For example, the Presbyterians of Edinburgh, Belfast and Princeton adopted different stances concerning evolutionary theories – despite their similar theological positions. Local circumstances played a very important role in determining attitudes.[8] Therefore, in reference to Roman Catholicism, it should not be surprising that, at national level, every Catholic community has had its own unique experience of modern science. The Irish Catholic experience is yet to be explored and elucidated.[9]

There is of course a critically important external or international dimension to be explored. The Vatican exerted enormous influence over the Roman Catholic Church, especially from the late nineteenth century onwards. Any analysis, therefore, has to take cognisance of what emanated from the capital of international Roman Catholicism. In matters of faith and morals, Irish Catholicism was profoundly affected by the pronouncements of the Vatican. Therefore, Irish Catholicism, to a large extent, reflected the Vatican's attitude towards science, especially concerning controversial scientific theories which created problems for the maintenance of traditional religious beliefs. There is, however, a danger of oversimplification here. Although there is an obvious and inextricable linkage between the papacy and Irish Catholicism, it does not follow that there were no socio-political agencies of change at work, unique to Ireland, which conditioned the formation of perspectives therein. These social and political conditions were in turn profoundly influenced by developments in Britain, especially before the creation of the Irish Free State.

There are two important aspects to the British dimension. Firstly, the views of English Catholics will be examined in instances where these impinge directly on Irish theological discourse. This necessitates an examination of the opinions of a number of authors, including John Henry Newman, St George Jackson Mivart, Bertram C. Windle and John S. Vaughan. Secondly, some eminent scientists in Britain, most notably Thomas Henry Huxley and John Tyndall, argued that religious faith, especially that of the Roman Catholic Church, was irreconcilable with science. Their polemical stance contributed very much to the emergence of some antipathy against mainstream science in Irish Catholic culture in the late nineteenth century.

In this book the period under examination will extend from the mid-nineteenth century to the dawn of the twenty-first. However, there are limits, imposed by necessity rather than by choice, to the ascertainment of Irish Catholic opinions. The ideas of Catholic authors are amenable to investigation, but cognisance must be taken of the fact that the vast majority of Irish Catholics never put their views about science on record. In this matter, and in others, they were not unusual. The subjectivity of religious belief and the lack of reliable statistical information rules out any definitive conclusions grounded on precise quantitative data.[10] It can be argued, in general terms, that writers do not necessarily represent the views of their readership and that the readership, especially in a population where there is very limited access to higher education, are not representative of the population at large. There is a distinction to be made between press opinion and public opinion. Records of meetings of societies, and private papers such as diaries and letters, allow very little progress to be made in evaluating public opinion with confidence.[11] Can we then know anything about Irish Catholic attitudes towards those scientific theories which impinged on Catholic doctrine? There is a strong argument for answering in the affirmative. Firstly, there was a very high degree of conformity in Irish Catholicism to the articles of Catholic faith as defined by Rome. Secondly, there was a very close relationship between the Irish Catholic clergy and the laity from the late nineteenth century to the late twentieth century. Indeed the bond between priests and people was so strong that an American bishop remarked that the Irish even believed in the infallibility of their priests.[12] On the basis of the above, it can be argued that those Irish Catholics who were aware of the theological implications of scientific theories generally deferred to the judgement of the institutional church. It is also highly probable that many Catholics, contending with poverty and deprived of access to higher education, were either unaware of, indifferent to, or unable to understand the controversies which sometimes troubled their more economically advantaged co-religionists.

On casual reflection it may seem that Ireland is a poor choice for this topic – a small country of little influence on the western edge of Europe, with a dismal record in scientific innovation and of little consequence in the vast international organisation of the Roman Catholic Church. Such a perception of Ireland would be grossly inaccurate on all counts – with the exception of the geographical description. Firstly, the small size of the Catholic population belied its role in international Roman Catholicism. In the nineteenth century Irish Catholicism became

> a world-wide phenomenon in the English-speaking world. Not only did the Roman Catholic Churches in England and Scotland become essentially Irish, but the Churches in the United States, English-speaking Canada, South Africa, Australia, and New Zealand were all strongly influenced by the developing values and mores of Irish Roman Catholicism.[13]

Secondly, Ireland has made important contributions to the progress of science and technology, especially from about 1780 to 1880. The achievements of Irish scientists have been discussed elsewhere and do not require elaboration here.[14]

The history of science is an essential element of cultural history and there is an increasing awareness of this. The publication of a number of books in recent years is indicative of such awareness. These books include *Science and Society in Ireland: The Social Context of Science and Technology in Ireland, 1800–1950* (1997), edited by Peter J. Bowler and Nicholas Whyte; *Nature in Ireland: A Scientific and Cultural History* (1997), edited by John Wilson Foster and Helena C.G. Chesney; *Science, Colonialism and Ireland* (1999) by Nicholas Whyte; *Prometheus's Fire: A History of Scientific and Technological Education in Ireland* (2000), edited by Norman McMillan; *Recoveries: Neglected Episodes in Irish Cultural History, 1860–1912* (2002), by John Wilson Foster; *Science and Irish Culture: Why the History of Science Matters in Ireland* (2004), edited by David Attis and Charles Mollan; *Science and Ireland: Value for Society* (2005), edited by Charles Mollan; *Communities of Science in Nineteenth-Century Ireland* (2009) by Juliana Adelman; and *Science and Technology in Nineteenth-Century Ireland* (2011), edited by Juliana Adelman and Éadaoin Agnew.

Social and economic changes in Ireland, and elsewhere, cannot be understood without taking cognisance of scientific and technological developments. Furthermore, the central role of the Roman Catholic Church in Irish society is not seriously contended. Therefore, there is considerable merit in examining the interaction between Irish Catholicism and science. A number of authors, including Juliana Adelman, Nicholas Whyte, Greta Jones, John Wilson Foster, Dorinda Outram, Thomas Duddy and Miguel DeArce, have addressed some aspects of Irish Catholic attitudes towards science. Some of my research work to date impinges upon, or is directly concerned with, this topic.[15] However, these works, collectively, have touched only lightly on the subject. There is still a pressing need for an in-depth study of Irish Catholicism and science.

'Science' in this work generally refers to the physical and natural sciences, encompassing a number of disciplines, including physics, cosmology, astronomy, geology, chemistry, biology and agricultural science. Irish Catholic periodicals gave attention to a diverse range of topics within these subject areas – evolution, thermodynamics, speculations about extraterrestrial life, the Heisenberg uncertainty principle, the Big Bang, the role of chemistry in industrial development, the extraction of iodine and potash from Irish seaweed, crop rotation, magnetism, radio astronomy, polymers, jet propulsion, atomic weapons, nuclear energy, photosynthesis, isotopes in biological research, and developments in electronics – to name but a few.[16] Not all of these matters will receive attention in this book – selective emphasis and exclusion is necessary if a clear narrative is to emerge.

What then is the basis for selecting some subjects for study whilst excluding others? Why are some subjects examined at great length while others are merely mentioned? Topics which receive the most attention are those which facilitate the elucidation of Catholic opinions about science and which had implications – positive or negative – for Catholic doctrine, provoking concern, and sometimes controversy. Therefore, evolutionary biology receives more attention than any other scientific subject.

Many journal articles were merely factual reports, summarising the latest discoveries in science, but were irrelevant to religious ideas and shed relatively little light on the status of science in Irish Catholic culture. There is little point in discussing, at length, the fine details concerning the extraction of iodine and potash from Irish seaweed, laboratory testing of silage and its potential to boost dairy production in winter, Robert Millikan's research on cosmic rays, or Hideki Yukawa's theory of nuclear forces – to give but a few examples. These subjects were examined in Irish Catholic periodicals[17] but were not recurring themes and were not especially relevant to Irish Catholic concerns. The first two examples are relevant to the history of science in twentieth-century Ireland but do not contribute significantly to an understanding of science in an Irish Catholic context. Some developments in science and technology, such as the development of nuclear weapons and genetically modified crops, are important issues for Catholic ethical discourse generally but have not received much attention from Irish Catholic authors, and thus will not be subjected to detailed scrutiny.

Consideration was given to the inclusion of a discussion on bioethical issues arising from developments in science and technology in recent decades. In view of the complexity of bioethics, it was decided to address such topics as *in vitro* fertilisation and stem cell research elsewhere.[18] Furthermore, there is very little in common between bioethical issues and the range of subjects studied in this text. There would, therefore, be a lack of thematic continuity between the ten chapters of this text and those addressing bioethics.

No book can be reasonably expected to provide the last word on its subject matter. A case in point is J.H. Whyte's excellent work, *Church and State in Modern Ireland*, first published in 1970. Similarly, there is much scope for further research about how Irish Catholics responded and contributed to developments in science. It is hoped that this book will play an important role in stimulating such research – which is long overdue.

1. Politics, Religion and Science, 1840s–1874

Catholic Under-representation in Science

In his seminal essay, 'Irish Thought in Science', Gordon L. Herries Davies observed that the top tier of the scientific profession in nineteenth-century Ireland was very much the domain of Protestants, despite their minority status. In a survey of fifty eminent scientists, Davies discovered only seven were Roman Catholic.[1] The work of James Bennett led to a similar finding. In his survey of scientists of 'significant standing', he found that only about 10 per cent were Roman Catholic and that a very large majority of Protestant scientists were members of the Church of Ireland.[2] Catholics were clearly under-represented in science in nineteenth-century Ireland.[3] Why did this occur? It might be assumed that there was something in Irish Catholic culture which was inherently anti-scientific. In her essay, 'Catholicism, Nationalism and Science', Greta Jones argued that there was nothing predetermined or inevitable about the marginalised status of science in Catholic nationalist Ireland. That strange collective entity, 'the Irish psyche . . . literary and intuitive rather than scientific and positivist' – created *ex nihilo* by some commentators on Irish culture – did not create the problem nor contribute to it.[4] This finding is supported by Juliana Adelman. She concluded in her *Communities of Science in Nineteenth-Century Ireland* (2009) that Irish Catholics were not averse to science. Although science did not feature strongly in the rhetoric and aspirations of the Irish nationalist movement – which became more and more associated with Catholicism – this was not due to a campaign by the Catholic Church in Ireland against science.[5]

Published works on, or relating to, the history of science in Ireland indicate that there were a number of interconnected social, economic and political reasons for the weakness of science in Irish Catholic culture. Catholic Ireland was predominantly rural, and lacking a strong and

1

diverse industrial base, did not have the resources to produce substantial numbers of scientists and engineers.[6] The central importance of agriculture in the economy would suggest that agricultural science would prosper. This did not occur. Faculties of agriculture were closed down in the Queen's Colleges in 1865 and in the Royal College of Science for Ireland a few years later because of the failure to attract sufficient numbers of students. Those who could afford to send their children to college did not generally have a high opinion of agriculture in terms of career prospects or as a way of life. Farm work was not held in high esteem relative to professions such as law. Furthermore, it seems that memories of the Great Famine of the 1840s worked against an interest in agriculture.[7]

The Great Famine had a devastating effect on lower-income Catholics, in particular. The constant struggle for survival and economic security would have made it extremely difficult to cultivate an interest in science. Those who were relatively affluent had much greater opportunities to pursue scientific study and research.[8] Privileged members of the Anglo-Irish Ascendancy had their 'places of knowledge' – such as libraries, observatories, botanical gardens and private museums;[9] and they engaged in intellectual debates taking place in England rather than in Ireland.[10]

Davies argued that Catholic under-representation in science could not be explained on the basis of a lack of good educational opportunities open to them. In support of this contention, he gave examples of English and Scots of 'humble origins' who had risen to eminence in science.[11] Nicholas Whyte, in his *Science, Colonialism and Ireland* (1999), took issue with Davies on this point. He argued that the poor educational opportunities open to Catholics, arising from their relatively poor economic status, needs to be considered in conjunction with the fact that Irish society was sharply divided at the time.[12] This social divisiveness worked against the progress of Catholics in science because the practice of science was carried out mainly in institutions dominated by the Protestant Ascendancy, such as Trinity College Dublin (the only college of the University of Dublin)[13], the Royal Irish Academy and the Royal Dublin Society. Whyte found that Catholics suffered discrimination at the hands of Protestants in these institutions.[14] Furthermore, the interest of many Catholics with the financial means to pursue higher education was probably diminished by their perception of science as an activity strongly linked to Protestantism and foreign influence.[15] There would have been considerable justification for opinions about foreign influence in this context. The institutions of Irish science came increasingly under the control of the English-based Department of Science and Art from 1853 when the department was founded. Irish science, therefore, was to a large extent controlled by civil servants in London.[16]

Adverse economic conditions, Protestant discrimination and the association of science with Protestantism and foreign influence do not entirely explain the weakness of science in Irish Catholic nationalist culture. The Irish Catholic bishops contributed very substantially to the problem, especially in relation to the issue of university education for Catholics (this will be discussed later). It can be argued that their authoritarian and censorial proclivities contributed to the weakness of science in Irish Catholic culture. The Irish ecclesiastical authorities were adverse to Enlightenment science and did not approve of Catholics participating in public debates about evolutionary theories.[17] They were hostile to intellectual freedom and feared the emergence of a secular intelligentsia that would challenge their own power and influence. Many of those who were intellectually gifted were recruited by the seminary at Maynooth. Such a repressive environment proved detrimental to higher learning, not least in theology. A consequence of this was that the church did not produce a single theologian comparable in eminence to John Henry Newman, Reinhold Niebuhr or Friedrich Schleiermacher.[18]

It would be easy to exaggerate the weakness of science in Irish Catholicism. Irish Catholic culture was certainly not devoid of science. Catholics who rose to prominence in science in Ireland include Fr Nicholas Callan (1799–1864), Sir Robert Kane (1809–1890) and William Kirby Sullivan (1822–1890). Callan, Professor of Natural Philosophy at Maynooth, undertook research in electromagnetics, an area of inquiry which posed no problems for theology. He made important contributions to the development of electromagnets, induction coils and electric batteries. In 1837 he sent a scaled-down replica of his induction coil to a fellow scientist and friend, William Sturgeon (1783–1850). Sturgeon in turn demonstrated it to members of the Electrical Society of London, many of whom copied it. Callan's scientific research contributed to later developments in science, such as innovations in the construction of electrical transformers, the generation of X-rays, electrical discharges in rarefied gases and advances in the study of atomic structure.[19]

Kane and Sullivan, both chemists, served consecutive terms as president of Queen's College Cork – Kane from 1845 to 1873, Sullivan from 1873 to 1890. Kane was one of the first Roman Catholics to graduate from the University of Dublin. In 1832 he became a licentiate of the King's and Queen's College of Physicians. However, his main scientific interests were in chemistry and he published several papers on this subject. He was also highly accomplished as an administrator and was director of the Museum of Irish Industry[20] (1845–1867) throughout its short existence.[21] In his best-known work, *The Industrial Resources of Ireland* (1844), he focused attention on the need for industrial education as part of a scheme to assess and exploit the island's natural resources. It was envisaged that this would in turn generate much-needed economic progress in Ireland. Kane's book greatly enhanced his reputation well beyond the scientific community and elicited praise from politicians, including the British Prime Minister, Sir Robert Peel, and Thomas Davis (1814–1845), a leading figure in the Irish nationalist movement, Young Ireland. Kane was a tireless advocate of popular scientific and industrial education without reference to 'class, creed or gender.'[22]

Kane's Museum of Irish Industry gave many people a measure of access to scientific and industrial education who otherwise would not have had the means to attend lectures. This was done under the Committee of Lectures' scheme from 1854 to 1865, worked out under the auspices of the Department of Science and Art in London. Information about plans to abolish the museum and place its resources under the control of the Royal Dublin Society was published in Irish newspapers in April 1863. This provoked such widespread opposition that the British government reversed its policy.[23] Kane's philosophy of access to education for all, regardless of class, religion or gender, continued when the museum was reformed in 1867 to become the Royal College of Science for Ireland (1867–1926).

In the mid-nineteenth century a public culture of science emerged in a number of European states. Science became more and more integrated into the cultural life of 'polite' society. Ireland was not an exception to this trend. The practice and promotion of science occurred in institutions such as Trinity College Dublin, the Royal Irish Academy, the Royal Dublin Society, the Queen's Colleges, St Patrick's College (Maynooth) and the Museum of Irish Industry. The importance attached to science was also evident from the activities of voluntary organisations such as the Belfast Natural History Society, the Dublin Natural History Society, the Cuvierian Society of Cork and the Galway Mechanics' Institute.[24] Increasing interest in science was further indicated by a number of developments, such as the conferences of the British Association for the

Advancement of Science held in Cork, Dublin and Belfast and the Dublin International Exhibition of 1853. The cult of science proliferated to some extent beyond urban centres to rural communities where scientific lectures, *conversaziones* and exhibitions were frequently held. Scientific knowledge was disseminated beyond the environs of academia and specialist societies to a much wider constituency through the medium of periodicals such as the *Dublin Penny Journal*, the *Dublin Literary Journal and Select Family Advertiser*, the *Belfast Monthly Magazine* and the *Kilrush Magazine and Monthly Journal of Literature and Useful Information*.[25]

Science was seen by unionists and nationalists alike as having an important role to play in the economic development of the nation. In theory, it had the potential to erode or even submerge political and sectarian tensions and was seen by some of those in government in this light. It was perceived as an antidote to intemperance, ignorance and immorality. Its pursuit would help to keep men away from the pubs, promote a spirit of self-improvement, and enhance intellectual development. Scientific endeavour would lead to an avoidance of vices arising from idleness. Science was seen as highly compatible with religious belief because it was thought to inculcate a way of reasoning that would condition the mind to be more receptive to religious truths. It is highly significant that it drew support from both Protestants and Catholics. The Catholic priest Daniel Cahill, although otherwise *persona non grata* in Protestant circles, received praise from Protestant clergymen for his provincial science lectures. It seems that the growth of the Catholic middle classes in the mid-nineteenth century was a critically important element in the increased interest in science amongst Irish Catholics.[26] Irish Catholic culture was clearly not totally without scientific enterprise. Nevertheless, relatively few practising scientists in Ireland were Catholic; and some of those that were, such as William Kirby Sullivan and Henry Hennessy (1826–1901), were aware that science as institutionalised and practised in Ireland, was not culturally or politically neutral.[27]

It can be argued that political developments in Britain and mainland Europe, adversely affecting the Roman Catholic Church, worked indirectly to consolidate a repressive cultural milieu in Ireland which made it more difficult for Catholics there to engage constructively with those controversial scientific ideas that seemed to contradict Catholic doctrine. The Catholic clergy of Ireland were very much aware of anti-Catholic tendencies in mainland Europe and in Britain.

In the nineteenth century, especially up to 1878, the Roman Catholic Church responded poorly to a wide range of social, economic, political and intellectual developments that were transforming Western Europe. Liberalism, frequently associated with anti-clericalism, was perceived as a grave threat to the church and elicited a hostile response from the Vatican. Pope Gregory XVI's encyclical *Mirari Vos* (1832) condemned principles such as the separation of church and state, freedom of religion, and freedom of the press. The *Syllabus of Errors*, issued with the encyclical *Quanta Cura* (1864), repudiated almost all the core principles of modern liberal democracies such as freedom of religious belief and practice (propositions 15, 77, 78), the separation of church and state (proposition 55), and the autonomy of academic disciplines such as philosophy (propositions 10, 11, 14 and 57). The eightieth and final proposition, that the 'Roman Pontiff can, and ought to, reconcile himself and come to terms with progress, Liberalism and modern civilization', was rejected outright.[28]

The *Syllabus* was written very much with Italian circumstances in mind, especially pertaining to the *Risorgimento*. Therefore, when the papacy refused to reconcile itself with 'progress, Liberalism and modern civilization', it was rejecting the Piedmontese government's version of these ideas, which, from a papal point of view, meant anti-clerical measures such as the closure of convents and monasteries and the establishment of secular education in direct opposition to the wishes of the Catholic church. The *Syllabus*, outside Italy, was generally not interpreted with Italian circumstances in mind, nor was it reasonable to expect otherwise. The Catholic hierarchies of most Western states experienced difficulties with their governments, and public opinion expressed its disapproval.[29] English Catholics attempted to explain, with very little success, that the pope condemned only the excesses and ideological errors of liberalism, and not liberalism as generally understood in England.[30]

The Catholic Church, under the pontificate of Pius IX (1846–1878), found itself increasingly in conflict with the political systems of Western Europe. After the revolutions of 1848 the power and privilege of the church declined sharply. At various times in the last half of the nineteenth century the governments of Italy, France, Germany, Spain, Austria and Belgium took action against the church which led to the closure of Catholic schools, the dissolution of monastic orders, and the confiscation of church property.[31] In September 1870 Italian troops entered Rome, extinguishing the last remnant of the Papal States and completing the process of Italian reunification.[32] This was a bitter blow to the prestige of the papacy, and Pope Pius IX thereafter regarded himself as a prisoner in the Vatican. In northern Europe, which was predominantly Protestant, the church frequently found itself on the defensive. In Germany, Chancellor Otto von Bismarck (1815–1898) presided over the *Kulturkampf* ('cultural struggle') against the minority Catholic population from 1872 to 1887. Bismarck regarded Catholics as enemies of the Reich. It seemed, from a conservative Catholic perspective, that the church was under siege from a convergence of enemy forces which were growing more powerful day by day.

Anti-Catholicism was also rife in England and permeated all social, political and religious sectors, from labourer to aristocrat, from Anglican to Protestant Dissenter, from right-wing Tory to left-wing Liberal.[33] It was expressed in a number of different forms and was at its most extreme amongst evangelical Protestants, who regarded the pope as the anti-Christ. Claims were frequently made that the Catholic faith was a gross distortion of Christianity. Liberals emphasised the church's restriction on the rights of conscience and rationalists denounced Catholicism as superstitious and detrimental to the progress of science. Those agnostics who had been Protestant remained anti-Catholic long after they had abandoned their faith. By the 1870s anti-Catholicism in England had declined but it still remained a powerful underlying force in society.[34] The promulgation of papal infallibility by Vatican Council I in 1870 worked against the amelioration of conditions of Roman Catholics in Britain. It greatly antagonised British Protestants, especially when it coincided with the growth of Anglo-Catholic practices in the Anglican Church.[35] Doubts were raised about the Anglican Church's ability to function as a reliable protector against the encroachment of Catholic power, which had grown robustly in England since the restoration of the hierarchy in 1850. Anti-Catholic sentiments were further intensified by developments in Ireland.

During the pontificate of Pius IX the papacy strengthened its control over the Catholic Church. In Ireland, Cardinal Paul Cullen acted as the pope's 'chief whip.'[36] The ultramontane or centralising movement within the church, concurrent with the 'devotional revolution',[37] was triumphant over the older and more independent form of Irish Catholicism. Under Cullen's primacy and reforming zeal, the Catholic Church in Ireland was brought into greater conformity with Rome, ecclesiastical discipline was sternly enforced, and there was a far greater standardisation of religious observances. In matters of doctrine the conservatism of the Irish Catholic clergy was based very much on the neo-Tridentine tradition and as the century progressed they became closely associated with the defensive policies of the papacy.[38] A close relationship existed between the priests and their congregations and the great majority of Irish Catholics were drawn into secure loyalty to Rome.[39]

In the late 1860s and early 1870s the growth and invigoration of Roman Catholicism, increasing electoral support for the Home Rule movement in Ireland, the convergence of interests between Irish Catholicism and Home Rule,[40] and the Vatican Council's decree of papal infallibility all combined to raise British Protestant fears that democracy would be subverted by Catholic priests. The Home Rule party was viewed as a puppet of the ultramontane Catholic hierarchy.[41]

The strong alignment between the Home Rule movement and the objectives of the Irish Catholic bishops, especially concerning the issue of denominational education, probably played a key role in creating considerable antipathy between Irish Catholicism and those who endeavoured to free science from external influences. John Tyndall (1820–1893),[42] Thomas Henry Huxley (1825–1895),[43] Sir John Lubbock (1834–1913), Sir Joseph Dalton Hooker (1817–1911) – all members of the X Club – were unionists;[44] so also were the majority of eminent scientists in late Victorian Britain.[45] Many scientists were opposed to Home Rule for political and religious reasons similar to those who were not scientists. Furthermore, they were frequently against Home Rule because they feared that the future of science in Ireland would not prosper under the jurisdiction of an Irish parliament. There was concern, against the background of the university question (which will be examined in the next section of this chapter), that the teaching of evolutionary theory would be curtailed to assuage Catholic theological concerns. It was also feared that the network of relationships between scientists in Britain and Ireland would be disrupted, which in turn would adversely affect science, especially in Ireland.[46] Tensions arose between the interests of science and the interests of Roman Catholicism in Ireland, which were due to a convergence of religious, political and economic developments internal and external to the island.

'Godless Colleges' and the Catholic University

Many Irish Catholic clergymen felt that their church was particularly vulnerable in a Protestant-dominated empire that had become extensively secularised. Their sense of vulnerability was clearly evident in their determination to exert control over the education of Catholics. In addressing the issue of higher education for Irish Catholics, the ecclesiastical authorities demanded a Catholic university for a Catholic people. This would satisfy three essential requirements. The institution would be set up on the basis of a Catholic ethos. It would be staffed by Catholic teachers, and its curricula would be in conformity with Catholic requirements.[47] The Irish Catholic hierarchy did not regard the University of Dublin (Trinity College Dublin), dominated by Protestants, as suitable for the education of Catholics because it was believed to be dangerous to their faith.[48] In 1845 the bishops insisted that six subjects – history, metaphysics, moral philosophy, logic, geology and anatomy – would be hazardous to the faith and morals of Catholic students if not taught by Catholic professors.[49]

The English liberal Catholic Wilfrid Ward stated, in evidence to the Royal Commission on University Education in Ireland (1901–1903), that the Irish Catholic bishops sought the fulfilment of four conditions if their approval of the Queen's Colleges was to be forthcoming. They sought a 'fair proportion' of Catholic professors and assurances of 'due influence' in the appointment of professors. They demanded dual professorships in history, metaphysics, moral philosophy, logic, geology and anatomy, which were perceived as often the medium of disseminating anti-Christian ideas. They insisted that any professor or any other member of staff who attempted to undermine a student's religious faith should be dismissed. Their fourth demand was for a salaried dean or chaplain.[50] The bishops persisted in their opposition to the Queen's Colleges because they believed that the faith of Catholic students was not safeguarded in these institutions.

The attitude of disapproval towards the existing system of third-level education by the Irish Catholic bishops was not unusual. In France the dominant role of the state in higher education, anti-clericalism, and the rigorous exclusion of religion from the system motivated the French bishops to set up five higher educational institutes in Paris, Lille, Angers, Lyon and Toulouse in 1875 – after nearly fifty years of struggle and at great cost to loyal Catholics.[51] In England and Wales the bishops there admonished Catholics not to attend Oxford and Cambridge. However, in 1895 the Catholic hierarchy of England and Wales relented. An enquiry directed by Cardinal Herbert Vaughan found that Catholics who attended the universities in defiance of the bishops were not losing their faith.[52] The Irish Catholic bishops, in contrast, were much more vigilant in protecting the laity against influences deemed inimical to the faith. Their formal disapproval of Catholics attending Trinity College Dublin, initiated in 1875, was maintained up to 1970.[53]

The attitude of the British Prime Minister Sir Robert Peel (1788–1850) towards demands for university education for Catholics in Ireland was influenced by his strategy of conciliation in dealing with the campaign to repeal the Act of Union (1800), which would have led to the restoration of a separate Irish parliament. In Britain, government and public opinion alike were very much opposed to the Repeal movement, fearing that the United Kingdom would be fatally weakened if it achieved its objective. But Peel's government realised that some degree of conciliatory action would have to be taken to pacify the restless Catholic majority. A number of measures, such as a large increase in the Maynooth Grant and the passing of the Provincial Colleges Act (1845), were intended to detach moderate Catholic support from the Repeal campaign, which had gathered momentum. However, Peel's initiative to meet the demands of the Catholic clergy and laity for an acceptable system of university education was not taken without due regard for the objections of British Protestant opinion to the setting up of denominational colleges in Ireland. Protestant sensitivities about Trinity College Dublin were also taken into account. The outcome of such a compromise did not meet with the approval of the Catholic hierarchy.

The three Queen's Colleges, in Belfast, Cork and Galway, created under the provisions of the Provincial Colleges Act (1845), were brought together under the Queen's University in Ireland, which was established in September 1850. No religious tests were to be imposed and religious considerations were not to feature in the appointment or dismissal of officials. Students would not be under obligation to study theology or to undertake any course of religious studies. The teaching of theology was permitted for the instruction of students of each denomination, but financial support for it was not to be sourced from public funds. The bill for the establishment of the Queen's Colleges was described by the Anglican (Low Church) politician Sir Robert Inglis as 'a gigantic scheme of godless education'. Daniel O'Connell (1775–1847) – from a different denominational perspective and mindful of Inglis's words – condemned the 'Godless Colleges' so vigorously that the term passed into popular usage.[54]

The non-denominational nature of the constituent colleges was regarded by the Irish Catholic bishops as incompatible with the ideal standards of Catholic education. Nevertheless, a strong minority of the bishops was prepared to co-operate with the institutions because of the pressing educational needs of Catholics. The bishops decided, unanimously, to refer the matter to the church authorities in Rome. The Vatican supported the majority view and the Sacred Congregation of Propaganda issued three rescripts against Catholic participation in October 1847, October 1848 and April 1850. The congregation was not satisfied with limiting its directives to condemnations of the Queen's Colleges. It also urged the setting up of a Catholic university similar to that founded at Louvain by the Belgian bishops in 1835.[55]

The Catholic bishops, assembled at the Synod of Thurles (1850) and mindful of Rome's wishes, issued a denunciation of the colleges. The opposition of the institutional church – in Rome and Ireland – worked against the aspirations of middle-class Catholics who endeavoured to gain access to higher education. This policy was sustained until the National University was set up in 1908 and greatly diminished Irish Catholic participation in scientific enterprise in the late nineteenth century.

The relationship between Roman Catholicism and Protestantism was characterised by mutual suspicion and animosity. The Catholic bishops continued to insist on a Catholic university to provide higher education for Catholics and, in 1854, the Catholic University of Ireland was established under papal authority. In July 1851 – three years before the university was set up – John Henry Newman (1801–1890) accepted an invitation from Cardinal Cullen to become its first rector, a position which he held until November 1858. Formerly a leading theologian in the Church of England, he had converted to Roman Catholicism in 1845. His elevation to the rank of cardinal by Pope Leo XIII in 1879 indicated his important status in the Roman Catholic Church.

Newman was a liberal by the standards of his time and he did not share the widespread conviction amongst the clergy that the laity could not be trusted to put religious duty before material interests.[56] He was convinced that educated and confident laity, working in close co-operation with the clergy, was the best antidote to agnosticism. Newman was critical of the patriarchal attitude of the Catholic bishops and priests and it seemed to him that 'no small portion of the hierarchy and clergy of Ireland think . . . Ireland will become again the Isle of Saints, when it has a population of peasants ruled over by a patriotic priesthood patriarchally'.[57]

In a series of lectures and addresses to the Catholic University of Ireland in the 1850s, Newman explained, at length, his opinions about the relationship between theology and science. He sensed that there was, 'in the educated and half-educated portions of the community', a perception that some religious beliefs could not be reconciled with science. This notion of incompatibility led some of those who were resolutely religious to adopt a hostile and prejudiced attitude against science. Newman regarded theology and the natural sciences as two great domains of knowledge. Theology was concerned with the supernatural, science was concerned with the natural. Their methodologies were different. Induction was the instrument of the natural sciences and proved harmful to the search for truth when introduced into theology. Deduction was the instrument of theology. Because they were separate domains they could not contradict each other.[58]

Despite all of the above Newman did acknowledge that there were points of intersection between theology and science. Revelation had advanced beyond its chosen territory, especially in the early chapters of the book of Genesis, which narrated the six days of creation and the global deluge. But the Roman Catholic Church had not dogmatically defined these narratives.[59] Therefore, Catholics could be assured that nothing could be discovered, in the physical or social sciences, which would undermine any dogma of their faith. They could be confident that 'if anything seems to be proved . . . in contradiction to the dogmas of faith, that point will eventually turn out, first, not to be proved, or, secondly, not contradictory, or thirdly, not contradictory to anything really revealed, but to something which has been confused with revelation'.[60]

If theology was to be secured against the threatening intrusions of science, then it was important to limit the disciplinary scope of science. Science was the philosophy of matter and was only concerned with phenomena amenable to sensory perception. It ascertained, catalogued and compared natural phenomena to discover and elucidate the laws of nature. It was based on the scientific methodology of Francis Bacon (1561–1626), who stressed the importance of experiment and inductive reasoning. The scientist, as a scientist, could not ask what external force sustained the universe and how it came into existence – although in a non-professional capacity he would have an opinion on the subject. Scientists were competent to address efficient causes, not ultimate or final causes. They could investigate the history of the natural world, but they had to do it on the basis of observation, by relying on 'internal evidence'.[61] But what if a particular scientific investigation seemed set to undermine or contradict some religious opinion? Newman argued that researchers should be allowed to carry out their work without fear of obstruction or censorship, provided that they did not contradict dogma or encroach on the intellectual territory of theologians, and provided that they refrained from 'scandalizing the weak'. Scientific research, by loyal Catholics, which seemed to contradict theology, was to be made accessible to a professional readership under conditions which were philosophically orthodox. Care was to be taken to exclude it from 'light' popular publications in order to protect the 'careless or ignorant' sectors of society.[62]

Although the importance of science was acknowledged in principle, all was not well in the Catholic University of Ireland, which was in a poor financial position. In 1858 staff of the faculty of science at the Catholic University issued a plea for an increase in funding through the medium of a pamphlet addressed to the bishops. The *Report of the Dean and Faculty of Science of the Catholic University of Ireland* (1858) indicated just how under-resourced the teaching and practice of science was in the university. The dean of the faculty of science, Robert D. Lyons, wrote that

> . . . the Natural and Experimental Sciences . . . constitute, so to speak, the objects in greatest demand in the educational market; and if our University does not supply them in all the abundance, extent, and variety required, our Catholic youth will and must, for they are forced so to do by the exigencies of the day, seek them elsewhere: – at what peril to faith is too well known to need comment here.[63]

Lyons pointed out that the faculty of science, now just in its second year of existence, was 'a most essential and indispensable' element of the Catholic university. But it was so under-resourced in terms of staff and equipment that it was not able to fulfil its educational functions.[64] It was in the interests of the Catholic bishops to limit the circulation of the above report – its contents could only have served to support the contention that educational standards at the Catholic University were not what they should be. And yet – as observed by historians Enda Leaney and Juliana Adelman – the Under-Secretary for Ireland (1853–1868), Thomas Larcom, succeeded in acquiring a copy.[65]

The Catholic bishops, despite ongoing staff shortages and inadequate facilities, continued to express confidence in the Catholic University of Ireland. They believed that Catholics would 'zealously avail themselves of the admirable opportunities' offered in science and literature at the university.[66] They envisaged that the Catholic University would fulfil a number of important functions in the service of Catholics. Its functions were to include: (1) the encouragement of intellectual development (2) the promotion of professional education, which in turn would contribute to the economic development of Ireland (3) the cultivation of science and literature at academic level, and (4) the improvement of educational standards for priests. The bishops alleged that the universities in Britain and Ireland discriminated against Catholics in science to such an extent that only those who were wealthy could practise it at a professional level. They insisted that secular education should not be separated from religious education. This was not meant to imply that there was a Catholic science of mathematics, or of chemistry, or of engineering, *et cetera*. Instruction in the natural sciences could be delivered by anyone with the appropriate professional qualifications, regardless of religion. Nevertheless, the training of the man, as distinct from the scientist, could only be safely entrusted to Catholics.[67] A non-Catholic university could be relied upon to produce educated men – but not educated Catholics.[68]

It was anticipated that most of the university professors would hold heterodox views and that Irish Catholic students would fall victim to error and infidelity. Bartholomew Woodlock, who succeeded Newman as rector at the Catholic University, believed that some professors were so highly accomplished in their chosen disciplines that they wielded 'incredible' influence – men such as the Anglican (High Church) Professor of Hebrew at Oxford, Edward Pusey, and Ernest Renan (1823–1892).[69] Renan was widely acknowledged as an authority on the origins and early history of Christianity but his *Life of Jesus* (1863) was distinctly heterodox, rejecting the miraculous and presenting Jesus Christ as purely human.[70] In the middle decades of the nineteenth century, historical studies and textual analysis eroded confidence in the infallibility of the Bible.[71]

Modern developments in philosophy were another great source of concern for the Catholic Church in Ireland. Before the publication of Charles Darwin's *Origin of Species* in 1859 the Catholic Church was already voicing its opposition to changes in the philosophy curriculum in the universities. In the last half of the nineteenth century, the ecclesiastical authorities clearly felt threatened by ideas arising from various schools of thought in philosophy, such as empiricism and positivism. They were concerned about the works of philosophers such as David Hume (1711–1776), John Locke (1632–1704), John Stuart Mill (1806–1873), Alexander Bain (1818–1903) and Herbert Spencer (1820–1903).[72]

The Irish Catholic clergy believed that wayward philosophical ideas, such as positivism, pantheism and materialism, had spread throughout Europe like a plague, especially in Germany, France and England. Irish Catholic fears, although based on gross exaggeration, had some basis in reality. In the mid-nineteenth century a number of scientists featured prominently in controversies about materialism in Germany and France. These included, most notably, Ludwig Büchner, Jacob Moleschott and Carl Vogt. They were political radicals who saw the popularisation of their materialistic science as a means of overcoming the forces of reaction which had led to the failure of the revolutions of 1848–1849.[73] The historian Owen Chadwick describes them as 'men of the laboratory' – especially the medical laboratory, rather than 'men of the Enlightenment'. Their outlook was occasionally expressed in epigrams such as 'no thought without phosphorous', and 'man is what he eats'.[74] Their books were widely circulated and won them notoriety. These included Moleschott's *Der Kreislauf des Lebens* ('The Circular Course of Life', 1852), Büchner's *Kraft und Stoff* ('Force and Matter', 1855), and Vogt's *Köhlerglaube und Wissenschaft* ('Blind Faith and Science', 1855).[75] In 1867 the anonymous author, or authors, of 'The Revival of Atheism' in the *Irish Ecclesiastical Record* referred specifically to the books of Moleschott and Büchner. The implication was that robust book sales exerted an extensive pernicious influence on the masses. However, the 'plague' of atheism, so prevalent elsewhere, had not yet spread to Ireland. Nevertheless, Irish Catholics were thought to be vulnerable because 'almost all the conditions calculated directly to foster a spirit of infidelity in the young' were to be found in the education system, especially in the university sector.[76]

Those scientists who were prominent in the materialistic controversy in the 1850s had gained professional expertise in either anatomy, physiology or zoology. They had dissected and examined the innermost structures of the human body and declared that there was no evidence of a soul therein. Therefore, humans had no soul. What they found instead was evidence of human kinship with other primates.[77] All this was a blend of philosophical speculation, half truths and comparative anatomy. Theologians were worried more about atheistic philosophy than its scientific appendage.

Charles Darwin's *Origin of Species* had been published in 1859 but Irish Catholic opinion did not seem to be troubled by its implications for theology in the 1860s. It was geology rather than the biological sciences that had disturbed the minds of theologians over the previous few decades. However, their concerns were soon assuaged when Fr Gerald

Molloy (1834–1906), Professor of Theology at Maynooth (1857–1874), wrote at length about how theology and geology could be harmonised when both were properly understood. Molloy's work was published in a series of nine articles in the *Irish Ecclesiastical Record* in the late 1860s.[78] It was greatly expanded and republished as a book, *Geology and Revelation* (1870). Molloy's harmony thesis indicated how a cautious departure from a traditionalist and literalist reading of the Bible could serve to accommodate its narratives to modern science.[79] For those Catholics who valued science this was not a matter of minor importance.

The harmonisation of science with their religious beliefs was highly valued by many Catholics who, if not highly educated and trained in science, at least appreciated its importance – both in intellectual and economic terms. However, there was another major problem to be addressed – this concerned the poor status of science in Irish Catholic culture. This issue was brought to public attention in November 1873 when seventy students and ex-students of the Catholic University of Ireland issued a 'Memorial' – appealing to the bishops to remedy the severe neglect of science at their *alma mater*. No other similar institution, insofar as they could discover, had neglected science to such an extent. The university library, for example, did not have any of the 'standard works' of modern science. The signatories argued that if the sciences were not adequately resourced then the ensuing intellectual deficit would have dire consequences, not only for the future status of the university but for the faith of many Irish Catholics who were distressed by a 'sense of their inferiority in science'. Irish Catholics were determined that such inferiority would not be allowed to continue and if scientific education was not provided by the Catholic University then they would seek it elsewhere – in the Queen's Colleges and Trinity College Dublin, or through private study. They would 'devour the works of Haeckel, Darwin, Huxley, Tyndall and Lyell' without the guidance of a Catholic professor who otherwise would bring their attention to differences between 'established facts and erroneous inferences'. Students, in these circumstances, were vulnerable to losing their faith.[80]

The signatories argued that the natural sciences were now the most highly regarded and were being used by the enemies of the church to attack both the Catholic faith and the credibility of Biblical narratives. The neglect of science at the Catholic University bolstered the argument that the Catholic Church was the enemy of science. One or two years previously 'a very distinguished Professor of Science' – Thomas Henry

Huxley – was reported to have urged that the British government should consider whether or not the hostility of the church to science 'ought not to be met by persecution'.[81]

Concerns were expressed by the signatories of the Memorial that the conflict thesis had more than a trace of plausibility. The ecclesiastical authorities had, after all, forbidden Catholics to attend universities and colleges where science was taught and then had not adequately resourced it in the only institution that they were permitted to attend. Critics of the Catholic Church claimed, with 'too much colour of truth', that the university authorities, after nearly twenty years since the university was set up, had not appointed even one of their own students to teach an elementary course in philosophy or science. It was alleged that standards of education were so low that the authorities were either too ashamed or afraid to do so.

Near the end of the Memorial the signatories urged the bishops to revive the publication of *The Atlantis*. This journal, 'conducted by Members of the Catholic University of Ireland', was devoted to the publication of scholarly articles in both the humanities and the sciences. It was intended for publication twice per year. But this policy objective was to prove unsustainable. An inserted note in the January 1862 issue of *The Atlantis* stated that future volumes would only be published when sufficient contributions had been received.[82] Those who signed the Memorial observed that the under-representation of Irish Catholics amongst those who were eminent in literature and science was due mainly to a lack of education, especially in the sciences. The scarcity of Catholics in the learned professions was particularly evident when examining the backgrounds of the members of the Royal Irish Academy. Only seven Catholic members were identified, including William Kirby Sullivan, Henry Hennessy and George Sigerson (1836–1925).[83] However, of far greater significance was the observation that if the academy was to lose the services of these members – all of them 'distinguished in science' – then no person would be found with sufficient qualifications to succeed them from the ranks of Catholics in Ireland.[84]

The Memorial was as provocative as it could be without being gratuitously offensive to the hierarchy. The signatories were careful to express respect for ecclesiastical authority by the use of such terms as 'we respectfully urge upon your lordships . . . we beg in the strongest manner to urge upon your lordships', and 'we entreat your lordships to place the most favourable construction on our action . . .'.[85] The Memorial, a pamphlet of about thirty pages, was circulated to each of the Irish Catholic bishops. It was more widely circulated through the medium of the press, where it generated some controversy.[86]

The poor condition of science at the Catholic University was seen by its sharpest critics as part of an underlying and much greater problem. It was alleged in the press that ecclesiastical control of the institution was becoming so repressive that it did not merit university status. The bishops were transforming it into 'a clerical school and nothing more' – an 'Irish layman's Maynooth'. They were seen as agents of a hostile foreign power, ruled over by a dictator whose pretensions of infallibility stood in the way of a sound diplomatic relationship with democratic states. The papacy had issued the Syllabus of Errors 'with its declarations of hostility to modern science and civilization'. The bishops were seen as unfit for governing an institution worthy of university status.[87]

In *The Times* it was argued that the censorial mentality of the bishops and rational enquiry were mutually incompatible. The Catholic Church was seen to be encountering difficulties in both literature and science – the twin pillars of education. The church's credibility in science was called into question because of its condemnation of Galileo in the seventeenth century. And it did not seem that British literature, which included the works of such authors as David Hume, Jeremy Taylor, Edward Gibbon and John Milton, could be taught safely to Catholics without extensive censorship. There would be 'no great danger to the Faith in reading aloud from a volume of elegant extracts, or in arranging a case or two of fossils . . .' Such education would have some value, but it would fall far short of university standards.[88]

Criticism of the bishops' stance on university education did not emanate only from non-Catholics. The 'defection' of William Kirby Sullivan from the Catholic University to Queen's College Cork in 1873 indicated a considerable level of liberal Catholic dissatisfaction towards the bishops concerning university education. Sullivan had accepted the position of Professor of Chemistry at the Catholic University in 1856 at Newman's invitation. Like Newman, he believed in the idea of a liberal Catholic university where laymen would be given positions of influence. However, by 1873 he had become disillusioned. He was critical of the hierarchy. The bishops, it seemed, were determined to create a seminary rather than a university. In a letter to his friend, William Monsell (MP for County Limerick, 1847–1874), Sullivan expressed concern that the bishops were planning to get rid of all the lay professors.[89] A policy of excessive ecclesiastical control effectively denigrated the role of the Catholic laity. Sullivan believed that this was in opposition to the aspirations of Irish Catholics. Furthermore, he was critical of the bishops for viewing science with suspicion because of the supposed dangers it presented to the Catholic faith. Their education, Sullivan claimed, did not enable them to apprehend the vital importance of science in secular education.[90]

The poor status of science in Irish Catholic culture can be seen as a clash of interests between British government policy and the Roman Catholic hierarchy in Ireland. The government, unionists and Irish nationalists were all aware of the importance of scientific and technical education as a means of efficiently exploiting Ireland's natural resources.[91] In government circles, science education was seen as neutral in religious and political terms and therefore as potentially useful in reducing political and religious tensions. The growing power of the restless Catholic middle classes was seen as potentially dangerous by both the Catholic hierarchy and the state. The state endeavoured to reduce the threat by providing secular education, of which science was an important part. The rationale was that prosperous contented citizens would be less rebellious. However, the Catholic bishops saw the secular colleges as a threat to their objective of preserving the influence of the church in Ireland.[92] Their opposition to the Queen's Colleges and Trinity College Dublin contributed greatly to a prolongation of Catholic under-representation in science at the highest levels, especially when science was grossly under-resourced in the Catholic University.

The Catholic University was very poorly equipped to promote the advancement of science in Ireland. It had more serious problems to contend with and these were inter-related. It failed to gain a charter and this greatly reduced its ability to attract students, which in turn impacted adversely on its financial viability.[93] Furthermore, the secondary school system in Catholic Ireland was poorly developed and inadequate to the task of supplying sufficient numbers of students for the university. Cardinal Paul Cullen's effective exclusion of his fellow bishops from exerting control over the university led to most of them losing interest, which, in turn, led to a sharp decrease of fund-raising for the institution. Newman's departure in 1858 was a further setback for the Catholic University, although it is unlikely that the decline of the institution would have been reversed if he had chosen to stay on as rector. By the mid-1860s indications of terminal decline were very much in evidence.[94] It was, in the words of its small student body, 'an institution of hope, founded in faith, on the basis of charity'. William Kirby Sullivan wrote to William Monsell in May 1873, giving a grim assessment of the university's condition and prospects. It was 'without suitable buildings . . . without endowments to pay the professors, without prestige, without the faculty of giving degrees . . . with the apathy of a large number of clergy and bishops; with the unconcealed hostility of a considerable number of priests; it is not possible to maintain a central Catholic university in Dublin'.[95] By the late 1870s the university had almost ceased to function.

The setting up of the Royal University of Ireland under the terms of the University Education (Ireland) Act of 1879 was another attempt to solve the complex problem of university education in Ireland. A major aim of the initiative was to conciliate Catholics, but progress on this was very limited. The Royal University, which replaced the Queen's University, was an examination body but it did not have a student body of its own. Students from other educational institutions, including those from the Queen's Colleges, were allowed to sit for its examinations. The new system enabled students of the Catholic University to pursue degrees without their university itself receiving a charter. The Catholic University of Ireland later became known as University College Dublin and was placed under the control of the Jesuits until it became a constituent college of the National University of Ireland, established under the terms of the Irish Universities Act (1908). Catholic students could continue their attendance at a select number of Catholic secondary schools to study for Royal University or University of London degrees. A Catholic ethos and Catholic teachers could be guaranteed, but a Catholic curriculum and Catholic texts could not be assured.[96] The Royal University was non-denominational, but care was taken to avoid offending any religious denominational interest when deciding the contents of courses.[97] However, the Irish Catholic bishops were still not satisfied with the system of university education. They continued to view the Queen's Colleges as godless and in dire need of reform.[98]

A Conflict of Interests

Up to about 1870 there was relatively little concern about the potential adverse impact of modern science on Catholic faith, although there are indications that some level of disquiet did exist about how science might be used to attack religion. In the early 1870s Irish Catholic concerns intensified. A hard-line attitude developed – evidently provoked by the anti-Catholicism of some leading evolutionists, especially

Thomas Henry Huxley and John Tyndall and by Charles Darwin's extension of evolutionary theory in the *Descent of Man* (1871) to include humankind. In the socio-political milieu of late-nineteenth-century Ireland, tensions between Irish Catholicism and science were to become increasingly evident.

Difficulties in reconciling science and scripture, arising especially from the idea of human evolution, created theological problems for the Christian churches in general, not least the Roman Catholic Church. There was a discernable reluctance in the Catholic Church to embrace mainstream science and to reassess traditional religious beliefs with it in mind. In Ireland, a combination of external and indigenous circumstances militated against a harmonious relationship between Roman Catholicism and science from the 1870s onwards.

There was probably a consensus amongst the Irish Catholic clergy that science could be misused, especially when there were apparent contradictions between revelation and reason. Under these circumstances science could 'eclipse the light of faith . . . and be degraded into the accidental tool of infidelity'.[99] There was a tendency to view science as something which was external and threatening, rather than as an instrument of progress and enlightenment.

The initiatives of Huxley, Tyndall and their allies to improve standards in the practice of science and free it from external influences militated against the development of a harmonious relationship between Catholicism and science, especially in Ireland. In the mid-nineteenth century many outspoken Victorian scientists had entered their profession from the fringes of middle-class society and from outside the main social and intellectual institutions of England. Men such as Huxley and Tyndall were highly talented and ambitious, and sought recognition from both their scientific peers and from the general public. They challenged the traditional intellectual elite, particularly the clergy,[100] who enjoyed enormous wealth, prestige and power – which was exercised through the pulpit and the education system, including the universities.

The struggle of Huxley, Tyndall and their allies was part of a much broader movement. A range of technical, medical and engineering practitioners were in a similar situation to the scientists. They too struggled to improve their status in society. By the 1860s many professional scientists were in high-ranking jobs in the state's administrative system and in the newly created technical institutes. They were now sufficiently influential to effectively challenge what they regarded as the unjustified interference by the clergy in practical matters beyond their competence.[101] They asserted their right to define the boundaries of their discipline and the epistemology, educational system, employment and social utility associated with it, regardless of religious or ecclesiastical considerations. Science would be taught on the basis of principles established by professional scientists, creating new areas of employment for graduates and enhancing both the economic and social status of the profession as a whole.

The endeavours of men like Huxley and Tyndall were not motivated entirely by professional interests. Ideological considerations played a major role. New interpretations of humankind, nature and society were proposed on the basis of scientific naturalism. This outlook was 'naturalistic' in that it would refuse to rely on causes which were not subject to observation in nature. It was scientific because it was based on three theories of central importance to mid-nineteenth-century science. These theories were concerned with the atomic structure of matter, the conservation of energy, and evolutionary biology. Leading figures in scientific naturalism besides Huxley and Tyndall included the scientists William Kingdon Clifford (1845–1879) and E. Ray Lankester (1847–1929), editor and literary critic Leslie Stephen (1832–1904), anthropologist Edward Tylor (1832–1917), philosopher Herbert Spencer, and populariser of science and banker John Lubbock.

Scientific naturalists frequently presented themselves as superior in ability to any other cultural group in the context of a leadership role in Britain's rapid development as a modern industrialised state. Furthermore, they argued that their discipline should not be circumscribed by the Bible or by clerical opinions.[102] The quest for intellectual independence by Huxley, Tyndall and other secular-minded scientists harmonised neatly with their quest for occupational and social prestige. They saw themselves as the pre-eminent educators in British society, as the natural successors of the Anglican clergy – whom they saw as deeply divided and tainted by Catholic ritualistic practices. The movement to professionalise science and to liberate it from external influences led to a conflict of interests between scientific naturalists and the Christian churches, especially Anglican and Roman Catholic. There was a lesser degree of friction with Protestant Nonconformists because of their demands, in the 1870s, for non-denominational education. Control over education was an issue of central importance for scientific naturalists such as Huxley and Tyndall.

Theological and ecclesiastical terms were applied to science and scientific institutions. Thus Huxley and his friends sang 'hymns to creation', preached 'lay sermons', were members of the 'church scientific' and entered the 'scientific priesthood'. The Victorian natural history museum was frequently referred to as 'nature's cathedral', and 'Bishop' Huxley sometimes admonished the religious faithful with cries of 'heresy' when they expressed opinions about science contrary to his.[103]

Scientific naturalists exerted considerable influence in Britain in the latter half of the nineteenth century.[104] However, their opinions were strongly challenged by scientists, popularisers of science, philosophers and others. Alfred Russel Wallace (1823–1913), co-discoverer of natural selection with Charles Darwin (1809–1882), placed the theory within a framework of theistic evolution.[105] The placing of evolutionary theory within a framework of theistic metaphysics found strong support amongst British idealist philosophers who, collectively, dominated British philosophy in the late nineteenth century. Proponents of scientific naturalism were especially challenged by the 'North British' group of physicists, including William Thomson (Lord Kelvin, 1824–1907), James Clerk Maxwell (1831–1879) and Peter Guthrie Tait (1831–1901). Although the scientific naturalists and the North British physicists engaged in heated debates about scientific issues (such as the age of the earth, the nature of molecules, and thermodynamics), there were underlying religious ideas (such as divine action in nature) which sometimes came to the surface.[106] However, notwithstanding their importance, there will be very little reference in this book to Wallace, the North British physicists or their allies – such as the physicist George Gabriel Stokes (1819–1903) – because they received correspondingly little attention by Irish Catholic apologists, who generally avoided acknowledging the merits of non-Catholic sources which could be used in defence of the church. The essential point here is that the scientific naturalism of Huxley, Tyndall and others, although considerably influential, did not dominate science, much less the intellectual landscape of Victorian Britain.

Huxley did not desire the extermination of all manifestations of religious belief.[107] What he did wish for was the elimination of religious dogma, especially when he perceived it in opposition to modern science. This outlook led Huxley to select the Roman Catholic Church as a prime target. Other advocates of scientific naturalism, including Herbert Spencer, William Kingdon Clifford and Leslie Stephen, joined him in contributing to anti-Catholic polemic. Collectively, they attained prominence in the expression of anti-Catholic sentiment. All this worked to the advantage of professional scientists, enabling them to benefit from anti-papal opinion in Britain.[108]

Huxley believed that if he was to oppose Roman Catholicism, effectively, he had to study it, sometimes at close quarters. His visits to Catholic seminaries[109] led him to Ireland's largest – St Patrick's College, Maynooth. It was here that he met Catholic professors and spoke candidly to them – as 'friendly enemies' during a 'truce'. Apparently, he was impressed by the encounter and acknowledged that the Catholic Church was a worthy adversary.[110] This was what he wanted – a powerful reactionary Catholicism posing a threat to the welfare of British society. This enabled him to present science as a powerful antidote to the baneful influences of a papacy suffering from delusions of infallibility. This populist notion of conflict in turn was vitally important for sustaining his ideological power base.[111] Not surprisingly then, Huxley's opinions on politics and religion were particularly offensive towards Irish Catholics. He claimed that Roman Catholicism was the great enemy of science[112] – 'the one great spiritual organisation which is able to resist, and must, as a matter of life and death, resist the progress of science and modern civilisation.'[113] His anti-Catholic opinions expressed at meetings of the London School Board received attention in the popular Irish newspaper *The Nation*. Acknowledged as an eminent scientist, he was denounced for his 'vulgar, foul-mouthed anti-Popery' and for working towards the extirpation of Roman Catholicism in common with many others who favoured non-denominational education.[114]

Huxley's conflict thesis was not unusual.[115] Two authors in particular popularised the notion that there was a conflict between religion and science. These were Andrew Dickson White, who served as president of Cornell University, and John William Draper, Professor of Physiology at New York University. White's book originated in the 1870s, from the text of a lecture entitled 'The Battlefields of Science', and from a small book, the *Warfare of Science*. After a number of editions it was published as *A History of the Warfare of Science with Theology in Christendom* in 1896. Draper's *History of the Conflict between Religion and Science* was published in 1874. Both books, it seems, were written as a response to the *Syllabus of Errors*, especially the eightieth condemned proposition. Both books were bitterly critical of institutional Christianity, but Draper's book focused its attack very heavily against the Roman Catholic Church and was put on the Vatican's Index of Forbidden Books in 1876.[116]

Strident anti-Catholicism occurred at a time when the Irish Catholic population were becoming more exposed to cultural influences from Britain. The Gaelic language was in sharp decline. English, the language of commerce, and the language of emigration, was becoming more widely spoken. Literacy levels were rising sharply.[117] Inexpensive periodicals were widely circulated. Little attention had been given to science in the 1840s and 1850s, but in the 1860s space was frequently allocated to scientific issues. In provincial Ireland readers had easy access to a broad range of literature, some of which originated from London.[118] It was against the background of these social conditions that the Irish Catholic bishops expressed their fears that newspapers, periodicals and books would lead unsuspecting Catholics astray. They were deeply suspicious that the press and the promoters of scientific materialism were working in harmony. In January 1873 they issued a pastoral letter which expressed their fears and contempt for 'the thought of the age' which was deemed to be diametrically opposed to the teachings of the church. The bishops declared that

> . . . never before has infidelity been found so thoroughly organised, so aggressive, so powerful . . . It is master of the press. In the newspapers which lie even upon the tables of Catholics, in the periodicals edited by infidels . . . in the handbooks which popularize the discoveries of science, and in the learned treatises which are the boast of the universities, its baleful forces are constantly at work . . . now crushing faith at a blow, and now again sapping it, by undermining the natural truths upon which the Christian demonstration rests. It assumes to be the dictator of the physical sciences; and its apostles, though they superciliously disdain even the bare knowledge of what Revelation teaches concerning the origin and destiny of man in the world, loudly proclaim to the youth, who, obeying the materialist tendencies of the age, throng in eager crowds to their schools, that faith cannot be reconciled with science.[119]

The bishops did not identify the books, magazines and newspapers which caused them so much concern, nor did they limit their condemnations to the press. They also condemned secret societies, singling out the Freemasons in Ireland for special mention. However, the main enemies of the church were politicians – especially Italian nationalists and the instigators of the *Kulturkampf* in Germany. No mention was made of Huxley and Tyndall at this point, but the bishops evidently had them in mind when they referred to the errors condemned by the First Vatican Council in its *Constitutio Dogmatica de Fide Catholica* – the Dogmatic Constitution on the Catholic Faith (24 April 1870).[120] These errors included the following:

> If anyone says that the one, true God, our creator and lord, cannot be known with certainty from the things that have been made, by the natural light of human reason: let him be anathema.
>
> If anyone says that human reason is so independent that faith cannot be commanded by God: let him be anathema.

Faith and reason were asserted to be compatible, truth was never in opposition to truth and, therefore, the Vatican Council maintained that 'all faithful Christians are forbidden to defend as the legitimate conclusions of science those opinions which are known to be contrary to the doctrine of the faith, particularly if they have been condemned by the church . . .'[121]

An alternative expression for 'the thought of the age' was 'modern thought' – a nebulous, all-embracing term used to indicate an anti-Catholic or non-Catholic outlook, meriting a plenitude of anathemas. It received extensive treatment in a series of five articles in the *Irish Ecclesiastical Record* (1873–1874). The anonymous author (or authors?) of 'The Church and Modern Thought' attributed the origin of modern errors to Protestantism, which in turn was supposed to have given rise to naturalism – a disbelief in the supernatural. Those whose outlook was conditioned by naturalism believed that man was nothing more than a highly developed primate. Agnostic evolutionists were criticised for straying beyond the boundaries of their competence and especially for making arbitrary statements on religious matters merely on the basis of assumptions. The attitudes of many scientists, as distinct from science itself, were seen as hostile to Catholicism. Furthermore, there seemed to be something in the scientific method, especially in Protestant cultures, that had drifted towards naturalism, which encouraged a type of scepticism that did not stop at the boundaries of science.[122]

It was argued that the Roman Catholic Church was not amenable to any social or historical analysis – it was 'too wide and deep' to be covered by any theory. The extension of Darwin's concept of natural selection, when applied to the discipline of history, failed to explain away the divine authority of the church, in view of the unprecedented durability and magnitude of its power and influence. The church, unlike scientists, did not have to concern itself with the burden of gathering evidence when pronouncing on points of doctrine. It was already in possession of the proof it required. The institutional church, in dealing with its members, would rely on faith, dogma and ecclesiastical authority. Its mission was to preach rather than to prove its doctrines. Adherence to dogma and the compelling force of 'solemn sanctions', rather than reasoning based on the discoveries of science, were to be the determinants of belief. The church was not reluctant to proclaim its doctrines, but it did not follow that all Catholics were sufficiently informed. Concern was expressed that Catholics were vulnerable to ideas which were incompatible with the basic principles of their faith. This danger was perceived to arise from a lack of religious education and from exposure to influences that were both anti-Christian and anti-Catholic. Apparently, some Catholics were unaware that they held views contrary to the teachings of their church. Therefore, some elementary principles needed to be explained to them. The church was confident that its illiberal stance was the correct position to maintain. Terms such as 'liberty of conscience', 'liberty of the press' and 'universal toleration' were denounced. The attainment of salvation was by far the most important mission in life and to achieve this it was necessary to submit to the authority of the church. This meant sacrificing any liberties which civil society might offer if such liberties were obstacles to saving one's immortal soul. 'Modern thought', in 'the garb of science' or 'in the vestments of philosophy', was incompatible with Roman Catholicism.[123]

The *Syllabus of Errors* impacted heavily on Irish Catholic clerical opinion. This document denied that 'the decrees of the Apostolic See and of the Roman congregations impede the true progress of science'.[124] However, the church's assertion that it was radiant with unadulterated truth and intellectual progress was regarded as highly implausible in view of the 'errors' censured in the *Syllabus*, which in turn were derived from allocutions, apostolic letters and encyclicals. Despite this, the mood of Irish Catholic opinion was not one of embarrassment – rather it was one of defiance. Claims that the church was the enemy of liberalism, hostile to progress and to science and motivated by obscurantism, were deeply resented. If the church seemed unreasonably intolerant of new ideas in philosophy then, it was argued, there was an underlying justification for its stance. Errors in philosophy could not be tolerated because philosophy interacted with theology and, sooner or later, philosophical errors would lead to heresy. Philosophical speculation, such as the scepticism of David Hume, had led to naturalism, which was thought to be the very basis of 'modern thought', which, in this context, was equated with 'modern error'.[125] Naturalism, with its kindred heresies of pantheism and absolute rationalism, was condemned at the beginning of the *Syllabus*.

It now seemed that the great confrontation of the age was not between Catholicism and Protestantism but between the natural versus the supernatural. Protestantism had lapsed into ineffectual opposition. No less an authority than Huxley was quoted in support of such a contention. Huxley had stated that the Roman Catholic Church was the great enemy of science and had to resist the progress of science and the incursions of modern civilisation if it was to survive. This antagonistic statement was gleaned from his *Lay Sermons, Addresses and Reviews* (1870).[126]

Tyndall and the Catholic University

Huxley's close friend John Tyndall was perceived as an eminent exponent of irreligious philosophy by the author of 'The Church and Modern Thought', published in the *Irish Ecclesiastical Record* (1874). He observed that Tyndall had declared his inability to answer any questions about God, believing any knowledge of the deity to be beyond the reach of human reason. Tyndall's sceptical opinions about miracles and the effi-cacy of prayer were widely disseminated through the medium of his *Fragments of Science*. From a Catholic perspective his professed lack of understanding was not regarded as a manifestation of intellectual integrity – rather it was believed that a 'conviction of superior knowledge' lurked beneath the expression of 'modest ignorance'.[127] Ignorance about the realm of the supernatural was, therefore, regarded as wilful igno-rance. This opinion is best understood when viewed against the background of Biblical criticism, questions concerning the efficacy of prayer and the occurrence of miracles in the 1860s and early 1870s in Britain and America.

The multi-authored *Essays and Reviews* (1860) had raised questions about the inerrancy of the Bible. Traditional views about prayer and mir-acles were called into question with greater frequency from the early nineteenth century. The English philosopher John Stuart Mill argued that miracles were not subject to proof. Tyndall published his sceptical views about prayer in a small book entitled *Mountaineering in 1861*. He rejected prayer on the basis that there was no evidence that it brought about any beneficial changes in the physical world. Prayer was not merely useless – it was harmful to society because it encouraged misplaced reliance on supernatural assistance and distracted attention from rational engage-ment with the real causes of scarcity and disease.[128] At this point Tyndall had gained some degree of notoriety, but he had not yet risen to promi-nence in controversies about science and religion.

Critiques of traditional Christian beliefs did not pass unanswered. In 1865 the Protestant theologian, James Mozley (1813–1878) spoke in defence of prayer in the Bampton Lectures. This series of lectures was later published as *Eight Lectures on Miracles Preached before the University of Oxford* (1867). Tyndall challenged Mozley on a number of fronts and in doing so brought the issues of prayer and miracles into a broader discussion concerning disciplinary boundaries and points of contact between religion and science. What could science usefully say about miracles? Even if a miraculous event, such as walking on water, was witnessed by men of impeccable honesty and eminent scientific stature, how could they know that it was not due to some natural phenomenon? Just because an occurrence was inexplicable at the time did not make it miraculous. The progress of science was constantly expanding the frontiers of human knowledge about nature and it was inappropriate for a scientist to move from what was unknown in nature to a miracle when proposing explanations.[129]

Tyndall's article on 'Miracles and Special Providences' was originally published in the *Fortnightly Review* (1867) and re-published in the second edition of his *Fragments of Science*. Irish Catholic opinion, as expressed in the March 1874 issue of the *Irish Ecclesiastical Record*, believed that Tyndall had made the mistake of equating Protestantism with Christianity when writing about 'Miracles and Special Providences'. At the intellectual level Tyndall was found to have won the argument against Mozley, but not of course against Roman Catholicism. It was observed that he had not ruled out, with absolute certainty, the occurrence of miracles. Miracles, although extremely difficult (if not impossible) to prove as isolated incidents, were amenable to proof if the historical context in each case was studied. Scientists ignored the 'proofs and evidences' that were to be found in revelation and in doing so had committed a fundamental error of judgement.[130] It was not at all clear what these 'proofs and evidences' were, however.

Exponents of scientific naturalism of Tyndall's stature were regarded as men of 'eminent intelligence', of 'exemplary candour', with 'admirable' powers of exposition. Their sincerity was not called into question. Yet they were disadvantaged by their Protestant backgrounds. Protestantism, lacking certainty due to the emphasis on private judgement, had fallen prey to rationalism. Protestants had immersed themselves in the natural sciences and persuaded themselves that any science outside the domain of the natural sciences was unworthy of the name. They were so preoccupied with natural science that they became intolerant of evidence which was not physical in nature. Tyndall was presented as the ideal example.[131]

Tyndall was very distrustful of Roman Catholicism and, consequently, he opposed the Home Rule movement for Ireland because he perceived it as a threat to the intellectual welfare and secular freedom of the country.[132] It seems that the meagre resources allocated to science at the Catholic University of Ireland exacerbated his worst fears. Tyndall probably became aware of the Memorial from reading a report about it in the newspapers. When he spoke at Belfast on 19 August 1874, as President of the British Association for the Advancement of Science, it seems that he was mindful of this document. His later 'Apology for the Belfast Address' indicates that his speech was very much influenced by the neglect of science at the Catholic University of Ireland.[133] At Belfast he exhorted his fellow scientists to 'wrest from theology the entire domain of cosmological theory'. He envisaged 'the mild light of science' as a powerful liberating influence on the youth of Ireland, and as an effective bulwark against any future 'intellectual or spiritual tyranny' which might threaten the welfare of Irish society.[134]

Nature was to be explained 'without the meddling of the gods'.[135] Believing as he did in 'the continuity of nature', he was convinced that matter had within it the potency to create life. However, evolutionary theory could not be proved on the basis of the experimental method. Nevertheless, Tyndall argued that its great strength derived from how well it harmonised with scientific thought. He declined, therefore, to 'stop abruptly where our microscopes cease to be of use' and proceeded to cross the 'boundary of the experimental evidence' to discern in matter 'the promise and potency of all terrestrial life'.[136]

Tyndall's Belfast Address elicited antagonised responses from both Catholics and Protestants, not only in Ireland but abroad also. His provocative opinions received widespread attention because of his status as President of the prestigious British Association.[137] In the polemical atmosphere of the early 1870s, exacerbated considerably by the publication of Darwin's *Descent of Man* (1871), the reaction against the Belfast Address was probably much sharper than it would otherwise have been.[138] His address, arguably, could be seen as more important than the Huxley-Wilberforce debate in 1860.[139] On that occasion Huxley had endeavoured to dissipate prejudice against Darwin's theory so that it could receive a fair hearing. Tyndall, in contrast, made much broader claims on behalf of science, proposing that it could explain the natural world and its origins without recourse to the supernatural.

The Irish Catholic bishops took the unprecedented step of issuing a pastoral letter on 14 October 1874. No other scientist had received such attention. The bishops were very much influenced by Newman in constructing their reply to Tyndall and quoted him at length to pursue two defensive strategies: firstly, to maximise the isolation of theology from science; and secondly, to limit the disciplinary domain of science.[140] Tyndall's vision of an unbroken evolutionary process was not supported by experimental evidence. From this the bishops judged that his conclusions were unscientific.[141] Irish Protestant clergymen also reacted strongly against Tyndall's address.[142]

The bishops observed how explicit Tyndall had been in anticipating that scientific education would lead young Catholics away from their faith. Tyndall's vision of a new Ireland, emancipated from the intellectual fetters of Roman Catholicism, served their interests. It gave additional justification to their stance that that part of the education system which was to serve the needs of Catholics should be under the control of the Catholic clergy.[143] Science would be taught under conditions which did not create problems for adherence to the doctrines of the church. In this way impressionable young Catholics would be protected from those who used science as an instrument of materialism.[144] The bishops took the opportunity of castigating those Catholics who were not fully committed to supporting a denominational system of education for Catholics, including a Catholic university. It is likely that those who were to the forefront of their thoughts on this point were Robert Kane, William Kirby Sullivan, a 'large proportion' of the clergy of Cork, and many of the prosperous families of that city who were resolute in their plans to give their sons a university education.[145] Furthermore, although the twenty-eight Irish bishops signed the pastoral letter, not all of them were genuinely in agreement with its contents.[146]

The collective stance of the Irish Catholic bishops reinforced Tyndall's opinion that Ireland epitomised the most pernicious effects of ecclesiastical power in retarding the progress of a nation. Ultramontanism and the 'Jesuitical system' had 'crushed out of Catholics every tendency to free mental productiveness', especially in Ireland and Spain.[147] The hierarchy's harsh treatment of liberal Catholicism, and the excommunication of one of its leading figures, Ignatz von Döllinger, served as a salutary lesson to Tyndall. Therefore, in his opinion, direct rule from London would hold the institutional church in check in Ireland and offer some prospect of enlightenment underpinned by science.

At this point it is evident that the remarkable juxtaposition of sectional interests, political allegiances and religious beliefs made it extremely unlikely, if not impossible, that science in the late nineteenth century – especially evolutionary theory – would be favourably received in Catholic Ireland. The theory of evolution, of central importance to biology, presented Christians – not least Roman Catholics – with major theological problems of how to reconcile faith and reason. In view of this, Irish Catholic attitudes towards evolution merits detailed study, which will commence with the next chapter.

2. Faith and Evolution,
1860s–1880s

Evolution by Natural Selection

A number of authors wrote about biological evolution years before the publication of Charles Darwin's *Origin of Species* in 1859. These included Jean Baptiste Lamarck (1744–1829), Robert Chambers and Darwin's own grandfather, Erasmus Darwin (1731–1802). In his *Vestiges of the Natural History of Creation* (1844), published anonymously, Chambers did not hold back from including humans in the evolutionary process. However, the scientific arguments in *Vestiges* were deeply flawed and scientists did not swing decisively in support of evolutionary theory. Darwin, in contrast, assembled a large volume of scientific evidence for the evolution of species, and used that evidence creatively.

Darwin's observations on the *Beagle* (1831–1836), and his reflections thereafter, led him to conclude that each species of plant and animal had not been created separately. His travels in South America and the Galapagos Islands played a central role in the formation of his evolutionary thesis. Charles Lyell's *Principles of Geology* (1830–1833) profoundly influenced his thinking and provided the vast time scale essential for the evolution of species by numerous small changes.[1]

The geographical distribution of species indicated a branching, open-ended process of change. The geographical distributions of giant tortoises, mocking birds and finches on the Galapagos Islands were especially important in this context. It did not seem plausible that God had specially created ranges of species unique to each of these tiny islands. Geographical distributions of plants and animals were best explained in terms of evolution and migration. New species would develop when a number of individuals were geographically isolated from the parent population under new environmental conditions. A species would gradually emerge in one local area. If successful, it would then extend its territory

33

and diversify, giving rise to a range of closely related species over a larger territory. This continuous process would explain why families and genera of plants and animals are frequently localised, and why extensive barriers to migration demarcate distinctive botanical and zoological domains.

Species competed for territory, but there was also competition between individual organisms within the same species. Individuals within species varied randomly from one another. Some were better adapted to their environment than others. Those who were best adapted were most likely to survive and reproduce, passing on favourable traits to the next generation. The gradual accumulation of favourable traits gave rise to new species of plants and animals over long periods of time.

In Chapter 1 of the *Origin of Species* Darwin wrote about artificial selection to help the reader understand how selection in nature (i.e. natural selection) worked. Human breeders generated artificial varieties from populations of domesticated plants and animals by selecting individuals with desired traits, rejecting those considered undesirable. There was an analogous process in nature driving change. The idea of natural selection in the *Origin of Species* was influenced considerably by Thomas Robert Malthus' concept of the 'struggle for existence' in his *Essay on the Principle of Population* (1797). Malthus observed that human population growth tended to outstrip food supply. In ideal circumstances, population growth would be checked by voluntary restraint. If not, the grim alternatives were war, famine and disease. Darwin applied Malthus' 'struggle for existence' to nature, where there would be no moral restraint. There was, instead, constant struggle where those organisms best adapted to existing environmental conditions would survive and reproduce. Those who were not would perish. Evolutionary development was not inevitably progressive although higher animals, including humans, had emerged from such a process.

Biological evolution was not compatible with a literal understanding of scripture. However, thoughtful Christians had already felt compelled to view the early chapters of Genesis in a new light when geological evidence indicated, beyond reasonable doubt, that the Earth was hundreds of millions rather than thousands of years old. There were precedents for the reinterpretation of scripture on the basis of overwhelming scientific evidence. But a similar exegetical imperative did not clearly apply in the case of Darwin's theory. There were several valid scientific criticisms to be answered. For example, if species descended from other species due to the cumulative effect of innumerable small changes, then why was there an absence of transitional forms in nature and in the fossil record? Natural selection seemed unable to explain why some species had remained unchanged over millions of years as indicated by the fossil record. It was difficult to conceptualise how organs of extreme complexity, such as the eye, could have evolved by natural selection. In the first edition of his *Origin of Species* (1859) Darwin acknowledged that there were valid criticisms to be addressed.[2] In later editions he attempted to answer additional criticisms, such as those put forward by the eminent British physicist William Thomson. Evolution on the basis of natural selection was a slow process and Darwin relied on the vast time scale of Charles Lyell's geological treatise to make it plausible. In the 1860s Thomson inflicted a heavy blow against the credibility of Darwin's theory when he estimated that the maximum age of the Earth was about 100 million years, based on its rate of cooling. This did not allow enough time for evolution by natural selection. But Thomson's calculations were grossly misleading because radioactivity – by far the main source of heat – was not discovered until 1896 by Antoine Henri Becquerel (1852–1908). Evolutionary biology seemed to contradict physics as then understood by scientists.

Darwin's replies to criticisms of his theory were not entirely satisfactory – mainly because science had not advanced enough to provide the necessary information.[3] Furthermore, he was considerably disadvantaged by his inability to explain variation within species upon which natural selection acted. When his book *The Descent of Man and Selection in Relation to Sex* was published in 1871, the science of genetics was not yet established. The results of plant-breeding experiments of Gregor Johann Mendel (1822–1884) were published in 1865–1866, but the importance of his work was not widely discerned until the early years of the twentieth century. Darwin was at a disadvantage in answering his critics without the means to explain how physical characteristics were transmitted from one generation to the next. Fleeming Jenkin highlighted Darwin's vulnerability when he argued, in harmony with the common understanding of inheritance at the time, that variation could not be maintained on the basis of blending paternal and maternal characteristics.[4]

Darwin's theory was frequently criticised on the basis that it departed from the inductive principle and was based on assumptions rather than facts. It was not underpinned by experimental evidence, nor indeed could it have been. No experimental evidence was presented to prove that any animal lineage had given rise to a new species over a number of generations. Darwin's critics maintained that he had deserted the authentic tradition in British science, initiated by Francis Bacon (1561–1626) and developed by Isaac Newton (1642–1727).[5] However, Darwin's supporters maintained, quite reasonably, that the long time scale associated with the formation of new species ruled out the possibility of direct evidence based on observation and experiment. Their argument was favoured by the greater inclination of scientists in the second half of the nineteenth century to adopt a more flexible methodology and to openly acknowledge the benefits of the hypothetico-deductive approach to scientific study.[6]

The general idea that old species had given rise to new species by a process of transmutation – despite all the scientific criticisms – was consolidated by the late 1860s. By the end of the decade the majority of biologists openly accepted the general theory of evolution.[7] The concept of natural selection, independently worked out by Alfred Russel Wallace, did not fare so well and the objections against it were not overcome in Darwin's lifetime. Even Thomas Henry Huxley – Darwin's most vigorous and influential supporter – was not persuaded about natural selection and argued that evolution might sometimes work through abrupt large variations (saltations) rather than through the selection of relatively small variations. In addition to the scientific objections there were also theological motives for expressing opposition to the Darwinian mechanism. Natural selection seemed to undermine a popular argument for the existence of God – the appearance of design in nature. It was now claimed that plants and animals were superbly adapted to their environment because only well-adapted creatures survived – not because they had been designed in a particular way. God's creatures were transformed into creatures of nature – brought into existence not by divine intelligence and benevolence but by an incredibly wasteful, long, cruel and bloody process of struggle and survival. And after all that it seemed to lack purpose.

The Rejection of Darwinism

Roman Catholics in Britain expressed their opinions about the troublesome implications of science through periodicals such as *The Tablet, The Rambler, The Month* and the *Dublin Review*. From 1859 to 1872 they advanced a number of arguments which, although highly contrived for the purpose of defending Catholic doctrine and humankind's special place in creation, were, nevertheless, highly resistant to rational assault. They endeavoured to minimise the contact between science (especially

Darwinism) and religion. Possibilities of conflict arose where the domains of science and religion overlapped. Where conflict was perceived, then it was argued that scientific investigation was incomplete, that there was insufficient evidence, and that scientific theory was subject to revision. When the scientific position could not be so easily dismissed then a further defensive argument was sometimes advanced – i.e. the interpretation of relevant scriptural passages had not yet been defined by the teaching authority of the Catholic Church. These two defensive strategies used in combination were particularly effective. If the scientific position was particularly strong, then changes in religious belief could be gradually and almost imperceptibly made, and presented as developments of doctrine. Furthermore, assertions of harmony between Catholicism and science were used to ignore difficulties and silence debate.[8] By the early 1870s Irish Catholic apologists were not without plausible arguments for repelling any attack which might be launched under the banner of the natural sciences.

The acceptance of biological evolution, including human origins, required unsettling changes in Catholic doctrine, especially pertaining to original sin. The Roman Catholic Church would only change its teaching when the weight of scientific evidence against it was overwhelming. Given that particular stance, it was in a very strong position. Archaeological findings, especially in caves at Brixham and Devon and in the gravel beds of the Somme valley, tended to support the idea of human evolution. Human origins were extended far beyond the few thousand years allowed for by the chronology of Genesis. However, the fossil record did not yield a single specimen which could be reliably taken as a link between humans and their hypothetical ape ancestors.[9]

In Ireland the theological response to evolution by natural selection was considerable. The response of Irish scientists, writing as scientists, was virtually absent in terms of published commentaries and reviews.[10] Darwin did, however, have some influential supporters in Ireland – this was indicated in 1866 when he was elected an honorary member of the Royal Irish Academy.[11]

The concept of natural selection was particularly reprehensible from an Irish Catholic perspective. In the May 1873 issue of the *Irish Ecclesiastical Record* a contributor, writing under the initials J.G.C., made use of some of the scientific arguments against Darwin's theory, such as the lack of transitional forms, past and present.[12] William Thomson provided him 'with some of the best weapons for an assault on Mr Darwin's position'.[13] He concluded that evolutionary theory was not only 'a scientific mistake' – it was 'unscientific in its methods, and mischievous in its tendency'.[14] However, J.G.C. was not in a strong position to judge the merits of evolutionary theory on a scientific basis. His lack of scientific knowledge was nowhere more conspicuously evident than when he stated that Darwinism was inconsistent with 'the facts of history, which tell us that the animals of to-day are, in unchanged characteristics, those of the pyramids, those known to the most ancient peoples who have left monuments . . .'[15]

J.G.C. did not give any indication of the sources for his argument from history which disclosed a complete lack of understanding of the vast time scale so essential for the tenability of Darwinism. It may have been based on the *Twelve Lectures on the Connexion between Science and Revealed Religion* (1837) by Nicholas Wiseman, who later became cardinal archbishop of Westminster when the Catholic hierarchy of England and Wales was restored in 1850. Wiseman rejected Jean Baptiste Lamarck's theory of biological evolution, which relied on the concept of the inheritance of acquired characteristics. He argued against Lamarck on the basis that no evolutionary changes had occurred over three thousand years as indicated by the mummified animals of ancient Egypt. This error was understandable in Wiseman's time when there was very little awareness that the age of the Earth was measured in millions rather than in thousands of years.[16] However, in the 1870s it displayed an inexcusable lack of understanding by an author who assumed himself competent to judge a scientific theory on the basis of scientific arguments. The lack of comprehension about the slow rate of evolutionary change, and the vast time scale it required, was not unique to J.G.C.[17]

The motives for attacking Darwinism were not primarily concerned with its scientific or philosophical faults. Science and philosophy provided opportunities for assaults on Darwinism – theology and hopes for eternal happiness gave rise to the motives.[18] J.G.C. was harshly critical of Darwinism because it called into question the status of humankind, concerning the existence of God and divine action in the natural domain. In Darwin's *Descent of Man* humans were seen as highly developed primates, as part of the evolutionary process and subject to natural selection like other species. Furthermore, Darwin had speculated about the origins of moral and religious beliefs and the social instincts of humans in purely utilitarian and scientific terms. Therefore, J.G.C. concluded that the obvious tendency of his doctrines is – if not to eliminate creative action altogether out of the universe of mind and matter, and to reduce the order of harmony of Nature to the results of blind fortuitous forces, which would be to obliterate God altogether – at least to place the Creator at such a distance from His works that His supervision, providence, and justice may be safely ignored.[19]

In the late nineteenth century God was expelled from scientific discourse, with considerable assistance from Darwin, but Christian scientists did not, generally, abandon their faith as a result of this development especially not in the United States.[20] Evolution was seen as a process determined by natural laws arising from the indirect action of God. However, evolutionary theory was also frequently associated with secularism, materialism and agnosticism. Irish Catholic opinion tended to see evolution in the latter context, especially against the background of Tyndall's Belfast address. The highly influential Jesuit priest Fr Thomas Finlay (1848–1940)[21] observed that well-established findings in scientific research were associated with, and used in support of, erroneous ideas. It was essential for Catholics to discriminate between 'undeniable scientific truths' and 'crude theories' which were in many instances 'absurd' and 'noxious'. Finlay, writing in the *Irish Monthly*, expressed the opinion that Irish Catholics were particularly vulnerable because they lacked the philosophical training to make the distinction between solidly established truths and ideas based on little more than speculation. Irish Catholics, so preoccupied with their own 'struggle for life' over the previous few centuries, were isolated from the 'wars of the learned' in mainland Europe and were unprepared for intellectual combat.[22] Under these circumstances evolutionary theory would be difficult to resist.

Finlay believed that the acceptance of Darwinism made it much easier to accept that there were no immortal souls in nature. Tyndall's presentation of evolution at Belfast left no room for the supernatural. This in turn overturned the moral principles upon which society functioned and eliminated all prospects for a blissful afterlife.[23] However, Finlay reassured himself and his readers that human thought could not be explained entirely on the basis of physical and chemical phenomena. The spirituality of the human soul was immune to the progress of science, as indeed was the vast corpus of Christian doctrine.

Finlay's opinion, associating scientific naturalism with the propagation of immorality and the prospect of social disintegration, was expressed against a background of an ongoing controversy in Victorian society where the same connections were at issue. In late-nineteenth-century Britain and Ireland critics of scientific naturalism and Darwinism frequently argued that the explicitly naturalistic science of Darwin and his supporters would provoke such a resurgence of immorality and corruption that it would even exceed the decadence of ancient pagan civilisations. *The Descent of Man*, where Darwin saw sexual desire and reproduction as critically important to the process of human evolution, and where he elaborated on the origins of moral beliefs in terms of natural selection, created some difficulties for repudiating such a charge. Tyndall, Huxley and other supporters of Darwin were vulnerable to misrepresentations of their views and were castigated for their apparent espousal of immorality. They frequently found themselves on the defensive in their attempts to maintain a reputation for moral probity.[24]

Finlay was evidently troubled by Tyndall's Belfast Address but he took comfort in the assertion by Vatican Council I's *Dogmatic Constitution on the Catholic Faith* that truth does not contradict truth, therefore revelation and science could never contradict each other. Some measure of protection could be assured if an isolationist – or at least a semi-isolationist – stance was adopted. Religious belief should not be dismissed on the basis that it could not be proven by scientific investigation. Finlay argued that the immortal soul of man could not be detected by the scalpel or the microscope. A corollary of this was that no amount of theological reasoning could construct the binomial theorem or ascertain the circulation of the blood. All this seemed to constitute a reasonable argument designed to prevent conflict between theology and science. But scientists had not stayed within their discipline. Finlay believed that the majority of contemporary scientific authors, due to a convergence of reasons which he had not ascertained, were hostile towards the Catholic Church. These included 'the leaders of modern progress' and 'the best representatives of the intellectual advancement of the age'. Thus the Catholic Church was stigmatised as the great opponent of enlightenment.[25] Finlay exaggerated the extent of the problem but there was some truth in his claim. It is significant that his observations were made when the X Club, consisting of only nine members, were exercising an influence over the scientific profession grossly disproportionate to their numbers. They were united in their 'devotion to science, pure and free, untrammelled by religious dogmas'.[26] Founded in November 1864, the club remained very active for two decades and included, in addition to Huxley and Tyndall, the eminent scientist Joseph Dalton Hooker and the philosopher Herbert Spencer. The protégés of Huxley had been 'sliding' into academic posts from Galway to Melbourne since the early 1860s.[27] These included W. Thistleton-Dyer (1843–1928), who accepted the post of Professor of Botany at the Royal College of Science, Dublin, in 1870 and Alfred Cort Haddon, who was appointed Professor of Zoology at the same college in 1880.[28]

From Finlay's perspective the prospect of reconciling Catholicism and mainstream science must have seemed rather limited. The dominant attitude among scientists towards the church seemed to be one of hostility or indifference. However, the advocacy of materialistic science, explicitly presented, stood little chance alone of detaching Irish Catholics from their faith. The greatest danger, it seemed, was that a subtle corrosive process would gradually lead the youth of Catholic Ireland to apostasy. According to Finlay, anti-Catholic scientists were mainly responsible for the formation of the various sciences and, therefore, Catholics would discover many ideas in scientific literature that would 'rudely shock' their religious beliefs. Furthermore, there seemed to be something in scientific methodology which was inimical to religious faith. On this latter point Finlay observed that modern scientific methodology would gradually inculcate 'a distaste for mere authoritative statements of truth' and 'an exaggerated sense of the force of scientific arguments against revelation'. Minds immersed in the study of the natural sciences would lose their appreciation of theological and metaphysical arguments. Thus the faith of science students would be exposed to 'a wearing, wasting process against which no precaution is excessive'.[29] Finlay's worries about the impact of science on religion were probably not very unusual.[30]

Finlay had very little reason to worry about the corrosive effects of science on religion. Few Catholic students, in Catholic secondary colleges or at university level, studied science – clerical apprehensions about science probably contributed substantially to this problem. The acute shortage of science graduates led to a scarcity of adequately qualified science teachers[31] and this in turn could only have propagated widespread ignorance of science amongst Irish Catholics.

Apes or Angels?

The theory of evolution in particular seemed to counteract the emergence of a positive attitude towards science in Catholic Ireland. Throughout the 1870s the church was not yet ready to accept that humans evolved from lower life forms.[32] Finlay rejected the extension of evolutionary theory to humankind because it was, in his opinion, 'directly opposed' to Catholic doctrine.[33] In their pastoral letter of 14 October 1874, the Irish Catholic bishops indicated their contempt for and intolerance of evolutionary theory, which they associated with Tyndall's agnosticism. They believed that if evolution was to be accepted, then humans would be degraded to the level of a 'brute'. The basis of morality would be eliminated, giving rise to 'a universal unchaining of all the worst passions ravenous for satisfaction', which in turn would cause social disintegration. Humans would be more vulnerable to suffering, especially when their hopes for a blissful afterlife were extinguished.[34] Evidently, the bishops placed little value on the potency of morality based entirely on secular values. However, the abandonment of religious belief did not necessarily lead to the demise of moral behaviour, a point exemplified in the promotion of Darwin as a virtuous person.[35] Darwin's virtues as a dedicated family man and a diligent scientist even received some acknowledgement in Catholic Ireland.[36]

Although Irish Catholic clergymen rejected evolution outright, on the basis that it contradicted revelation, their opinions were not representative of the Catholic Church's official position. No dogmatic pronouncement emanated from Rome on the issue, not even after St George Jackson Mivart's *Genesis of Species* was published in 1871. The book elicited favourable reviews in the Catholic press, especially in *The Tablet* and the *Dublin Review*, and met with some mild approval in *The Month*. Mivart (1827–1900), the most eminent Catholic scientist in England, argued that evolution and Catholicism were compatible. He became one of Darwin's most eminent critics in the 1870s and downplayed the significance of Darwin's evolutionary mechanism of natural selection. Mivart put forward several scientific arguments, supported by a large volume of biological data.[37] He maintained that humankind originated from an evolutionary process under God's guidance, not from the blind process of natural selection. Finally, he referred to the works of St Augustine, St Thomas Aquinas and the Jesuit Francisco de Suarez to assert that theistic evolution was 'thoroughly acceptable to the most orthodox theologians'.[38]

In the July 1871 issue of the *Quarterly Review* Mivart bitterly criticised Darwin's *Descent of Man*, published earlier that year. Huxley responded aggressively in defence of Darwin through the medium of another British periodical, the *Contemporary Review*, arguing that evolution and Roman Catholicism were incompatible, and that Suarez would have 'damned' Mivart 'forty times over' for the views he expressed.[39] The Vatican would have disagreed. Papal approval of his work was indicated in 1876 when he received an honorary doctorate in philosophy from Pope Pius IX.[40] The way seemed clear to embrace theistic evolution, extended to include humankind. But would such liberty of thought be granted to Catholic Ireland? It seemed not!

From a traditionalist Catholic perspective the special creation of man was still sacrosanct. Evolutionary theory threatened man's privileged status and had to be resisted – even in the heart of rural Ireland. In the late nineteenth century there was an exceptional popular interest in natural history and this was due mainly to the cultural aspirations of middle- and upper-class Protestants who had both the time and the resources to study nature.[41] Many field clubs organised excursions to the countryside and hundreds of people from English industrial towns were shuttled in chartered trains to rural destinations.[42] Apparently, visiting scientists were not shy about propagating the gospel of evolution in the Irish countryside, especially in 1878 when the British Association for the Advancement of Science held its annual meeting in Dublin.[43] This caused some concern amongst the Irish Catholic clergy. Canon H.E. Dennehy, parish priest of Kanturk, County Cork, complained that:

> They march about in triumphal procession, and everyone appears to applaud them. They are thrown upon our shores under the name of the British Association, and they are fêted everywhere. In the morning they inspect our caves and climb our mountains, in the company of honest and believing men, to tell us before night that we are the descendants of apes and baboons, and that our life has originated in a chance combination of atoms! It is a dangerous thing to wrestle with a giant. And hence timid men, though learned, retire from them, and bold men content themselves with flatly denying their conclusions without proving these conclusions to be false.[44]

He claimed that the speculations of scientists about the origins of man had proven detrimental to the faith of the young generation. Unbelief, he believed, was rampant, especially in France, Germany, Italy and England.[45] Even in Ireland

> whose faith is a proverb, young men educated under liberal scientific professors show a tendency to free themselves, from moral and intellectual restraints. Everywhere a pride of intellect is being generated which is widening the area of rebellion against revelation . . . Where is it to end? . . . To stem the coming tide is clearly the duty of staunch

> believers in revelation. And yet how few opponents have the philoso-
> phers had to encounter![46]

Catholic apologists were apprehensive, confronted as they were by the superior intellectual forces of the richly endowed British scientific community which evidently enjoyed considerable influence in the so called 'godless' colleges. Very few Irish Catholics enjoyed the benefits of university education and were extremely disadvantaged in challenging modern scientific theories. The Roman Catholic Church in Ireland did not have any scientist of its own, of the calibre of Tyndall or Huxley to champion its cause. Catholic clergymen, therefore, had to look abroad, frequently referring to the writings of Darwin's most eminent critics, especially St George Jackson Mivart and George Douglas Campbell (the eighth Duke of Argyll).

The training of priests left much to be desired, but Ireland was not exceptional in this way. Throughout most, if not all, of the pontificate of Pius IX there were very few Catholic centres of scholarship outside Germany which could match the standards of rationalists and Protestants.[47] Walter McDonald (1854–1920), who later became Professor of Dogmatic Theology at Maynooth in 1881, gave an account of his experiences in *Reminiscences of a Maynooth Professor*. Seminarians were subjected to

> a dead grind of some old, traditional statements of doctrine, proofs,
> and answers to objections; all very bald and imperfect – very unlike
> what one meets in the real world. Darwin was then revolutionizing
> thought; but we overturned him in two or three brief sentences.[48]

He believed that Maynooth was behind the times, too preoccupied with Protestantism to address the new danger posed by the rationalists – 'slaying foes that had been disabled or killed long ago'.[49] Some of those in religious life experienced great difficulties in confronting the arguments presented by the rationalists. The strong emphasis on tradition greatly restricted innovative thinking. McDonald found the conservatism of the church so difficult to endure that it threatened both his sanity and the very foundations of his faith. He suspected that the Bible contained errors and contradictions. All this had a long-term effect on him and he was troubled with doubts throughout the rest of his life.[50]

McDonald was critical of the unscientific outlook and unquestioning faith of the college professors and associated it with the lack of prepara-tion by seminarians for the intellectual challenges of the late nineteenth century. He was critical of the tendency of the professors to smugly dismiss the great controversies of the time. Their 'strong childlike faith' kept them 'safe in the Middle Ages' – but for him, and some of his fellow seminarians, this was not good enough.[51] McDonald's knowledge and understanding of natural science was not at an advanced level but he did appreciate its importance.[52]

The Irish Catholic antipathy towards mainstream science in the late nineteenth century was probably not unusual in the English-speaking world – especially considering the pivotal role Irish Catholicism played in the development of Catholic communities in Britain, the United States Canada, South Africa, Australia and New Zealand. The lack of genuine intellectual discourse, the excess of unquestioning faith, and naïve views about evolution, which McDonald referred to, were probably typical of English-speaking Catholicism in the early 1880s. Mivart, from his extensive social contacts with his co-religionists, found widespread ignorance of science and prejudice against evolution.

In his self-assumed role of reconciler of theology and science Mivart was, in correspondence with Cardinal Newman, critical of the role of the clergy. Newman responded that priests did not have enough time to educate themselves about science to enable them to respond competently to irreligious critics who maintained that science and Catholicism were irreconcilable. Furthermore, Newman maintained that the antipathy of priests towards science arose because theories, rather than established facts, were used to criticise the Bible. The tendency of priests, therefore, was to wait for these theories to be undermined by new scientific discoveries, rather than spending much time and energy in challenging erroneous opinions.[53] Ignoring the problem would solve it.

Newman's opinion was probably more applicable to Irish Catholicism than to English Catholicism, where circumstances were very different. English Catholicism, unlike Irish Catholicism, benefited from a stream of intellectually gifted converts from the mid-nineteenth century to the mid-twentieth century.[54] These converts formed the nucleus of liberal Catholicism in England,[55] which had no comparable counterpart in Ireland. There were strong similarities as well as differences – both religious communities had suffered discrimination at the hands of the British state. In Ireland and England pressing social and pastoral concerns tended to distract attention away from matters regarded as intellectual rather than of practical value. In Ireland, after the suppressive effects of the Penal Laws, the church felt compelled to make enormous efforts in institutional reconstruction, such as the building of schools and churches and the setting up of charitable organisations. In England, the Catholic Church was under severe pressure to cope with the huge influx of poverty-stricken Irish Catholics who emigrated in the years of the Great Famine and afterwards.

English and Irish Catholics suffered self-imposed intellectual isolation because their respective ecclesiastical authorities forbade attendance at the universities. Attempts, in both cases, to set up an alternative Catholic university did not prove satisfactory, especially in England, where the Catholic University at Kensington, which had opened in 1875, closed in 1877 amid scandal and heavy debts.[56] Scientific education in both countries suffered because of its neglect in the seminaries.[57]

The intellectual condition of Catholicism in the other English-speaking countries was probably poorer than that of Britain and Ireland. For example, the Catholic Church in the United States was mainly an immigrant church. Poverty, lack of education, and little leisure time militated against the acquisition of the minimal standard of education necessary for participation in scientific debates. Most American Catholics were too preoccupied with the practical requirements of life, such as the building of homes, schools and the setting up of businesses, to sustain an interest in the merits and demerits of evolutionary theory. The clergy were too concerned with pastoral duties and those Catholics who were well educated, and had sufficient leisure time to reflect on topical issues, were primarily concerned about the preservation of the faith and did not view science as potentially helpful in this regard.[58]

Irish Catholics tended not only to reject Darwinism but also evolution in general. Caricatures of the Irish as monkeys or apes could only have reinforced their resistance to the theory. Evolution cartoons were sometimes used to communicate opinions about gender, race and social and cultural hierarchies. In the late nineteenth century it seems that the Irish were frequently the nation of choice for illustrating similarities between humans and monkeys or apes.[59] There was probably some awareness of this abuse of evolutionary theory amongst Irish Catholics.

Rejection of evolution was unnecessary from a liberal theological point of view. Many scientists were able to reconcile their Christian faith with their belief in an evolutionary process. Nevertheless, Irish Catholic apologists felt too threatened to seriously contemplate coming to terms with it. Furthermore, some modern ideas in other disciplines, such as in philosophy and history, also posed serious doctrinal problems for them.

In early 1884 Cardinal John Henry Newman cautiously suggested, in the *Nineteenth Century*, that there might be minor errors of detail in scripture, irrelevant to matters of faith and morals.[60] He did so with historical, scientific and geographical inaccuracies in mind and was taken to task by John Healy (1841–1918), a professor of theology at Maynooth.[61] Healy's harsh criticism was published in the February issue of the *Irish Ecclesiastical Record*. In the debate that followed Healy revealed a critical weakness in his position when he refused to take account of modern historical scholarship.[62] In this instance, theological orthodoxy took priority over the consensus of experts in secular scholarship.

Murphy versus Vaughan and Mivart

Irish Catholic apologists were adamant that no ground would be conceded to the social or natural sciences when findings in these disciplines conflicted with, or seemed to conflict with, points of Catholic doctrine. In the September 1884 issue of the *Irish Ecclesiastical Record* Fr Jeremiah Murphy urged his clerical colleagues to study science so that they would be in a strong position to challenge those who used science to discredit revelation.[63] It was essential to keep scientists 'rigidly' to 'the established facts of science'.[64] Defenders of revelation had nothing to fear.

Murphy argued that Christian doctrine had, for centuries, provided a perfectly satisfactory explanation of human origins. It was not reasonable to set it aside to make way for the acceptance of an unproven scientific theory. The burden of proof was on scientists, not just to prove their theory but also to 'disprove, utterly' the arguments in favour of revelation which were found to be cogent and persuasive.[65] Revelation, of course, was defined by the Catholic Church and could only be defended – effectively – by the same institution. Murphy took the opportunity to castigate Protestantism – with its 'cognate broods of heresy', beneath contempt as an adversary and helpless in the face of scientific naturalism.[66]

Darwinism was an unfounded assertion and Darwin himself was reduced to 'little better than an average specimen of the Rationalistic school', whose achievements had been grossly exaggerated. In contrast, those who opposed him were described as 'competent authorities', 'eminent men', 'most eminent Naturalists' and 'distinguished'.[67] These included the Scottish historian and social critic Thomas Carlyle (1795–1881), the Swiss anatomist and embryologist Rudolph Albert von Kölliker (1817–1905) and the Paris physician Constantin James. The reference to James is of particular interest. His book, *Du Darwinisme ou l'homme-singe*

(1877), attacked Darwin and other evolutionists with greater scurrility than any other French book of the period. It is highly significant that the 1892 edition of the book reproduced a letter of praise from Pope Pius IX[68] – the same pope who had honoured the work of Mivart.

Many Catholic scientists, especially in France, had declined to accept evolution on the basis that there was inadequate evidence for it, and denied that their opposition to evolution was motivated by religious considerations.[69] Murphy was not reticent about declaring his religious bias. The prospect of science undermining the very foundations of faith was evidently distressing for him to contemplate. Darwin had speculated in his *Descent of Man* about the origins and development of human social instincts, codes of morality, intellect, the immortal soul, and belief in God.[70] He claimed that it was arrogance and prejudice which caused opponents of evolution to deny that humans shared a common ancestry with other vertebrates.[71] All this was regarded as reprehensible by Murphy and he asserted that:

> Science condemns it; reason revolts against it; Revelation anathema-
> tizes it . . . Man . . . in his foolish effort to escape from his Creator's
> hands he brings himself down to the level of the beasts, and deliber-
> ately claims kindred with them. Such are the dreamings which our
> scientists offer as a substitute for our faith. They would take from us
> the God whom our fathers adored, the religion that is our sole conso-
> lation here and our passport to happiness hereafter, and as a substitute
> they would give us – nothing, absolutely nothing.[72]

Murphy read the polemical exchanges between Mivart and Huxley which had occurred in the early 1870s. Although his sympathy was with Mivart, he believed that Huxley was the clear winner of the argument that theology could not be reconciled with the evolution of humankind.[73] But were Roman Catholics permitted to believe that humans evolved from lower forms of life? There was considerable uncertainty about this because the teaching authority of the church had not issued any clear pronouncement on this specific issue.[74] However, the dominant view amongst the Irish Catholic clergy in the nineteenth century was opposed to the acceptance of evolutionary theory applied to humans. Jeremiah Murphy argued at length, in the *Irish Ecclesiastical Record*, that Roman Catholics were obligated to repudiate the theory of humankind's lowly origins. The application of evolutionary theory to other forms of life did not interest the church, but faith did not permit 'coquetting with the evolution system' when the body and immortal soul of man was being considered.[75] What was the theological basis for such a stance? Murphy claimed that Darwinism attacked the very foundations of faith because it denied intelligent design in nature. But was it permissible to believe in an evolutionary process, operating through natural laws, initiated and maintained by God? Mivart advocated the acceptance of an evolutionary process which included the human body – but not the immortal soul. Murphy read Mivart's *Genesis of Species* and *Lessons from Nature as Manifested in Mind and Matter* (1876) but he was not persuaded by Mivart's thesis which harmonised Catholic theology and human evolution. He regarded the English biologist as a loyal, well-intentioned, but misguided son of the church.[76]

Murphy's position on the issue was weak. He was unable to discover a definitive statement of a general council, or an authoritative papal decree, asserting the immediate creation of the first humans. However, this did not prevent him from invoking the authority of the church. He claimed that the theologians and teachers of the Roman Catholic Church asserted 'with the most extraordinary unanimity' the immediate creation of Adam and Eve.[77] Catholics were bound to comply with an assertion by the 'ordinary' magisterium of the church as if it had been defined by a general council or by a pope teaching *ex cathedra* (i.e. as infallibly true). The *Dogmatic Constitution of the Catholic Faith*, promulgated at the First Vatican Council, was quoted to support this point:

> . . . by divine and catholic faith all those things are to be believed which are contained in the word of God as found in scripture and tradition, and which are proposed by the church as matters to be believed as divinely revealed, whether by her solemn judgement or in her ordinary and universal magisterium.[78]

Furthermore, the *Syllabus of Errors* was also mentioned in the above context. The twenty-second condemned proposition was: 'The obligation under which Catholic teachers and writers are bound applies only to those things which are proposed by the infallible judgement of the Church as dogmas of faith.'[79]

Murphy argued that the Biblical account of the creation of mankind was so precise that if evolution had really occurred then the scriptural text could not have been better calculated to deceive its readers if this had been the intention of its inspired writers.[80] But he did not regard the scriptural texts as conclusive proof of the immediate formation of Adam's

body. Instead, he relied on the church fathers and theologians to determine the meaning of scripture and this, he claimed, had been done so
that the literal interpretation of Adam's creation was now a *res fidei* – a
revealed truth. If the 'gospel' of human evolution was a true interpretation of the creation narrative in scripture, then it was

> strange that no Catholic for 1800 years should have even a remote
> conception of this meaning. For all that time the Church taught the
> above revealed proposition, and for all that time the faithful believed
> it; and yet all along the Fathers and Theologians were ignorant of what
> she taught, and the faithful ignorant of what they believed – that is if
> Evolution be applicable to man![81]

When discussing the beliefs of the church fathers, Murphy noted that the
writings of St Augustine had been cited frequently by Christian evolutionists as a basis for their viewpoint. Murphy rejected their claim, stating
that St Augustine's language was too obscure and that the evolutionary
concept could not have occurred to him.[82] But this argument undermined his position also. He had asserted that the writings of the church
fathers supported his point of view, but he also acknowledged that these
theologians had no knowledge of modern evolutionary theories and
could not therefore have been expected to explicitly disagree with it.[83]

Murphy thought it most unreasonable that the church was expected,
in some quarters, to 'bend and strain Revelation to suit the speculations
of even well-meaning men'. The only science that was 'real' was science
that was in harmony with Catholic orthodoxy. However, the acceptance
of evolutionary theory, as applied to humans, was becoming 'too
common' amongst Catholics.[84] This trend, he believed, was a threat to the
faith of many Catholics, although he did concede that some of its advocates had good intentions towards the church.

An English Catholic priest, John. S. Vaughan, challenged Murphy's
views.[85] It is significant that no Irish priest chose to do so. This can
reasonably be taken as an indication that there was extremely strong
opposition to the idea of human evolution amongst the Irish Catholic
clergy. It is likely that some priests – probably a tiny minority – saw no
theological objection to it but, out of deference to ecclesiastical authority,
chose to keep their opinions to themselves. Ireland, unlike England, did
not have a liberal Catholic movement in the 1880s.

Vaughan expressed a more tolerant and broad-minded approach
towards science and he robustly criticised the restrictions which Murphy

advocated. His views, communicated through the *Irish Ecclesiastical Record*, exposed a number of weaknesses in Murphy's dogmatic stance:

1. When the six 'days' of creation were each believed to be twenty-four hours in duration, the idea of a slow and gradual evolution of Adam's body was not tenable.
2. That God formed man's body and infused it with a living soul was not in doubt. What was open to question was the method. Was Adam's body created in an instant or did it take years? The Bible was silent on this matter. Furthermore, although it was of historical and scientific importance, it was not theologically significant because it was deemed to be irrelevant to one's attitude and duties to God.
3. Theologians, past and present, were not unanimous and even if they were this was not in itself binding on future generations because the instant and direct creation of the first humans was not affirmed as a doctrine of faith. There was an important distinction to be made between divinely revealed facts and the consensus of theologians.
4. What was fundamentally wrong with the theory of man's ape ancestry? There was no sustainable theological objection. The church had not defined its position.[86]
5. The advances of the natural sciences (notably geology and astronomy) had in the past compelled a reinterpretation of scripture. The *prima facie* interpretation of scripture was not always the correct one.[87] This was a particularly strong argument. There were precedents for the abandonment of literal interpretations of some scriptural narratives.[88]

On the basis of the above points Vaughan believed that it was permissible for Roman Catholics to believe in a theory of evolution applied to the creation of the human body. He believed that Murphy's stance was narrow-minded and contributed to acrimonious exchanges between theologians and scientists, which in turn were detrimental to the advancement of both theology and science.[89] He was convinced that if an attempt was made to force Murphy's views on Catholics it would 'put their faith and obedience to a cruel test'.[90] Catholics were free, without fear of heresy or eternal damnation, to make up their own minds. However, Vaughan was careful to state that he would accept, 'unreservedly', any decision the church might make on the issue.[91]

Murphy did not concede his position. He believed that it would be 'suicidal' for Catholics to reinterpret scripture for the purpose of reconciling it with evolutionary theory.[92] He expressed the opinion that the traditional belief in Adam's creation was now becoming less widely held.[93] This was a source of concern to him and he believed that if the theological ideas he opposed became widely accepted then Vaughan and himself would have little to defend.[94]

The two priests had been quite prepared to debate with each other through the pages of the *Irish Ecclesiastical Record*. This journal had a considerable influence on the intellectual formation of priests in Ireland. Cardinal Paul Cullen had founded it for the purpose of creating closer links between the Irish church and Rome.[95] The main function of the *Irish Ecclesiastical Record* was to facilitate the discussion of issues 'intimately connected with the professional studies of a priest' but it also included articles pertaining to literary, scientific, historical and archaeological topics which were the subject of public attention.[96] In the nineteenth century most of the articles about scientific topics focused on the biological sciences – especially biological evolution and its 'alleged implications' for the interpretation of the Bible and Catholic doctrine.[97] Although opposite views on evolutionary theory had been discussed within its pages, there was a different attitude towards a more open forum.[98] When the evolutionary issue was discussed in *The Tablet*, Fr Murphy protested that it was inappropriate in a journal circulated to the general public. He believed that statements which pointed to man's primitive ancestry 'must be a severe shock to the faith of ordinary Catholics'.[99] He wished, like Cardinal Newman, to protect Roman Catholics against novel ideas which might threaten their faith.

The opinions of Murphy and Vaughan were published in a series of five articles in the *Irish Ecclesiastical Record* from December 1884 to November 1885. Both priests had referred to the works of well-known Catholic authors for support.[100] Most Catholic theologians were opposed to human evolution, regarding it as 'rash', but only a few went so far as to assert that the direct divine creation of Adam's body was an article of faith. Murphy and Vaughan drew their sources of inspiration from opposite ends of the spectrum of clerical opinions that accepted or rejected evolutionary theory relating to human evolution.[101]

As the debate between Murphy and Vaughan was still in progress, Mivart responded to Murphy's first article on 'Evolution and Faith' through the medium of the English periodical, the *Nineteenth Century*.[102] In the July 1885 issue, he asserted that scientists enjoyed far more intellectual freedom than had been previously supposed – not just in the natural sciences, but also in political economy, sociology, history and Biblical criticism. Conclusions in the social and natural sciences would be determined by a rational evaluation of evidence, not by ecclesiastical authority. The censorship of the Copernican hypothesis and the persecution of Galileo in the seventeenth century indicated clearly to Mivart that it was in the best interests of the Roman Catholic Church to respect the independence of scholars in all scientific disciplines. Murphy was seen as one of 'the ever-recurring band of obstructives who always turn out to have been in the wrong'.[103]

Murphy responded to Mivart in the May 1886 issue of the *Nineteenth Century*, expressing resentment for being cast in the role of a narrow-minded and incompetent 'obstructive'. Mivart's assertion of the rights of intellectual freedom was dismissed as 'wanton license, the offspring of intellectual pride, a license which loyal Catholics have never claimed, and which the Catholic Church has never granted'.[104] The debate between Mivart and Murphy ended on a bitter note. Mivart, as a self-professed liberal Catholic, castigated ultramontane Catholicism which for him indicated obscurantism, the abuse of ecclesiastical power, an unscientific outlook and an aversion to enlightenment and progress. He feared that some educated young Catholics, especially those knowledgeable about biology, were losing their faith because of 'an approved divergence' between Catholic doctrine and science. Murphy epitomised the 'intolerant and aggressive faction' of Roman Catholicism. According to Mivart some members of the Irish clergy did give him 'hearty sympathy', but he did not give names or any indication of how many. Murphy's 'intolerably pernicious' opinions had stirred him to action in defence of liberal Catholicism and science.[105] Murphy's opinions probably exerted considerable influence in the Catholic Church outside Ireland. His anti-evolutionary views featured in a polemic between Mivart and the Benedictine bishop of Newport (Britain), John Cuthbert Hedley. Of greater significance is the fact that the Congregation of the Index took cognisance of Murphy's arguments when examining John Zahm's *Evolution and Dogma* (1896) in 1898 (see Chapter 3).[106]

Mivart had to struggle on two fronts to reconcile Roman Catholicism and science. In science he had to contend with the Darwinians and found himself ostracised by many of his fellow scientists, most notably Thomas Henry Huxley, who had been a personal friend.[107] Within the Catholic Church he received criticism from a number of his co-religionists and it is highly significant that, in recounting his experiences in 1900, he singled out Fr Jeremiah Murphy for special mention.[108] At around this time he sensed a deep hostility from Irish and English Roman Catholics.[109] However, up to 1887 he had not even received a hint of ecclesiastical disapproval for his views on evolution.[110]

The absence of censure did not mean approval. The Roman Catholic hierarchy did not condemn human evolution outright, at least not publicly. Nevertheless, it is likely that some bishops adopted a policy of discreet disapproval and probably, when circumstances seemed to demand it, persuaded their priests not to advocate controversial scientific theories. Fr John Vaughan, who had defended the right of Catholics to believe in human evolution in 1885, seems to have changed his attitude when he returned to the subject four years later. Writing under the provocative title of 'Man or Monkey?' Vaughan vigorously attacked the materialistic account of human evolution without making any reference to the alternative theistic version. Humankind's primate ancestry was dismissed as a mere 'superstition'.[111] Like other Catholic apologists he was particularly incensed about Darwin's statement in the *Descent of Man* which claimed that the difference in mind between humans and animals was one of degree, not one of kind.[112]

Vaughan, with materialistic evolution in mind, presented a grim picture of life on earth. Man's body was a 'corruptible vesture of vile clay . . . made to feast the worms'. Life was 'a veritable nothing: utterly valueless except in so far as it is related to eternity'.[113] The possibility of no afterlife was distressing to contemplate, evoking as it did feelings of futility and insignificance. Man's glory was in his immortal soul, not in his body. With scripture (Hebrews 2: 7) in mind, Vaughan argued that man was created 'a little lower than the angels', not 'a trifle higher than the brutes'.[114] Humans were destined for greatness and made in the image of God.[115] Materialistic scientists had overlooked man's higher interests, creating a considerable amount of apathy in spiritual matters when they promoted Darwinism.[116] The reason for this, he believed, was their tendency to consider only what could be ascertained by sensory perceptions and by scientific investigations.[117]

The threat posed by science was associated with its prestige and with the success of its applications. However, there was also a tendency in Irish Catholicism to see scientific study in a positive light. Fr Gerald Molloy wrote about the combustion process of a lighted candle to explain the carbon cycle. He saw 'traces of that mighty hand' throughout nature.[118] The Italian Jesuit astronomer Fr Angelo Secchi (1818–1878) was praised as an exemplary Catholic scientist whose discoveries inspired reverence for the Creator.[119] Astronomy was seen as a powerful stimulus to thoughts which elevated spiritual sensibility over material concerns.[120] The Royal Dublin Society was praised in the *Irish Ecclesiastical Record* for hosting a series of public lectures ranging from astronomy, physics and chemistry to the philosophy of science. The lectures were seen as 'a kind of Lenten Exercises', illuminating the fundamental point that science was 'the hand-maid of religion'.[121] Fr Henry Bedford's series of science articles in the *Irish Monthly*, written under the general heading of 'Scientific Gossip', empha-sised the harmony between religion and science. Diligent research in science, when pursued in 'the right spirit', would help one draw closer to the Divine Creator who revealed himself through his works.[122] Bedford's presentation of the harmony thesis was not merely defensive – it was not limited to a reiteration of the concept that science does not contradict rev-elation. It was expressed positively to make the point that scientific knowledge led to a greater appreciation of God's wisdom and power.[123]

Bedford's expositions made scientific and technical subjects such as astronomy, thermodynamics, telephones and Crookes tubes comprehen-sible, at the elementary level, to the readers of the *Irish Monthly*. He viewed his subject matter in a broad interdisciplinary context. This was nowhere more clearly evident than in his two essays on the telephone, which not only explained how the mechanism worked – the physiology of speech and hearing also received close attention. Medical scientists had worked out, in considerable detail, the role of anatomical structures such as the diaphragm, vocal cords and the cochlea. But, as Bedford observed, scientists knew very little about the nervous system. This raised the question about the origins of thought in the speaker and their interpretation by the listener. Bedford believed that scientists would never be able to explain thought in purely natural terms. Thoughts were 'evident tokens of what is divine: thus far can we go, but no farther . . . The power which made them is divine, and some knowledge He thinks fit to keep to Himself.'[124] It was not philosophically sound to infer the existence of God on the basis of the unknown but this does not seem to have troubled Bedford. He was so at ease with science that he could refer to the scientific works of Tyndall and Darwin without animosity.[125]

The implications of scientific theories for theology evidently con-cerned Irish Catholic authors from time to time, but not to the exclusion of earthly considerations. In his review of Gerald Molloy's *Gleanings in Science* (1888), Fr Francis Lennon (1838–1920), Professor of Natural Philosophy at Maynooth, envisaged that scientific knowledge would enable the efficient use of natural resources. Hydroelectricity, for example, was a potential source of energy for industrial development throughout many villages, towns and cities.[126] The priest novelist Canon

Patrick A. Sheehan (1852–1913), who frequently used fictitious characters to discuss controversial issues, wrote eloquently about the
achievements of science. Through the medium of an imaginary scientist
he acknowledged human ingenuity.

> We have captured the lightnings, and compelled them to carry our
> messages around the earth; we have weighed the sun, we have put
> the ponderous planets in the scales; . . . we have taken the suns of
> other systems, whose distance is so great that it paralyses the imagi-
> nation, and told you the very materials of which they are composed;
> we have walked among the nebulae of the Milky Way . . . We have
> torn open the bosom of the earth and shown you in stony manu-
> scripts the handwriting of Nature in the days of the mammoth and
> leviathan; and as the service of man is the only service we acknowl-
> edge, we have bade 'the little god of this planet' to rest from labour,
> for Nature shall be compelled to work for him. For him we harness
> its most dreadful powers . . .[127]

And science had so much more to offer because it had yet 'only touched
the fringe of Nature's garment'. But Sheehan's perspective was radically different from that of Molloy, Bedford and Lennon. There was a horrendous
price to be paid for what science had to offer because scientific practice
was subservient to secular interests and not in accordance with Christian
ethics. Sheehan, therefore, saw science as an agent of destruction rather
than an instrument of progress. Using one of his fictitious characters as a
mouthpiece, he associated science with the extensive destruction of the
natural environment and with the ruthless exploitation of men, women
and children in the factory system of *laissez-faire* capitalism:

> It is true you, men of science, have revealed certain secrets of Nature,
> but how? By laying sacrilegious hands on her awful face! You have cut
> and delved, and maimed and sacrificed Nature and her children, until
> her beautiful face is scarred . . . and the hideous ugliness has fallen
> upon the souls of the children of men . . . [Y]ou, from an advanced
> platform of scientific inquiry, would not only sacrifice to your sinful
> curiosity the poor beast that licks your hand in his agony, but you
> would even exhume your father's remains for the sake of an experi-
> ment. And after all, what have you done? Does the sun give more light
> or heat to our earth since you discovered that he is a furnace of liquid
> fire? . . . Is mankind better or happier since you drove him from the
> green fields and the blue skies to the cloudy and choking city,
> which . . . drags the strength from his limbs . . . Is childhood more

pure and joyful since you brought it into your factories . . . and chased
the roses from its cheeks, and the laughter from its lips, and the light
from its eyes . . . and the tender love of God from its heart? . . . You
can, no doubt, explain to us all about the sunsets; but the smoke of
your towns and factories has made it impossible for us to see one.[128]

Despite all its wonderful offerings, science was ultimately detrimental
to the idyllic way of life imagined by Sheehan – rural and deeply spiritual. However, Catholic apologists were worried mainly about eternal life
and salvation. The preservation of rural bliss was of much lesser importance. In the early 1890s evolutionary theory, especially Darwinism, was
still seen as a vehicle for agnosticism. In view of the strong perception in
Irish Catholic circles that scientific studies were very much under the
influence of those hostile to Roman Catholicism, it was extremely difficult for any Catholic to openly advocate that human evolution could be
reconciled with Catholic theology.[129] Nevertheless, the Catholic hierarchy
still refrained from issuing any pronouncement explicitly condemning
the idea of human evolution. But this limited toleration for those who
cautiously advocated theistic evolution was being eroded by developments in Rome.

3. Catholicism and Science, 1890s–1903

Converging Themes

Negative opinions about evolution from a theological perspective would suggest a relationship of conflict between Irish Catholicism and science. However, in this chapter it will be clear that the interaction between scientific and religious thinking was not so one-dimensional. This is certainly true of Irish Catholic culture from the early 1890s to the early years of the twentieth century. In this chapter cognisance is taken of developments indigenous and external to Ireland. Irish Catholic opinions are explored with reference to mainland Europe – with a particular emphasis on Rome and the English-speaking world – especially focusing on Britain. Evolutionary theory continued to be a theme of central importance – but it was not the only concern. Controversy about the Galileo case, Draper's conflict thesis, and theoretical physics also received attention. At this point it will be evident that discourse about religion and science did not take place in isolation from broader cultural, political and philosophical influences. Irish Catholic responses to evolutionary theory, for example, were conditioned by concerns about the influence of the popular press and the supposed susceptibility of English Protestant culture to irreligious ideas. Furthermore, Irish Catholic responses to evolution were not entirely negative. Evidence will be presented to indicate some degree of acceptance of evolution. There were even speculations about the theological implications of extraterrestrial life. In this chapter, therefore, there is no single theme, no simplistically linear narrative. Rather, a number of converging themes are addressed to elucidate the complexity of Irish Catholic opinions about science.

The Ascendancy of Ultraconservatism

In the 1890s the Vatican's censorious responses to Père Marie Dalmace Leroy's *L'Évolution Restreinte aux Espèces Organiques* (*Evolution Restricted to Organic Species*, 1891) and Fr John A. Zahm's *Evolution and Dogma* (1896) strongly indicated theological disapproval in the higher echelons of the Roman Catholic Church towards evolutionary theory, especially concerning human origins. Leroy, a French Dominican, and Zahm, a professor of physics at the University of Notre Dame (USA), argued, like Mivart, that evolution was compatible with Catholic theology. In February 1895 Leroy was summoned to Rome and was persuaded to publish a retraction of his views shortly afterwards in the periodical *Le Monde* (Paris). Zahm was persuaded to take measures to minimise the circulation of his book. In May 1899 his submission to ecclesiastical authority was made known through the medium of the periodical *Gazetta di Malta*. The following month it was republished in the journal of the Vatican Jesuits – *La Civiltà Cattolica*.[1]

Two Catholic bishops, Geremia Bonomelli (1831–1914) of Cremona (northern Italy) and John Cuthbert Hedley of Newport (England), also found themselves in difficulties for their tolerance of evolutionary theory. Bonomelli gave it some attention in his book *Seguiamo la Ragione* ('Let Us Follow Reason', 1898), but did not condemn it. This was regarded as an unacceptable omission and he was persuaded by 'friendly, kind and very competent persons' to make public, through the medium of *Lega Lombarda* (late October 1898), that evolutionary theory – extended to humans – was 'not perfectly in conformity with the teaching of the Church'.[2]

Hedley wrote approvingly of evolution in a review of Zahm's book in the *Dublin Review* (October 1998) and was criticised by *La Civiltà Cattolica* (7 January 1899). He then wrote to the English Catholic periodical *The Tablet*, conceding that the Mivartian thesis was no longer sustainable (14 January 1899). However, by 1902 Hedley had expressed scepticism about theological objections to Mivart's thesis in a letter published in *England and the Holy See* by Rev. Spencer Jones. In April of that year the ever vigilant and highly influential Jesuit authors of *La Civiltà Cattolica* indicated in their response to Hedley that Leroy and Zahm did their utmost to withdraw their books from circulation because of disapproval from the 'Supreme Tribunal of the Holy See'.[3]

The 'Supreme Tribunal of the Holy See' indicated the Holy Office.[4]

Known today as the Congregation for the Doctrine of the Faith, this congregation was the highest ranked of the Vatican congregations. It was concerned with a broad range of doctrinal matters and issued directives to other congregations. It could, for example, instruct the Congregation of the Index to add specific published works to its Index of Prohibited Books. The Congregation of the Index was not officially empowered to examine or condemn a specific doctrine. It performed a lesser role of ascertaining the dangers to the faith of the Catholic readership, presented by specific publications.[5]

The research of Mariano Artigas, Thomas F. Glick and Rafael A. Martínez found no evidence in the archives of the Holy Office of any official action on its part against Leroy and Zahm. The congregation which acted officially against these authors was the Congregation of the Index. In their *Negotiating Darwin: The Vatican Confronts Evolution, 1877–1902* (2006), Artigas, Glick and Martínez found that the Jesuits of *La Civiltà Cattolica* misled their readers into assuming that the Holy Office, rather than the Congregation of the Index, had taken formal action to limit circulation of the published works of Leroy and Zahm.[6]

The Vatican refrained from issuing a definitive and public condemnation of evolutionary theory, probably because it feared that the credibility of such a pronouncement might be undermined by future discoveries in science. In the absence of a definitive statement from the Vatican there was widespread misunderstanding about the church's position. The letters of Leroy, Zahm and Bonomelli were re-issued in English in *The Tablet* (24 June 1899).[7] Some members of the Irish clergy were probably aware of these letters. Leroy's retraction and Hedley's letter (published on 14 January 1899) received attention in the *Irish Ecclesiastical Record* in May 1899 – this will be addressed later. However, it will be clear from the previous chapters that Irish priests and bishops did not require any directives from Rome to repudiate evolution.

Memories of anti-Catholic opinions expressed by Huxley and Tyndall were still fresh in the minds of those Catholic authors who concerned themselves with the theological implications of evolutionary theory. In a letter published in *The Irish Times* (1 August 1891), Huxley wrote that the Irish were 'the most charming people in the world' to do business with, provided that one did not require 'punctuality, accuracy', or 'moral courage'. He continued to see the strong connection between the Roman Catholic Church and the Home Rule movement as a threat to the security of Britain. 'The Irish difficulty', he believed, was very much due to papal initiatives 'to make Ireland the base of operations for the religious reconquest of Britain'. The Irish Catholic bishops supported Home Rule and the price of such support would be the endowment of their schools and colleges.[8] Tyndall's comments about Home Rule and Irish Catholicism were even more conspiratorial and acerbic. At a public meeting in Belfast on 28 January 1890 he spoke out against Gladstone's Home Rule policy, condemning attempts to place this 'great community of the North' under the control of an unholy alliance – the political wing of which was the Parnellite 'rabble'. Pre-eminent in the religious wing was the Archbishop of Cashel, Thomas William Croke (1824–1902), and his 'myrmidons' (henchmen) – 'backed by the ignorant and excitable peasantry of the South'.[9]

The derogatory statements of Huxley and Tyndall elicited a reciprocal response from Irish Catholic authors. A contributor to the *Irish Ecclesiastical Record* wrote that the main impact of Huxley's work was to popularise Darwinism and to 'spread unbelief amongst the people, to undermine Christianity'. Comments on his scientific work were not complimentary – 'as a man of science his performance is of little value'; 'no great discovery remains after him'; and 'he has done so little that is original or of any permanent value'.[10] Tyndall was reviled as a leading exponent of irreligious ideas. The Irish professor had dared to level a charge of ignorance against the Irish clergy. For such an offence he was denounced as a 'vain, sullen, canker-hearted unbeliever' who had 'broken away from his old theological moorings, and developed an insane hostility to his native country'.[11] But the Irish Catholic clergy had little reason to fear the influence of Tyndall or Huxley.[12]

The association of Darwinism with Huxley and Tyndall could only have worked against Irish Catholic acceptance of it as a valid scientific thesis. But a scientific theory could not be rationally repudiated simply because of its misuse or association with those who were professed enemies of the Roman Catholic Church. It had to be evaluated on the basis of scientific criteria. When the well-known Irish Anglican astronomer Sir Robert Ball (1840–1913) expressed his approval of Darwinism in the concluding chapter of his book *In Starry Realms*, he was criticised by E. Gaynor (C.M.) in the *Irish Ecclesiastical Record*. Ball observed that the nebular hypothesis, which explained the formation of solar systems, had much in common with Darwin's theory – both were theories of evolution. But Gaynor asserted that Ball's support for Darwin was little more than a series of baseless assertions and erroneous analogies.[13] The emphasis on facts ascertained from observation and experiment (induction), rather than reliance on deductive reasoning, was frequently employed by Catholic authors when challenging what they saw as the uncritical acceptance of evolutionary theory. Furthermore, it was argued that not only was there a gross deficiency of evidence for evolution, there seemed to be strong evidence against it. Gaynor pointed to the research of Louis Pasteur (1822–1895), the founder of modern bacteriology, whose findings were seen to weigh heavily against the idea of spontaneous generation. If life had not emerged spontaneously from inanimate matter, to give rise to primitive life forms, then purely naturalistic explanations of the evolutionary process were undermined at the very beginning.[14] But, of course, the results of Pasteur's experiments did not mean that life could not have developed very gradually from inanimate matter early in the Earth's history when physical and chemical conditions were very different to those in modern times. Furthermore, the rejection of evolution by some Catholic authors was discredited by the overwhelming support for it amongst professional scientists.

Socio-economic and political conditions in Britain had favoured the acceptance of evolution far beyond the scientific community. The evolutionary process was seen as inherently progressive. This appealed to middle-class entrepreneurs who sought the termination of long-standing restrictions designed to preserve aristocratic privileges at their expense. Progressive evolutionism was associated with socio-economic advancement, and also with notions of racial superiority. The idea of progress was also widely accepted in the religious domain. It seemed that evolution was used by the Creator as a means to create the higher mental and moral faculties in humans. Liberal evangelicals in the Free Churches reconciled evolution with their religious beliefs. There was also broad support for teleological evolution amongst Anglicans, many of whom were influenced by Charles Gore's *Lux Mundi* (1889). However, progressive evolution was not without theological difficulties, especially in relation to Original Sin.[15] This introduced an element of regression inconsistent with the notion of continuous progress. In Ireland, George Sigerson (1836–1925), writing in the *New Ireland Review,* maintained that the idea of progress could not be sustained in the light of history. Sigerson, a physician and scholar who was later to serve as Professor of Biology at University College Dublin and as a member of the Senate of the Irish Free State (1922–1925), argued that civilisations, such as those of ancient Egypt and Greece, had risen to great heights only to collapse over time. In prosperous England the notion of progress was popular because it was flattering to the national self-image.[16]

Although there were theological difficulties associated with evolutionary theory, especially concerning humankind, it nevertheless began to make inroads into Catholic thinking outside Ireland. In Europe five international congresses held by Catholic scientists between 1888 and 1900 indicated a softening of attitudes towards evolution. Catholic scientists became increasingly aware of the critically important difference between evolution as an ideological weapon against religious belief, and as a valid scientific theory.[17] In the United States there was a favourable shift in Catholic opinion from 1890 to 1905, influenced in no small measure by the German Jesuit entomologist Erich Wasmann.[18] Barry Brundell, in his 'Catholic Church Politics and Evolution Theory', wrote of a 'dissonance' between the centre and periphery of Catholicism.[19] Greta Jones, in reference to Brundell, observed that in secular Catholic cultures like France, or in mainly Protestant cultures like the United States and England, there was a strong tendency amongst Catholic writers to avoid intellectual isolation. Their attempts to reconcile theology with evolutionary theory were consistent with such a tendency. However, Irish society was neither predominantly Protestant nor highly secularised. Social and political conditions facilitated a close affinity with traditionalist attitudes emanating from the Vatican.[20] It will be recalled, from the introduction to this text, that the Catholic Church in Ireland exerted a profound influence on the development of its counterparts in English-speaking countries. This, to some extent, probably counteracted the dissonance between core and periphery mentioned above. It is likely that the anti-evolutionary stance of the Irish Catholic hierarchy made itself felt in the newly settled Catholic communities of Australia and New Zealand, where it would have been further consolidated by the tendency of rationalists to use evolutionary theory in polemical discourse against Christianity.[21]

There is some evidence that members of the Irish Catholic clergy propagated anti-evolutionary views in the United States. Monsignor Michael O'Riordan of Limerick, inspired by little more than wishful thinking, declared in New York's *Freeman's Journal* (30 July 1898) that evolution had been discredited and abandoned by scientists, leaving only those who were poorly informed to support it. The American author and biologist William Seton responded vigorously to O'Riordan's article through the pages of the same journal. Seton was unusual, if not unique, as an outspoken Catholic Darwinist. In the course of the debate O'Riordan conceded that he knew very little about science. He repudiated evolution on philosophical grounds, not on the basis of science – a discipline deemed inferior to philosophy. If evolution was not scientifically sound then it followed that 'good' scientists would reject it. O'Riordan 'grasped at every straw in the scientific wind, magnifying each criticism by Mivart, qualification by Huxley, word of caution from England's Lord Salisbury, and barb from the pen of Virchow' until he was convinced that only atheists and 'tenth rate' scientists supported the theory. Seton denounced the idea that one could claim competence to evaluate the merits of Darwin's work while ignorant of the natural sciences. He argued that the best way to safeguard the church was to rely on evidence rather than ecclesiastical censorship.[22] However, the Vatican, as indicated by the cases of Leroy and Zahm, was not in a tolerant mood, and ecclesiastical authority would determine what was theologically permissible and what was not.

Evolution, Extraterrestrials and the Incarnation

The advocacy of theistic evolution by Catholic authors was a hazardous enterprise because some of their vigilant co-religionists, who opposed evolution, tended to report deviations from strictly orthodox thinking to Rome.[23] A precautionary strategy, therefore, was to make extensive reference to St Augustine's commentary on Genesis – *De Genesi ad Litteram*. This tactic was employed for centuries by Catholic apologists who feared censure from the ecclesiastical authorities.[24]

In view of the dominance of ultramontanism and the pervasiveness of censorious attitudes, it might be expected that no Catholic author would dare to express pro-evolutionary opinions and that if he did, he would not be facilitated by an Irish Catholic periodical. Yet, despite the dominance of ultramontanism in Catholic Ireland, there is some evidence of liberal thinking. In 1899 the *Irish Ecclesiastical Record* published two very different opinions on evolutionary theory against the background of Zahm's *Evolution and Dogma*. Zahm claimed that it was St Augustine who first proposed the principles of contemporary theistic evolution. God created matter directly and impressed on it certain properties – the *causales rationes* ('causal reasons') – to enable it to change and develop over time, thus effectively putting in place an evolutionary process. Therefore God worked indirectly through secondary causes after the creation of matter.[25] Fr Philip Burton (C.M.) studied Zahm's book but came to a different conclusion about St Augustine, concluding that he was really a creationist. Creationist in this context meant that God's action was 'immediate and constant'. There was 'no evolution of species from species, no transformation of species, no mutability of species'. Nevertheless, Burton did concede that there was 'something to be said for the Catholic evolutionists who claim his patronage'.[26] Fr Patrick F. Coakley (O.S.A.) expressed an opinion diametrically opposed to Burton's, concluding that St Augustine was an evolutionist. He was careful to distinguish theistic evolution from irreligious versions of the theory. Reference was made to Huxley's infamous statement – that evolution, 'in addition to its truth, has the great merit of being in a position of irreconcilable antagonism to that vigorous enemy of the highest life of mankind – the Catholic Church'.[27] Coakley believed that in the heat of controversy the doctrines of the church and the concept of evolution were both misunderstood. Under these circumstances it was 'highly convenient' for Catholics who opposed evolution to deny to their pro-evolutionary co-religionists the theological support of St Augustine's *De Genesi ad Litteram*. Now that polemical discourse had subsided it was difficult to see how St Augustine could not be seen as an evolutionist.[28]

In his second article Burton stated that even if St Augustine was to be considered an evolutionist there would still be no justification for quoting his work in support of evolution because the modern theory was extended to include humankind. Burton was aware of Leroy's retraction from reading *The Tablet*. He also quoted Hedley's letter, published in *The Tablet* on 14 January 1899, when the bishop conceded that the 'Mivartian theory', allowing for human evolution, was judged by the Vatican to be theologically 'rash and something more'.[29] Burton's observations are highly significant because they suggest, by virtue of the fact that they were published in the *Irish Ecclesiastical Record* – a journal issued under the imprimatur of Archbishop William Walsh of Dublin – that the Irish Catholic clergy, especially bishops and seminary professors, were aware of the Vatican's aversion to the concept of human evolution. Their opinions were closer to those of Burton than of Coakley.[30]

There was an excessive tendency in authoritative circles to condemn new ideas. This was even expressed in the pages of the *Irish Ecclesiastical Record* when a contributor defended the integrity and motives of Walter McDonald whose book, *Motion: Its Origin and Conservation*, was published in 1898.[31] McDonald was deeply influenced by St George Jackson Mivart,[32] who asserted that human evolution was compatible with

Catholicism. However, Mivart was denied access to the sacraments in January 1900, not for his views on evolution but for his persistence in challenging ecclesiastical authority and his refusal to give his assent to the dogmatic teachings of the church when pressed by Cardinal Herbert Vaughan to do so.[33] McDonald believed that he had only narrowly escaped the same fate as Mivart and was mindful of the constant danger of harsh disciplinary action. He struggled to harmonise Catholic theology with the discoveries of modern science but, in the course of his studies, felt compelled to reject some traditional beliefs which were non-dogmatic. This brought him into conflict with conservative theologians.[34]

From June 1894 onwards McDonald's abstruse ideas about harmonising modern scientific theories of motion with the theology of grace provoked opposition from some of his colleagues in Maynooth, especially Daniel Coghlan (or Cohalan, 1858–1952), Professor of Theology since 1886. McDonald refused to withdraw his thesis, seeking instead a wider forum to express his contentious views. On 18 August 1897 he spoke about 'The Kinetic Theory of Activity' at the International Catholic Conference in Freiburg, urging that Catholics should not 'hurl anathemas at those who maintain a doctrine in physics which is based on so much scientific authority'.[35] This paper was published in the *Irish Ecclesiastical Record* (October 1897).

McDonald elaborated his views about physics and theology at great length in his book *Motion: Its Origin and Conservation* (1898). Its subject matter was vast and complex, comprising elements of the natural sciences, theology and metaphysics. McDonald, mindful of his limited scientific knowledge, did not pretend that his work was free of error. Its purpose was to serve as a basis for discussion. McDonald proposed that there was a direct connection between all causes of motion and God's will. A major theological difficulty was identified with this thesis. If it was true that God directly activated every cause of motion, then where was the scope for human free will?[36] Nevertheless, McDonald believed that there was nothing proposed in the text that was dangerous to the faith. He expected that it would be read only by philosophers and theologians – 'neither the book nor the opinions would set the Liffey on fire'. Furthermore, McDonald showed the text to a number of readers before it was published, including – most importantly – the official ecclesiastical censor, Louis Hickey, a Dominican. Hickey saw nothing censorable in it and advised Archbishop Walsh that publication should be permitted. However, despite the imprimatur, the Sacred Congregation of the Index issued a condemnation of his book on 15 December 1898. McDonald was ordered, insofar as it was possible, to withdraw all copies of his book from circulation. No precise criticisms of the text were communicated to him.[37]

McDonald pointed out to his clerical colleagues that some of their debates were based on principles of physics no longer held by physicists. Their books were 'stuffed with arguments based on principles in which no man of Science believes – which would be laughed out of existence if paraded . . . where men of science could hear what we say and ridicule us'.[38] The suspicion and hostility towards scientists and towards new ideas, which seems to have been so widespread in clerical circles, worked very much against the enterprising spirit of McDonald and others of a similarly progressive outlook.

The Catholic response to Darwinian evolution was very much conditioned by the exclusion of intelligent design from the process. But there was a limited and cautious level of acceptance of evolutionary thinking. The nebular hypothesis, elaborated by Pierre Simon de Laplace and William Herschel, explained how solar systems were formed from massive clouds of gas under the force of gravity. The millions of stars evident from telescopic observations indicated the existence of a vast number of planets. This in turn suggested the high probability that intelligent species existed in other worlds. Of course, there was no direct evidence for such extraterrestrial life forms but, on a statistical basis, it seemed very likely. Furthermore, there was a strong theological argument in favour of it – the principle of 'plenitude'. Why would God create millions of lifeless solar systems? To insist that He had done so implied that His creative actions were wasteful – this was unacceptable. To insist to the contrary also created theological difficulties – centred around questions of redemption and whether or not Jesus Christ was incarnated on other planets.[39] E.A. Selley (O.S.A.) wrote about the theological implications of extraterrestrial life in a short series of articles in the *Irish Ecclesiastical Record* in 1902–1903, inspired by a range of published works which included those by Sir Robert Ball,[40] *The Heavens* by Amédée Guillemin, *Elementary Lessons in Astronomy* by Sir Joseph Norman Lockyer (1836–1920) and *More Worlds Than One* by Sir David Brewster. In his introductory paragraph Selley stated that no definitive answer could be given to the question of whether or not extraterrestrial life existed. Theologically, revelation was silent on the issue. Scientifically, there was no direct evidence and there was very little hope that there would be in the future. Nevertheless, Selley maintained that there were

, sound arguments for believing that extraterrestrial life did exist. He argued on the basis of 'plenitude' – although he did not refer to the principle by name – that intelligent beings did live on other planets. He was open to the possibility that revelation, including fundamental Christian doctrines of the Fall and Redemption, were applicable to the inhabitants of other worlds.[41]

Selley's speculations about intelligent extraterrestrial life diminished the relative importance of mankind in God's universal plan. Furthermore, it was clear from observations in astronomy that the Earth and its solar system were incredibly tiny when cognisance was taken of stellar numbers and distances. This apparent antithesis of anthropocentrism was probably not well received by the clerical readership of the *Irish Ecclesiastical Record*. A letter writer, under the initials M.F.H., argued that it did not seem possible that the 'excess of Divine love', represented by the sacrifice of Jesus Christ, was matched or exceeded elsewhere. Humankind, therefore, was the pre-eminent species in the universe. With this in mind it seemed appropriate that planet Earth was located in a very special position in the vastness of space. The stars of the night sky, apparently of random distribution, were, in reality, deliberately positioned by the Creator to illuminate the Earth and to serve as signs for days, seasons and years (Genesis 1: 14–15).[42] A view which contrasted sharply with M.F.H.'s was offered by an English priest, Canon John S. Vaughan of Westminster. He believed that the Earth was 'a very inferior planet indeed' and speculated that future discoveries might reveal 'vast numbers and varieties of rational animals, scattered through the universe', of which humankind might be 'a very poor and inferior specimen'.[43]

Some members of the Catholic laity were probably aware of the theological implications of the nebular hypothesis and may have questioned Selley about it.[44] The formation of stars, planets and moons was presented as an evolutionary process and Selley believed that scientific evidence in favour of the hypothesis was 'exceedingly strong'. In view of this it would be 'somewhat harsh' for 'the great *Mater docens*' (the hierarchy) to condemn it. Selley referred, fleetingly, to Zahm and was probably aware of the condemnation of *Evolution and Dogma*. He argued that it was within the bounds of orthodoxy to believe that God was a 'Creator-Evolutionist', creating primordial matter at the beginning of time and, thereafter, working through secondary causes to eventually create life. He declared his wish to write strongly in support of 'moderate evolutionists' but felt compelled to proceed cautiously because

'Creationists' had put forward 'grave difficulties' in reconciling evolution with Genesis. It was even questionable whether or not the evolution of plants and animals, excluding humans, could be accepted as compatible with Catholic doctrine. In reference to the question of humankind, Selley stated that:

> We know that the evolution theory dare not be applied, *salvâ fide*, to any mediate creation of Adam's soul. We know that it would be, at least, rash, if not proximate to heresy, to apply it to creation of his body; because even in the latter case, the *traditio Patrum* and the *consensus theologorum* are against it.[45]

Selley regarded evolution as a satisfactory explanation of change and development in nature, provided that Darwinism and irreligious ideas associated with it were discarded. God had to be acknowledged as the creative force behind the process. Another contributor to the *Irish Ecclesiastical Record*, John Meehan, argued that if evolution was ever proved then it would bestow a new depth and grandeur to the concept of God – the 'Continuous Evolver' – working through the mechanism of secondary causes.[46] However, the overriding tendency of Irish Catholic authors was to reject evolutionary theory, especially applied to humankind, but not to assert, with absolute certainty, that it could not have occurred.

Catholic authors were especially hostile to Darwinism. This is, to some extent, understandable. Darwinism was frequently associated with anti-Catholic, and sometimes anti-Christian, ideas. Rejection of Darwinism by Catholics was especially likely when natural selection failed to sustain widespread support from biologists in the decades around 1900. The Irish Catholic bishops were averse to Darwinism but they did not issue an absolute condemnation of it in any formal sense. This indicates that they were well informed about the Vatican's attitude. The ecclesiastical authorities in Rome, mindful of the legacy of the Galileo case, were determined to avoid issuing any public statements which could be perceived as signalling a conflict with modern science.[47] However, the hostility of the bishops towards Darwinism was clear enough to those who were well informed about matters of religion and science in Ireland.

Despite the eclipse of Darwinism there is some evidence to indicate that it considerably influenced the thinking of Irish scientists.[48] A number of eminent Irish scientists – even including those who were probably sceptical of natural selection – were resentful of the church's intervention in debates about Darwinism because they saw it as an issue of academic freedom in the universities – in this case, the right to teach science free of external interference.[49] This probably generated considerable tension between traditionalist Irish Catholic and mainstream scientific thinking in the years around 1900.

In Defence of the Faith

The church was frequently regarded as hostile to the natural sciences by those who were anti-Catholic. As the nineteenth century drew to a close, polemical exchanges about Galileo had spread from scholarly discourses to popular culture.[50] In Britain, Mivart castigated the ecclesiastical authorities for their refusal to come to terms with the historical criticism of the Bible and modern science. Angered by the restrictions imposed by the papal encyclical *Providentissimus Deus* (1893) and the censorship of Leroy and Zahm, Mivart maintained that the church had erred in condemning Galileo and drew two conclusions from this. Firstly, the Holy Office presided over by the pope could make mistakes in matters pertaining to the interpretation of the Bible. Secondly, scientists 'may have truer religious perceptions imparted to them, than any Roman Congregation'.[51] The church had intruded into the scientific domain and had committed a grievous error of judgement – it could never be trusted again.

Mivart's criticism of the church sparked a controversy which received extensive coverage in the secular and religious press in England. In Ireland, John M. Harty took issue with Mivart's stance in the February 1900 issue of the *Irish Ecclesiastical Record*. He rejected Mivart's contention that the church has no authority in matters of science when these impacted on scriptural narratives. Harty conceded that the Holy Office, with the pope's approval, had made a mistake in pronouncing on the meaning of scripture. But the church did not undermine its authoritative position because its declaration was not issued on the basis of the doctrine of infallibility.[52] Harty returned to this theme again in April, arguing at length that no infallible declaration had been issued against the Copernican hypothesis and Galileo's advocacy of it. He conceded that the Roman Congregations were wrong but that there were strong mitigating circumstances. The Copernican hypothesis had not been proved and Galileo had used arguments, such as the ebb and flow of tides, which were disputed at the time and were subsequently shown to be false. There was some merit in Harty's argument. In the seventeenth century it seemed that both science and theology favoured the stance of the ecclesiastical authorities. Members of the Inquisition viewed the question of the Earth's mobility as a choice between Biblical certainties and unfounded scientific speculation.[53] Nevertheless, the progress of science vindicated Galileo. Harty did not, and could not, deny that the Roman Congregations erred when they stood in judgement of Galileo Galilei. But he maintained that the error was small and rare. Therefore, loyal Catholics were obligated to respect the decisions of the Roman Congregations as they would respect the decisions of civil tribunals when rare mistakes made by the latter institutions did not undermine their authoritative status.[54] The church, it seemed, had little if anything to apologise for.

John William Draper, in his widely read book *History of the Conflict between Religion and Science*, made a number of false claims against the Roman Catholic Church. He claimed, for example, that Copernicus's *De Revolutionibus Orbium Coelestium* (*On the Revolutions of the Celestial Spheres*, 1543) 'incontestably established' the heliocentric hypothesis, and that Galileo was forced by members of the Inquisition to 'deny facts' which they, like him, 'knew to be true'.[55] The doctrines of the Roman Catholic Church, he believed, were hopelessly at variance with science. This opinion, understandably, grated on Catholic sensitivities. One way of responding was to ask the rhetorical question: Why were so many eminent scientists Roman Catholic? For example, Copernicus, Galileo, Stenson, Pasteur, Buffon, Coulomb, Ampère, Volta, Galvani, Avogadro, Foucault, Lavoisier and Pasteur! On this basis it was argued that Catholicism and science were reconcilable.[56] This was a straightforward argument with some merit.[57] However, it did little to address substantive issues concerning the need to reinterpret the Biblical narratives in the light of modern science. There was a pressing need to depart further and further from literal interpretations of some scriptural passages, especially in Genesis. But departures from literal interpretations carried their own risks. If many Biblical passages, traditionally understood in a literal sense, were reinterpreted metaphorically or allegorically, then this might undermine the credibility of scripture.

Fr Peter Coffey (1876–1943), appointed Professor of Philosophy at Maynooth in 1902, endeavoured to adopt an innovative approach to the Bible and the natural sciences, regarding both as 'hidden' books. The Bible was 'full of mystery', containing 'a vast, hidden wealth of meaning'. Mindful of the guiding principles of *Providentissimus Deus*, Coffey argued that science did not, and could not, contradict scripture. Science could only overturn a particular interpretation of scripture. Therefore, when hostile scientists attacked the church by denigrating the Biblical text, they were fundamentally in error because they were only disproving provisional interpretations of Catholic scholars. The Roman Catholic Church had never committed itself, dogmatically, to any particular interpretation of the Mosaic cosmogony.[58] This strategy adopted by Coffey and others was very shrewd because it enabled the custodians of faith to shelter safely behind the vagueness of the Hebrew text. Coffey was aware of Huxley's cynical view of this exegetical principle from reading the *Nineteenth Century* (November 1885–February 1886). Huxley, in controversy with William Gladstone, expressed 'great faith in the pliancy of that tongue [Hebrew] in the hands of Biblical exegetes.'[59]

The ongoing struggle to reconcile the scriptural narratives with the firmly established findings of modern science and history gave rise to different schools of thought such as concordism, critical literalism, idealism and revelationism. All of these were flawed or questionable to some extent. Catholics were permitted some scope for speculating about new systems of interpretation. There was 'sufficient obscurity' to allow for differences of opinion. But Catholics were admonished not to lose sight of the divine authorship, inerrancy and inspiration of the Biblical texts. Furthermore, they were to 'enquire diligently' about 'the mind and feeling of the Church' and readily submit to its teaching. As Catholic exegetes struggled to ascertain the true meaning of many scriptural passages, the church declined to pronounce definitively on any particular interpretation.[60] Obscurity endured and if its persistence antagonised those who yearned intensely for truth, it offered the not inconsiderable advantage of greater flexibility in deflecting, sidestepping or resisting the onslaught of irreligious critics. In the 1890s and early years of the twentieth century, Irish Catholic apologists were still concerned about the irreligious opinions of eminent scientists such as Huxley, Tyndall and Haeckel.

In 1895 Catholic Ireland's main seminary, St Patrick's College, Maynooth, celebrated its centenary. A large number of bishops attended, from Britain as well as from Ireland. These included Cardinal Michael Logue of Armagh and Cardinal Herbert Vaughan of Westminster. Vaughan encouraged the formation of the Maynooth Union – an association of past students of the college. The association was to give financial support to facilitate the growth and development of the college. Vaughan pointed to the English Catholic colleges – Ushaw, Stonyhurst, Old Hall, Downside and Oscott – as examples worthy of emulation. He spoke about the development of Catholic higher education in the context of the church having to do battle with 'a world armed with science and literature and with all the facilities of modern education'.[61]

The Maynooth Union was formed with the approval of the Irish hierarchy. The association held its inaugural meeting on 27 June – the last day of the centenary celebrations. Walter McDonald played a leading role in its formation. Before an audience comprised of Cardinal Michael Logue, several bishops and many priests, he read a paper entitled 'A Maynooth Union, as a Social and Academic Memorial of the Centenary'. McDonald expressed concern about an intellectual deficit with reference to the Irish clergy in the late nineteenth century. He emphasised the pressing need to remedy this problem because it posed a serious threat to the welfare of the church in Ireland. He told the assembly:

> Our people are not what they were . . . the faithful generally in our towns, and many even in country districts – those of them who read the newspapers, and especially those who dabble in periodicals – have become critical not only of our conduct, but even of our doctrines.

Those who were most educated amongst the laity, especially university graduates, were now conversant with modern literature. A new threat had emerged – Lutherans and Calvinists were no longer the church's bitterest enemies – these had been superseded by materialists, rationalists, socialists and 'Revolutionists'.[62] This opinion was probably not uncommon.[63] The appropriate response to the perceived danger, McDonald argued, was that his fellow priests should become more intellectually active. If priests were to continue to give leadership to their people, then they had to cultivate a taste for serious study to enable them to discuss and challenge modern ideas. Furthermore, their training in the seminaries was in dire need of improvement – the 'musty wisdom' imparted by their professors was no longer adequate.[64] McDonald anticipated that a major benefit of the Maynooth Union would be to increase the inclination for study amongst the Irish priesthood.

In the late nineteenth century the increased circulation of newspapers and books, and the spread of literacy, meant that Irish Catholics, especially the younger generation, were more likely to become familiar with evolutionary ideas. As evolutionary theory seemed to be contrary to Catholic doctrine, some of the clergy feared that scepticism would become rife amongst the laity.[65] In the closing years of the nineteenth century scientists were still regarded with suspicion and hostility and this was evident from some of the speeches made at Maynooth. The Very Rev.

M.J. Murphy spoke of a conflict between religion and pseudo-science waged through the medium of newspapers and magazines.[66] Maynooth professor Daniel Coghlan viewed scientists as part of an anti-Christian movement, especially in England. He declared that science, and philosophy, had broken free of religion. If progress in natural science was to be made, then science had to be reconciled with the teachings of the Catholic Church. He acknowledged that Irish Catholics had achieved very little in the natural sciences, but he defended their dismal record by arguing that, in the absence of a Catholic university, it was not possible for them to contribute substantially to the progress of science. Because of a lack of higher education, Irish Catholics were unable to counteract the widespread acceptance of ideas among scientists that could not be harmonised with the teachings of the church.[67]

At subsequent meetings of the Maynooth Union priests and theologians expressed strong views on a range of issues concerning the spiritual welfare of the people. Generally, they believed that Catholics were vulnerable to the acceptance of ideas contrary to their faith because of the poor education of the laity and the more widespread distribution of literature. Michael Hickey, Professor of Irish at St Patrick's College, Maynooth, observed, with alarm:

> The rapid spread amongst our people of the reading of periodical literature of various kinds is, I believe, one of the most remarkable and noteworthy developments of our time. Even so late as thirty years ago, few daily papers found their way into the rural districts, and but a comparatively small number into the provincial towns and villages. Even the weeklies had, outside the cities and larger towns, a comparatively small circulation. To rural residents . . . the London 'penny dreadful' was practically unknown. What a change has been effected in the interval! The weeklies, and to some extent the dailies, now find their way everywhere.

Hickey was of the opinion that the press exerted a powerful influence over public opinion. To a large extent it was a force of evil, frequently pandering to 'depraved taste', propagating erroneous principles, and misleading the 'thoughtless and unwary'. The best response was to improve the education of the priests and the laity. A number of measures needed to be pursued – better teaching methods in the seminaries, a considerable improvement of religious instruction in primary and secondary schools, and the setting up of parochial libraries well stocked with publications in harmony with Catholic doctrine. Simple faith and piety were no longer adequate to meet the challenges of the modern age.[68]

Some priests perceived that Irish Catholicism was singularly disadvantaged. Catholics were handicapped by a feeling of inferiority[69] and by a pervasive 'intellectual apathy'.[70] Furthermore, it was claimed that the 'simple and unquestioning faith' of the people was rapidly becoming a thing of the past.[71] It was believed that these internal weaknesses of Irish Catholicism made it particularly vulnerable to external threats – which seemed to emanate mainly from England.

In Britain, Huxley had popularised agnosticism in some quarters, especially amongst the middle classes. In the 1890s middle-class agnostics organised Ethical Societies which were precursors of the modern humanist movement. Low-priced editions of books critical of Christianity were published by the Rationalist Press Association. Many of these volumes were concerned with the idea of science in opposition to religion.[72] At this time the Catholic Church in Ireland was becoming more closely associated with the nationalist anti-colonial movement. Scientific studies and research probably suffered as a result of this development because science was largely in the hands of the Protestant Ascendancy.[73] After the political demise of Charles Stewart Parnell (1846–1891) in 1890, the 'demand was for symbols of the Celt, not the scientist'. Science was associated with British imperial domination.[74] Such an association was not inevitable. Ireland's unique flora and fauna was potentially a fertile area for studies in natural history, which could have appealed strongly to the intellectual proclivities of Irish nationalists and British unionists alike. There was a convergence of interests in studies of the Irish language, Irish antiquities, the Irish landscape and Irish natural history. Some common ground existed between this broad-based cultural nationalism and political nationalism for a number of years.[75]

The perceived association of science with foreign domination provides at least some explanation for the extreme views expressed by Rev. J.M. O'Reilly at a meeting of the Maynooth Union on 21 June 1900. O'Reilly told his audience that the Irish Catholic 'mind' was being gradually erased by the 'English mind'. This collective consciousness from abroad was subjected to a tirade of abuse. The 'English mind' was

> . . . a fleshly spirit . . . unmannerly, vulgar, insolent, bigoted; a mind whose belly is its God . . . a mind to which pride, and lust, and mammon are the matter-of-course aims of life . . . a mind where every absurd device, from grossest Darwinism to most preposterous

> spiritualism, is resorted to . . . a mind essentially without God in the world. . . .[76]

O'Reilly believed that the only effective defence against the invading tide of English ideas was the Irish language, but there was little support for such a proposal amongst the clergy.

O'Reilly's antipathy towards English culture was probably not uncommon. Fr P.J. Dowling (C.M.), Honorary Secretary of the Irish Technical Instruction Association, railed against the education system with reference to England. In the *Irish Ecclesiastical Record* he maintained that:

> We are unconsciously allowing ourselves to be trailed at the heels of a decadent country. Our methods and our means are English, and are seldom even English at first hand . . . Nature study is there now, it will probably reach us in a decade or so when its futility is fully apparent even to English educationalists . . . in our National Schools mathematics, the backbone of technical progress, is being silently strangled, whilst the force of Continental example is making its study an indispensible item in the English schools . . .[77]

There was a 'barrenness of intellect' in England, even in science. Dowling declared that the only remarkable invention in England in the previous thirty years was the steam turbine designed by Charles Algernon Parsons (1854–1931).[78] England had been overshadowed by the 'intellectual nations' of the world, such as Germany. All this had dire implications for science and technical education in Ireland. Many teachers recruited for technical instruction schemes and the teaching of science were from Britain due to a shortage of suitably qualified Irish teachers.[79] Dowling deeply resented the control exercised by the Department of Science and Art over a number of Irish educational institutions. This department was centred in South Kensington, London – hence Dowling's expression of despair – '. . . we are being South Kensingtonised here in Ireland.' The department was, in his opinion, 'probably the most costly, the most wasteful, and the most stupid of our educational shams . . .'[80] There was probably an intense dislike of the department in the highest echelons of Irish Catholicism.

A few months after the publication of Dowling's article, the *Irish Ecclesiastical Record* facilitated further criticism of the Department of Science and Art when the solicitor George F. Fleming argued that it failed to adequately fund science and technical instruction in Ireland. Central funding was being administered in such a way that it discriminated against Ireland and in favour of Scotland.[81] Gerald Molloy was more positive in his assessment of science education in Ireland. He had been appointed rector of the Catholic University of Ireland in 1883, and also served as vice chancellor of the Royal University of Ireland. Although he acknowledged a shortage of competent science teachers and a scarcity of laboratory facilities in secondary schools, he argued that considerable progress had been made in the teaching of science since the setting up of the Department of Agriculture and Technical Instruction (DATI) in 1900.[82]

As observed in Chapter 1, Molloy had argued that there was no incompatibility between revelation and geology. In a liberal intellectual milieu he would probably have applied his harmony thesis to human evolution, perhaps even in terms of natural selection. Molloy, according to Walter McDonald, had done some work on a manuscript called the *Antiquity of Man* a few years before his death in 1906, 'but, having satisfied himself on certain points, thought it more prudent to keep his conclusions to himself. He had no taste for martyrdom.'[83] There was little toleration for evolutionary theory applied to humans, much less for Darwinism.

If godless Darwinism ever posed a threat to Irish Catholicism, then it was grossly exaggerated, especially in the 1890s. Darwinians in Ireland were probably few in number – and those of the 'godless' variety fewer still. Darwinians were to be found especially amongst the staffs of the anthropometrics laboratory in Trinity College Dublin, the Royal College of Science, and the Dublin Science and Art Museum. Staff at the Dublin Science and Art Museum presented Irish natural history in terms of natural selection. Nevertheless, they sought to avoid controversy. For example, they did not explicitly mention Darwin because of the frequent association of Darwinism with materialism. Furthermore, no reference was made to human evolution. Staff at the museum aimed to stimulate a widespread interest in Irish natural history, not to engage in the promotion of materialistic evolution. Their cautious presentation of biological exhibits indicates that there was a strong resistance to Darwinism in Ireland.[84]

Agnosticism[85] was also in a very poor position to challenge the influence of Roman Catholicism in Irish society. Although it won some support in Britain,[86] there is no evidence to indicate that it gained a significant following in Ireland. Yet Irish Catholic apologists still wrote about agnosticism as if it presented a major threat to the church's future. The teaching of St Thomas Aquinas was seen by theologians and priests as providing a robust defence against agnosticism and other unorthodox ideas. Pope Leo XIII, especially in his encyclical *Aeterni Patris* ('Of the Eternal Father', 1879), had encouraged the study of the works of St Thomas Aquinas (circa 1225–1274). An objective of fundamental importance in Thomism was to restore the notion of a First Cause to a position of primacy in scientific philosophy so that science would cease to be the main contributor to anti-religious beliefs. Some Catholic writers became obsessed with the idea that modern science and Thomism could be reconciled.[87] It was argued that every effect had to have a cause. One could not simply put forward the cosmic vapour as the ultimate explanation of the origin of the universe. The notion of eternal matter did not solve the problem. The notion of a universe without a Creator was regarded as irrational – like an effect without a cause. The Catholic mind recoiled against such an idea. It was unthinkable that the universe, incredibly more complex than the works of man, was not designed by an intelligent power.[88]

From a Catholic perspective agnosticism was potentially lethal to religious faith, but Catholicism was not without its strengths. Fr Michael O'Riordan, speaking at the International Catholic Scientific Congress at Freiburg in August 1897, told his audience that only the certainties of Catholicism, rather than the doubts of agnosticism, would satisfy the human mind. Humans, unable to free themselves from 'the ghost of religion', needed a personal God, not the great emptiness of Spencer's Unknowable. The church asserted that it could satisfy this basic human need, and presented itself as the source of God's revelation to man – truths which unaided human reason could never discover. Its great strength, in its battle with wayward scientists, was that it offered certainty, guidance and consolation in a harsh, competitive world. O'Riordan asserted that the Roman Catholic Church was the only effective defence against scientific naturalism. In support of this contention, he referred to Huxley's visit to Maynooth when that eminent exponent of agnosticism singled out the Roman Catholic Church as the only worthy opponent of scientific progress.[89]

Catholic apologists castigated Protestantism for the emergence of irreligious philosophies. From a Catholic perspective, the rejection of the teaching authority of the Catholic Church, and the emphasis on individual judgement, exposed Protestant thinking to the full onslaught of rational thinking, which in turn so weakened Protestant faith that it became vulnerable to pernicious Enlightenment philosophies – of which agnosticism was but one. Peter Coffey's understanding of agnosticism was that it was an assertion that everything beyond the realm of sensory perception was unknowable to humankind. Huxley, Tyndall, Spencer and Matthew Arnold were harshly criticised, not for their inability to know God but for their unwillingness to know Him.[90] Coffey viewed agnosticism as a monstrous predator and denounced it in the following terms:

> Abroad stalks the demon of human pride, deceiving the doubtful, waylaying the wavering, whispering in the name of Modern Science, Rationalism, and Freethought, that 'It is man's privilege to doubt'; even assuming the shape of an angel of light – that spirit of false humility which permeates modern, up-to-date Agnosticism – to seduce the weak and the unwary, and lead them away from the path of truth.[91]

The growth of agnosticism in England was presented as a logical and gradual development of the philosophical errors of John Locke, David Hume and George Berkeley. Their ideas were propagated and developed in an intellectual milieu of free thought and private judgement which were implanted and promoted by the Reformation.[92] Coffey condemned the tendency amongst agnostics to regard Catholics as superstitious and unscientific, maintaining that the converse was true. Agnostics, the most eminent of whom were natural scientists, embraced unsubstantiated theories full of contradictions.[93] If natural science posed a threat to the credibility of the Catholic faith, as Coffey seemed to think, then it was appropriate to cut it down to size. Its diminished status in the hierarchy of knowledge would render it innocuous as a prop for agnosticism. And, by some strange twist of logic, scientific theories were to be regarded as similar to the doctrines of Roman Catholicism in terms of epistemological status. Science was accepted 'by the millions, not on the evidence of demonstration, but on the authority of those eminent men of science who form its *Ecclesia Docens*'.[94] Agnosticism – 'the cult of the Unknowable' – was viewed as an aberration of modern science, which abandoned Christ and the Bible and embraced 'nature-worship' and evolution instead.[95]

Coffey regarded Herbert Spencer as the greatest contemporary philosophical exponent of scientific agnosticism. He did not know how much Spencer's philosophy influenced popular opinion. But it was, in his opinion, the most determined attempt yet to construct an elaborate system of philosophy, ethics and 'religion', underpinned by a fusion of evolutionary theory, empiricism and subjective idealism.[96] This initiative was absolutely reprehensible to Coffey because it served to

> empty the mind of faith and hope, to deprive it of the vitalizing warmth of truth, and to leave it a cold barren waste parched by the blighting winds of doubt and despair; while it is only the philosophy of truth, the wisdom of Christianity, that can solve the enigma of life, give a reason for all things and bring peace and happiness to the heart of man.[97]

With this perception of reality, the allurement of Christianity seemed irresistible.

Irish Catholic apologists believed that the most influential representatives of science, especially Darwin, Huxley, Tyndall, Spencer and Haeckel, had deceived many people with their pseudo-science. The view was expressed that irreligious proponents of scientific theories had so skilfully constructed their arguments that 'immature or untrained minds' were 'readily captured to take delight in the insolence of half-knowledge'.[98] There was a strong tendency in clerical circles to exaggerate the vulnerability of young Catholics to the ideas of those who would lure them astray. This made it extremely difficult for the British government and the Irish Catholic hierarchy to reach agreement on much-needed reforms of the university system in Ireland.

4. Commissions of Enquiry, 1901–1907

Restraining the Scientists

The setting up of the Royal University had not satisfied Catholic demands for a satisfactory system of university education. On 1 July 1901 the Conservative government of Lord Salisbury (Robert Gascoyne Cecil) established the Royal Commission on University Education in Ireland under the chairmanship of Lord Robertson (James Patrick Bannerman). It was set up to put forward proposals on university education but its terms of reference explicitly excluded Trinity College Dublin.

Edward Thomas O'Dwyer, Bishop of Limerick, gave oral evidence to the commission from 19 September to 21 September 1901. He informed the commission that the Roman Catholic Church in Ireland had rejected the Queen's Colleges 'not because there would be secular Science taught there with an insufficient amount of Catholic doctrine', but that 'there was no security that the secular Science would be taught without infringing Catholic doctrine'.[1] The concerns of the hierarchy about protecting the faith of Catholic students in colleges of higher education in Ireland raised the question of upholding intellectual freedom so essential for maintaining and promoting high academic standards. O'Dwyer's attention was directed to a point made by Cardinal Newman in one of his lectures that professors of the physical sciences had the right to freely teach their subjects without interference from those motivated by theological considerations provided that the science professors kept within the boundaries of their discipline. O'Dwyer agreed with this in principle and played down the probability that any conflict would occur between theology and science. The church had very little to say about mathematics or the physical sciences. Indeed a man would have to be 'very originally-minded' if he was to find conflict between Catholic doctrine and mathematics or the physical sciences.[2]

81

O'Dwyer emphasised the importance of distinguishing between hypotheses and ascertained facts, and stressed the need to correctly identify and respect disciplinary boundaries. If these conditions were maintained then there would be no need for the church to seek the imposition of restrictions. The bishop referred to Thomas Henry Huxley, whom he acknowledged as an eminent biologist. There would have been no problem with Huxley teaching biology to Catholic students – if he confined himself strictly to that subject. But scientists sometimes ventured beyond their discipline to take on the role of philosophers. O'Dwyer would have let Huxley 'go on as long as his Science did not come in collision with Revelation'. If Huxley had challenged doctrines about revelation or denied the supernatural in his lectures then O'Dwyer, if he had the power, would have taken action to prevent a recurrence.[3] The defence of theology on the basis of strict adherence to one's disciplinary domain was sustainable to some extent. Biologists, speaking only within the professional competence of their discipline, could not say anything meaningful about revelation or the supernatural. But enquiring minds did not so rigidly compartmentalise theology, philosophy and the sciences when addressing important questions of natural history. The implications of scientific theories for theology could not be simply ignored by constructing strictly defined impermeable boundaries between academic disciplines. This was acknowledged by O'Dwyer. He told the commission that the Catholic ideal of education was that religious and secular knowledge could not be separated. It was impossible to teach secular knowledge without it impacting on religious issues in some way.[4] Therefore, in Catholic colleges the appropriate interdisciplinary connections would be made – but not by infidels such as Huxley.

Some branches of science were not sources of worry for those concerned with the education of Catholics. William Delany, a Jesuit priest and president of University College Dublin, told the Robertson Commission that subjects such as electrical engineering, applied mathematics, and mathematics did not present any problems for adherence to Catholic doctrine. But biology and geology were in a different category – requiring vigilance – because it was in these subjects in particular that scientists tended to stray beyond their disciplinary boundaries and express opinions about the implications of their dicipline for religious doctrines.[5] Delany gave an example of how this might occur. A professor might tell his students, on the basis of scientific evidence, that the Earth was 300,000 years old – much older than the several thousand years indicated by a literal reading of the Bible. Delany would not take disciplinary measures against him for this. But if the professor then proceeded to state that the Biblical narratives were untrue, Delany would intervene. The geologist was obligated to teach geological theories only. He was not authorised to interpret the Bible.[6] The strict demarcation of disciplinary boundaries was not without its problems. There was always the possibility that a student might ask about the apparent contradiction between geology and Genesis.[7] Under such circumstances a scientist's resolve to stay within his discipline would be severely tested.

Delany stated that a Catholic university would not exclude modern science from its courses. He referred to the Catholic University of Louvain (Belgium) to make the point that science could flourish in a Catholic university environment.[8] Even the 'most progressive' science would be facilitated because it could be neutralised as a threat to the Catholic faith by instilling an awareness of disciplinary boundaries and, when necessary, dictating the appropriate interdisciplinary connections.[9] Furthermore, the Catholic Church would decide, in its own educational institutions, what 'progressive' science really was.

There was some surprise amongst the commissioners when they were told by Delany that there was great scope for intellectual freedom at University College Dublin. Not all professors at the college were Roman Catholic. There was so few Catholics in Ireland sufficiently qualified in the natural sciences that it was considered necessary to employ Protestants.[10] Some Protestants, including clergymen, attended lectures at the college.[11] Students were permitted to read the works of modern philosophers – for example, René Descartes, Immanuel Kant, George Wilhelm Friedrich Hegel, Benedictus Spinoza, Jeremy Bentham, Auguste Comte and John Stuart Mill – including those on the Vatican's *Index Librorum Prohibitorum* (Index of Prohibited Books). Examples of such works were Kant's *Critique of Pure Reason* (1781) and Mill's *Principles of Political Economy* (1848). Such freedom was not seen as dangerous to the faith of students. Not only were students permitted to read books listed on the Index – they were required to do so for the purpose of disproving the errors therein. However, the intellectual freedom supposedly permitted at University College Dublin was more imaginary than real. The study of modern philosophy took place under carefully controlled conditions – Catholic professors were close at hand to administer 'the antidote'.[12]

The Robertson Commission pressed forward in its enquiries about the Catholic Church's attitude towards intellectual freedom. Delany was informed about Cardinal Paul Cullen's evidence to the Commission on Education in 1869. Cullen was reported to have stated that: 'If a man teaching Chemistry or Geology were to assert that the cosmogony of Moses was in opposition to the order of things at present existing I would remove him from his teaching.' Delany used this question as an opportunity to stress the broad scope of thinking within the church. What did 'the cosmogony of Moses' mean exactly? The chronology of Genesis, the meaning of the word 'day', and the extent of the Deluge were all open to debate – the church had not defined its position, thus permitting great freedom for debate. Therefore, it was not at all clear what Cullen was responding to.[13] The inference from Delany's response was that the church was not refusing to accept soundly based findings in geology, chemistry or any other branch of science. What it was refusing to accept was that there was a conflict between established facts in science and a correct interpretation of scripture as defined by the church.

In her 'Catholicism, Nationalism and Science', Greta Jones observed that there was some concern among scientists, and those supportive of science, that the control exerted by the Catholic hierarchy over appointments at University College Dublin would lead to the exclusion of some scientific subject matter from the college courses. Secularisation of the universities was regarded as an essential condition if science was to flourish within these institutions. The attitude to Darwin's theory within a college or university was often seen as a good indicator of whether progress of this kind had occurred or not.[14]

James Alfred Ewing, Professor of Mechanism and Applied Mechanics at the University of Cambridge, enquired about whether or not there would be restrictions of scientific freedom in a Catholic university. He thought it likely that many of his fellow scientists believed that the conditions imposed on academic staff in institutions controlled by the Catholic Church would have the effect of 'somewhat emasculating the teaching of the sciences'. Ewing, a member of the commission, then asked: 'Would not a Professor find his hands somewhat tied in the teaching of certain branches of science with the constant fear before him of saying something which might be held by the Bishops to be contrary to faith and morals as determined by the Church?' Delany replied that such a problem could only arise if a professor of science went beyond his discipline to advance his own ideas – illogically deduced from scientific facts, which would, within a few years, fail to withstand scientific scrutiny.[15]

Evidently, Ewing was still unclear about the attitude of the Catholic

Church towards science. He enquired, 'would you give a Professor of Comparative Anatomy, or a Professor of Embryology, a free hand in regard to Darwin's theory of natural selection?' Delany replied, 'Certainly not, if he taught students that the scientific facts he advances conclusively proved that all things, including the human soul, have been evolved by the mere play of physical forces from non-living matter.' He then pointed to the distinction between science and the theories and deductions from science advanced by some scientists. Implicit in Delany's response was that scientists could not say anything meaningful about the immortal soul which was clearly beyond the domain of science. Furthermore, he reiterated the point about the instability of scientific theories – implying that natural selection was in this category.

Ewing continued to press for clarification of the Catholic Church's attitude towards science and asked whether or not Delany would allow a science professor 'to teach as a scientific possibility, to say nothing more, that the human species was developed in that way from lower organisms – in the same way as the development of other species can be traced?' Delany answered:

> If he advanced as a mere speculative theory that there appeared to be considerable evidence to suppose that his human body may have been developed from some simious [sic] animal I should say he was trenching on ground which was dangerous; but I should ascertain, before condemning him, that his teaching was not merely in disaccord with my own personal opinion, but condemned by the Catholic Church in that particular form.[16]

There was an element of ambiguity in Delany's response but there was also an indication that the freedom of science would not be respected. Scientists were clearly within their rights to advance human evolution as a scientific thesis – a right which Delany did not clearly concede. In reply to further questioning by Ewing, Delany took the opportunity to emphasise that during his eighteen years in office he had never reprimanded or disciplined any professor under his authority.[17] It was critically important for Catholic representatives to impress upon the commission that a Catholic university or college, benefiting from state funding, would respect the rights of academic staff to pursue their research free from interference by the church authorities.

The Irish Catholic bishops had moderated their demands concerning the setting up of a state-funded Catholic university or college which probably assuaged the concerns of the Robertson Commission. In a statement issued on 23 June 1897 the bishops had stated that they did not insist on: (1) religious tests (2) a majority of clergymen on the governing body or (3) the endowment of a theological faculty from public funds. The bishops believed that a prudently chosen Board of Visitors would give 'reasonable protection' to professors while at the same time providing for 'absolute security' for faith and morals in the university.[18]

The protection of faith and morals was seen as heavily dependent on a good education system. Irish Catholic representatives who appeared before the commission complained time after time how deficient this system was and laboured the point that Catholics were disadvantaged relative to Protestants, especially in relation to Trinity College Dublin. Patrick O'Dea, Vice President of St Patrick's College, Maynooth, informed the Robertson Commission that a broad and sound education was essential for the defence of religion. Isolation from secular knowledge would lead to estrangement and a lack of harmony between conclusions drawn from theology and science. There was a pressing need for Irish Catholic clergymen to acquire expertise in the sciences as well as in theology so that religion could be defended against false claims – O'Dea made no mention of the Catholic laity in this context.[19] But St Patrick's College, Maynooth did not have the resources to adequately provide for science education. There was no museum to enhance the teaching of the natural sciences and there were no laboratories which seminarians could avail of.[20]

Catholic laymen were similarly disadvantaged, at least those who complied with the admonitions of the bishops not to attend Trinity College Dublin or the Queen's Colleges. Delany informed the commission that University College Dublin was hopelessly under-resourced to teach mathematics, natural philosophy, engineering, and the applied sciences. Furthermore, there was no incentive for Catholics to study mathematics and the sciences because career prospects in these disciplines were so poor.[21] Fellowships of the Royal University compared very unfavourably with those of Trinity College Dublin. In his evidence to the commission Delany stated that

> the reason we have not Catholic Professors of eminence in certain branches of education, especially in Mathematics and the Natural and Physical Sciences, is that we, Catholics, have not what exists in Trinity College, an inducement for taking up the study of those branches of knowledge, with the prospect of obtaining a dignified position, or even a competency in life.[22]

In the secondary school system some Catholic schools were equipped with laboratories.[23] At local level the clergy worked in co-operation with the Department of Agriculture and Technical Instruction (DATI) to advance technical education in the schools.[24] J.D. Burke, Superior of the Christian Brothers' Schools in Cork, told the Robertson Commission that there were 160 laboratories in the physical sciences under the direction of DATI. But there was such a severe shortage of qualified science teachers that these had to be recruited from Britain. The examination system focused almost entirely on theoretical questions rather than on practical or experimental work.[25] The gross inadequacy of the secondary school system was nowhere more bluntly expressed than in the evidence of Bishop O'Dwyer. About eight thousand pupils throughout Ireland presented themselves for examinations under the Intermediate school system each year. About 75 per cent of these were Catholic. Even those Catholics who achieved excellent results were 'half educated' with 'a smattering of Classics . . . a smattering of Mathematics' and 'a smattering of Modern Languages'. Unlike Protestants, with prospects of education at Trinity College Dublin, they had, in the vast majority of cases, no career prospects.[26] Delany's evidence reinforced that of O'Dwyer. He claimed that Protestant schools were far better supplied with competent teachers to teach the mathematical and physical sciences than Catholic schools.[27]

Catholic secondary schools were comparatively disadvantaged. These educational institutions had no 'direct endowments'. A member of the commission, William J.M. Starkie, pointed out that a teaching career in Ireland was almost closed to Catholic laymen. They, unlike their Protestant counterparts, had to contend with celibate Catholics devoted fulltime to religious life who could undertake teaching duties at much lower rates of pay. Catholic schools, because of their meagre financial resources, were economically compelled to employ members of the clergy and those in religious orders. Secondary schools would not be economically sustainable without this cheap source of labour. Student fees were not sufficient to meet the running costs of the schools if laymen were employed. Delany agreed with Starkie, and referred to Clongowes Wood College (County Kildare) as a case in point. Over twenty Jesuits were employed as teachers in this school.[28] But, as observed by Patrick O'Dea, the Irish Catholic clergy were poorly educated in the sciences.

The physicist George Johnstone Stoney (1826–1911) was not optimistic about the prospects for intellectual progress in Catholic Ireland. His outlook was radically different from that of the Catholic representatives who appeared before the commission and seems to have been influenced by eugenics – a term coined by Francis Galton (1822–1911), a cousin of Charles Darwin. In the late nineteenth century and early twentieth century, controversies were generated by the idea that human populations could be improved by selective breeding. Galton argued that the only way of improving the human species was to restrict the reproduction of individuals with inferior traits while promoting increased numbers of children from parents with desirable traits.[29] In Ireland, around 1901, there was little or no debate about eugenics.[30] Nevertheless, Stoney's evidence to the commission on 20 December of that year indicates some familiarity with the subject matter of eugenics. He pointed out that there were about three thousand priests in Ireland. In addition to this figure, Catholic Ireland supplied nearly all the priests of the English-speaking world. The church 'snapped up' so many of the most intellectually gifted young men for the priesthood that it virtually depleted the numbers of those who had the potential to benefit from university education. Stoney believed that this would prove to be disastrous for the Irish Catholic population over a number of generations because Catholic priests did not father children – in effect the antithesis of eugenics. If, generation after generation, all or most of the most intelligent young Catholics were drawn to a life of celibacy then 'anyone breeding cattle even will know what the effect of that must inevitably be.'[31] On a shorter timescale Stoney saw the campaign for a Catholic university as part of a plan by the Catholic bishops to further their own interests at the expense of the people of Ireland.

The poor condition of Irish Catholic education was acknowledged by the Robertson Commission when it issued its final report in July 1903. The commission declined to pass judgement on whether or not the Irish Catholic bishops were justified in their opposition to the Queen's Colleges. Their opposition, whether right or wrong, was 'disastrous to the interests of education.'[32] The Royal University, created to overcome 'the religious difficulty', had not succeeded. University College Dublin had also fallen far short of the ideal – it was 'crippled on the side of the practical sciences'. The commission found that:

> Roman Catholics, even more than the members of other denominations, have failed to obtain through the Royal University and the Colleges connected with it, that combination of general education with technical knowledge which is required by the social conditions now prevailing in Ireland. Young men who might find useful careers in

industrial and practical pursuits are drawn away by the cheap attrac-
tions of an Arts Degree that can be obtained simply by examination
results. There appears to be a dearth of the trained capacity necessary
for professional posts in the several departments of applied Science.[33]

The commission referred to the evidence of Horace Plunkett to make the
point that his Department of Agriculture and Technical Instruction
needed qualified inspectors of agriculture and teachers of the applied sciences but the need for these skills could not be met from within Ireland.[34]
The Catholic clergy exerted enormous influence over the educational
system but the majority of these men were of 'inadequate culture' and
lacked university education. Unlike in Britain, no teacher training
courses were offered by the universities. In Roman Catholic secondary
schools less than 10 per cent of teachers had been awarded university
degrees. In Catholic primary schools less than 1 per cent of teachers had
graduated.[35] The commission found that the 'evils' due to the lack of university education were 'far-reaching' and penetrated 'the whole social and
administrative system.'[36]

The commission acknowledged that if a new system of university
education in Ireland was to succeed then it was critically important to
gain the approval of the Irish Catholic bishops. It observed that, in the
Queen's Colleges, every professor, on appointment, was obliged to sign a
declaration, undertaking to 'abstain from teaching or advancing any
doctrine, or making any statement derogatory to the truths of revealed
religion, or injurious or disrespectful to the religious convictions' of any
sector of his class or audience. Furthermore, in his capacity as professor,
he was not permitted to introduce or discuss any subject that was politically or religiously controversial. In the Queen's Colleges the College
Council, and ultimately the state authorities, could define what 'the
truths of revealed religion' were in the case of a prosecution. The
Catholic bishops would be empowered to issue such a definition in a
case pertaining to a Catholic college.[37]

With concerns of the Catholic bishops in mind the commission proposed that the Royal University should be reformed as a federal teaching
university, comprised of four constituent colleges – the three Queen's
Colleges and a new Catholic college in Dublin.[38] The Catholic college
would be Catholic in the sense that it would provide a safe environment
for the faith and morals of its Catholic students. This concession to the
Roman Catholic Church in Ireland would have to be balanced against the
need to uphold academic freedom.[39] The commission also recommended

that courses at the Royal College of Science should be accepted as quali-
fying, entirely or in part, for some degrees of the new university.[40]

Members of the Robertson Commission were deeply divided on the
issue of university reform and nearly all of them expressed qualifications
and criticisms in notes appended to the final report which detracted
greatly from the force of its recommendations. Furthermore, the exclusion of the University of Dublin from the terms of reference of the
commission greatly diminished the value of its findings. The British government did not regard the proposed scheme of university reform as
satisfactory and continued to look for alternatives.[41]

Joly's Critique

In autumn 1903 the Chief Secretary of Ireland, George Wyndham,
drafted a scheme of university reform in consultation with the under-secretary, Sir Anthony MacDonnell, and the archbishop of Dublin, William
Joseph Walsh. The scheme was published in the press in January 1904
under the name of Lord Dunraven. It proposed the expansion of the
University of Dublin to include two new colleges. These were Queen's
College, Belfast, and a new college for Roman Catholics – King's College
– to be established in Dublin. This scheme was favoured by many
Catholics but gained little support amongst Protestants and was not
implemented by Arthur Balfour's Conservative government.[42]

When the Liberal Party, under Sir Henry Campbell-Bannerman,
regained power in December 1905 it quickly set about seeking a solution
to the university problem. On 2 June 1906 it set up a commission under
the chairmanship of Sir Edward Fry to enquire and report about Trinity
College Dublin and the University of Dublin in the context of addressing
the question of university reform. The antipathy of the Irish Catholic
bishops towards Trinity College was a major obstacle to progress. Trinity
College was for centuries associated with English rule and the governing
elite in Ireland. Before 1793, like Cambridge and Oxford, its doors were
open only to Anglicans. In that year legislation was passed to permit the
admission of students and the conferring of degrees without religious
tests. But legally based discrimination for religious reasons still persisted.
In 1873 Fawcett's Act removed all remaining religious tests. All emoluments were now open to competition from Catholics. There was strong
support for Henry Fawcett's initiative from within Trinity College where
many members of staff wished to present the institution as non-sectarian.[43] The Catholic bishops were not pleased. In 1875 they responded

by issuing a ban on Catholics attending Trinity College.[44] Their antipathy towards Trinity lingered on and is evident from their statement to the Fry Commission on 25 July 1906. They believed that Trinity was still tainted by an anti-Catholic and anti-Nationalist tradition although they conceded that those few Catholics who did study there were treated with 'special consideration'.[45] The bishops informed the commission that they would be prepared to accept any of the following: (1) a university for Catholics (2) a new college in the University of Dublin or (3) a new college in the Royal University. They were resolutely against any scheme of mixed education at Trinity College. Their preference was for a Catholic university. Roman Catholics, they argued, comprised 74 per cent of the population and they had a right to a university set up on principles in harmony with their religious beliefs.[46]

If a college rather than a university was offered to Catholics, which university would they choose for it? William Delany, in his evidence to the commission on 12 November 1906, was critical of the University of Dublin. He saw it as unsuitable for Catholics because of its traditional hostility to Roman Catholicism. He also believed that educational courses at Trinity were not suited to the needs of Ireland. There was an excessive focus on mathematics and classical studies to the detriment of commerce, modern languages and the applied sciences – such as agricultural science. Delany expressed a clear preference for the Royal University and was at that point a member of its senate for twenty-one years. The Royal was not restricted by too strong an adherence to tradition. Delany anticipated that the Royal, unlike Trinity, would be more flexible in responding to the country's educational needs. If the least preferred option – association with Trinity in the University of Dublin – was granted, then the new college for Catholics would have to be resourced to such an extent that it would be of equal status to Trinity.[47]

The financial cost of setting up a new college or university for Catholics could not be ignored. One way of reducing expenditure would be to organise shared access to expensive laboratory facilities for students with their counterparts in Trinity College. Delany was asked whether or not the mingling of students in the laboratories and lecture rooms was acceptable or not. He stated that there would be strong objections to such a proposal. He also rejected the idea of university professors teaching in both Trinity and in the Catholic college. There would be problems concerning procedures of appointment and control over teaching.[48] Control over the teaching of biology was a particularly sensitive issue. Delany told the commission: 'I have known students who have taken up Haeckel's books, because Haeckel is supposed to be an authority in Biology, and not a few have given up all belief in Christian revelation.' To avoid any misunderstanding that the Roman Catholic Church was exceptionally vulnerable to the works of Haeckel, Delany declared: 'I know no difficulty we Catholics make with regard to Biology which all believers in Christ are not bound to make. We have no special tenet of the Catholic Church which is contradicted by the teaching of Biology which is not common to all Christians.'[49]

The commission returned to the question of sharing laboratory facilities. Did Delany think it acceptable for students of the new Catholic college to do some of their work in the Royal College of Science? Delany dismissed the idea. He asserted that education and training at the Royal College was not of university standard – it was 'really a sort of higher technical school'.[50] However, the most serious objection seemed to be religious. Civil, electrical and mechanical engineering were not a problem. But biology, in the wrong hands, seemed to be full of hidden dangers to the faith. Brewing, for example, required an extensive knowledge of cellular physiology. But it was not possible to anticipate what a professor might say about the cell, or 'the powers of the cell'.[51] There were eight professors at the Royal College, all were Protestant, and anecdotal evidence indicated that at least one Catholic student there was on the road to perdition, having dismissed Christianity as a fiction.[52]

A measure of ecclesiastical control was required but this had to be balanced against the right to undertake scientific research without exposure to disciplinary action if theological sensitivities were offended. Archbishop William Walsh was aware of the hostility towards the idea of a state-funded college or university under the control of the Irish Catholic bishops. He informed the commission that the bishops did not demand a majority of Catholic clergymen on the governing body. A college or university for Catholics did not inevitably lead to clerical interference with secular studies. There would be no restriction of learning. A university for Catholics would not be exclusive to Catholics. Protestants would not be prohibited on the basis of their religious status from applying for all posts and emoluments in the new institution.[53]

On 18 October 1906 John Joly, Professor of Geology and Mineralogy at Trinity College, attended before the commission to give oral evidence. His opinions will receive considerable attention in this chapter because they yield an insight into how the Roman Catholic Church in Ireland was perceived by those outside the fold, especially in matters pertaining to intellectual freedom and the inter-relationship between science and faith.

Joly's opinions were taken as representative of the views of many of the academic staff of Trinity College.[54] He was asked whether or not it was right for a professor in a Christian college such as Trinity to teach anything contrary to Christian doctrine. Joly replied that it would not be right for a professor to venture beyond his discipline 'to make any attack or cast any aspersion upon the credibility of the Holy Scriptures'. Nevertheless, he maintained that a professor should be able to lecture with freedom, provided that he restricted himself to 'the facts and the received theories of science'.[55] What the 'facts' and 'received theories' of science were in relation to evolution was of course a matter of contention.

Did Joly think a professor had a right to teach anything which was 'contrary' to Christianity? Joly replied: 'No; nothing in the nature of an attack upon Christianity.' There was of course an important distinction to be made between attacking Christianity and saying something contrary to it. The commission pressed for clarification. Joly was asked: 'You do not consider any of the facts of science are contrary to the doctrine of Christianity, do you?' Joly prudently replied: 'That is a very difficult question to answer.' Joly was then told that the Catholic bishops were particularly concerned about safeguarding the faith of Catholic students in circumstances where professors might express opinions critical or disrespectful of religious convictions. The declaration which professors in the Queen's Colleges were obliged to sign, abstaining from expressing such opinions, was quoted at length. Joly declared that he did not have 'the slightest objection' to signing the declaration. But it is highly significant that he added, 'some people imply by Christianity a wider scope of belief than others.' But it was 'a hard question' to explain what Christianity meant in its 'wider sense'.[56] What Joly probably meant, without wishing to state it explicitly, was that the Catholic faith, as defined by the Catholic bishops, was less adaptable to the broadly accepted theories of science than liberal Protestantism. There seemed to be a very high risk of inadvertently offending Catholic sensitivities when teaching science.

In addition to his oral evidence to the Fry Commission, Joly submitted a document concerning the role of Trinity College and the University of Dublin in the future of higher education in Ireland. He pointed out that almost the entire staff membership of Trinity College was opposed to the creation of a second college within the University of Dublin where appointments to the governing body might occur for reasons other than academic merit. Joly feared that Catholics might gain so much power in such a reformed University of Dublin that Protestant influence would be dissipated. What was at stake for him, and the vast majority of his colleagues, was the prestige of the university and the high esteem in which its degrees were held. He saw Catholic and Protestant theories of education as fundamentally and irreconcilably different. The right to think for oneself was considered by the Roman Catholic Church as 'dangerous to faith and morals'. Most Protestants disagreed. In Trinity College – a Protestant institution – independence of judgement was prized as the foundation of education. It was immoral and detrimental to education to restrict free enquiry on the basis of safeguarding dogma. It was not good enough to teach a student 'the facts of Science' and then to 'train him to close his eyes to obvious deductions' from those facts. This principle of education retarded the development of independent thinking and rationality – qualities of vital importance to research.[57]

The Catholic Church's attitude towards evolution was not far from Joly's mind when he was making the above points. He referred extensively to the evidence submitted to the Robertson Commission by Bishop Edward O'Dwyer and William Delany. As observed earlier in this chapter, Delany had been asked by the Robertson Commission if he would permit a professor in University College Dublin to teach human evolution as a scientific thesis. Delany replied that his decision would be based on the judgement of the Catholic Church on the matter. Joly was clearly angered by this when he wrote:

> In other words, it is not a question of the right of evolution to rank as a credible generalisation on the support of facts of Palaeontology, Embryology, and Comparative Anatomy. It is not a question of the weight of scientific authority in its favour. The question is whether or not, in the judgement of theologians, it is contrary to their reading of Scripture . . . How far is this an advance on the days of Galileo?[58]

Joly observed that Delany and O'Dwyer were in agreement over the issue of evolution. O'Dwyer had criticised scientists for engaging in philosophy on the basis of developments in science. Joly dismissed this criticism as unreasonable. Were not scientists to think critically? He argued that the restrictions demanded by the Catholic Church would not be tolerated in any of the great universities of England, America or Germany. The administration of Delany's 'antidote' against evolution, as a substitute for 'calm, judicial, scientific evidence', would be considered 'lamentably deficient' by those who could speak authoritatively about biology. If

Trinity College was ever subjected to the Catholic ideal of education then great men of science and literature, of the stature of Charles Darwin, Mathew Arnold, Herbert Spencer and Oliver Goldsmith, would not be welcomed within its halls. The exceptional merit of their work would not be recognised. In view of this, it would be impossible to reconcile the ideal of education prevalent in Trinity with that of the Roman Catholic Church.[59] Joly was not opposed to the admission of Roman Catholics to Trinity College. On the contrary he, in common with many of his colleagues, favoured reforms which would encourage the entry of a greater number of Catholic students.[60]

Joly believed that Catholic representation on the governing body, the recruitment of Catholics to the teaching staff, and making provisions for the care of the Catholic faith would make Trinity more attractive to Catholics. On the third point, for example, the Office of Catechist could be set up to care for the spiritual needs of Catholic students. However, safeguarding the faith of Catholic students in Trinity was subject to a qualification of fundamental importance. Joly argued that

> this safeguarding of inner convictions must not hamper the honest teaching of secular facts and theories. So long as a lecturer in Science (for instance) is teaching the facts and theories of Science, he must be above rebuke . . . No inquisitorial supervision or impeachment of the published work of sane and honest men should be permissible . . .[61]

The final report of the Fry Commission was published on 21 January 1907. The commissioners did not anticipate that any scheme of reforms would make Trinity College acceptable to the Catholic bishops. They failed to reach broad agreement about what measures to take for the higher education of Catholics in Ireland. With one exception, they agreed that a college for Catholics should be established in Dublin but they failed to agree on a scheme for this.[62] Consensus was not reached on whether or not to set up the new college within a reformed Royal University or within an enlarged University of Dublin alongside Trinity.

On 25 January, James Bryce, the Chief Secretary of Ireland, announced a plan, with cabinet approval, at Dublin Castle which envisaged the establishment of an enlarged University of Dublin – a national university – encompassing Trinity, the Queen's Colleges at Belfast and Cork, and the new college in Dublin. Bryce, within a few days of leaving office to take up his new role as ambassador to the United States of America, anticipated that Queen's College Galway, Magee College, and the Arts Faculty at St Patrick's College might becomes affiliated colleges to the national university. The new university was to be completely non-denominational – free of religious tests for members of the governing body, professors, lecturers, examiners and students. Alternative courses were to be provided in controversial subjects such as history and philosophy. Bryce believed that examiners should issue alternative papers in controversial subjects to avoid causing offence to some students. Many subjects of course were non-controversial, such as mathematics. There was, Bryce declared, no such thing as Catholic mathematics and Protestant mathematics.[63] This of course was true, but seemingly non-controversial subjects – even mathematics – might provoke controversy if credence was given to extreme opinions where dangers to the faith were perceived at every turn. Professor Daniel Coghlan of Maynooth submitted the following opinion to the Fry Commission, which was published in the appendix to its final report:

> There can be grave danger from non-Catholic teachers and fellow-students, even in purely secular or scientific classes. A teacher could, for example, make a covert hostile allusion to the principle of authority in the Church even when teaching mathematics, by remarking significantly that mathematical conclusions are not received on authority, that scientific work and authority are mutually incompatible.[64]

There was intense opposition from Trinity College Dublin to proposals which would alter its status as the only college of the University of Dublin. In February the Dublin University Defence Committee was formed to preserve Trinity's unique relationship with the University of Dublin. The incompatibility between Bryce's statement about mathematics and Coghlan's statement to the Fry Commission did not escape the attention of the committee.[65] The scope for conflict seemed to be much broader than that anticipated by Bryce.

In its public repudiation of the Bryce proposals, the Defence Committee asserted that Trinity College had accepted the principle of equality in education since 1873. Trinity was explicitly presented as a non-sectarian university, open to Roman Catholics on terms of equality with Protestants. Few Catholics were attending Trinity, but the Catholic bishops were held responsible for this. From the viewpoint of Trinity staff, non-denominationalism was associated with the rightful freedom of teaching and research across a wide range of academic disciplines, including science. The Defence Committee claimed that a new college for Catholics in the University of Dublin, alongside Trinity, would be a futile attempt to bring together two incompatible principles of education. On the Trinity side there was freedom of thought; on the Catholic side such freedom was curtailed by authority. It was unacceptable to Trinity that 'the boundaries of science should be fixed, directly or indirectly, by ecclesiastical authority, or the impulse of speculation arrested by clerical intervention'. Conflicting views between the two colleges would give rise to 'occasions of strife and bitterness' which could only lead eventually to one of the institutions losing its identity. There could be no fruitful union between the two colleges 'so sharply divided by principle and tradition'. Internal conflict within the governing body of the university would be so bad that it would adversely impact on policy issues, erode standards of education, and shake public confidence in the institution.[66]

John Joly played a very active role in the campaign to preserve the independence of Trinity College. He was involved in the organisation of public meetings in England in support of Trinity. In February 1907 he left Dublin to attend these meetings and to meet Augustine Birrell, newly appointed Chief Secretary for Ireland (1907–1916) after Bryce's departure. He stated that in his twenty-four years of teaching at Trinity his research had never been held back by the fear that he was 'under the supervision of those who viewed Biology, Geology or Science generally as curbed by boundaries fixed on theological grounds and immovable for all time'. But now a new university was to be created which would bring about the restrictions he feared. Joly's concerns for the future of Trinity had been intensified by a close reading of the evidence submitted by O'Dwyer and Delany. As a constituent college of the new university, Trinity College would be vulnerable to interference from the Catholic hierarchy. Lay Catholics on the governing body of the university would be submissive to the bishops – and the authority of the bishops would be a barrier to scientific progress. The bishops, advised by theologians, would decide to what extent evolutionary theory would be taught. Evolutionary theory was important for both geology and biology. Joly pointed out that he could not teach palaeontology without teaching evolution. He protested that 'it is no longer a question of the scientific evidence . . . but of what theologians define on theological grounds to be *a priori* true or false.' The Bryce scheme would expose teaching and research to external influences which would damage both.[67]

Joly expressed his opinions at great length in a sixty-eight page booklet under the title of *An Epitome of the Irish University Question*. He referred again to the views of O'Dwyer and Delany. For Joly the imaginary curtailment of Huxley by O'Dwyer left little doubt that scientific studies would be greatly impaired if the bishops had their way. He declared that theologians, who knew nothing about biology, would decide what it was – and this was 'intolerable'. But was it not inappropriate, as O'Dwyer had claimed, for scientists to venture beyond science to engage in philosophical discourse? Joly thought not and took guidance from Tyndall and Huxley in responding to this point when he wrote:

> Here the Roman Catholic ideal seeks to restrict the man of Science to the microscope, chemical balance, and electroscope. But the greatest discoveries are those which have come from that nebulous region where, like summer lightning, the scientific imagination lightens the darkness; the region where fact and conjecture meet.[68]

Rational speculation and imagination were essential elements of scientific enterprise. The boundaries between 'facts, probable truths and speculation' could not be precisely defined – contrary to the assertions of the Roman Catholic Church. Joly pointed to a correlation between the church's concern to safeguard the faith of its students and a censorial attitude towards education which would prove to be excessively restrictive on the teaching of science. Similar restrictions would be imposed in other disciplines, such as history and English literature.

Joly gave particular attention to Delany's evidence to the Robertson Commission when questions about human evolution were raised. He pointed out that 'Dr. Delany is everywhere explicit and candid as to his views on the limitations of Science, and the fact that the Church is the sole arbiter of those limits. He refers to the limitations of Darwinism which must prevail in a Roman Catholic College.'[69] Joly was now confident that he understood the principles of the Catholic Church in education, especially towards science. He concluded:

> We see here, as elsewhere, that the Catholic Church is to be the ultimate arbiter in deciding the limits of controversy. This is really the kernel of the whole matter, and on this point the Roman Catholic witnesses have been so perfectly explicit and perfectly frank that it is only needful to quote a very few of their statements. They speak for all.[70]

Joly returned to addressing the question of how to increase the numbers of Roman Catholic students in Trinity. He was aware that proposed reforms to attract greater numbers of Catholics to Trinity might not succeed in doing so. Reforms might be carried too far, leading to the estrangement of non-Catholics without any compensating benefit to Catholics. Joly acknowledged that Trinity should contribute to the initiative to meet increasing demands from Catholics for university education. But a principle of critical importance had to be complied with. Trinity was held to be of equal status to Cambridge and Oxford. It would retain that position if intellectual freedom was respected. Any proposed changes that threatened Trinity's status had to be vigorously opposed.[71]

The fears expressed by Joly and others did not come to pass. A 'hands off Trinity' campaign gained powerful political support in Britain and had the desired effect.[72] Trinity was left untouched under the terms of the Irish Universities Act (1908). The Royal University was dissolved. Two new universities were created which, like Trinity, were legally non-denominational. Queen's College, Belfast became the Queen's University of Belfast and catered very much for the needs of non-conformist Protestants, especially Presbyterians. The National University of Ireland (NUI) was comprised of three colleges: University College Dublin and the former Queen's Colleges in Cork and Galway. St Patrick's College, Maynooth, became a 'recognised' college in 1910 and attained constituent college status in 1967. The exclusion of Trinity and Queen's University Belfast from the NUI ensured that it would be predominantly Catholic and nationalist.[73] There had been formidable obstacles to the establishment of an all-inclusive national university. The British government eventually opted for university reform on the basis of a partitionist rationale, which can be seen as a harbinger of the partition of Ireland in 1921.[74]

The Irish Universities Act can be seen as the outcome of an attempt to put in place a broadly acceptable compromise in the face of irreconcilable demands – the persistent opposition of the Catholic bishops to mixed education and the espousal of intellectual freedom by Joly and others.[75] The NUI, although not a Catholic university, was effectively a university for Catholics. The Catholic bishops grudgingly gave their consent. The external threat of Protestantism and other unholy influences had been reduced to acceptable levels of risk. But a new and formidable danger to the faith was perceived – and it was emerging from within the Catholic Church itself.

5. Anti-Modernism,
1907–1920s

The Campaign against Heresy

In the late nineteenth century Catholic scholars struggled with a range of exegetical problems arising from the latest findings in archaeology, history and the natural sciences. Modernist initiatives in theology were not unique to the Roman Catholic Church and occurred in other Christian denominations also.[1] However, theological controversies in the Protestant churches, arising from developments in historical research and the natural sciences, started about forty years earlier and were less intense than in the Catholic Church.[2] Theologians and Biblical scholars in the Catholic Church were particularly disadvantaged. They had to work within the excessively restrictive parameters of Thomism. Furthermore, the new pope, Pius X (1903–1914), was extremely intolerant of even moderately liberal opinions in theological discourse. Cardinal Rafael Merry del Val, whom he appointed as secretary of state, was also of a reactionary disposition.

The modernist crisis which arose in the first decade of the twentieth century was the greatest intellectual upheaval in the church since the Reformation. Thomism failed to bring about the intellectual unity hoped for by the ecclesiastical authorities and served mainly to exacerbate the crisis.[3] Modernist authors put forward a number of proposals which were at variance with a core doctrine of the Catholic Church concerning the immutability and infallibility of the apostolic deposit of faith – the *depositum fidei*. Their outlook in this matter was based on an evolutionary perspective.[4] Two leading figures in the modernist movement, Alfred Loisy and George Tyrrell, argued that the organisation and dogmas of the church had developed in response to the social milieu and needs of Catholics throughout history.[5] All this was reprehensible to many Catholics, especially those in the upper echelons of power.

Pope Pius X acted decisively against the modernists.[6] Catholic writers found their works condemned – especially theologians and Biblical scholars. Anti-modernist pronouncements issued forth from the Vatican. In July 1907 the Holy Office published the decree *Lamentabili Sane Exitu* ('A Lamentable Departure Indeed'), condemning sixty-five propositions concerning theology and exegesis. On 8 September 1907 Pius issued the encyclical *Pascendi Dominici Gregis* ('Feeding the Lord's Flock'), which condemned modernism in the harshest terms. On 1 September 1910 he issued the *motu proprio*,[7] *Sacrorum Antistitum*, obliging the vast majority of the clergy to take an anti-modernist oath.[8]

Pius instructed the bishops to enforce the study of scholastic philosophy, based on the works of St Thomas Aquinas, in Catholic colleges and seminaries and to exercise vigilance in the censorship of unorthodox literature.[9] The pope's encyclical strengthened the position of reactionaries within the church. Liberal Catholic periodicals and newspapers were suppressed. Professors and lecturers in seminaries who were suspected of holding heterodox ideas suffered censorship, disgrace and dismissal from their posts. Some of those who were denounced as modernists, such as Loisy and Tyrrell, had strayed far beyond the dogmatic teaching of the church. But many Catholic scholars, although innovative and liberal in their approach to theology and the scriptures, had stayed within the limits prescribed by dogma. Ardent anti-modernists often failed to discriminate between these two categories of Catholic writers. Catholic scholars were spied upon by networks of informers – the most infamous of which was Monsignor Umberto Benigni's *Sodalitium Pianum* (League of St Pius V). They were discouraged from pursuing new lines of enquiry, especially in Biblical studies. This had a devastating impact on the quantity and quality of research publications.

The vast majority of Roman Catholics did not cultivate intellectual interests affected by modernist controversies. Generally, Roman Catholics accepted that their church was the arbiter of truth and provider of religious certitudes and were not inclined to confront the complexities, abstractions and enigmas of theology.[10] There is no reason to suppose that the Catholic laity of Ireland were exceptional in this regard. However, the Irish Catholic clergy, in common with their counterparts elsewhere, were very much aware of the intellectual turmoil within the church. The dominant tendency was to regard modernist ideas as a threat to the very foundations of the faith. Daniel Coghlan (or Cohalan) was particularly intolerant of ideas not clearly in conformity with the teachings of the magisterium. He had been bitterly critical of Walter McDonald.[11] That Coghlan's outlook, rather than McDonald's, was the dominant one amongst the bishops and priests is indicated by the fact that Coghlan was promoted to the rank of bishop (of Cork) while McDonald was censured and carefully watched by his clerical colleagues.

Coghlan presented modernism as a fusion of Kantian philosophy and Darwinism – embellished with only a veneer of Christian terminology. It is likely that he had McDonald in mind when he claimed that a number of Catholic apologists were repeating the error of rashly proposing changes in doctrine – influenced by a desire to accommodate scientific theories which they understood to be sound but that were likely to be rejected by scientists in the future. Some Catholic writers, he believed, had been arguing, implicitly rather than explicitly, that the origins of Catholicism could be explained by recourse to natural selection.[12] Coghlan believed that Loisy had led the way in applying Darwin's theory to explanations of the origins and development of Catholic religious beliefs.[13] According to this exposition of Loisy's published works, the Roman Catholic Church, as a social organisation, had transformed itself through the centuries in a manner analogous to the adaptive changes in plant and animal species. Morality was a product of natural selection. Its function was to curb anti-social behaviour and to promote social virtues, thus contributing to the survival of the human species. The institutional church, like all living organisms, was subject to the law of natural selection and the fundamental tenets of Christian faith were merely ideals with no basis in reality. When the church acknowledged its own evolutionary development, then it would be able to make peace with science.[14]

Coghlan's critique of modernism linked heresy with evolutionary theory and showed how science might be used to undermine religious belief.[15] Other Irish Catholic writers also condemned modernism, associating it with the agnosticism of misguided scientists and philosophers.[16] Catholics were admonished to approach science with the utmost caution. Theological students were advised that they were permitted to believe in an evolutionary process provided that it was held to be under divine guidance and allowed for occasional divine intervention.[17] All this could only have generated feelings of suspicion and fear of science in Irish Catholicism. Anti-modernism, extending outwards from Rome, militated against the emergence of a strong scientific culture in Catholic Ireland.

Walter McDonald and some of his colleagues were deeply distressed by the censorial attitude of the church authorities. McDonald was a moderniser, not a modernist, and rejected the contention that there was an inevitable conflict between Catholic doctrine and modern science.[18] He believed that scholastic metaphysics was in dire need of revision because of the many advances in science since Copernicus. Developments in metaphysics would in turn bring about changes in theology.[19] McDonald wrote against a background where there was a pressing need for progress in theology. Theology had stagnated in the aftermath of the Enlightenment and had revived in several European countries at different times and for different reasons, from the early nineteenth century to the first decade of the twentieth century. These countries were Germany, France, England, the Low Countries and Italy. There was very little contribution to theological and Biblical scholarship from other countries with large Catholic populations.[20]

McDonald wished to promote scholarly enterprise in the faculty of theology in Maynooth and with this in mind he set about establishing a new journal of theology. In his opinion the *Irish Ecclesiastical Record* was so firmly under the control of the hierarchy that debates on 'burning questions' had been stifled.[21] The enterprise of McDonald and his colleagues was looked upon with deep misgivings by a number of Catholic bishops. Despite this they pressed ahead with their project and in January 1906 the first issue of the *Irish Theological Quarterly* was published.[22] However, McDonald's published work came under such close scrutiny from a number of bishops and from the authorities in Rome that he deemed it necessary to sever his connection with the journal. He was in no doubt about the adverse impact of anti-modernist excesses when he stated:

> We were unfortunate in the time at which our project was commenced, as the Modernists not only lamed but killed us. They aimed at progress, so did we; therefore we were Modernists. It was of no avail to disclaim Modernistic views . . . If we were not Modernists, should we not be content with the I.E. Record?[23]

McDonald was critical of the modernist movement which he believed had greatly counteracted progress in the Catholic Church. He was particularly bitter towards Loisy and Tyrrell. The heavy hand of censorship stifled theological enterprise with the result that the *Irish Theological Quarterly* did very little to extend the boundaries of theological science.[24]

McDonald worked out his own views on a number of theological questions which had, for him, required the abandonment of some traditional beliefs. However, he found himself under constant suspicion and the bulk of his work was refused an imprimatur, or would have been refused an imprimatur if he had sought it.[25] He identified his predicament with that of St George Jackson Mivart who had been so harshly treated by the church shortly before his death. McDonald maintained that censorship alone would not protect the church against the infiltration of unchristian ideas percolating into Ireland from abroad through the medium of the press.[26] But he exerted little influence in an institution which set itself so resolutely against modernity.[27]

The church's aversion to mainstream intellectual trends was nowhere more clearly evident than in its excessive emphasis on medieval Thomism. For centuries the works of St Thomas Aquinas provided the Roman Catholic Church with plausible arguments for the existence of God.[28] But the arguments of St Thomas were greatly weakened, if not undermined, in the eighteenth century by the German philosopher Immanuel Kant (1724–1804) and the Scottish philosopher and historian David Hume (1711–1776).[29] This did not dissuade the Vatican from elevating Thomism to a position of primacy in Catholic theology. It rejected philosophies of the Enlightenment and resorted to Thomism as an antidote to the intellectual ills of the modern world. Since the late nineteenth century no Catholic was allowed to hold a professorial position in a Catholic institution who did not accept fully the teachings of St Thomas as interpreted by the Vatican authorities.[30] The imposition of Thomism enhanced the influence of reactionary elements in the curia and created a culture of intolerance towards other theological schools of thought during the pontificate of Pius X.[31] Catholic scholars who did not revere St Thomas quite as much as their rigidly conservative co-religionists had to express their opinions about the shortcomings of Thomism with extreme caution.

Although great merit was seen in St Thomas's arguments for the existence of God, it was deemed necessary to concede that these same arguments were of limited value when used in response to difficulties presented by modern science.[32] Walter McDonald tactfully observed that non-Catholics defended religion on grounds far removed from St Thomas's *Summa Theologica*. Many discoveries about the natural world had been made since the writing of the *Summa Theologica* and it was reasonable to speculate that St Thomas Aquinas would have considerably changed his defence of theism if he had the benefit of new knowledge. McDonald was aware that evolutionary theory had inflicted some damage on St Thomas's fifth argument. The thirteenth-century philosopher contended that natural objects displayed intelligent design and purpose and, because they could not design themselves, it was reasonable to conclude the existence of a Designer – God. However, McDonald believed that 'the modern scientific mind' now tended to view the evolutionary process, working within the framework of natural laws, as capable of providing satisfactory explanations of everything in the universe with no need to invoke God as an external and underlying cause. This outlook, he maintained, was groundless. He was convinced that modern science, rather than weakening the tenability of theism, was of great benefit to religion because of major gaps in the continuity of the evolutionary process. McDonald referred to the opinions of the German physiologist Emil du Bois-Reymond, although he did not identify the exact source. Du Bois-Reymond was of interest to McDonald because he was a proponent of materialistic evolution.[33] This atheistic stance required a belief in the continuity of the evolutionary process. Despite this du Bois-Reymond identified seven major 'enigmas' or gaps in scientific explanations of natural phenomena. These pertained to:

1. The nature of matter and energy.
2. The origin of motion.
3. The origin of life.
4. The apparently designed order of nature.
5. The origin of sensation and consciousness.
6. The origin of rational thought and speech.
7. Free will.

McDonald believed that theists could confidently maintain that all but the first required divine intervention. The physical sciences were therefore supplying 'bases of proof more tangible, and . . . more serviceable' than those proposed by St Thomas.[34] McDonald's subtle and mild critique of Thomism indicated that Catholic apologists were looking for other and more satisfying proofs of God's existence. An alternative and more persuasive approach, therefore, was to identify weaknesses in the arguments of atheists who believed in an unbroken evolutionary process. The lack of evidence for the development of life from non-living matter, for example, seemed to weaken the case for materialistic evolution. Scientists believed that, early in the earth's history, and over many millions of years, chemical substances of greater and greater complexity had formed until primitive life forms arose entirely from the innumerable interactions of complex organic molecules. This complex process was an essential element of evolution, linking inanimate with living matter, an essential element of evolutionary development from the primordial nebular cloud to the emergence of *Homo sapiens*. In the words of R. Fullerton, a contributor to the *Irish Ecclesiastical Record*, the process of cosmological development was seen as an 'unbroken record of the evolution of gas into genius'.[35]

McDonald observed that there was no evidence for the emergence of life from inanimate matter in modern times but he did not assert that this absence of evidence undermined the idea. He warned his readers not to rely too much on scientific proofs. He feared that if such negative scientific proofs were ever overturned then it would lead those who were 'weak either in faith or in philosophy' to distrust similar arguments in future.[36]

McDonald's clerical colleague at Maynooth, Peter Coffey, wrote extensively about the interconnections between theology, philosophy and science, mainly in the *Irish Ecclesiastical Record*. In his historical survey of modern philosophy Coffey presented René Descartes (1596–1650) as the greatest influence. Although Cartesian philosophy fragmented into many conflicting schools of thought, they all shared in common an underlying subjective scepticism which failed to engage with the serious problems of life or to satisfy those who searched earnestly for truth. Scientists, inspired by the inductive method of Sir Francis Bacon, had little use for the vague subjectivist speculations of mainstream philosophy. However, when scientists distanced themselves from this type of philosophy they also abandoned the 'moderate realism' of scholastic philosophy, often failing to distinguish it from Cartesian philosophy. The poor relationship between science and philosophy created difficulties in science concerning the scope of scientific methodology and the interpretation of data. This in turn led to the widespread misunderstanding that science and religion were, somehow, in conflict.[37]

Coffey maintained that science was 'sick' since its separation from scholasticism and that it lacked a sound philosophy.[38] Not only had scientists rejected scholastic philosophy – many Catholic philosophers had done likewise. Was there any reasonable basis for expecting that scholasticism might be revived beyond the walls of institutions controlled by the ecclesiastical authorities? It seemed not, despite some degree of resurgence. Coffey observed that Pope Leo's elevation of Thomism had disappointed many learned Catholics and was generally dismissed as unworthy of serious consideration by non-Catholics.[39] The 'ordinary' man regarded scholasticism as slightly 'less archaic than Babylonian bricks'. The possibility that scholasticism would 'overleap the walls' of the seminaries, infiltrate the universities and, through the medium of the press, capture the interest of the public was not likely.[40] Coffey was aware that scholastic philosophers were sometimes grossly ignorant of physics.[41] Therefore, scholasticism needed to give rise to neo-scholasticism. It had to be purged of its medieval errors, revised, and harmonised with modern science if it was to influence modern thought in Ireland and elsewhere.[42]

Coffey believed that a harmonious relationship between neo-scholasticism and science would not only serve the best interests of scientists and philosophers – it would also be in the broader public interest. Science was serving 'well enough the lower wants of man . . . procuring bodily comfort and luxury'.[43] The general public was 'amazed, overawed' and 'subdued' by the 'astonishing' discoveries, theories and speculations of scientists that had transformed the world into a 'veritable fairyland'.[44] But science, devoid of guidance from a sound philosophy, was dangerous to the welfare of humankind, in both the earthly and spiritual spheres, and was not without its defects in intellectual matters. Coffey, it seems, feared that science would eclipse not only theology, but religious belief generally. Therefore, it was necessary to attack the prestigious position of science.

Science was misused in the production of armaments, thus giving rise to the 'scientific savagery of modern warfare'.[45] On the intellectual front science was not omnipotent. Coffey repudiated the notion that physical laws explained all the great mysteries of nature. It was, for example, preposterous to him that the mental faculties of humans arose entirely from the 'mere mechanical dance of material or electrical particles'. He expressed concern about 'pseudo-scientific truths' expounded by 'second- or third-rate popularizers', which were being disseminated through the medium of newspapers and periodicals. These erroneous ideas were 'calculated to disturb common Christian beliefs' and sometimes, he believed, they had the intended effect.[46] Coffey's worries and alarmist views about the adverse impact of scientific theories were not unique amongst Catholic writers.[47] The best response to this problem, in Coffey's opinion, was for Catholics to keep themselves informed about the new discoveries concerning God's creation, bearing in mind the fundamentally important distinction between facts and theories.[48]

A much simpler and radically different opinion to Coffey's was expressed by the lay polemicist Alfred O'Rahilly (1884–1969). O'Rahilly asserted that censorship could be used – justifiably – to counteract the threat of ideas that were deemed incompatible with Roman Catholicism. He argued that the Catholic Church had been right to censor Galileo to protect the faith and happiness of its members. In modern times many souls had been lost to the church because of the 'fervent dogmatism' of Huxley, Tyndall and Haeckel. Men were still being led astray by the publications of 'rationalist charlatanism' and were abandoning their faith. The people needed to be protected. After all, what was more important – speculative science or the happiness and salvation of the masses?[49] O'Rahilly's opinion was probably not unusual amongst Catholic apologists. An article in the *Irish Theological Quarterly* gives an insight into conservative Catholic thinking about the assumed hazards of unfettered enquiry. The suppression of intellectual endeavour was justified on the basis that 'free thought is as disastrous as free love'. Reason did not cohabit easily with the unquestioning acceptance of Catholic dogmas. Many well-educated men did 'not suffer their intellect to be led into captivity', and were unable to sustain their faith. Ignorance was bliss – or so it seemed. Heaven awaited those who surrendered their intellect to the church, while retaining their own judgement in worldly matters.[50] All this was in perfect harmony with anti-modernist sentiments which permeated early-twentieth-century Roman Catholicism, not least in Ireland.

Evolution and Apostasy

Not all those who chose to challenge atheists, agnostics and sceptics of every complexion were ranked amongst the clergy. Members of the Catholic laity who wrote in defence of their church included, most notably, Sir Bertram Alan Coghill Windle (1858–1929) and Professor Alfred O'Rahilly. Both men were scientists and served as president of University College Cork (Queen's College Cork, 1845–1908) – Windle from 1904 to 1919, O'Rahilly from 1943 to 1954. Both men were devout Roman Catholics and scientists. They wrote on the relationship between Catholicism and science, but agreed on little else.[51]

Windle, a British Anglican, had converted to Roman Catholicism in 1883. He was led by his reading to the threshold of the church, and one of the books which had influenced his decision was John Henry Newman's *Apologia Pro Vita Sua* (1864). Both men lived in Birmingham and subsequently met. After his conversion, Windle corresponded with Mivart who impressed upon him the importance of overturning a commonly held idea in the English-speaking world that science and Catholicism were not compatible. Mivart believed that if this objective was to be achieved then England had to produce many Catholic scientists. With this in mind he urged Windle to serve his church by rising to eminence in his chosen profession. Windle, it seems, was deeply influenced by this advice.[52] The zeal of the convert worked in tandem with a dedication to science and stimulated a prodigious output. Windle's books include *What Is Life? A Study of Vitalism and Neo-Vitalism* (1908), *Twelve Catholic Men of Science* (1912), *A Century of Scientific Thought and Other Essays* (1915), *The Church and Science* (1920), *The Evolutionary Problem As It Is Today* (1927) and *The Catholic Church and Its Reactions with Science* (1927). Windle's dedication to the Catholic Church did not go unacknowledged. Pope Pius X conferred him with a knighthood of St Gregory and he received an honorary doctorate from Pope Pius XI.[53]

Windle, notwithstanding his dedication to the Roman Catholic Church, acknowledged a genuine problem in reconciling religion and science. The *modi operandi* of scientists made it difficult for them to embrace faith. In a letter to a friend Windle declared that, in science, ideas were constantly changing because of new discoveries. Religion, in contrast, was governed by faith and immutable 'truths'. He experienced difficulties because

> . . . it is hard to keep these two attitudes in water-tight compartments
> . . . What I meant about science was this: when one is working at it
> one learns to accept nothing that one cannot actually demonstrate.
> Now in Religion one must take certain things on faith, as naturally I
> am prepared to do. But I think it is harder for a scientific man in some
> ways, though he has this help, that he knows there are a whole lot of
> things which he must accept tho' he can't understand them.[54]

Windle's dilemma was probably not unusual amongst scientists.[55] Evidently, he was able to subdue any doubts he had about Catholicism and, as a loyal Catholic, he was anxious to counteract the anti-Christian ideas of those 'enterprising journalists' who sensationalised and misrepresented science to capture the attention of an 'ignorant' public.[56]

If Windle's faith was severely tested by the critical and sceptical attitude appropriate to science, it also appeared to find support from the subject matter of science. It was argued, quite reasonably, that there was a fundamental difference between living and non-living matter. However, the unsubstantiated claim was made that life was more than physicochemical phenomena, that living organisms were animated by some vital or extra-physical life force. In Ireland the idea was vigorously advocated by a few Catholic writers, especially by Windle, whose book *What Is Life? A Study of Vitalism and Neo-Vitalism* was entirely devoted to the subject.

Vitalism had been discredited in the mid-nineteenth century by the mechanistic worldview of Newtonian physics. In the late nineteenth century it was revived by the German scientist and philosopher Hans Driesch (1867–1941). Driesch renamed it neo-vitalism to make it seem less archaic. Neo-vitalism gained very little acceptance amongst biologists and this acceptance was short-lived. But the idea did influence many biologists to critically examine the limits of mechanistic philosophy. These scientists hoped for the construction of a theory which, although subject to the laws of physics, would not depend entirely on physics. An integrative mechanism or principle, peculiar to the domain of biology, was pursued as an alternative to the reductionism which viewed life as merely the outcome of physicochemical phenomena. Many biologists, although opposed to a mechanistic approach to the study of life, did not accept Driesch's neo-vitalist system. Instead, they embraced other concepts which would facilitate explanations peculiar to biology, such as holism and organicism. Some neo-vitalists were theologically motivated. They argued that there was a distinctly non-material force in every organism; therefore, supernatural intervention was required to explain its origins.[57] Some Catholic authors associated neo-vitalism with the scholastic philosophy of the church.[58]

The advocacy of neo-vitalism epitomised the tendency of some Catholic apologists to seek out the limitations and discontinuities of scientific knowledge as a means of proving the existence of God. But what proof was there of a vital force in nature? Windle argued that it was quite evident from casual observation and common sense that nature, in all its complexity, required more than physical and chemical laws to sustain and operate it. On this basis the burden of proof lay with materialists whom Windle associated with the rejection of neo-vitalism.[59] The fact that the neo-vitalistic concept of life was incompatible with the law of the conservation of energy did not present an insurmountable problem because, Windle thought rather conveniently, that the law in question might be inaccurate or incomplete.[60]

This mysterious life force was used to explain how humans differed in kind – not just in degree – from other animal species. The higher intelligence of humans distinguished them from the rest of the animal kingdom but this, it was asserted, could not be explained in purely physical terms. Thought was 'wholly immaterial' and brain tissue, without this vital force, could not become self-conscious. Matter could not think – it could not reflect on itself.[61] It did not seem possible that

... all the phenomena exhibited by living bodies, including the poetry
of Shakespeare and Wordsworth, the profound reasonings of Aristotle
or Sir Isaac Newton ... and all minor manifestations of life are expli-
cable and may, therefore, some day be explained in terms of chemical
equations and physical experiments.[62]

There was a resistance among Irish Catholic apologists to the idea that
complex arrangements of inanimate atoms could give rise to a living,
feeling, conscious organism. But an understanding of life was not to be
found by looking at the constituent atoms. For species to evolve, function
and procreate, atoms had to organise into highly complex molecular
structures – therein lay the secret of life. Neo-vitalism was not scientifically demonstrable and very few biologists were influenced by it.

Life, and the origins of life, were, from a scientific point of view,
underpinned by physical and chemical laws. There was no conflict with
Catholic theology here, or so it seemed. Catholics could view these laws
of physics and chemistry as secondary causes put in place by the Creator.
But theological issues arising from evolutionary theory were not so easy
to address. There was still the fear that the idea of human evolution was
dangerous to one's Catholic faith – even if it was tentatively expressed and
referred only to the human body and not the immortal soul.

Catholics were not the only Christians to express concern about the
theological implications of evolution. Some members of the Church of
Ireland also experienced similar difficulties. However, in the early twentieth century it seems that there was considerable support for the idea
that evolution was God's creative *modus operandi*. Two influential
Church of Ireland clergymen (the Reverend Charles Grierson, Dean of
Belfast and later Bishop of Down and Connor; and Charles Frederick
D'Arcy, Bishop of Armagh (Anglican Primate of Ireland) from 1929 to
1938) were not reticent about expressing positive opinions about the
theory.[63] These Anglican prelates did not, it seems, have their counterparts in the Irish Catholic Church.

Evolution presented theologians with a major problem because they
experienced difficulties in reconciling it with the Genesis account of creation and with the doctrine of Original Sin. How did Windle, as a
scientist and a Catholic, reconcile theology with evolution – especially
human evolution? In his book *The Church and Science* (1920), Windle
indicated his submission to ecclesiastical authority on this contentious
issue. He was aware that 'certain able theological writers' had written in
favour of Mivart's teleological version of human evolution and had

'retracted their advocacy' when the ecclesiastical authorities in Rome
expressed disapproval. The Vatican was very reluctant to concede that a
new interpretation of scripture could be 'freely taught' in order to harmonise it with a theory which had not been proven. What was required
from the scientists was incontrovertible evidence. In the meantime it was
expected that loyal Catholics would 'adapt' their thinking to the 'mind'
of the Church and would accept its guidance, even when its teaching was
not put forward as infallible.[64]

Catholic antipathy towards evolutionary theory seemed to originate,
to some extent, from the perception that it offered support to atheists and
agnostics who asserted that religious belief was based on ignorance,
unfounded superstition and wishful thinking. For those with grossly
exaggerated fears, evolution seemed poised to displace religion in intellectual discourse:

> Everyone nowadays, from the high-class specialist . . . to the coal-
> heaver . . . is prepared to discuss nebular hypotheses, geological
> periods, missing links, and all the rest of it . . . It is evolution every-
> where, all evolution, and nothing but evolution; everything is
> explained, the world is an open book. . .[65]

The grim spectre of materialism loomed large in this bleak intellectual
landscape as 'worshippers' assembled at 'the shrine of science'.[66]
Evolutionary theory, so closely connected to philosophy and theology,
was tainted with a tendency to explain everything on the basis of physical
and chemical laws, without any reference to God. It was so convincingly
put forward that it represented a 'grave danger' to the Catholic laity.[67] Fr
Garrett Pierse (1883–1932), who was appointed Professor of Theology at
Maynooth in 1914, expressed his fears of apostasy in the pages of the
widely circulated and extremist Catholic monthly periodical the *Catholic
Bulletin* (1912). Many workers and their families at the time endured
extreme poverty, probably enhancing the impact of his dire prognostica-
tion. Claiming that the Rationalist Press was determined to popularise
materialistic science, he declared that

> . . . the ordinary people – the toilers – are selected as the disciples of
> this godless enlightenment. These workers have not many of the joys
> of this life. Popular science would rob them of the future life. The only
> hope which might sustain them in the miseries of their daily lot is the
> soothing hope supplied by the Catholic faith; but of this they are being
> deprived by a materialistic science.[68]

Under these circumstances it might have been expected that the clergy would endeavour to communicate with the laity to counteract anti-Christian or non-Christian ideas. But it seems they chose to remain aloof on such issues. The author William Patrick Ryan (1867–1942) observed in his book *The Pope's Green Island* (1912) that many Irish priests regarded themselves as so intellectually superior to the laity that they were '. . . a great caste apart, which indeed the multitude was privileged to approach and be given what was considered good for it. That the masses wanted more they could not be made to realise.'[69] In Ireland the clergy did not enter into public debate about controversial scientific issues such as the theory of evolution. Ryan was of the opinion that:

> Generally speaking, official Maynooth seems in no hurry to deal with philosophical or psychical or mystical questions in which so much of the rising generation is interested. It wants to go on believing that Ireland consists, and will always consist, of an incurious Catholicism headed by a professional Catholicism.[70]

Some clerical writers were aware of a 'curious' Catholicism but this did not lead to a dialogue between the clergy and the laity to any significant extent. They acknowledged that piety alone was inadequate to safeguard the faith and stressed the need to educate the public in matters of science, through the school system and through the medium of the Catholic press.[71]

And yet science was not always seen as a great intellectual threat to the Catholic faith. The great strides in the formation of major scientific theories, which so characterised the mid-nineteenth century, were followed by a growing fragmentation and specialisation of scientific studies in the early twentieth century. The new branches of knowledge grew so rapidly and so unevenly that there was a lack of interdisciplinary interaction. All this counteracted a fruitful synthesis.[72] Theoretical pluralism and the increasing tendency to regard theories as working hypotheses demolished the unfounded assumption that scientific explanations provided an exact account of physical reality. The philosophy of Friedrich Nietzsche, which had become very influential from the 1890s onwards, tended to undermine grand explanatory schemes based on notions of truth which were in turn associated with scientific laws. In some intellectual circles it became fashionable to speak about the limitations of science.[73] It was against the background of these intellectual developments that Canon Patrick Sheehan had written in 1903:

> Science has passed from great principles into mere experiment.
> Instead of being mistress of great minds, she has become an artificer
> of toys for men's hands and human convenience . . . Darwin and
> Owen, Huxley and Tyndall have vanished, and Edison and Marconi
> remain. Great principles, for right or wrong, are no longer laid down,
> fought for, assailed, accepted, or rejected.[74]

Science was seen to have descended to the level of mere technicalities.
Sheehan believed that the age of great intellectual ideas had passed – not
just in the natural sciences but in other disciplines also. The innovative
application of such ideas was all that remained. In his opinion civilisation was intellectually bankrupt.[75] Sheehan was typical of Catholic writers
who wished to diminish the status of science but his apparent complacency about the intellectual impotency of science was probably not
shared by the majority of those of his co-religionists who were mindful of
its implications for Catholicism.

A number of developments within science, and external to it, exposed
it to criticism and Catholic apologists were not reticent about taking
advantage of the opportunities. Darwinism had been extrapolated
beyond the biological sciences and had given birth to social Darwinism,
with its central tenet of 'survival of the fittest'. This ideology influenced
social and political thinking. It conditioned, to some extent, the outlook
of European leaders prior to the outbreak of the First World War in 1914
and was invoked to underpin imperialism, communism and fascism.[76]
Thus it was observed that social Darwinism was contrary to Catholic
doctrine, which maintained that the primary purpose of civil society is to
promote justice rather than foster a competitive and warmongering
ethos.[77] R. Fullerton, writing in the *Irish Ecclesiastical Record*, took issue
with notions of racial superiority underpinned by social Darwinism. He
argued that 'backward savage races' were not intellectually inferior to
those of 'high-class' civilisation. All they required was the opportunity –
a favourable environment – to make progress. The literature of Western
civilisation, it seemed, indicated degeneration, not progress.[78] However,
in the discipline of anthropology, very much permeated by Darwinism,
the theory of degenerationism was greeted with professional contempt.
Degenerationism rejected the contention that human society had
progressed from barbarism to high civilisation and was associated with
very conservative religious attitudes.[79]

Darwinism itself had not recovered from its decline in the biological
sciences in the late nineteenth century. The concept of natural selection

as an evolutionary mechanism sank to its lowest level of support in the period before the outbreak of the First World War.[80] The rediscovery of Gregor Mendel's published work should have led to the widespread acceptance of the evolutionary mechanism proposed by Darwin – but initially it did not because it seemed to offer an alternative to the notion of gradual change. When carrying out his research Mendel had deliberately chosen characteristics of his plants which differed from one another in an all-or-none way. Geneticists now assumed that new characteristics would arise through inheritable changes in genes, termed mutations, leading to drastic transformations rather than very small changes. Since mutations were regarded as the only source of genetic novelty, it was widely believed that the main impetus of evolutionary change was the random accumulation of favourable genetic changes. Darwin's key principles of natural selection and gradual change were frequently dismissed as inconsequential. In the first decade of the twentieth century evolutionary biologists were deeply divided between the Mendelians, Darwinians and Lamarckians.[81] Consensus proved elusive until the 'modern synthesis' when Mendelian genetics was fused with a revised Darwinism. Therefore, in the early decades of the twentieth century Catholic apologists found it relatively easy to emphasise the many weaknesses of evolutionary theory.

The most reprehensible aspect of evolutionary theory, from a conservative Catholic point of view, was the concept of natural selection because it seemed so contrary to divine purpose and intelligent design. Darwinism had been eclipsed to such an extent that it was thought to be in terminal decline as an important evolutionary theory. Eberhart Dennert's book *At the Deathbed of Darwinism* (1903) was typical of this expectation.[82] There was some rejoicing in theological circles that Darwinism was 'on its deathbed' while the ideas of the leading geneticists Hugo de Vries (1848–1935) and William Bateson (1861–1926) were deemed to be very similar to successive creation theory.[83] However, the demise of Darwinism was greatly exaggerated.

Although scientists were deeply divided about how evolution occurred, the vast majority of them accepted that it had actually occurred. There was some recognition of this by Catholic apologists.[84] Nevertheless, there was a distinction to be made between what scientists claimed and what they could demonstrate. Taken to its extreme, this meant that science was mostly based on faith.[85] As such, it would not be in a stronger epistemological position than Catholic doctrine and therefore it would not pose a major threat to the Catholic faith.

Catholic writers were not content with merely defending their faith against agnostics and atheists who endeavoured to discredit religious belief with the findings of modern science. Some of them counter-argued that science could prove, or at least strongly indicate, the existence of God. One such argument was concerned with the origins and nature of life. Bertram Windle maintained that there were only two explanations for the origins of life: the spontaneous emergence of life from non-living matter or creation by God.[86] He did not concede the probability of extra-terrestrial origins.[87] The experimental work of the French chemist Louis Pasteur undermined what had been considered evidence for the origins of living organisms from inanimate particles. However, Windle was aware that although no direct evidence had been discovered for the emergence of life from inanimate matter in the present era, this did not mean that it could not have happened in prehistoric times when physical and chemical conditions were completely different.[88] Yet in the absence of evidence, Windle dismissed this speculation as 'misplaced faith'.[89]

It was so much easier to defend the integrity of scripture against an unsound theory. It was argued that palaeontology was the main evidence for biological evolution – but its findings were not conclusive.[90] Although palaeontologists had 'ransacked the bowels of the earth', many important missing links had not been found and the record of evolutionary development remained very incomplete.[91] It was not regarded as satisfactory to argue that the scarcity of transitional forms could be explained away by the imperfection of the geological record. Furthermore, even if the palaeontologists succeeded in finding many of the missing links, this would not constitute proof of evolution. It would not prove that one species evolved from another – only that one species succeeded another in time.[92]

Some criticism of evolutionary theory revealed a gross ignorance of the subject. R. Fullerton, a contributor to the *Irish Ecclesiastical Record*, failing to understand the enormous time-scale of the evolutionary process, wrote

> ... the sheep is as stupid to-day as it was when Abel tended his flocks, and birds have not improved on nest-building since the days of Moses; dogs have made no progress in moral virtue since the home-coming of Ulysses, nor have asses advanced in intelligence since the time of David. Why has there been no advance? Why no variation? As far as we can know the different species of animals are in the same condition now as they have ever been in the past.[93]

The theory of evolution was not only groundless, it was held to be probably beyond the reach of proof.[94] If it was ever proved then it would make no difference to the faith of Catholics.[95] And yet there was that unshakable and disturbing awareness that the vast majority of scientists accepted the general idea of evolution as the only sensible explanation of the origin of species. Although there was a persistent resistance to evolutionary theory, there was some acknowledgement of how important modern science was and the need to avoid conflict between theology and science. Fullerton urged theologians to revise their teaching in the light of the substantiated findings of science. He made the point that:

> No good, but only harm, can come from ultra-orthodox defenders of Christianity refusing to recast their doctrines and bring them into conformity with the true conclusions of progressive science, for unnecessary conservatism will injure religion just as immoderate liberalism will tell against science.[96]

This conciliatory attitude towards science was probably influenced by the pronouncements of the Pontifical Biblical Commission 'On the historical character of the first three chapters of Genesis' (30 June 1909). The commission found that in some instances reason dictated the abandonment of a literal interpretation of scripture. And it conceded that the Hebrew word *yôm* for 'day' in the first chapter of Genesis could be taken to mean an indefinite period of time.[97] That same year the University of Cambridge celebrated the centenary of Charles Darwin's birth and the fiftieth anniversary of the publication of his *Origin of Species*. Canon Henri de Dorlodot attended as representative of the Catholic University of Louvain. In his lecture at Cambridge de Dorlodot praised the achievements of Darwin.[98] His opinions met with the approval of the 'élite' of English Catholics and were disseminated to a broader public in *The Tablet*.[99] Even at the high point of the anti-modernist movement there was an emerging tolerance, not just for evolution but for Darwinism. In Ireland, however, such toleration was hard to find. There was scarcely a mention of the Pontifical Biblical Commission, which offered greater latitude in thinking relative to that expressed by Irish Catholic apologists.[100]

Developments in modern science generated demands for a revision of theological thinking on Genesis. Of course, the problems associated with the early chapters of Genesis could be explained away by a plethora of miracles – God was omnipotent. Plants, for example, could be miraculously sustained before sunlight penetrated to the surface of the Earth.

Fossils could be dismissed as inexplicable features of stone. But all this was not only unscientific – it was also regarded as theologically unsound.[101] Catholic writers did not candidly admit that Genesis was historically inaccurate and unscientific. The narrative of creation was still held to be true, although not in a strict literal sense. It was maintained that:

> To see falsehood in it would only be the mark of a narrow and illiterate pedantry. The writer is not bent upon a scientific or scholastic treatise . . . he is the inspired seer whose chief purpose is to bring it home to the people committed to him that God is the One Supreme Creator of all . . .[102]

Even with all their defensive arguments in place against the troublesome implications of scientific theories, there still seemed to be an unshakable fear amongst Irish Catholic apologists that science could somehow inflict great harm on the Catholic faith. The road to perdition, it seemed, was paved with scientific ideas. Fear led to evasion, apathy and neglect.

Science was in decline in Ireland since about the 1890s and continued to decline until the middle of the twentieth century.[103] Irish Catholics, at least up to the 1960s, were noted more for their piety than their scientific achievements.[104] In this period the power of the church over its people was perhaps greater than in any other country. This provoked a polemical response from some hostile writers who regarded the institutional church as an obstacle to economic progress and detrimental to the welfare of society.[105] Irish Catholicism was described as 'the narrowest and least advanced form of Catholicism', 'unenlightened' and without 'intellectual vigour'.[106] Even friendly observers commented on the intellectual weakness of Irish Catholicism. In 1907 the French writer Louis Paul-Dubois found 'a certain form of intellectual apathy very widespread, a distaste for mental effort, a certain absence of the critical sense' among Irish Catholics, even amongst those of a liberal disposition. He found that Irish Catholicism was 'unhealthy and abnormal' because there were so few amongst the laity who were well educated.[107] The majority of priests were also poorly educated. This, to a large extent, can be attributed to the fact that seminarians in Ireland received a low standard of education in the late nineteenth and early twentieth centuries. Severe discipline, rote learning and an anti-intellectual bias militated against the emergence of original contributions to theology and cognate disciplines. The emphasis was on strenuous pastoral work rather than the innovative application of

Christian principles.[108] Catholic Ireland did not produce any philosopher or theologian of the intellectual stature of Karl Barth (1886–1968), Paul Johannes Tillich (1886–1965), John Henry Newman or Karl Rahner (the first two were Protestant).[109]

Sir Horace Plunkett (1854–1932), a leading figure in the co-operative movement in Ireland, wrote about some traits of Irish Catholicism which, in his opinion, were holding back economic progress. In his *Ireland in the New Century*, first published in 1904, he argued that the excessive emphasis on authority, the suppression of individuality, and the inordinate concerns about life after death stifled initiative and self-reliance, especially amongst poor Catholics who lacked educational opportunities.[110] He was critical of extravagant church-building in communities with scarce economic resources. The growth of monasteries and convents, at a time when the population was declining, was proving detrimental to economic development.[111] Technical education, so important for the living conditions of the people, was inadequate.[112] But progress was being made. In 1900 the Department of Agriculture and Technical Instruction (DATI) was established under the terms of the Agricultural and Technical Instruction Act (1899), which had been inspired by Plunkett. A system of technical education was set up with a strong emphasis on practical applications, especially in relation to agriculture. One of the problems which DATI had to contend with was the shortage of suitably qualified teachers. There was little interest amongst teachers in the teaching of science or applied science. Nevertheless, courses were organised to train teachers in science, but they met with a limited measure of success.[113]

Plunkett's *Ireland in the New Century* was widely criticised.[114] Rev. M. O'Riordan responded at great length in his *Catholicity and Progress in Ireland*, taking issue with numerous points raised by Plunkett. In addressing the contentious issue of denominational education, he pointed to the success of the medical faculty of the Catholic University (in Cecilia Street, Dublin) and maintained that, in its early years, the university promoted the teaching of science in Dublin, especially through the provision of laboratory facilities.[115] Nevertheless, the poor intellectual condition of Irish Catholicism was clearly evident in the natural sciences in the early years of the twentieth century. It is highly probable that the suspicious attitude of the church towards science was a major contributor to this problem. In her essay 'Heavenly Bodies and Logical Minds', historian Dorinda Outram observed that the church did nothing to promote the integration of the natural sciences with the culture of Irish nationalism.[116]

Before the Irish Free State was established in 1922 there was a pressing need for scientific education and training. In 1919 the priest and scientist Henry V. Gill observed that the public interest in, and knowledge of, science was much less than it had been thirty years previously. There was still a widespread ignorance of science, even amongst those who were well educated.[117] In Irish periodicals political issues and questions about social reform received considerable attention but very few articles were devoted to science. Furthermore, the devastating effect of the First World War, and its aftermath, seems to have adversely affected the output of scholarly publications.[118]

The allied forces of Irish national culture and Catholicism did not allow much scope for moral values derived from scientific theories and Enlightenment philosophy. Little importance was attached to objectivity, rational analysis and individual autonomy – all of which were fundamentally important to science.[119] Irish Catholics were exceptionally disadvantaged relative to many of their counterparts in mainland Europe because of the adverse indigenous influences at work. In view of this, it is likely that their attitudes towards science were amongst the least progressive in Western Europe.

6. Evolution, Entropy and Electro-Magnetics, 1920s–1930s

Science before and after the Treaty

Nicholas Whyte, in his *Science, Colonialism and Ireland* (1999), rejected the idea that Irish nationalism was incompatible with science because of science's essential internationalism. Ascendancy scientists were, after all, 'not so much internationalists as British nationalists'. Commitment to a political cause at national level did not necessarily hinder dedication to science at international level.[1] In the early twentieth century some positive attitudes towards science were expressed in Sinn Féin circles, especially in relation to technological applications and potential economic benefits.[2] But support for science was not deeply embedded in Irish national culture. Science was in noticeable decline from about the 1890s and this downward trend lasted until about the mid-twentieth century. A survey of literature on the subject points to a number of probabilities for the decline of science in the late nineteenth century and early twentieth century. Gordon L. Herries Davies put forward a number of suggestions for consideration in his essay 'Irish Thought in Science' (1985).[3] Firstly, the population base from which scientists could be drawn was halved in the years from 1845 to 1936. The decline of the Protestant sector of the population, which had produced a disproportionately high number of Ireland's scientists, was greater than that of the general population. In the southern Irish state it fell from 468,000 to 144,000 in the century from 1861 to 1961. Secondly, Davies tentatively suggested that selective emigration may have played a role. A disproportionately high number of the most intelligent members of the population may have emigrated, thus reducing the average intelligence of the population. However, Davies did not produce any solid evidence in support of this point. Thirdly, international science was becoming increasingly competitive, especially due to the development of scientific institutions in countries such as the United States and Germany. Thus, in relative terms, it was becoming increasingly difficult for Irish science to maintain its position. Fourthly, the economic cost of scientific research was increasing and Ireland was very poorly resourced to undertake the necessary invest- ment. Fifthly, science (especially field studies in geology) was adversely affected in the years from the Land War to the Civil War. Concerns about security arising from political unrest inhibited investment and research.[4] A sixth reason for the decline of Irish science, proposed by Davies, was that the Irish Free State (established in December 1922) failed to promote a culture conducive to the growth of science. It was probably too inward- looking, so preoccupied with literary censorship and with attempts to revive the Gaelic language that it neglected to cultivate an international perspective so essential for science. Furthermore, in Irish society there was a tendency, for political reasons, to devalue, or dismiss as foreign, the outstanding achievements of many Irish scientists because of their Protestant Ascendancy identity.[5]

Opinions expressed by a number of authors support or at least are consistent with some of the points proposed by Davies. Richard Kearney observed that the majority of Ireland's most accomplished scientists, whose background was Protestant, were disowned as English.[6] Steven Yearley and Sean Lysaght made the point that successive Irish govern- ments in the early years of the state, especially through the education system, were too preoccupied with their devotion to Roman Catholicism and the revival of the Irish language to give adequate attention to science. There was also a heavy emphasis on nationalist history in the educational curriculum of the new state.[7] Science was dropped from the primary school curriculum so that more time could be allocated to the teaching of Irish.[8] There was very little appreciation of science as an essential part of secondary education.[9] In 1953, T.S. Wheeler, Professor of Chemistry at University College Dublin, observed that many students entering univer- sity knew virtually nothing about science – failing to understand elementary facts such as the difference between a compound and an element. In the absence of such foundational knowledge, it was extremely difficult for departments of science in Irish universities to train students to a level consistent with international professional standards.[10] It was the late 1950s before the first measures were taken to address very low stan- dards in the natural sciences.[11]

Technical education fared no better than science. In 1926 Fr Timothy Corcoran (S.J.), Professor of Education at University College Dublin, observed that technical schools set up since 1900 had experienced 'very grave intrinsic difficulties' and that 'in the vast majority of cases they did not at all correspond to their title'. There were major deficiencies in the education system, such as the poor attendance of pupils at primary schools, which needed corrective action before progress could be made in technical education.[12] Corcoran also argued against the teaching of rural science to pupils under fourteen years of age on the basis that it would be at the expense of other more important subjects and would impact adversely on the essential skills of reading, writing, arithmetic and drawing.[13] He saw even less scope for the teaching of agricultural science. If agricultural science was to be taught, then a school needed access to a nearby farm. Furthermore, the subject should only be taught to post Intermediate Certificate pupils who had prospects of an agricultural livelihood.[14]

State investment in science and technology, when it did occur, was very much determined by anticipated economic benefits. Corcoran's fellow Jesuit Fr Henry V. Gill pointed to the construction of the hydro-electric dam at Ardnacrusha (the Shannon Scheme) and the development of the Drumm Battery as examples of state initiatives which demonstrated the merits of scientific research.[15] This raised the question of how much time and how many resources should be given to science in the education system. Gill had studied physics for two years under Sir Joseph John Thomson (1856–1940), the Cavendish Professor of Experimental Physics at the University of Cambridge. At the time, Thomson, winner of the Nobel Prize for Physics in 1906, was turning the Cavendish Laboratory into one of the leading physics research centres in the world. Gill sustained his interest in science after leaving Cambridge, especially in the fields of atomic structure, electricity and seismology.[16] He saw government support for scientific training and research in the universities as critically important if science-based enterprise was to flourish. His attitude towards science in the second-level school system was not so positive. He regarded classics and literature as the core elements of a sound educational programme and believed that much less time was needed for the study of science. Nor did there seem to be much demand for science! Gill, writing in 1932, observed: 'Long established tradition has secured for literary studies their proper recognition. It is not so with science; until comparatively recently science in the schools has been "regarded with jealously by the staff, with contempt by the boys, and with indifference by the parents". Furthermore, there was a danger that an interest in science, like so many other intellectual pursuits, might 'monopolise the mind to the exclusion of other interests'. The interest that was uppermost in Gill's mind was religion.[17]

Gill's concerns about science were unfounded. The interest in science was not so strong that it might push the Catholic faith to the outer margins of Irish social life. When science was perceived as a threat, evolutionary theory was usually the main focus of attention. But there were many aspects of science which were unrelated, or only tenuously related, to Catholic theology. Ireland's economy was predominantly agricultural, therefore it should not be surprising that agricultural science received some attention from time to time in Catholic periodicals, especially *Studies*.[18] Attention was given to a wide range of topics relating to science and economic growth such as the production of synthetic chemicals, the critical role of electricity for industrial development, the extraction of iodine and potash from seaweed, and the production of vegetable oils and medicinal herbs.[19] Authors included Thomas Wibberley (Professor of Agricultural Research at University College Cork), Henry Kennedy (scientist), W.J. Williams (Lecturer in Education at University College Dublin), Rev. Edward Leen (President of Blackrock College, Dublin), John J. Nolan (Professor of Experimental Physics, University College Dublin), Hugh Ryan (Professor of Chemistry, University College Dublin, and Director of the State Laboratory, Dublin), Thomas J. Nolan (Assistant State Chemist), Thomas Dillon (Professor of Chemistry at University College Galway) and Joseph Reilly (Professor of Chemistry at University College Cork).

Leen, the only member of the clergy in the above list of authors, was lukewarm in his support for the inclusion of science in secondary school education. He acknowledged that science was an essential element of a well-balanced education, but he immediately added that it should not be overrated. Those who were to play leading roles in society would need an understanding of human affairs mainly derived from the study of history, art and classical literature – 'a true education' would be 'humanistic'. It would be 'fatal' to national progress to use the education system as an instrument for 'turning out a nation of mere scientists or mathematicians' – as if there was such a prospect. Science and mathematics imparted quantitative and factual knowledge – but not wisdom. With the Shannon Scheme in mind, Leen asserted that science and technology had a very limited role in elevating national culture to 'a higher and more intelligent concept of life'.[20] Leen was not the only author who was lukewarm in his appreciation of science. Hugh Ryan believed that it mattered little that a student entering university to study chemistry had not previously studied the subject. Classical and mathematical studies, in contrast, were held to be indispensible.[21]

Thomas Dillon, like W.J. Williams, Thomas J. Nolan and Thomas Wibberley, was unambiguously supportive of scientific education and research. In his essay 'Chemistry in the Service of Man' he emphasised how advances in chemical research generally stimulated industrial growth in the manufacture of a broad range of products including dyes, drugs and synthetic fibres. The economic policy of the Irish Free State was committed to promoting industrialisation. However, as Dillon pointed out, this policy would be deeply flawed if the state failed to provide resources for scientific training and research. He urged that 'we must in fact build up our industry on the brains of our people'. Policy-makers decades later would use terms such as 'the smart economy' and 'the knowledge economy' to express the same basic idea.

Dillon was critical of the Department of Education for the decline of science in the education system. He was also critical of school principals, many of whom he believed disliked science and had no scientific training. Inadequate scientific training at second level impacted adversely on the university system because many school leavers were not sufficiently prepared for science courses, or, if totally unprepared, did not attempt to study science at university. There was an attitude problem to contend with, especially in relation to chemistry. Chemistry was generally held in low esteem and there was a widespread failure in Ireland to appreciate its potential contribution to industrial and agricultural development. There was also an intellectual dimension to be considered. The majority of Irish university graduates did not understand the principles of science which so profoundly influenced 'modern life and thought'.[22]

Dillon, writing in 1943 about 'The Relation of Chemical Research to the Development of Our Industries', asserted that, not only was the second-level education system failing to provide the foundation for the training of scientific researchers, it was counterproductive to such an essential enterprise. The system vigorously discouraged the kind of critical and independent thinking which was so indispensable to scientific development.[23] Dorinda Outram, writing in 1988 about the novels of John Banville, would have agreed with Dillon on this point. She observed that major obstacles to the modernisation of Ireland in the twentieth century were the non-acceptance of Enlightenment values of rationality and progress, and a lack of due regard for individual autonomy. Outram found that the limited resources of the state probably put 'big science' beyond its reach. She pointed to the Roman Catholic Church in Ireland as a powerful influence against the emergence of a strong scientific culture. The church was deeply suspicious that the natural sciences would be instrumental in the spread of materialism and atheism. Furthermore, the Irish church had a narrowly constructed theology of nature. It neglected nature in the broadest sense, concentrating on 'one single natural object, the body and more particularly its reproductive history'. The church – occupying a dominant position in Irish social life – did not use its resources to make science an important aspect of Irish national culture. The dominant Irish Catholic nationalist perspective in the southern Irish state identified science with 'all that Ireland . . . was not' – Protestant, monarchist, foreign, modernising and pluralistic as distinct from Roman Catholic, republican, Gaelic, traditional, culturally monolithic, and with an emphasis on history, folklore and literature.[24] There is merit in Outram's thesis for the years shortly after the attainment of independence, but it is deeply flawed when applied to the years from 1988 to the early years of the twenty-first century – this matter will receive further attention in Chapter 10.[25] Another problem with Outram's thesis concerning the role of the Catholic Church in Ireland is that she did not give due attention to its restricted scope for reform within an international organisation still in the grip of anti-modernism.

Nicholas Whyte asserted that 'the case against either Irish nationalism or Roman Catholicism as despoilers of science remains to be proven'. In the case of nationalism there was some support for science – but it was very limited. Therefore, as Whyte conceded, 'it was after 1921 that opportunities were not grasped by policy makers . . .'[26] As if to underscore how far removed science was from mainstream Irish nationalist thinking, Whyte quoted extensively from Éamon de Valera's St Patrick's Day address (1943), when the Taoiseach spoke longingly for an Ireland in terms of Christian spirituality and frugal comforts – an Ireland which in this particular context did not seem to attach much importance to science and technology.

The case against the Catholic Church, contrary to Whyte's assessment, is more complicated than that against Irish nationalism. Whyte argued that

> although the Catholic church took about sixty years to accept that Darwinism was compatible with its teaching, this was little different from the scientific world as a whole. There is no evidence that at any

> point the Irish hierarchy used the threat of dangerous Darwinist ideas
> as an excuse for discouraging the teaching of science or for deterring
> research by Catholic scientists . . . Apart from the case of McDonald,
> who was not a scientist, there is no evidence of the church restraining
> or attempting to restrain scientific research for theological reasons.[27]

Evidence for the Irish church's attitude indicates that scepticism, not only
of Darwinism but of evolutionary theory in general, was sustained right
up to the late 1950s. It was only around the centenary of Darwin's *Origin
of Species* that a conciliatory attitude of acceptance became evident. This
is much longer than the sixty years approximation of Whyte.

It is true, consistent with Whyte's contention above, that no direct evidence has been adduced to prove that the church authorities in Ireland
deliberately obstructed any programme of scientific research by any scientist, or took steps to impose censorship on the teaching of any specific
science course in the interests of theology. But the thesis of non-conflict
between Irish Catholicism and science is of limited value if constructed
on such a narrow basis. A broader analysis is necessary to adequately
address the complexity of the issue. The opposition of the institutional
church – both in Rome and in Ireland – to the Queen's Colleges greatly
restricted Catholic participation in science in the late nineteenth century.
The considerable influence of the Catholic bishops over the constituent
colleges of the National University of Ireland after 1908 did little to
reverse the adverse effects of such a policy.

Near the conclusion of his *Science, Colonialism and Ireland* Whyte
continued to defend the Irish Catholic Church's role *vis-à-vis* science,
when he stated that

> . . . the Catholic church's role in the promotion of science in Ireland
> was probably as positive as financial and political constraints allowed.
> Debate of the latest scientific ideas even flourished in ecclesiastically
> sponsored journals such as the *Irish Ecclesiastical Record*, the *Irish
> Theological Quarterly*, and from 1912 Corcoran's *Studies*.[28]

The points made here by Whyte are not sustainable. The Roman Catholic
Church in Ireland occupied a powerful position in the newly created state
of southern Ireland. It exerted enormous power and influence over the
education system.[29] Even taking into account the limited resources of the
state, the church could have influenced successive governments to fund
education and training in science and technology to a much greater
extent than it did.

A survey of Irish Catholic journals does not reveal a series of vigorous debates about contemporary scientific ideas. In fact the only debates about scientific theory discovered to date occurred in the *Irish Ecclesiastical Record* – between Jeremiah Murphy and John S. Vaughan in 1884–1885, and between Philip Burton and Patrick F. Coakley in 1899. Many articles were published about science from 1900 to the late 1950s, especially concerning biological evolution, but there was very little debate. Instead, readers were subjected to uncontested opinions that were sharply critical of scientific theory (especially evolution), and sometimes of scientists.

The Catholic nationalist movement led eventually to the overthrow of what Greta Jones has referred to as the 'Huxleyite project' in Ireland. A central feature of this project was the creation of a system where scientific education and research could be conducted free from denominational influence. In the years following the Irish Universities Act (1908) the viability of the Huxleyite project was eroded as the intellectual milieu of the constituent colleges of the National University of Ireland became less and less non-denominational. It finally met its end with the establishment of the Irish Free State. The education system came increasingly under denominational control in independent Ireland. Connections between the scientific communities of Britain and Ireland were adversely affected and allocations of resources to science in Ireland were greatly diminished.[30]

Evolution – Continuous or Discontinuous?

During the War of Independence (1919–1921) conditions in Ireland were far from ideal for ruminating on such profound issues as the origins of humankind. Yet it was still possible for the scholarly mind to seek answers to a number of important questions safely removed from heated political debates and the armed struggle. Dr D.T. Barry, a medical scientist and lecturer, was not clear about what Catholic doctrine had to say in relation to biological evolution. When writing about the subject in the *Irish Ecclesiastical Record* (January 1920) he made it clear that he was not intentionally disagreeing with any theological pronouncements of the church. If any statement he made did contradict Catholic doctrine then this was due to his lack of understanding and was not deliberate. The purpose of his article was to elicit a response which would clarify what exactly he was bound to accept or reject. Barry asserted that the dismissal of the theory of evolution simply on the basis that it was 'only a theory' was an act of intellectual indolence. Evolutionary theory was of central importance in biology. Barry observed that many students were fascinated by Darwin's theory of natural selection but there was a commonly held belief that the Roman Catholic Church condemned it as 'godless and untenable'. Was this opinion correct? And was it acceptable to believe in the evolution of humankind?

Barry consulted the *Catholic Encyclopaedia* for enlightenment and noted that evolutionary theory was broadly acceptable. This concession to science 'apparently' extended to human origins – Barry was not quite sure about this. Neo-Lamarckism and natural selection were condemned. But Rev. Erich Wasmann, one of the contributors to this section of the volume, had, apparently, expressed a more liberal theological view concerning natural selection and human evolution in a separate work (*Modern Biology and the Theory of Evolution*). Barry was somewhat confused by this lack of consonance and by Wasmann's tendency not to be explicit.[31] His confusion was further aggravated by an article in the *Irish Ecclesiastical Record* by Fr Thomas J. Agius which seemed to him to rule out the acceptance of human evolution on the basis of 'an insuperable theological difficulty'.[32] Near the end of his article Barry referred to the eminent zoologist and theistic evolutionist Conwy Lloyd Morgan (1852–1936) to make the point that although biological evolution lacked 'absolute confirmation', it was nevertheless the best explanation of the facts established by scientific research.[33] This was a fundamentally important point in evaluating the merit of the theory. It was a point frequently missed by Irish Catholic critics, who too readily associated evolution with those secular philosophies which were antagonistic to Roman Catholicism. In the late nineteenth century such a tendency was, perhaps, excusable. In 1920 the Maynooth theologian Garrett Pierse observed that Huxley, Tyndall, Haeckel and Spencer had enlisted the support of evolutionary theory in their conflict with theology. Theologians too had made errors of judgement, confusing their own interpretations of scripture with theological dogmas. Errors occurred on both sides of the divide. Now that the relationship between religion and science was much less belligerent, Pierse felt confident in declaring that the general theory of evolution was compatible with theism.[34] However, in the upper echelons of the Roman Catholic Church there was a much lesser degree of confidence in reconciling theism and Darwinism. This can be seen from Raf de Bont's 'Rome and Theistic Evolutionism: The Hidden Strategies behind the "Dorlodot Affair", 1920–1926'.

Canon Henri de Dorlodot's *Darwinism and Catholic Thought* was published in French in 1921, and in English in 1925. Dorlodot – a priest, theologian and Professor of Geology at the University of Louvain (Belgium) – argued that Darwinism and Catholic doctrine were compatible. The book provoked a strong reaction from the traditionalists in Rome. Cardinal Willem van Rossum and Dom Laurent Janssens, president and secretary respectively of the Pontifical Biblical Commission, issued 'reprimands' against the canon. They were supported by the veteran antimodernists – Cardinal Merry del Val, Louis Billot and Gaetano de Lai. Attempts were made to intimidate Dorlodot to publish a retraction of his view that Darwinism was compatible with Catholic doctrine. The canon steadfastly refused to comply. He was not without friends in high places and looked to a number of prelates for support, including Francis Bourne, Pietro Maffi (archbishop of Pisa) and Francis Gasquet (archivist at the Vatican archives). Paulin Ladeuze, rector of the Catholic University of Louvain, and Archbishop Désiré Mercier played important roles in his defence. No official condemnation was issued against Dorlodot. However, it seems that the strong opposition to Darwinism influenced Dorlodot to abandon his declared intention of writing a second volume about the origins of humankind. Although the progressive wing of the church did not gain entirely what it wished for, there were indications that the power of the traditionalists had considerably weakened since the pontificate of Pope Pius X.[35]

The intrigues of Dorlodot's detractors and defenders took place behind closed doors. It is most unlikely that information about attempts to censor him reached any of the Catholic clergy in Ireland. Therefore, inferences could only be made from what was in the public domain. Henry V. Gill observed that Dorlodot's book received the approval of the ecclesiastical authorities of the University of Louvain. This, he anticipated, would exert a 'considerable influence' on Catholic teaching. But if evolutionary theory was to be accepted it would be under conditions favourable to religion. Gill's version of evolution was essentially a theory emasculated by a dependency on divine intervention at certain stages of development. If animal and plant species were not directly created by God, then they had to emerge through evolutionary development. This meant that the earliest forms of life had to originate from non-living matter. But Gill argued that there was no evidence for this, nor was there ever likely to be. Therefore, this lack of evidence testified to the need for divine intervention to ensure the continuity of evolution. And if, somehow, a scientist succeeded in creating life under laboratory conditions it could not be used against Catholic doctrine because medieval

Catholic philosophers believed that lower life forms developed spontaneously from inanimate matter. Nevertheless, the continuity of evolution depended on God. Gill argued that there was some evidence for the evolution of the inorganic universe but it was 'very slight' and could not be asserted with confidence.

The Anglican modernist Canon Ernest William Barnes (1874–1953) had spoken at the Cardiff meeting of the British Association for the Advancement of Science (August 1920) about a continuous evolutionary process from 'some fundamental stuff' to life, to mind, to 'spiritual consciousness'. He was criticised by Gill in the *Irish Ecclesiastical Record* on the basis that there was no direct evidence for such an idea, except perhaps a little for the evolution of chemical elements.[36] The cut and thrust of Gill's argument was to weaken a potentially harmful scientific theory with reference to the inductive method and then prop it up with divine intervention – a 'god of the gaps' argument where God would be invoked to fill the spaces as yet unoccupied by scientific knowledge. In this way modern science would be reconciled with Catholicism and could be used to support rather than undermine theism – much more satisfying than a purely defensive stance.

As observed earlier, Gill had studied physics at the University of Cambridge. But his scientific training, in what must have been a very stimulating intellectual environment, did not lead him to adopt a positive attitude towards evolutionary theory similar to that of Dorlodot. Irish priests who did not have the benefit of Gill's advanced scientific training were far less likely to express views consistent with mainstream scientific thought when, all too frequently, evolutionary theory was associated with a rejection of Christianity.

Irish Catholic apologists were very much aware of debates about religion and science in Britain. This is indicated by reference to such authors as Conwy Lloyd Morgan, John Arthur Thomson (1861–1933), Oliver Joseph Lodge (1851–1940), Arthur Stanley Eddington (1882–1944) and James Hopwood Jeans (1877–1946) – all of whom were on the side of religion; and those who were not, including Edwin Ray Lankester (1847–1929), Herbert George Wells (1866–1946), Bertrand Russell (1872–1970) and Julian Huxley (1887–1975) – a grandson of Thomas Henry Huxley. Controversies about the religious implications of evolutionary theory did not cease with the passing of the nineteenth century. Irish Catholic writers who wrote in defence of the church, most of whom were priests, were not reluctant to express critical views about non-Catholic Christian authors who argued for reconciliation between religion and science and who sometimes were seen to indicate a degree of confidence in evolutionary theory unwarranted by the evidence. Speeches made at meetings of the British Association for the Advancement of Science and the Gifford Lectures were of particular interest.

The continuity of the evolutionary process, and the emergence of life and mind from matter, were themes of central importance when discussing the relationship between science and religion. When Professor J. Arthur Thomson pointed to the limitations of science in his book *Science and Religion* (1925), it elicited comments of approval from John Ashton (S.J.) in the *Dublin Review*. Science could not ask what was behind nature or address questions of meaning. But when Thomson wrote about the continuity of evolution, from 'the whirling nebula' to the emergence of *Homo sapiens*, Ashton was critical, even though continuous evolution, in Thomson's opinion, suggested the existence of God.[37] There was another way of looking at the continuity of evolution which was obvious to Ashton and which had disturbing implications for religious faith. What was meant by the 'continuity of process'? Did it mean that the primordial matter of the universe was 'a closed system, containing within itself the potentialities of life, mind, spirit?'[38] If the answer was yes, then it greatly strengthened the case for materialistic evolution because God could be quite easily disposed of, as in Newton's mechanistic universe.

Discontinuities in evolution would greatly strengthen theistic arguments – or so it seemed. Ashton was aware of a number of formidable counterarguments. Thomson contended that discontinuity suggested that God made mistakes at the beginning of Creation and had subsequently found it necessary to intervene to remedy the defects in the evolutionary process. There were other difficulties to be addressed which were highlighted by ongoing debates in Britain and elsewhere which Ashton referred to but did not adequately address. He referred to Professor Andrew Seth Pringle-Pattison's claim that many theologians had abandoned the notion that God gave evidence of His existence by 'spasmodic interferences' in nature and 'lived in the gaps of our scientific knowledge', and whose existence was increasingly threatened by advances in scientific knowledge. Henry Drummond's *Ascent of Man* (1894/1904) was also quoted to make the point that Christian apologists 'ceaselessly scan the fields of Nature and the books of Science in search of gaps which they fill up with God. As if God lived in "gaps".' Ashton argued that since scientists themselves had identified many gaps in nature, it was reasonable to invoke the 'gaps' argument. God intervened in nature through miracles. In doing so He was not acting against nature but in harmony with its 'highest laws'. Ashton did not indicate what these supposed laws were.[39]

In 1926 Michael Browne, Professor of Moral Theology at Maynooth since 1921 and a future Bishop of Galway (1937–1976), addressed 'Modern Theories of Evolution' in a series of four articles in the *Irish Ecclesiastical Record*. Browne seemed familiar with scientific literature and referred to the works of such luminaries as Ernest Rutherford (1871– 1937), Arthur Stanley Eddington, James Hopwood Jeans, J. Arthur Thomson and Conwy Lloyd Morgan. At the first opportunity Browne set about emphasising the limited competence of science. Cosmic evolution started with the spiral nebulae. But where did they come from? The inability of contemporary scientists to answer this question was used to support the contention that science could not answer questions of 'ulti-mate origins'. Before the universe there was nothing and therefore nothing for experimental science to investigate. Browne stated that deductive reasoning in philosophy could prove the existence of an 'Intelligent First Cause'. However, this was not reconcilable with his latter comments that 'it is debatable whether reason would in point of fact have reached knowledge of creation if there had been no revelation . . . all agree that reason cannot prove that creation took place in time'. Knowledge about creation was derived from supernatural revelation which was 'on a different plane' to the 'truths of empirical research'.[40] Browne acknowledged that there was nothing in the 'creed' of an evolu-tionist to prevent him from believing in the doctrine of creation. In view of this, it might seem that the idea of continuous evolution could be con-ceded as a strong possibility. But no such concession would be granted by Catholic apologists, writing in journals of limited circulation and preaching to the faithful. In this context a sceptical attitude towards evo-lution provided a second line of defence, comforting and impregnable.

Browne was critical of what he regarded as the widespread uncritical acceptance of evolutionary theory. From his study of chemistry he con-cluded that evolutionary theory suffered 'a very sharp rebuff' concerning the evolution of the elements.[41] In biology he found that confidence in evolution was so great that it had been elevated to the status of a dogma – which was most unscientific because dogma was the antithesis of the inductive method. Dogmatism in turn had led to 'materialistic deter-minism'. If dogmatic evolutionism threatened to expel God from the universe, then an unproven doubt-ridden version would bring Him back in. Browne reiterated the point, now well established in Irish Catholic apologetics, that if somehow an unbroken sequence of evolutionary developments could be proven beyond reasonable doubt, the arguments for the existence of God and the system of revealed religion would still not be adversely affected.[42]

Browne argued against the development of life from inanimate matter on the basis that the work of Louis Pasteur had undermined it. Modern microbiology, in medicine and in food processing, worked on the basis that it did not occur contemporaneously.[43] This, however, did not mean that it did not occur early in the Earth's history when conditions were very different. Browne also argued against the transformation of species on the basis that the element of continuity in evolutionary theory seemed inconsistent with discontinuities in nature, such as mutations in biology and the quantum theory of Max Karl Planck (1858–1947) in physics. Furthermore, no matter how much evidence was accumulated in support of the evolution of species, it could never be accepted as certain because new discoveries might overthrow it. Newton's laws of motion, for example, had to be modified when the theory of relativity was formulated. There could be no finality in empirical science. Scientific theories were, by their very nature, tentative and provisional. And yet Browne felt compelled to acknowledge that 'transformism', rather than the fixity of species, harmonised with 'a large series of facts', had been 'a most fruitful' mechanism of discovery, and was supported by the 'vast majority of scientists'. This observation did not cause Browne much concern. Scientists would jettison the latest idea of continuity in evolution when they became aware of the limited competencies of science.[44]

Browne's attitude could only have served to propagate the notion that there was some degree of tension between scientists and theologians. Bertram Windle adopted a more conciliatory stance, not just between religion and science but also between Protestantism and Roman Catholicism. He even went so far as to observe that the great agnostics of the nineteenth century, Thomas Henry Huxley and Herbert Spencer, were not without religious sensibilities.[45] Windle worked hard to dispel the notion that Roman Catholicism and science were incompatible.[46] In his book *The Catholic Church and Its Reactions with Science* (1927), aimed at a non-specialist readership, he laboured the point that there was no real conflict between these two great fields of knowledge. In reference to the general theory of evolution he stated that the church did not condemn it. Rather, it condemned materialistic or atheistic evolution.[47]

The more sensitive question of human origins was addressed by Windle in another book, *The Evolutionary Problem as It Is Today*, also published in 1927. Windle maintained human evolution was not likely to be proved. Even if it was, it would not be in opposition to 'any solemn, ordinary, or official teaching of the Church'. Therefore, Catholic teachers were quite reasonable in adhering to the traditional interpretation of the second chapter of Genesis which stated that the body of Adam was created directly by God. However, Windle did not rule out the possibility that humans had evolved and urged his co-religionists to refrain from anti-evolutionary triumphalism. The danger of associating Catholic orthodoxy with an unrelenting rejection of evolution was that if this scientific theory was ever established on a strong empirical foundation, then it would give greater confidence to the enemies of the Christian faith.[48]

Patrick J. Gannon (S.J.), Professor of Theology at Milltown Park in Dublin, also promoted the idea of conciliation. His article 'The Conflict between Religion and Science' in the Jesuit periodical *Studies* (1926), reviewed five books, including G.K. Chesterton's *The Everlasting Man* (1925) and *Science, Religion and Reality* (1925), edited by the Anglican Marxist scientist Joseph Needham (1900–1995). Chesterton made 'no claim to erudition or research' but, nevertheless, sarcastically dismissed the plausibility of human evolution. This met with the approval of Gannon, but it does not seem to have occurred to him that someone lacking professional training in science might be in a weak position to dismiss, with even a semblance of credibility, a theory accepted by the vast majority of scientists. Furthermore, the rejection of evolution would only tend to aggravate rather than diminish tensions between religious and scientific worldviews.

In his review of *Science, Religion and Reality* Gannon noted that, of the ten 'eminent' authors, none were Roman Catholic. Although he thought that this greatly diminished the quality of the work, he also saw an advantage – that no critic could claim that 'the fear of Roman anathemas' had stifled the free expression of opinion[49] – as if such a fear was groundless. The excesses of anti-modernism in the universal church stifled Catholic Biblical scholarship in the early decades of the twentieth century.[50] Anti-modernism repressed creative thinking throughout the church. Ireland did not escape its repressive effects.[51]

Gannon addressed the subject of evolution again in 1928, influenced to some extent by Windle's *Evolutionary Problem as It Is Today*, but was probably mainly motivated by Sir Arthur Keith's presidential address to the British Association for the Advancement of Science held in Leeds in August 1927. The text of this speech was later published under the title *Concerning Man's Origin* (1927). Keith, an eminent anatomist and pale-oanthropologist, was actively involved in the Rationalist Press Association since 1922. His research on the structure of the brain had led him to the acceptance of a materialistic worldview. His materialistic opinions, expressed at the Leeds meeting, elicited harsh criticism from the popular press.[52] Evidently, this did not escape Gannon's attention.

Gannon denied that theologians were in 'a sort of panic-stricken conspiracy' to persuade themselves and others to deny scientific 'truths' in defence of the Christian faith. Neither did theologians expect scientists to suppress or distort scientific evidence to safeguard religious beliefs. Evolutionary theory, in a strictly scientific sense, was not directly or formally condemned by the church. The church pronounced only against those versions of evolution which were contrary to the dogmas of faith, such as those which denied the existence of God. Even when considering the evolution of the human body, Gannon stated that there was no theological objection on the grounds of Catholic dogma. But it had to be dependent on God's creative power and the immortality of the human soul had to be defended. On this latter point Gannon argued that a spiritual, immaterial and immortal substance could not develop from something which did not have any of these characteristics.

The human mind seemed to lie at the interface of the body and immortal soul. Could it have evolved? Gannon maintained that any attempt to prove that we were evolving apes would be self-defeating. If one accepted 'that thought is nothing more than molecular movement in the grey matter of the brain, then it becomes impossible to establish any system of epistemology which will give us *episteme* or knowledge'.[53] Why the human mind, functioning entirely on the basis of physical and chemical laws, should be, for that reason, inherently incapable of formulating sound philosophical principles in relation to science was not at all clear. Gannon may have had Darwin in mind. Darwin questioned the reliability of his own convictions and asked if the human mind, evolved through multitudinous generations from the lowest animals, was capable of drawing sound conclusions in response to such profound questions as to whether or not the universe existed by chance or by design.[54]

The conservative Catholic concession to science was minimalist. The admission that human evolution did not contradict any dogma of the Catholic Church was not as liberal-minded as it seemed. It was merely to clear the ground for a hasty retreat in the event of scientists making one or more groundbreaking discoveries which might put human evolution beyond reasonable doubt. Holding scientists rigidly to the inductive method seemed more intellectually credible than invoking theological anathemas. In addition to this, some impenetrable barriers had to be constructed to halt the onward march of science in the evolutionary context.

Gannon derived some comfort from the observation that there was a huge difference in intelligence between humans and their closest animal relatives. This tended, in his opinion, to greatly weaken the prevailing scientific idea that such a difference was one of degree, not one of kind. Even if it had to be conceded that there was unbroken developmental continuity leading upwards to the human mind, this was the absolute limit of evolutionary progress. Gannon was adamant that the spiritual soul could not develop from any physical substance. Its origin, nature and existence was beyond the domain of science. So also were the dogmas of revelation. The church proclaimed that these dogmas were 'not the discovery of reason or of human industry'. Catholics were not asked to accept church dogmas on the basis that the institution could 'prove them biologically, geologically or zoologically'. Acceptance or rejection would be for reasons outside the domain of science.[55] From this it may be inferred that a heavy burden of proof could be imposed on science, and not on theology. Science, therefore, would be greatly weakened relative to theology and would, as a result, be less capable of harming religious belief.

Near the end of his essay Gannon acknowledged that the doctrine of creation gave rise to 'some delicate issues'. Controversy surrounded the interpretation of the opening chapters of Genesis, which were difficult to interpret. The church had not pronounced definitively on the points in question, but Pope Leo XIII's *Providentissimus Deus* (1893) and the findings of the Pontifical Biblical Commission (30 June 1909) laid down general principles to guide scholarly research. Gannon maintained that these principles allowed Catholics great freedom in what they might choose to believe in. On this basis he concluded that there was no conflict between Roman Catholicism and science, only between Roman Catholicism and pseudo-science.[56]

Evidently, some Catholics were deeply concerned about how the doctrines of their church could be reconciled with the findings of modern science. But Protestants had to struggle with similar difficulties, especially those who adhered to an excessively literal reading of the Bible. In 1925 this became conspicuously evident when a young schoolteacher,

John Thomas Scopes, was prosecuted for violating a state law prohibiting the teaching of human evolution in public schools in the state of Tennessee. His trial attracted international media attention. Although Scopes was found guilty as charged, the creationists were sharply criticised by the media and their legislative campaign lost its momentum by the end of the 1920s.[57] Those who actively promoted the idea of special creation failed to gain a platform for their views in journals controlled by 'orthodox' scientists. The Scopes trial itself, and subsequent developments, indicated the difficulty in finding any support for an alternative to evolution amongst scientists.[58]

The publication of *Evolution and Theology: The Problem of Man's Origin* (1931) by the Catholic theologian Ernest C. Messenger indicated a consolidation of tolerance in the Roman Catholic Church for the idea of human evolution.[59] Messenger, who had translated Dorlodot's *Darwinism and Catholic Thought* from French to English, claimed that there was no sustainable theological objection to the theory of evolution extended to humankind.[60] But there was, of course, an important distinction to be made between toleration and acceptance.[61] Messenger's book was reviewed by Professor Michael Browne of Maynooth in the *Irish Ecclesiastical Record*. Browne sustained his sceptical attitude towards evolution and criticised Messenger on a number of important points. Messenger had not given a concise account of evolutionary theories relating to cosmology, the emergence of life from inanimate matter, and the transformation of species, and this omission 'considerably diminished' the quality of the book. Browne strongly disagreed with Messenger's reading of evolution into the works of the Church Fathers, such as those of St Gregory of Nyssa. Nevertheless, he praised Messenger's painstaking research and high standard of scholarship, concluding that *Evolution and Theology* was a book of 'first-rate theological importance'.[62]

Censorship

It would be misleading to create the impression that the theological implications of evolutionary theory were the focus of intense interest amongst Roman Catholics in the early 1930s. There were more pressing concerns. The collapse of the financial markets in the United States in October 1929 was quickly followed by an international economic crisis. Loans to European countries were called in, which in turn pushed them into economic depression. The United States raised tariffs, which caused a decline in the importation of goods. Agricultural prices also fell and this exacerbated the economic downturn. Rural communities were unable to purchase industrial goods as before, so factories closed and shops went out of business. Millions of people lost their jobs and their homes and were left destitute. As industrial output sharply declined, so also did the demand for raw materials, which impacted heavily on Latin Amercia, Africa and Asia. *Laissez-faire* policies were abandoned in favour of protectionism. In Europe, the economic crisis had a destabilising effect on political systems. Democratic regimes in Germany, Portugal and eastern Europe gave way to dictatorships. Furthermore, the failure of governments to deal adequately with the global economic crisis proved to be a major contributor to the deterioration of international relations and the outbreak of the Second World War in 1939.[63]

In the 1930s Irish Catholic authors expressed deep concern about the loss of civil liberties in states governed by fascist and communist regimes and were critical of the capitalist system. Some of these, inspired by Pope Pius XI's social encyclical *Quadragesimo Anno* (1931), advocated sweeping political and economic reforms in the Irish Free State.[64] Fr Edward J. Coyne, an Irish Jesuit well known for his writings on Catholic social teaching, viewed European society as the product of European thought slowly evolving over the centuries. He believed that the masses of Europe had been influenced by philosophical ideas inimical to Christianity and were slowly drifting towards atheism. In a lecture delivered at Ruskin College, Oxford on 30 July 1934, he declared that scepticism was the philosophical outlook of the majority of Europeans. This scepticism was influenced by 'a certain half-doubting belief in materialistic evolution and some form of determinism'. Enlightenment philosophy had spawned a 'whole brood of errors'. The dissemination of these ideas was facilitated by the printing press and the growth of literacy so that 'error' had taken on the qualities of a pandemic.[65] By the end of the nineteenth century the philosophical errors of centuries had spread from the environs of academia to the ranks of 'ordinary' citizens and this in turn had determined the transformation of society, either through vigorous action or passive tolerance.[66] Marxist ideology was ranked high in the list of errors and it was associated with Darwinism, both of which, it seemed, permeated the popular consciousness. Coyne declared that:

> Marxism has an enormous, if unconscious, influence on the average man today. It stands in much the same position as the theory of biological evolution associated with Darwin. Indeed, it owes much of its popular success to the popular success of Darwin. It contains about

the same amount of hidden truth, and the same amount of very plausible falsehood or half-truth. Nine men out of ten, I suppose, believe
vaguely in biological evolution as a final explanation of the world.[67]

In the Irish Free State there was an inordinate fear of communism in
some quarters.[68] However, there was very little support in Ireland for the
communist utopia envisaged by Karl Marx and Friedrich Engels. And,
notwithstanding Coyne's observations of contemporary European
society, there was virtually no support for materialistic evolution in the
Irish Free State.

The heavy hand of censorship militated against the emergence of
ideas subversive of either church or state. Lobbying by Catholic pressure
groups led to the passing of the Censorship of Publications Act (1929).
Over the next three decades a number of major literary works of the
twentieth century were banned arising from the judgements of the
Censorship Board. Some Irish authors fell victim to its overzealous proclivities. The censorship rigorously imposed by the state was supported
by unofficial censorship. Artists and writers deemed to have offended
against moral standards were singled out for harassment. Booksellers and
libraries came under pressure not to stock certain undesirable published
works or, if they had done so, to remove such books which had somehow
escaped or survived the scrutiny of the state apparatus.[69] Between 1930
and 1939 approximately twelve hundred books and about one hundred
and forty periodicals were banned. Opposition to these draconian measures was weak. Some of those who objected did so through the pages of
The Irish Times. Despite the suppressive measures in place, there was dissatisfaction in some quarters that censorship policies were not being
implemented with due diligence and that the legislation in place did not
allow for sufficiently robust censorship.[70]

It is likely that many authors outside of Ireland took a dim view of its
censorship laws. The eminent philosopher Bertrand Russell (1872–1970)
wrote in his *Scientific Outlook* (1931) that the Catholic Church had made
no significant progress towards enlightenment since the trial and abjuration of Galileo. His criticism was particularly directed against Irish and
American Catholicism. He bluntly stated that 'Wherever it has power, as
in Ireland and Boston, it still forbids all literature containing new ideas.'
Russell then proceeded to make the grossly exaggerated claim that
Galileo's 'few proved truths' had undermined the entire philosophical
basis of Catholic doctrine, destroying 'the scintillating firmament of
medieval certainties.'[71]

The press was still seen as a potent threat to the Catholic faith in Ireland and elsewhere. A contributor to the *Irish Monthly* (1932), G.C. Heseltine, observed that, although the old Victorian notion of a conflict between Catholicism and science had been undermined by the 'practical evidence' of religious scientists such as Louis Pasteur, there was a lack of recognition of such a development. The press had facilitated the revival of the notion of conflict. Low-priced publications for popular consumption had acted as a platform for rationalists. Heseltine claimed that 'the greatest scientists' had abandoned the idea of conflict. But the idea still lingered in the minds of 'the less brilliant professional scientists', science teachers, students and journalists, all of whom lacked the necessary philosophical skills to distinguish between science and 'pseudo-science'. The great danger of 'pseudo-science' was that the 'ordinary' readership – accounting for 'at least ninety per cent' of the total – could not distinguish it from its orthodox counterpart. Some science writers were themselves deceived. Therefore, in these circumstances the blind were leading the blind. Some of them were invoking science with a social or political agenda in mind. Others simply sought public attention. Whatever their motives, the press was pleased to publish their views because pseudo-science was more sensational than science. Sensational news generated greater sales and higher profits.

In his article, Heseltine was particularly critical of Bertrand Russell's *Scientific Outlook*, denying that the church had a case to answer when it persecuted Galileo and rejecting the contention that there was an unavoidable clash between the inductive method of science and the deductive method so important to theology. Eminent Catholic scientists, such as André Ampère (1775–1836), Luigi Galvani (1737–1798), Gregor Mendel, Angelo Secchi and Alessandro Volta (1745–1827) were given as examples to bolster the argument that Roman Catholicism and science could be easily reconciled. The 'greatest' scientists had no quarrel with religion.[72] The point that many eminent scientists were Catholic was a recurring theme in the works of Irish Catholic apologists.[73]

Mind over Matter?

The first law of thermodynamics, also known as the principle of the conservation of energy, declared that energy could not be created or destroyed but could be changed from one form to another. For example, energy could be transformed from thermal to mechanical, chemical or electrical. The second law of thermodynamics was first explicitly elaborated by the

Cambridge geophysicist and mathematician William Hopkins in 1852. A revised version of the law was published by Rudolf Clausius (1822–1888) in the 1860s. The second law stated that the total energy available for work within a closed system inevitably and irreversibly decreases. In such a system, entropy – a measurement of disorder determined by mathematical physics – tends towards a maximum. By the end of the nineteenth century these laws were consolidated in theoretical physics. It soon became clear that if there was a finite amount of energy in the universe, and that if it was being continuously dispersed, then the 'heat death' of the universe was inevitable. It seemed that the universe would simply run down to become dark, cold and lifeless. This realisation stimulated debates about the beginning and end of time, and provoked questions about God's role. Some authors took the view that a dying universe undermined confidence in a beneficent deity. For others it indicated the existence of God.[74] The entropic creation argument was used occasionally from the late nineteenth century to about 1920, but after this period it rarely featured in Christian apologetics.[75] It received widespread attention when Pope Pius XII claimed that entropy 'eloquently postulates the existence of a necessary Being' in his address to the Pontifical Academy of Sciences on 22 November 1951.[76]

The Jesuit priest Francis J. McGarrigle was clearly influenced by St Thomas Aquinas's five arguments for the existence of God. The thirteenth-century theologian had argued that a series of cause and effect relationships could be traced back to God. There had to be a first cause for everything.[77] For McGarrigle, thermodynamics seemed to reinforce the logic of St Thomas. He assumed that the universe could not have emerged spontaneously out of nothing. If it had a beginning then it had to be created by an 'Infinite Being'. But what if there was an infinite series of causes? The universe might be infinitely old. McGarrigle rejected this notion on the basis of deductive reasoning, probably based on the philosophy of the theologian Bonaventure.[78] He argued that if the past was infinite then we could never have reached the present because infinity, by its very nature, could not be traversed. In other words, if the past was infinite the present would be unreachable. After labouring this point, he then turned to thermodynamics for additional proof of God's existence. If the universe was infinitely old then all its energy would have been completely dispersed, leaving it in a state of inertia. Since this was clearly not true, McGarrigle confidently concluded that the universe had a beginning; therefore, God's existence was secured.[79]

Evolution was rarely, if ever, far from the minds of Irish Catholic authors when constructing arguments for the existence of God. Fr Henry V. Gill observed that there was no evidence for the emergence of life from non-living matter. He summarily dismissed the highly speculative idea of extraterrestrial origins, i.e. that 'some seed was somehow wafted' across outer space to Earth from some distant planet. The idea of extraterrestrial origins was rejected on the basis that it put the answer to the problem further out of reach – because life on that other planet would then have to be explained. The 'simplest and most scientific explanation' was to concede that life was created by God. The emergence of life could not be accounted for on the basis of physical and chemical laws and the random motion of atoms. Furthermore, evolution and entropy were incompatible. Biological evolution was the development of less organised and less complex matter to a state of higher organisation and greater complexity. Therefore, the theory of biological evolution contradicted the well-established physical law of entropy. Evolution could not be established on a 'rationalistic' basis. To work it required 'continually active interference' from the Creator. In the course of relating entropy to biological evolution, Gill cautioned his readers against attaching 'too much importance' to this 'proof' of God's existence.[80] Gill's argument here was deeply flawed because he did not take cognisance of the fact that entropy applied only to closed systems. Decreases of entropy could occur in some parts of the universe (such as the development of life on Earth), at the expense of increasing entropy elsewhere (such as the emission of energy from the Sun). This was well known for decades.[81]

The argument from thermodynamics seemed more convincing than emphasising the lack of evidence for the development of the earliest forms of life in Earth's history. This latter argument relied too heavily on gaps in scientific knowledge. The argument from thermodynamics seemed to be stronger because of its apparent basis in well-established laws of science. It was particularly satisfying because it seemed to be so conclusive, and it had the added advantage of simplicity. Gill pointed to temperature differentials across the universe. Given that energy was constantly dispersing, there would be no temperature differences if the universe was infinitely old. This was clearly not the case – therefore the universe was of finite age. If it had a beginning in time then it was created. Or so it seemed! This argument assumed that there was no mechanism of renewal in the universe.

Around 1900 the entropic creation argument was accepted by many German Jesuits – the same religious order as Gill – but some of them did not accept it as a valid proof of God's existence.[82] Generally, Catholic apologists were cautious not to overestimate the entropic creation argument.[83] The history of the entropic creation argument is quite complex and is explored in great detail in Helge S. Kragh's *Entropic Creation: Religious Contexts of Thermodynamics and Cosmology* (2008). From *Entropic Creation* it is clear that there was no simple alignment of participants in the debate. It was not simply a case of Christian apologists invoking entropy for a universe with a beginning and hence a creator, versus atheists arguing for an infinitely old universe and therefore no creator. The atheistic philosopher Bertrand Russell, for example, accepted that the universe had a beginning on the basis of the entropic argument – but he did not then conclude that it was divinely created. Arthur Eddington, one of Britain's leading astronomers and a Quaker of strong religious conviction, held a diametrically opposite view – he did not accept that the universe had a beginning.[84]

Thermodynamics and cosmology were not the only subjects in theoretical physics which were thought to have profound implications for theology. New theories in physics provoked Catholics, and other Christians, to re-examine their beliefs, especially in relation to divine activity in nature and the doctrine of free will. Some attention will be given here to twentieth-century physics before examining Irish Catholic opinions about free will.

The mechanical world of classical Newtonian physics seemed rock solid in the late nineteenth century. It had dominated theoretical physics for over two centuries. However, between 1895 and the 1930s it was superseded by the new physics which was based on fundamentally different ideas of space, time, causality, energy transformations and the nature of wave-particles relating to both matter and radiation. At the subatomic level quantum mechanics and the principle of uncertainty overturned the mechanistic view of matter by demonstrating that the behaviour of particles was subject to statistical laws and could not be ascertained with absolute accuracy.[85] Theoretical physics at the astronomical level also underwent radical change. Albert Einstein (1879–1955) played a central role. By the 1920s his general theory of relativity had come to prominence and it overturned ideas of absolute space, time and motion and proposed a four-dimensional universe.

The new physics was frequently misused to both defend and attack traditional Christian beliefs. On balance it seemed more supportive than detrimental to a Christian worldview. It seemed to overcome the implied determinism and materialism of Newtonian physics. The principle of uncertainty or indeterminacy formulated by Werner Heisenberg (1901–1976) in 1927 showed that there was a limit to the accuracy of determining both the position and the momentum of sub-atomic particles. If, for example, a scientist chose to ascertain an electron's position, then the opportunity was lost to discover its momentum. Scientists became aware that they, as observers of natural or induced phenomena, were part of every experiment, and that there was no means of effectively distancing themselves to ensure that their findings were consistent with objective reality.[86] Heisenberg's uncertainty principle led some authors to conclude that the universe was not deterministic and that there was considerable scope for God and human free will. In the twentieth century there was, for reasons not entirely understood, a greater degree of theological orthodoxy amongst physicists than amongst their colleagues in the biological, social and behavioural sciences.[87]

Bertrand Russell, in his *Scientific Outlook*, observed that clergymen were quick to take advantage of the principle of uncertainty to shake off the burden of ubiquitous physical laws. He argued that the principle of uncertainty in no way diminished the universality of physical laws. The principle of uncertainty was a problem pertaining to measurement, and was not concerned with physical causality. Russell envisaged that further experimental research might circumvent the obstacle of uncertainty to yield major insights into atomic physics. Therefore, it was 'very rash to erect a theological superstructure upon a piece of ignorance' which might be very short-lived.[88] Russell was particularly critical of Arthur Stanley Eddington, and of the British physicist James Hopwood Jeans, both of whom saw consonance between modern theoretical physics and the plausibility of God's existence. From Jeans's *The Mysterious Universe* (1930) it seemed that God had a passion for mathematics. Russell cynically observed that theologians had 'grown grateful for small mercies' and were willing to accept any kind of God that scientists might offer them.[89]

Eddington and Jeans were not only criticised by Russell but also by Henry V. Gill, although of course from an entirely different perspective. Gill's 'Physics and Free Will', published in the *Irish Ecclesiastical Record* (August 1932), was concerned with the relationship between mind and matter, and indicated familiarity with the works of Eddington and Jeans. Eddington had stated that:

> The new physics . . . opens the door to indeterminacy in mental phenomena, whereas the old deterministic physics bolted and barred it

completely. If the atom has indeterminacy, surely the human mind
has an equal indeterminacy; for we can hardly accept a theory which
makes out the mind to be more mechanistic than the atom.[90]

What was the connection between the indeterminacy of atoms and sub-
atomic particles and free will? Gill could not see it but pointed to what he
saw as the underlying assumption – that the functioning of the mind is
subject to the laws governing matter. This was unacceptable because it
was only 'slightly removed' from materialism which was incompatible
with science. The 'greatest scientists' believed that the human mind was
'not subject to the limitations of matter'. Even when determinism was
seen in material things, this did not lead to a denial of free will in
humans. Scientists did not say that the human mind was 'indeterminate'
– rather their position was that the human mind 'determines itself'.[91]

Some of those who were religious accepted that the mind could be
seen as an outcome of physical actions in the brain. But for them physical
activity in the brain did not rigidly predetermine mental activity, thus
leaving considerable scope for free will.[92] Free will, if it was to be truly
free, was not predictable. It was speculated that indeterminacy at sub-
atomic and atomic levels could lead to indeterminacy at higher levels of
organisation in nature. But it was frequently argued that random or
chance events in the brain at the microscopic level could undermine
responsibility for one's actions rather than consolidate it.[93] Gill drew no
support for free will from the principle of uncertainty. He observed that
indeterminism in modern physics was another name for 'chance' or randomness, which was applicable to electrons. However, he did not accept
that it was correct to apply the physical principle of uncertainty to mental
activity and even if it was, it would not 'prove' the existence of free will. It
'would only go to show that the workings of the mind are as capricious as
those which the principle of uncertainty attributes to atoms and electrons
which apparently have no cause'. Therefore, uncertainty and randomness
in physics did not offer any support for free will.[94] In other words, if mind
arose entirely from physical matter, then the idea of free will was unsustainable, regardless of whether it was subject to mechanistic determinism
or statistical probabilities.

Gill acknowledged that very little was known about mind and
matter.[95] In the case of matter there was much uncertainty 'at both
extremes of the scale of creation' – in astronomy and atomic physics.
What was the nature of this uncertainty? Gill pointed to the limitations
and imperfections of human knowledge, and the limited potential of

scientific instrumentation. There was a distinction to be made between what was unknown and open to discovery and what was unknowable. For example: did the uncertainty about electron motion arise because of an innate property of electrons? If this was true then even God could not know the position and velocity of individual electrons. Gill was unwilling to place such an avoidable restriction on God's omniscience. He specu- lated that scientists might someday be able to ascertain both the velocity and position of electrons by using some method other than X-rays. [96]

Gill was concerned to uphold the principle of physical causality. Heisenberg had argued that, in quantum physics, it was impossible to state definitively that a precise set of physical conditions would definitely cause another precise set of physical conditions. Predictions were based on probabilities rather than on the laws of classical causality.[97] However, Gill argued that the assumption of cause and effect as a working principle had served science well – this was proof of how sound a principle it was. Furthermore, the principle of causality was philosophical – not scientific. It could not be disproved by any scientific observation or experiment.[98] The uncertainties in nature were not due to a lack of causes but rather to a number of interacting causes which made the 'visibility very low'.[99]

Despite the lack of knowledge about mind and matter, Gill was confi- dent in stating that: 'In the case of the mind we know that we are free without knowing how this comes about. We see our minds from the inside.'[100] This hardly qualified as a rational argument. But for Gill rational argument was only of secondary importance. The human mind was intimately bound up with the idea of the immortal soul, and 'the spiritual operations of the soul' were 'on a different plane altogether from those of matter'.[101] This point was reiterated by another contributor to the *Irish Ecclesiastical Record*, F.R. Hoare, who asserted that 'the will is called free, not because its acts are uncaused, but because it is the cause of its own acts'. The ultimate cause of human acts was God, but this cause was not so restrictive that it violated free will.[102]

Hoare argued that, although physicists could not predict the course of an individual particle, its course was nevertheless determined and consis- tent with the principle of causality.[103] But all this was irrelevant to the question of free will. Psychology – rather than mathematical physics – was the appropriate discipline to examine whether the concept of free will was sustainable or not. At this point Hoare conceded that some human acts lacked freedom. He argued that a drug addict might not resist temptation because 'the involuntary craving' might be 'overwhelming' – totally unrelated to the determinacy or indeterminacy of electrons in the constituent atoms of his body. The freedom of some actions could be diminished for a number of reasons – for example, by pathology, intoxication or the habits of everyday life.[104] Nevertheless, some acts were undeniably free. There was an intellectual dimension where choices were made concerning objectives in life and the means to achieve them.[105]

Irish Catholic authors were confident that modern science did not present any difficulties for upholding the doctrine of free will. As Gill had observed, very little was known about mind and matter. There was no short- to medium-term prospect that scientists would be able to comprehensively explain the human mind in terms of biochemistry, physiology and anatomy. In the absence of a satisfactory scientific explanation for mental activity, there was a tendency to look to the supernatural. The enormous void in science gave sanctuary to the immortal soul, provided a comforting assurance that death was not the end but the gateway to eternal life.

Scientific Consensus and Catholic Dissent

In the early twentieth century biological evolution was still the primary focus where points of contact between science and theology were concerned. The most objectionable aspect of evolutionary theory in general, from a religious perspective, was the mechanism of natural selection. In the early twentieth century those who were critical of evolution could take comfort in the apparent incompatibility between natural selection and Mendelian genetics. But in the 1930s and 1940s biologists forged a synthesis between these two schools of thought. The evolutionary process was now seen to be driven on the basis of natural selection suppressing or favouring genes that had mutated. Natural selection was revived on the basis of extensive research by many specialists, including zoologists, population geneticists and palaeontologists. Amongst those who made important contributions were Sergei Chetverikov (1880–1959), Theodosius Dobzhansky (1900–1975), Ronald Fisher (1890–1962), John B.S. Haldane (1892–1964), Ernst Mayr (1904–2005), George Gaylord Simpson (1902–1984) and Sewall Wright (1889–1988). Julian Huxley (1887–1975) also played an important role, although not in terms of scientific research. His contribution took the form of integrating a diverse range of scientific findings in his *Evolution: The Modern Synthesis* (1942). His survey gave the 'Modern Synthesis' its name.[106] Neo-Darwinism was firmly established in mainstream science on the basis of experimental genetics and population statistics. Therefore, Irish Catholic apologists who hoped that evolutionary theory would be weakened rather than consolidated by scientific research were to be disappointed – or, if they were not, then they were very much out of touch with developments in science. One such apologist was the Catholic dean of Cork, Mgr P. Sexton, who displayed gross ignorance of his subject when he wrote about science in the *Capuchin Annual* (1933).

The main thrust of Sexton's article was that no established finding in science contradicted any aspect of Catholic doctrine, properly understood. However, after giving a garbled account of the Galileo controversy, he maintained that the sun-centred theory was still 'only a theory, and even today it is not regarded as a fact'. Contemporary scientists viewed it as 'a very big probability'.[107] Sexton was blissfully unaware that Newton's laws of gravity, the observation of stellar parallax by the German astronomer and mathematician Friedrich Wilhelm Bessel (1784–1846) in 1838 and the experiments of the French physicist Jean Foucault (1819–1868) had placed the Copernican system far beyond reasonable doubt.[108]

Sexton's account of biological evolution was as incoherent as his version of the Galileo affair. Natural selection, he declared, had been rejected by mainstream science and was 'practically dead'. Sexton's lack of understanding about evolution is, to some extent, understandable. At this time it was not unusual in Britain for authors to maintain that evolution was not proven and that natural selection was very unlikely. The notion that Darwinism was 'dead' sometimes featured in debates between Christian apologists and those who attacked religion on the basis of evolutionary theory.[109] In Britain this occurred against the background of the acrimonious debate between H.G. Wells attacking Roman Catholicism and Hilaire Belloc and G.K. Chesterton defending it. However, Belloc and Chesterton, both of whom believed that mainstream science had abandoned natural selection, had a poor understanding of what was actually happening in science. Darwinism was being transformed and was coming to occupy a position of central importance in theory formation in the life sciences. Furthermore, news of its revival was transmitted beyond the environs of the scientific community to a broader readership.[110]

Sexton indicated a very superficial acquaintance with the substance of the debate between Belloc and Wells and with the 'higher criticism' of the Bible. But his credulous and unscientific outlook must have become obvious to many of his co-religionists when he wrote that although the falling of manna was a miracle when God used it to feed the Israelites in the desert, it was a frequently occurring and natural event in Armenia. Armenians gathered it before sunrise to make cakes and he had been promised one by a local bishop. After narrating this incredible tale, Sexton then wrote about the 'stupendous' discoveries of scientists. But he feared that some Catholics might be so overawed by the remarkable achievements of scientists that they would lose confidence in theologians. They might come to regard scientists as pre-eminent. He addressed this fear with the assertion that theology, with its 'handmaid' philosophy, alone had the right and the power to answer, with 'unerring certainty', the most important questions of life.[111]

Sexton was not reticent about expressing his opinions to an audience outside the readership of the *Capuchin Annual*. In October 1928 he had spoken publicly, and disparagingly, about the universities. His anti-academic and anti-intellectual proclivities again found expression in April 1932 when he spoke out against university professors, suggesting that they should limit their activities to the education of their students. Sexton's opinions are significant because his general outlook may have been representative of the views of a substantial section of the Cork clerical community. At the time the Catholic hierarchy tended to resent and distrust independent-minded lay Catholic intellectuals, even when they were unambiguously orthodox.[112]

Irish Catholic authors were much more aware of what was happening in Britain than in continental Europe in matters where the intellectual domains of science and religion overlapped. There was very little specific reference to the Vatican or to relevant documents of central importance, such as the decrees of the Pontifical Biblical Commission or *Providentissimus Deus*. In October 1936 Pope Pius XI redefined the role of the Pontifical Academy of the New Lincei and brought it directly under papal control. The reformed institute was renamed the Pontifical Academy of Sciences. The pope appointed seventy academicians, including such notable figures as the physicists Niels Bohr (1885–1962), Guglielmo Marconi (1874–1937), Max Planck (1858–1947) and Erwin Schrödinger (1887–1961) to the institute.[113] The academy was to serve as the 'scientific Senate' of the Holy See, and was to promote harmony between Roman Catholicism and science.[114] This provided an opportunity for Irish Catholic authors to reject the assertion that the church was averse to progress in science. Fr Henry V. Gill took advantage of such an opportunity and wrote about the papal initiative in the *Irish Ecclesiastical Record*.

Gill maintained that the setting up of the academy indicated the positive attitude of the church towards science, contrary to common perceptions.

If the church rejected the latest findings in science then it was merely being 'cautious', as with Galileo in the seventeenth century. Galileo had not proved his case, and therefore the censorious attitude of the ecclesiastical authorities in Rome was nothing more than 'apparent hostility' to the progress of science. Gill maintained that the church had never condemned evolutionary theory except when it was associated with atheistic philosophy. Nevertheless, he believed that there was a widely held view – presumably he meant outside of the Irish Free State – that Catholic priests were 'reactionary and ignorant of science'. He gave two reasons why the Catholic priesthood was held in such low esteem. Firstly, in matters of science the Sunday papers served as a public platform for a small number of scientists who expressed opinions hostile to the church. He gave no details about the offending newspapers, or about the scientists. Secondly, he associated the epithet of reactionary with the church's opposition to 'certain practices of birth control', including sterilisation, and 'certain means of eliminating the unfit'. Gill gave no details about eugenic practices, but he was probably thinking about the racist policies of Nazi Germany. In reference to birth control, Gill probably had in mind Pope Pius XI's encyclical *Casti Connubii* (December 1930), which condemned artificial means of contraception in contrast to the less restrictive position adopted by the Anglican bishops at their Lambeth Conference earlier the same year. Gill's comments were made against the background of opposition by both church and state to artificial means of contraception.[115] He concluded his article by quoting at length Pope Leo XIII's *Providentissimus Deus* (1893), to make the point that, despite occasional apparent contradictions, there was complete harmony between science and Catholic doctrine.[116]

Alfred O'Rahilly, Professor of Mathematical Physics at University College Cork, advocated the harmony thesis, in common with other Catholic apologists. His greatest contribution to science, *Electromagnetics: A Discussion of Fundamentals* (1938), was jointly published by Cork University Press and Longmans, Green & Company (London). It was about nine hundred pages in length and was a painstaking synthesis of numerous mathematical equations in advanced physics. Its advanced mathematics put it far beyond the comprehension of the non-specialist reader. O'Rahilly was severely critical of Albert Einstein's special theory of relativity and declared his intention to write a detailed rebuttal of the general theory of relativity at a later date. The works of other scientists were also subjected to criticism, including those of Jeans and Eddington. O'Rahilly believed that there was such an excess of deference to eminent physicists such as Einstein that it stifled much-needed constructive criticism within the discipline. His declared aim was to reawaken physicists from their 'dogmatic slumber'.[117] However, his aspiration of making a major contribution to theoretical physics was not well served by his tendency to express opinions which were unnecessarily offensive towards many of his fellow scientists.[118]

Electromagnetics did elicit comments of approval from a few scientists, but it was generally not well received by physicists. O'Rahilly was to pay a heavy price for his unorthodox scientific opinions. He was persistently ignored by the scientific community at large, to such an extent that he felt compelled to abandon further studies in physics. This was a source of bitter disappointment to him.[119] O'Rahilly, the scientific heretic, was effectively 'excommunicated', somewhat like St George Jackson Mivart in the late nineteenth century. Those scientists who were sharply critical of the prevailing consensus in their profession were vulnerable to marginalisation in the international scientific fraternity.

7. From De Valera's Institute to the Big Bang, 1939–1950

The Dublin Institute for Advanced Studies

In the Irish Free State there was little public appreciation or understanding of the need to allocate resources for scientific education and research consistent with the state's finances. Generally, the attitude of politicians reflected public thinking on this issue. An exception, to some extent, was Éamon de Valera, leader of Fianna Fáil, and Taoiseach without a break from 1932 to 1948. On 6 July 1939 he introduced a bill in Dáil Éireann to make provision for the establishment of the Dublin Institute for Advanced Studies (DIAS). Initially, it was to consist of a school of Celtic studies and a school of theoretical physics. De Valera left open the possibility of setting up schools in other disciplines at a later date.

The DIAS was de Valera's own idea.[1] It resonated well with two of his main intellectual interests – Gaelic (Irish) language studies and mathematics. Furthermore, it seems that he was inspired by the setting up of the Institute for Advanced Study at Princeton in 1930, which served as a sanctuary for a number of well-known scientists (most notably Albert Einstein) who were refugees from Nazi Germany.[2] Several weeks after the introduction of de Valera's bill in Dáil Éireann the Second World War broke out in Europe. It was hardly an appropriate time to set about the establishment of an institute of higher learning. But de Valera was not dissuaded by the anticipated exigencies of wartime. In 1938 he had been informed of the plight of the eminent Austrian physicist Erwin Schrödinger. Schrödinger was dismissed from his professorial post at the University of Graz at the behest of the Nazis who were now firmly in control of Austria after the announcement of Anschluss (union with Germany) on 13 March 1938. Schrödinger, regarded as politically unreliable by the authorities, thought it prudent to leave Austria while he still could. De Valera, through intermediaries (including the British

153

mathematical physicist Edmund Taylor Whittaker), arranged a meeting with Schrödinger in Geneva. Schrödinger's plight was de Valera's opportunity. It seems that de Valera had first thought of appointing Schrödinger to a senior position at the DIAS after reading a newspaper report about his sacking at Graz.[3] Schrödinger was invited to Dublin, although the DIAS had yet to be set up. On 21 November 1940 he was appointed Director of the School of Theoretical Physics – a post which he resigned from on 14 December 1945 to become Senior Professor so that he could devote his time entirely to scientific research.[4] Schrödinger's 'Long Exile' lasted until 1956.[5]

De Valera personally directed the legislation for the setting up of the DIAS through both houses of parliament. His declared ambition was to restore the status of science in Ireland to what it had been in the mid-nineteenth century. When making reference to nineteenth-century scientists he mentioned Sir William Rowan Hamilton (1805–1865), James MacCullagh (1809–1847), George Francis FitzGerald (1851–1901), Sir George Gabriel Stokes and William Thomson – Tyndall was omitted.[6] According to de Valera, Hamilton was regarded as the most accomplished of Irish scientists. He loved his country and had worked to enhance its prestige.[7] Implicit in de Valera's remarks was that Tyndall, an eminent scientist, did not merit distinction as an Irish scientist because of his staunch unionist attitudes and support for the Orange Order.

De Valera envisaged that Ireland's status on the international stage would be enhanced as it became a centre of advanced learning in carefully selected specialised areas of study. He had hoped to set up a school of experimental physics but decided not to do so because the cost of establishing and maintaining it would be too expensive, especially due to the cost of the equipment.[8] However, he argued that all that was required for theoretical physics was the professional staff, paper and a library.[9] Such expenditure, therefore, could be justified in view of the potential benefits. The political opposition did not agree and fears were expressed that the universities would be adversely affected. Some support was expressed for Celtic studies but not for theoretical physics.[10] De Valera was exceptional amongst Irish politicians in appreciating the crucial importance of the connection between basic science and applied science.[11] Scientific knowledge was important for its own sake but it was also valuable for the economic benefits which were likely to flow from it. Applied science frequently benefited from discoveries that initially had no apparent practical or economic value. De Valera's parliamentary colleagues did not understand this fundamental point. Amongst parliamentarians there was little interest in theoretical science which did not carry with it the prospect of material gain.[12] Their views were probably broadly representative of public opinion on this matter. The DIAS was established because of de Valera's determination to promote Celtic studies and theoretical physics. But successive Irish governments, including those led by de Valera, did not make adequate provision for scientific education and research.

Those in the upper echelons of political administration did not seem to have a clear vision about the importance of science in terms of intellectual, social and economic benefits.[13] But was it reasonable, given the extremely difficult economic conditions of the early 1940s, to increase government spending on science? A cursory examination of the issue indicated that any substantial increases in expenditure would be extravagant. However, a more thoughtful analysis indicated otherwise – the state could not afford to neglect science. So argued Thomas Dillon through the medium of *Studies*. He drew on the history of chemistry and physics to make the point that there was no reliable demarcation between scientific research for industrial purposes and for purely academic reasons. For example, Michael Faraday's research on electromagnetic induction had no apparent practical application when it was undertaken but was of immense practical importance in later years. No entrepreneur would have financed the work of Paul Sabatier, Professor of Chemistry at the University of Toulouse. But Sabatier's study of the role of metals as catalysts for the hydrogenation of unsaturated hydrocarbons later found widespread application in the conversion of fish oils into solid fats for food processing and soap production.

Although there was a very strong case for funding science in hard times, Dillon viewed Irish public opinion as a major obstacle. The Irish were, generally, 'severely practical' in their attitude towards science. They were supportive of 'applied science' only and were not well disposed towards those who wished to undertake research for theoretical reasons with no provable practical value prior to investment. This attitude greatly impeded industrial development.[14] Implicit in Dillon's observations was that leading politicians would not promote science when public opinion did not support such a policy.

Dillon was knowledgeable about the history of science in Europe, including Ireland. In discussing eighteenth- and nineteenth-century Ireland, he referred to a number of scientists who played key roles in promoting physics and chemistry – William Higgins (1763–1825), Sir Robert Kane, William Kirby Sullivan, Hugh Ryan and John A. McClelland. He argued that those scientists who worked in the nineteenth century to promote the application of science to Irish industry achieved very little because of the political circumstances of their time. The people of southern Ireland were now independent and thus would only have themselves to blame if they failed to use science as an indispensable instrument of industrial development.[15]

Dillon was a voice in the wilderness. The *Commission on Vocational Organisation Report*, published in 1944, gave little reason for optimism. From 1934 the teaching of rural science was no longer compulsory in primary schools. This facilitated the allocation of more time for the teaching of the Irish language. By 1943 the number of primary schools teaching the subject fell from 3,200 to 350.[16] Furthermore, very few secondary schools taught rural science. The commission was sharply critical of this policy. The vast majority of children, many of whom were to become farmers, would not proceed to secondary school. Depriving them of instruction in rural science was depriving them of foundation knowledge essential for subsequent training in agriculture on a scientific basis. The commission found that agricultural education was neglected in primary, secondary and vocational schools. This was 'highly unfortunate' because the Irish economy was mainly agricultural and failing to provide adequately for education in this subject area adversely affected the country's ability to compete with other agricultural economies in the international market.[17] The neglect of rural science and agricultural science in the education system continued for many years after the publication of the *Commission on Vocational Organisation Report*.[18] Provision for technical training for the industrial sector was also in poor condition. The commission found a lack of planning and co-ordination in the state departments of agriculture, industry and commerce, and education. And there was a failure to take full advantage of university laboratory facilities.[19] It was the late 1960s before the state began to address the pressing need for technical education and applied science with the setting up of the Regional Technical Colleges and National Institutes of Higher Education.[20] In the 1940s there were no indications that any initiatives, from the state or from the Catholic Church, were about to stimulate the emergence of a vigorous culture of science in Ireland.[21]

Alfred O'Rahilly – Defender of Roman Catholicism

In 1939–1940 external threats to the Irish Free State, arising from the escalation of military conflict in Europe and the disruption of trade, and the internal threat due to the subversive activities of the Irish Republican Army (IRA), were, apparently, not the only dangers to be contended with. In some quarters there was also deep concern about the spiritual welfare of the Catholic population because of the widely disseminated opinions of irreligious authors such as Herbert George Wells and Bertrand Russell. Wells had studied under Thomas Henry Huxley in 1884–1885 and was intellectually 'bewitched' by him for the rest of his life.[22] Sales of his book *The Outline of History* (1920) reached over two million copies in a few years and made him a wealthy man. In this volume Wells was critical of the Roman Catholic Church. His anti-Catholicism intensified rather than subsided over the years.[23] In August 1939 his literary assault on Roman Catholicism was renewed with the publication of *The Fate of Homo Sapiens*. As a student in the 1880s he had come to the conclusion that science thoroughly undermined the 'simple fundamentals' of Christian 'mythology' – the doctrines of creation and Original Sin, and the story of the flood. Instead of the images evoked by the Genesis narratives he saw a vast universe illuminated by countless nebulae and stars where life evolved upwards.[24] The 'most highly organised and active expression' of Christianity was to be found in the Roman Catholic Church.[25] At the intellectual level he viewed Roman Catholicism as 'the most extraordinary jumble of absurdities and incompatibilities that ever exercised and perplexed the human intelligence',[26] from which scientific knowledge was excluded.[27] The great strength of Roman Catholicism was the enormous diversity of its doctrines. There was something there for everyone and, because the 'mighty jumble sale of its entirety' was far beyond the competence of any single person to understand it, potential converts could ignore the most disagreeable articles of faith.[28] Wells then asked, rhetorically, how intelligent people could embrace 'this strange heap of mental corruption'.[29] There was no great complexity in the answer. Catholicism offered guiding principles and directives for all the main issues in life and in doing so it gave comforting reassurances. In return for such bountiful blessings the church required a suspension of one's critical faculties. Wells singled out his arch antagonist Hilaire Belloc as a prime example of a devout Catholic who somehow managed to suppress his intelligence for the duration of every Mass he attended.[30]

Wells viewed the institutional church as a great force of evil in the world, allied to nefarious governments such as the fascist regimes of Benito Mussolini and Francisco Franco. All that was required of such leaders, for ecclesiastical approval, was an adherence to the precepts of Catholicism.[31] Catholic prelates were frequently well intentioned but were 'extremely ignorant' men.[32] Ignorance then was a gateway to evil!

After this scathing attack on Roman Catholicism Wells then turned his attention to the church in Ireland. The dominant role of the church in education, and the Catholic-inspired system of state censorship, kept young Irish Catholic men 'as blankly ignorant of the modern world as though they had been born in the thirteenth century'.[33] Many of these men were obsessed with bringing Protestants in Northern Ireland under Catholic control in the name of national unity. Irish republicans were committing acts of terrorism in Britain in an attempt to persuade the British state to abandon Northern Ireland. Desiring to cleanse their souls of murderous deeds they would simply go to Mass and 'purify their souls by confession'.[34] These extreme opinions were expressed against the background of an IRA bombing campaign in Britain which began in January 1939. In that year at least seven people were murdered and nearly two hundred were wounded.[35] From the viewpoint of Wells it was as if all Irish Catholics were supporting republican terrorists. He maintained that the Roman Catholic Church in Ireland would continue to keep young Irishmen ignorant and predisposed towards terrorism. The Irish and the Spanish, he believed, were temperamentally very close. It was in their nature to engage in 'vindictive massacres and pitiless wars'. Enlightened Irishmen living abroad hoped that some day their nation would break free of 'priests, piety and patriotism' and contribute once more to 'world civilisation'.[36]

This vitriolic attack against Roman Catholicism did not go unnoticed in Catholic Ireland, especially when Irish Catholicism had been singled out for special attention. Excerpts from *The Fate of Homo Sapiens* were published in the British newspaper *Picture Post* in November and December 1939. The editor of *Picture Post* then publicly extended an invitation to the editor of the *Irish Catholic*, or a person chosen by him, to reply to Wells. This in turn prompted Francis O'Reilly, the executive secretary of the Catholic Truth Society, to telegraph the editor of *Picture Post* stating that Professor Alfred O'Rahilly – 'the most eminent publicist in Ireland' – was willing to respond to Wells through the medium of the London periodical. O'Reilly then confirmed his telegram by letter but received no reply.[37] Wells, it seems, expressed a preference for one of two of his old adversaries, Archbishop Richard Downey or Hilaire Belloc.[38] This may have been the main reason why O'Rahilly's offer was declined. But even if O'Rahilly had been facilitated he would not have been able to reach his readership in Ireland. *Picture Post* was officially banned in Ireland on 22 December 1939, apparently on the grounds of obscenity and indecency. The ban was maintained for a period of several months at the behest of the Censorship Board. O'Rahilly felt compelled to use another medium in challenging the offensive opinions of Wells. An alternative newspaper was the Catholic weekly *The Standard*, with a circulation figure of about 50,000 in 1939.[39] O'Rahilly was able to reach a large readership, which was to grow even larger. His series of several articles, published from 12 January to 1 March 1940, stimulated much public interest and were credited with nearly doubling the sales figures of the newspaper.[40]

In his sixth article, published on 9 February 1940, O'Rahilly addressed a number of derogatory opinions about Irish Catholicism. He conceded that the Censorship Board might have made 'a few mistakes' – which was quite an understatement. O'Rahilly objected to Wells lecturing the Irish about the injustice of censorship when he and many of his fellow Irishmen had risked their lives during the War of Independence to express their opposition to British 'tyranny'. The Irish were now asserting their freedom and national identity, and were resisting exploitation propagated through the medium of 'British commercialised vice'.

O'Rahilly next addressed what he regarded as censorship in science. Evidently, he was still bitterly disappointed about his fellow scientists generally ignoring his refutation of Einstein. In recent years he had discovered that there was 'authoritarianism in physics' and 'a much stricter orthodoxy in science than in theology'. It was pointless arguing against Einstein, Eddington and Jeans – 'one is met not with counter-arguments but with a supercilious smile. Verily, the ways of the scientific heretic are hard.' Adherence to scientific orthodoxy demanded homage to 'certain tutelary deities' – such as Darwin in biology and Maxwell in electromagnetics.

O'Rahilly was not troubled by the assertion of Wells that the general outlook of young Irishmen was more typical of the thirteenth century than of the twentieth. His preferred century was the thirteenth. He lamented the fact that his fellow countrymen knew so much about the modern world and so little about the thirteenth century. Wells had overestimated the power of the church. O'Rahilly pointed to the competing influences of cinema and foreign literature, state support for Protestant schools, and the independence of the universities. What the country needed was greater control by the Catholic Church over the education system to counter the stifling effects of bureaucracy.

The simplistic and biased commentary of Wells on Northern Ireland drew a robust response from O'Rahilly. He maintained that the Protestant minority in the Irish Free State did not suffer injustice. The same could not be said about the Catholic minority in Northern Ireland. O'Rahilly pointed to the abolition of proportional representation and the gerrymandering of local electoral areas which gave Protestants a disproportionately high level of political representation. Furthermore, Catholics had to endure the Belfast pogroms and the bigotry and jobbery of the Orange Order. O'Rahilly expressed abhorrence at the atrocities of the IRA. However, he maintained that these terrorists were representative of only a very small minority of Irish Catholics. To condemn the entire national community for the acts of a few was 'ludicrously unjust, and unbalanced'. And the British state itself was not reluctant to support acts of terrorism to promote and defend its interests. O'Rahilly referred to acts of arson, torture and murder perpetrated by the Black and Tans during the War of Independence, and to a long history of persecution by the British. If Irish republican terrorists engaged in 'the misuse of religious practices' to sustain themselves in their struggle, this did not constitute a valid objection against religious belief itself. Otherwise it could be reasonably contended that Haeckel's notorious falsification of embryonic structures cast doubt on the merits of biological studies, and that the errors of Wells brought the value of historical studies into question.[41]

O'Rahilly exposed the prejudices and mere assumptions underlying many of Wells's opinions about Roman Catholicism. But his literary crusade against Wells was considerably devalued by his tendency to descend, like Wells, to the level of gratuitous insults, and to issue offensive remarks of a personal nature against his opponent. Wells had a 'shoddy mind', was 'an uncritical and gullible follower of agnostic bigwigs',[42] and was 'entirely incapable of independent research'.[43] He was 'too old to be spanked . . . too noisy to be ignored . . . too cocksure to be argued with' and 'too obstinately ignorant to be enlightened'.[44] O'Rahilly's defence of Roman Catholicism would, understandably, have won widespread support from Irish Catholics who would not have been indifferent to the bitter attack of Wells. Wells in turn could have relied on anti-Catholic sentiment amongst some Protestants and rationalists of all hues. But it is highly probable that the majority of those readers, initially uncommitted to either side, would have remained neutral. O'Rahilly's intemperate language would probably have alienated many potential supporters in Britain if published in the *Picture Post*. Perhaps the most important point to be made about O'Rahilly's energetic defence of the Catholic faith was that it was essentially superfluous. Wells did not pose a major threat to Catholicism, especially in Ireland where there was unswerving loyalty to the church. Furthermore, Ireland had not produced any home-grown irreligious authors as eminent as Wells, or Russell. There was no real debate in Ireland, unlike in Britain, where Belloc and Wells engaged in an acrimonious exchange of views. But O'Rahilly's campaign against Wells was probably of some value – it served to increase the sales figures of *The Standard* and it added a measure of drama to everyday life – for both the author and his readership.

O'Rahilly was exceptionally gifted intellectually. The merit of his *Electromagnetics* was indicated by a growing demand for the book by scientists in the 1960s. It was republished in London, New York and Toronto in 1965 with some minor corrections.[45] In the 1990s O'Rahilly's book was still referred to by physicists to address some aspects of Einstein's special theory of relativity.[46] Perhaps if he had been more tactful and less severe in his criticisms of Einstein and other eminent scientists he would have gained due recognition from the international scientific community, something which he would have greatly appreciated. But he was unable to restrain the polemical impulse.

In early 1944 O'Rahilly delivered nine lectures on religion and science which were broadcast by Radio Éireann. The texts of these lectures were published, without amendment, by *The Standard* newspaper in 1948, appropriately under the title of *Religion and Science: Broadcast Talks* (1948). The slim volume received the imprimatur of Daniel Cohalan, Bishop of Cork. O'Rahilly quickly set about emphasising the limited competence of science. Although he acknowledged that biological evolution was a valid scientific theory, he expressed extreme scepticism of it, declaring that natural history was little more than conjecture and was beyond scientific proof.[47] Metaphysical truths could not be ascertained on the basis of physical processes.[48] Science was 'purely descriptive' and was not concerned with ultimate causes. It was not able to address questions pertaining to the meaning of life or to the 'validity of knowledge'.[49] Neither could it offer a proof or a disproof of God's existence.[50] God was to be found through philosophy instead, especially through the five arguments of St Thomas Aquinas.[51]

O'Rahilly believed that many people harboured a 'sneaking suspicion' that science, somehow, made God less probable or more remote. He asserted that the idea of God in retreat before the progress of science was fostered by agnostic scientists.[52] But there was no logical connection between the loss of faith and scientific advancement.[53] Most of science stood in isolation to the main articles of faith. There was no such thing as Catholic chemistry or Catholic biology. Catholic anthropologists were not under obligation to uphold the common origin of all humans from Adam and Eve.[54] In view of such a high degree of mutual isolation there was correspondingly little scope for incompatibility between Roman Catholicism and science.

In defending the idea of harmony between Roman Catholicism and science O'Rahilly discussed the Galileo affair. His conclusions were predictable enough, when he found that the ecclesiastical authorities were essentially in the right. But he had to admit, although grudgingly and with an emphasis on mitigating circumstances, that the ecclesiastical condemnation of Galileo was 'deplorable'.[55] This admission did not provide a basis for the claim that the church was the enemy of science. The greatest enemy of science was not the church, but the state. Evidently with the Scopes trial (1925) in mind, O'Rahilly observed that it was the state of Tennessee – not the Catholic Church – which opposed evolution. O'Rahilly argued that the inventions of science, such as the printing press, the aeroplane, the machine-gun and the radio, were being used by the state as instruments to increase its control over society. Scientists and medical doctors were docile collaborators in schemes of creeping totalitarianism, readily joining the civil service to become part of the state machine. O'Rahilly was critical of scientists for not speaking out in defence of moral and intellectual freedoms. They were 'too busy dehumanizing man, proposing discrepant biological claptrap, devising schemes for mental and bodily enslavement of the masses' and attempting to undermine the Roman Catholic Church, which was the great defender of corporate freedom against 'growing Statolatry'.[56] Some of them dabbled in theology and 'quite a number of them' were communists.[57]

As a Roman Catholic, O'Rahilly felt compelled to take a stand against contemporary scientists. The theory of 'man's bestiality' had undermined respect for human life.[58] It was much easier to manipulate nature than to channel scientific knowledge towards serving the best interests of humankind. O'Rahilly feared that science would be misused to serve the totalitarian state. In this political system, which did not seem so remote in early 1944, he feared the imposition of such measures as artificial contraception, sterilisation and euthanasia. Humans would be treated as mere things.[59] O'Rahilly referred obliquely and fleetingly to eugenics when he stated that medical doctors and scientists, as servants of the state, wished to 'educate us, to inspect us, to sterilise us'.[60] Evidently, O'Rahilly was very much aware of the eugenics movement which had influenced government policies in many states, especially in Nazi Germany, where thousands of people were forcibly sterilised and millions were murdered in concentration camps. Even in democratic states such as the United States and Canada, eugenic sterilisation laws had been passed in violation of human rights.[61] These laws were also contrary to the teachings of the Roman Catholic Church.[62] O'Rahilly condemned artificial contraception, sterilisation and euthanasia, all of which he claimed had been advocated by scientific specialists who violated the dignity of their fellow human beings and treated them as mere 'things'.[63]

O'Rahilly castigated, and occasionally ridiculed, scientists and non-scientists alike, both living and dead. These included Charles Darwin, Thomas Henry Huxley, Sigmund Freud, Julian Huxley, Sir Arthur Keith, H.G. Wells, Bertrand Russell, John B.S. Haldane and Albert Einstein. Wells in particular was singled out for derision. Those scientists whom O'Rahilly admired included the Jesuit astronomers of the seventeenth and eighteenth centuries, such as Roger Joseph Boscovich, Christopher Scheiner and Orazio Grassi – the latter two had clashed bitterly with Galileo on the nature of sunspots and comets respectively.[64] Nineteenth-century scientists who met with his approval included the Augustinian botanist Gregor Mendel, whose concepts proved to be of fundamental importance to modern genetics; and St George Jackson Mivart, who was an eminent critic of Darwinism.

O'Rahilly's denigration of mainstream science and scientists would not have enhanced his reputation among scientists. However, it is likely that very few scientists listened to his broadcasts. His fears of the growing power of the state are, to some extent, understandable against the background of the rise of dictatorships in Europe in the 1930s. By late 1940 only five democratic states had survived – Britain, Ireland, Sweden, Switzerland and Finland.[65] In Britain and Ireland the exigencies of wartime demanded greater state intervention in their respective national economies. Nevertheless, it was possible to be unduly pessimistic about the future of democracy. O'Rahilly served on the Commission on Vocational Organisation (1939–1944) and he, like a number of other influential members of the commission, was excessively critical of the civil service and of state intervention in matters of social and economic concern.[66]

O'Rahilly believed that the error of the ecclesiastical authorities in so harshly disciplining Galileo proved to be beneficial to the church in the long term, despite the distortions and exaggerations of those authors who were hostile to Catholicism. It promoted the autonomy of science and influenced theologians to be moderate. However, O'Rahilly also maintained that some theologians learnt the lesson of Galileo 'too well' and adopted an attitude 'too subservient' to science when, in the nineteenth century, geological and evolutionary theories seemed to contradict the early chapters of Genesis.[67] Various versions of concordism had proved to be unsustainable. The Bible was not meant to teach science. Genesis was an 'ingenious literary scheme' to convey the meaning of God's creative power.[68] O'Rahilly expressed his 'calm conviction' that science could never contradict his religious faith.[69] The strategy of minimising the contact or overlap between the domains of science and religion greatly reduced the danger that scientific studies would undermine any articles of faith. The strategy of isolation had its limits. Catholic doctrine could not be isolated completely from the historical and natural sciences. O'Rahilly conceded that some aspects of belief would have to be revised but insisted that the essential Catholic dogmas were immutable.[70]

O'Rahilly was scathing in his criticism of those scientists who dared to venture beyond the confines of their laboratories to speculate on their findings to such an extent that it took them beyond science. He saw Erwin Schrödinger as one such offender. Schrödinger's interests turned towards a synthesis of physics, chemistry and biology. In February 1943 he delivered a series of lectures at Trinity College Dublin under the auspices of the DIAS. He influenced scientists to undertake research on genes based on methods from physics and chemistry, which in time led to the discovery of the structure of deoxyribonucleic acid (DNA). When he attempted to have his lectures published in Ireland, however, he experienced difficulties. The proposed book was deemed offensive to Catholic sensibilities. An appointee to the supervisory board of the DIAS, Monsignor Patrick Browne (S.J.), objected to the implied materialism in Schrödinger's work.[71] The Austrian scientist had to look abroad for a publisher and, in 1944, Cambridge University Press published his manuscript under the title of *What Is Life? The Physical Aspect of the Living Cell*.[72] O'Rahilly's Catholic sensitivities were offended and in *The Standard* of 23 February 1945 he castigated Schrödinger's failure to understand the Aristotelian-Thomistic theory of life and was sharply critical of his incursion into philosophy and religion.[73] According to the *Catholic Herald* this scathing review caused a 'greater stir' than Schrödinger's book.[74] This may have been true of Ireland but it is extremely unlikely that O'Rahilly's opinions attracted much attention abroad. Schrödinger prudently refrained from being drawn into controversy with O'Rahilly.

O'Rahilly persisted in trying to discredit the 'tutelary deities' of science, especially Charles Darwin. Other famous personalities, both living and dead, were also singled out for frequent criticism. These included the Huxleys, H.G. Wells and Bertrand Russell. So trenchant was his criticism that a journalist with *The Irish Times* wrote:

> A most serious fault is the note of personal animus against the Huxleys (past and present), H.G. Wells, Bertrand Russell, and others . . . [T]he O'Rahilly method may leave some people under the mistaken impression that his quarrel with Darwinism or Materialism is the outcome of a personal feud with the Huxleys and their friends . . . He goes over this ground so often . . . Little harm might result if Radio Eireann declared a closed season on Darwin and the Huxleys for a few years . . .[75]

O'Rahilly was the most vigorous, the most persistent and the most publicised defender of Roman Catholicism in Ireland when scientists and theologians crossed the intellectual boundary which so incompletely separated them. Scientists were frequently presented as the aggressors, eager to discredit religion as irrational and unsubstantiated. Therefore, O'Rahilly, in common with other Catholic writers, tended to emphasise the limitations and weaknesses of science as a means of defence.

Gill's *Fact and Fiction in Modern Science*

Henry V. Gill's book *Fact and Fiction in Modern Science* (1943), published under the imprimatur of Archbishop John Charles McQuaid, was mainly or entirely comprised of a collection of revised essays, previously published in the *Irish Ecclesiastical Record*, *Studies*, *The Month* and *Thought* – some of which have already been examined in this text. According to Monsignor Patrick J. McLaughlin, who served as Professor of

Experimental Physics at Maynooth, the book met with 'immediate success' and was sold not only in Ireland but also in England, the United States, and Portugal.[76]

Gill was aware of the epistemological upheaval in the natural sciences and was not reticent about elaborating on it. Like many other Irish Catholic apologists, he tended to present the progressive nature of science in a negative way. Scientific knowledge was imperfect, incomplete, and based on assumptions that could not be proved. In other words, there was a substantial element of faith underpinning science. Scientists had a very incomplete knowledge of the physical properties of matter and were constantly trying to integrate new data with previously acquired information, which often resulted in apparent contradictions.[77] No matter how much scientists discovered about matter, they would never get close to 'the ultimate reality of material things'. There were realities beyond the reach of sensory perception and the human intellect.[78]

Gill believed that there was insufficient emphasis on the speculative nature of scientific theories. This was, he argued, particularly evident when the earlier versions of the atomic model proposed by Niels Bohr contradicted the widely accepted laws of electromagnetic theory.[79] Furthermore, there seemed to be a number of persistent and important contradictions between scientific theories. Gill reiterated the old fallacy that biological evolution was not reconcilable with the strongly established second law of thermodynamics.[80] The corpuscular theory of light could not be reconciled with the wave theory of light.[81] However, Gill acknowledged that scientists were aware of deficiencies and flaws in scientific theories which sometimes gave rise to contradictions.

Attempts were made by scientists to address the inconsistencies which had arisen. For example, in 1935, Bohr, in dialogue with Einstein, maintained that the classical ideal of causality was no longer tenable in view of recent findings in quantum mechanics and that a radically different approach to the problem of ascertaining physical reality was imperative. Photons, as well as electrons, exhibited wave and particle properties under different and defined experimental conditions. Bohr introduced the concept of 'complementarity' to address the apparent anomalies between wave and corpuscular properties applying to light and electrons. This idea acknowledged that data derived from different experimental procedures could not be understood within a single conceptual framework, and that the observer invariably influenced the behaviour of his object of interest when observing it.[82] This was not an admission of an illogical element in scientific thinking; it was merely an acknowledgement that scientific investigative methods were not omnipotent and infallible. It was reasonable to provisionally adopt two theories in science which were mutually incompatible, when these, collectively, provided the best possible explanation of experimental results at the time. Gill, by so strongly emphasising the inconsistencies of scientific theory, failed to adequately appreciate this point.

Gill argued that, because the development of life from non-living matter was irreconcilable with the strongly established second law of thermodynamics, there was a 'vital principle' which elevated life to 'a higher plane of existence', where it was protected from the effects of entropy. Materialistic evolution could not be established on a rational basis because it could not reasonably substitute 'spontaneous generation' for the vital principle which was activated when God 'breathed life into the slime of the earth'.[83] Despite the fact that Gill found the emergence of life from inanimate particles scientifically untenable, he quoted the French edition of Canon Henri de Dorlodot's *Darwinism and Catholic Thought* to make the point that Catholics were free to accept it.[84]

Gill was concerned that the 'half-educated classes' were vulnerable to false claims based on misunderstandings of science which would, if unchecked by a sound system of science education in the schools, undermine the very basis of religious belief. He disapproved of Jeans' and Eddington's incursions into theology. Nebulous statements about a 'mathematically minded creator' were not supported by valid conclusions from the natural sciences.[85] He was critical of those who viewed the benefits of science almost entirely in terms of promoting economic progress. It was necessary to safeguard the faith by teaching science in conjunction with a system of philosophy approved of by the Catholic Church.[86] Gill saw a vital role for scholastic philosophy in the study of science. He was confident that modern science was slowly moving towards the scholastic theory of matter.[87] However, contrary to Gill's optimism, modern scientists had little use for obsolete medieval concepts such as the *materia prima* and the *forma substantialis*.

Gill expressed his disappointment at the 'limitation of outlook' evident in the statements of eminent figures in twentieth-century science and philosophy, such as Jeans, Eddington and Alfred North Whitehead (1861–1947). It was here that science was devalued, almost to the point of dismissal, as a useful contributor to the human quest of ascertaining truth pertaining to the existence of God. Scientific speculations about nature could at best lead only indirectly to knowledge of God. Physicists could only provide a little information relating to God, and even this was subject to great uncertainty. But the 'process of pure reasoning' would lead 'immediately' to the Creator. The 'ordinary man', with his 'ordinary intelligence', was quite capable of examining the 'metaphysical evidence provided by causation, motion, contingency, etc.', and on the strength of this could arrive at a sufficiently clear understanding of the nature of God.[88] From Gill's perspective, philosophical proof of God's existence was remarkably simple. The existence of anything, physical or spiritual, was testimony to the existence of a First Cause – i.e. God – which had no beginning. However, it was unlikely that significant numbers of 'ordinary' men in Ireland (Gill did not mention women) studied the five arguments of St Thomas Aquinas to reassure themselves that God was not a figment of the human imagination.

Gill maintained that reason by itself was inadequate as a means of ascertaining the important truths of life. It was 'wholly unscientific' of 'devotees of science' to ignore Christianity.[89] Science was in need of guidance from an external source. Gill found it disturbing that modern scientists, when addressing the subject of God, made very little reference to the teachings of Jesus Christ.[90] Furthermore, he asserted that no scientist, even as eminent as Newton or Kelvin, could ever devise 'a thoroughly satisfying theory of the universe' if he declined the opportunity to be guided by the Roman Catholic Church.[91] Thus it seemed that the only viable formula for a good relationship between Roman Catholicism and science was for scientists to surrender their intellects to the church.

Gill's views were not consistent with those of mainstream science. His scepticism of the evolution of life from non-living matter, his idea that evolution was incompatible with entropy, and his failure to understand that Einstein's theory of relativity had undermined the idea of the ether (a hypothetical medium previously deemed necessary to support the propagation of electromagnetic radiation in outer space) all indicated that well-informed scientists would not agree with what he categorised as fact or fiction.[92]

Gill's book discussed, in broad terms, the philosophy of science and how science, properly understood, was consistent and supportive of Catholic doctrine. Philosophy, in harmony with the precepts of Catholic teaching, led one inevitably to know that God existed. But Gill somewhat diminished the significance of this assertion when he placed it in the context of Catholicism as a community animated by faith. There was an inverse relationship between the strength of a religious conviction and the desire for evidence to consolidate it. In making this point, Gill may have been influenced by an article written by the American author W.A. Hauber, published in the *Ecclesiastical Review* (March 1942). Hauber wrote:

> A Catholic knows that God is everywhere, that all things are done by Him. The Christian thinker is so sure of himself on this point that, having expressed his mind, he is tempted to stop thinking. In this matter it is quite natural for him to fall into an error of excess. He is inclined to ascribe to the direct intervention of God what St Augustine long ago explained is accomplished through secondary causes.[93]

Gill observed that:

> We reason very little concerning things about which we have strong convictions, and the stronger our convictions the less do we reason about them. Where the faith of a people is intense, there is an absence of religious discussion . . . The average man speculates very little, if at all, on the facts of human life; and even educated people think but seldom concerning first principles in relation to what they see and hear around them.[94]

This intellectual apathy did not surprise or trouble Gill because he believed that the 'most important truths require no subtle proof; they are too evident to need it'. Although Gill believed that strong faith lessened the inclination to undertake an intellectual examination of religious belief, he did express some surprise that educated Catholics were not more interested in studying God 'as a branch of science'. The reason for this, he believed, was that the vast majority of people were more interested in advancing their knowledge of things amenable to sensory perception.[95]

Gill believed that the misrepresentation of science posed some danger to the faith, but he does not seem to have regarded it as a major threat. He was writing at a time when the Roman Catholic faith was above and beyond any serious threat of scepticism in the Irish Free State.[96] Faith was inculcated by indoctrination from infancy onwards. Generally, loyal Catholics received the sacraments regularly and kept their critical faculties well under control in religious matters. The power of the church was propagated and maintained through an unusually high level of control over the education system and through a vigorous system of censorship.

Those who dared to criticise the church were dismissed as cranks and disloyal misfits, and were relegated to the ranks of those who were deemed to be out of touch with the mainstream values of Irish society. In such an environment, science would not disturb the tranquility of faith, nor did it have much to contribute – scientific arguments for the existence of God were superfluous.

Gill's *Fact and Fiction in Modern Science* received words of praise from Rev. Patrick McLaughlin in the *Irish Ecclesiastical Record*. He believed that Gill's book was especially well written for educated Catholics who did not have an in-depth knowledge of science. McLaughlin also referred to O'Rahilly's *Electromagnetics* (1938), observing that it was addressed to specialist readers, but concluded that it lacked 'the persuasive touch, unfortunately'. McLaughlin focused on the epistemological difficulties in atomic physics to make the point that materialists and Marxists who placed their confidence in contemporary understandings of the nature and structure of matter were now in an unenviable position in view of the great uncertainties which had become so entrenched in the discipline.[97] In the 1930s several eminent scientists in Britain, including J.B.S. Haldane, John Desmond Bernal (1901–1971, an Irish Catholic turned atheist)[98] and Joseph Needham (1900–1995), became Marxists and believed that if the applications of science were to benefit the common good then scientists could not remain aloof from politics. There was also a strong tendency towards materialism amongst these radicals.[99] McLaughlin was critical of the connections between Marxism, materialism, and science and singled out Haldane for criticism in this context. Evidently, he took some comfort in the illusion that modern physics had reached the limits of its potential to probe the innermost workings and structure of matter. But for all its limitations, real and imaginary, McLaughlin observed that the prestige of the natural sciences was growing 'steadily, if not menacingly'. The progress of synthetic chemistry was so impressive that it now seemed possible, contrary to an old proverb, to make silk purses from sows' ears.[100]

Gill's book was also reviewed by Alfred O'Rahilly, who expressed approval of Fr Gill's 'calm and critical' analysis. It was a mark of distinction not to be 'too "popular,"' unlike, for example, Jeans and Eddington. O'Rahilly then referred to the fact that his 'severe criticism' of these two eminent scientists had been ignored. Gill was probably not pleased with O'Rahilly's assessment of his work. The professor's complimentary remarks were devalued considerably by the statement that some of the republished essays in the book were 'rather slight' and should have indicated a 'greater acquaintance with the relevant literature'. This criticism was justified. Gill's list of quoted authors after the table of contents listed only thirty-four names and there were very few footnotes throughout the text. A minor criticism of O'Rahilly's referred to Canon Henri de Dorlodot's *Darwinism and Catholic Thought*, which Gill quoted but did not criticise. O'Rahilly maintained that de Dorlodot 'should be accepted only with caution', because his interpretation of the church fathers was very much open to question and he had confused Darwinism with evolution.[101]

It is significant that two influential Irish Catholic scientists chose not to concur with the liberal-minded opinions of de Dorlodot, whose work indicated a growing tolerance, and probably a greater acceptance, of Darwinism in the universal church. Perhaps in the case of Gill it may be best understood against the background of the lapse of academic standards in the Irish province of the Society of Jesus in the early decades after political independence.[102]

In the 1940s two related developments indicated a relaxation of anti-modernist attitudes in theology and cognate disciplines. The publication of the papal encyclical *Divino Afflante Spiritu* (30 September 1943) led to a relaxation of anti-modernist strictures and gave Biblical scholars greater scope for re-interpreting scripture in the light of modern scholarship, ranging across disciplines from archaeology, textual criticism and the natural sciences.[103] The publication of this document stimulated an interest in Biblical studies, especially amongst the clergy.[104] In the early years of his pontificate Pius XII issued two other theological encyclicals which stimulated creativity in theological studies. These were *Mystici Corporis Christi* (29 June 1943) and *Mediator Dei* (20 November 1947). The three encyclicals collectively exerted a liberating effect on Catholic theology[105] – contributing greatly to the emergence of a 'new theology' (*nouvelle théologie*), which was particularly strong in France. But the new theology does not seem to have made any significant impact on Irish Catholic thought.

In the May 1944 issue of the *Irish Ecclesiastical Record* Rev. John O'Flynn, Professor of Scripture at Maynooth, quoted extensively from *Divino Afflante Spiritu* to urge the restraint of those who exercised 'intemperate zeal' in defending orthodoxy because they imagined that 'whatever is new should for that very reason be opposed or suspected'.[106] This was probably more than a subtle protest against reactionaries whose censorious attitudes had stifled creative thinking in the church.

Postwar Pessimism

The Second World War alerted public opinion in many countries to the fact that science could be used for good or for evil. The atomic bombing of Hiroshima and Nagasaki in August 1945 demonstrated the incredibly destructive potential of scientific knowledge when misused. In Ireland, Liam Brophy, a contributor to the *Irish Ecclesiastical Record* and the *Irish Monthly*, wallowed in nostalgia for medieval European society and issued dire prognostications with great intensity. Modern science was not presented in a favourable light. Brophy was convinced that the golden age of European civilisation extended from the rise of Christianity to the Reformation. It was then generally believed that man was part of a cosmic plan devised by an omniscient deity. Pre-Reformation man was at peace with himself – 'the cries of futility and utter pessimism which sweep through modern literature were unknown because even the meanest serf knew and believed that his life had purpose and meaning.' He knew that 'he had a place in the social and political scheme of things and in the vaster plan of the cosmos'.[107] What more could 'theological' man desire? Post-Reformation rationalism challenged this anthropocentric view. The 'hideous doctrine' of Darwinism presented humanity as a product of blind chance, nothing more than an intelligent animal. Humanity was deprived of its divine destiny. Brophy, paraphrasing Sigmund Freud, declared

> . . . while Newton banished God from nature and Darwin banished Him from life, Freud drove Him from His last fastness, the human soul. And now modern man finds himself stripped and lonely . . . robbed of his God and of his own soul.[108]

Protestantism and humanism were blamed for giving rise to a number of ideologies, such as empiricism, idealism, utilitarianism and positivism, which threatened to bar modern man from heaven. A dismal portrayal of this unhappy creature, inspired by Hermann Hesse's *Der Steppenwolf* (1927), was presented to the reader. Modern man was 'roving restlessly hither and thither in the endless and loveless desert that is Western civilisation, and hideously crying out his hunger and thirst for Eternity'.[109] More desolate thoughts were gleaned from Bertrand Russell's *Free Man's Worship*, which had been first published in the *Independent Review* in December 1903. Russell was quoted at length.

> . . . Man is the product of causes which had no prevision of the end they were achieving; that his origin, his growth, his hopes and fears,

his loves and his beliefs, are but the outcome of accidental collocations of atoms; that no fire, no heroism, no intensity of thought and feeling, can preserve an individual life beyond the grave; that all the labours of the ages . . . are destined to extinction in the vast death of the solar system . . . and that the whole temple of Man's achievement must inevitably be buried beneath the debris of a universe in ruins . . .[110]

Brophy triumphantly declared that the utopian aspirations of H.G. Wells had been swept away by two world wars. In *The Fate of Homo Sapiens*, Wells had lapsed into a mood of depression, especially in the concluding chapter.[111] Brophy was evidently pleased about this – his faith in Roman Catholicism was vindicated. Only a return to the Age of Faith, rather than misplaced reliance on science, could save man from his self-destructive proclivities.

Brophy fulminated against the philosophies of the Enlightenment, especially that of René Descartes (1596–1650) and Auguste Comte (1798–1857). In the *Irish Monthly* he wrote that there was a tendency amongst modern humanists to view science as a substitute for religion. Communist ideology, and that sector of Protestantism under the spell of modernism, also both featured prominently in the new humanism. Brophy believed that Marxism would not endure – pointing out that it was based on materialism. But materialism was based on determinism which had been undermined by the new physics – specifically by the principle of indeterminacy. He reserved most of his criticism for H.G. Wells, who had renewed his attack on Roman Catholicism in his *Crux Ansata* (1943).[112] In this book, Wells expressed extreme and irrational views about the papacy and about Roman Catholicism generally, much of which was irrelevant to science; it was little more than a reiteration of anti-Catholic opinions from militant Protestants and freethinkers.[113]

The intemperate language of Wells was equalled by the extreme opinions of Brophy who, facilitated by the Jesuit periodical the *Irish Monthly*, continued to see science more as a threat than a blessing. His article 'Will Men Be like Gears?' was very much inspired by Samuel Butler's sharp criticism of Darwin and proponents of Darwinism. Brophy emphasised the deleterious effects of science. Men had become so enslaved to machines that their creative thinking was greatly reduced, much to the detriment of art and literature. Humans were becoming increasingly dependent on machines to such an extent that their intellectual independence was being compromised.[114] In a further article about the blessings and evils of science, also published in the *Irish Monthly*, Brophy maintained that the limited blessings of science were outweighed by its 'giant evils'. The 'acids of modernity, secreted by science' had inflicted harm on the souls of millions. Scientific materialism had eroded faith, the use of atomic bombs had destroyed the notion that scientific progress would give rise to a new paradise, and the many labour-saving applications of science generated massive unemployment. [115] All this represented an extremely unbalanced and hostile attitude towards science. Furthermore, Brophy failed to distinguish between science *per se* and the misuse of science – which was something very different.

Brophy's claim that scientific theories had proved detrimental to the religious faith of millions may have been confirmed in the minds of some of his readers by the irreligious opinions of Bertrand Russell. Russell spoke about 'The Faith of a Rationalist' on a BBC Home Service broadcast on 20 May 1947. The text of this radio talk was published in *The Listener* on 29 May. Russell admired two qualities in particular – kindness and veracity. Kindness was conducive to happiness. There was no need for a supernatural order. Russell disagreed with the contention that some beliefs, which were comforting and deemed to be morally beneficial, should not be critically examined. He rejected such a stance, arguing that no sound morality could be sustained on the basis of evasion. Happiness which was dependent on beliefs maintained only because of their pleasantness was not deserving of commendation. Russell quoted the English philosopher John Locke (1632–1704) to make the point that the best way of pursuing truth was not to accept any proposition with greater confidence than the 'proofs' upon which it was based would allow. But absolute proof was not attainable. Therefore, it was necessary to settle for the next best position – proof based on sensory perception and the principles of logic and mathematics. If proofs could not be ascertained on this basis then intellectual integrity demanded a confession of ignorance.

Near the end of his radio talk Russell spoke about the human soul and the question of whether or not it survived after death. In answering this question Russell regarded mind and soul as synonymous. He observed that the mind developed like the body, was affected by diseases and drugs, and was intimately associated with the functioning of the brain. There was no scientific reason for assuming that the soul, or mind, acquired an independence of the brain after death which it did not have before death. This was not presented as a conclusive argument but Russell argued that, aside from the 'slender evidence' provided by 'psychical research', there were no grounds for believing in the immortality of the human soul.

The relative insignificance of the Earth in astronomical terms, and the ephemeral existence of humankind, strongly indicated to Russell the absence of an omnipotent creator. It was difficult for him to accept that a creator would require so vast a scheme for such a small and 'transitory' result. But he did not claim to know – with certainty – that God did not exist. He acknowledged that his knowledge was too limited to sustain such an assertion. However, he stated with confidence that the knowledge of his fellow humans was also insufficient to reach a reliable conclusion.[116]

Russell's contention that there was no scientific basis for believing in the existence of a supernatural order was particularly irritating to Garrett FitzGerald – probably the same Garret FitzGerald (1926–2011) who became leader of Fine Gael in 1977 and served as Taoiseach in the 1980s. FitzGerald, writing in the *Irish Monthly*, maintained that some decisions in life would have to be taken against either a belief or disbelief in life after death. Individuals could not postpone these decisions indefinitely. But FitzGerald failed to address the substantive issue of evidence raised by Russell. It was as if an arbitrary decision, taken without due regard for weighing the evidence, was somehow automatically better than no decision. Furthermore, FitzGerald missed the point that Russell's advocacy of kindness and veracity were two fundamental guiding principles which were, arguably, adequate to the task of determining how people should live their lives.

FitzGerald conveniently sidestepped the difficulty of discussing the 'reasonableness of the claims of religion' when asserting the 'unreasonableness' of Russell's philosophy. When Russell expressed the opinion that no one, including himself, knew whether or not there was divine purpose in the universe, FitzGerald denounced the statement as if it was an intolerant prohibitive dogma, failing to discern what was an expression of honest opinion (albeit vigorously presented) based on an extensive knowledge and understanding of philosophy and science. FitzGerald then accused Russell of bigotry, of failing to live up to his own rational principles, and of callously 'destroying common men's beliefs'.[117]

In 1947 and 1948 the *Irish Monthly* presented its readership with a harsh assessment of the natural sciences in terms of their alleged adverse impact on the material, intellectual and spiritual welfare of humankind. Scepticism and criticism of evolutionary theory was still prevalent amongst Catholic authors in Ireland. From March to October 1948 the

Irish Monthly facilitated the anti-evolutionary opinions of Geoffrey Taylor, a biologist with a special interest in entomology. Taylor's series of five articles in the *Irish Monthly* were based on broadcasted talks from Radio Éireann in January, April and May 1948. In his first talk Taylor associated 'evolutionism' with communism, describing the two as the 'great secular faiths' of modern times. In view of the antipathy towards communism in Ireland, this claim could only have been calculated to appeal to those Catholics whose opinions might otherwise drift towards the evolutionary worldview. Taylor dismissed biological evolution as a very plausible and elegant theory, but one which lacked evidence. However, there was still that uncomfortable fact that had to be explained away – the overwhelming support amongst professional scientists for evolutionary theory since the late nineteenth century. Taylor's explanation was that evolution, as proposed by Charles Darwin, was highly plausible. The initial success was also due to theoretical affinities between notions of progress, nineteenth-century materialism, and the competitive nature of capitalism. Taylor not only rejected Darwinism but evolution in general.[118]

From Taylor's perspective it seemed that scientists were rather dim-witted, failing to discern the strong evidence against evolution, failing to appreciate how weak the theory really was, and filling in the many deficiencies of data with broad assumptions. The fossil record indicated against evolution. There were so many gaps, and these were so large, that the evidence of the rocks supported the idea of creation rather than evolution. How then did scientists sustain their 'evolutionary faith'? Taylor declared that he did not know. John Milton's *Paradise Lost* and the book of Genesis appealed more to his imagination and sense of reason than evolutionary theory.[119] After rejecting evolution Taylor was asked what evidence did he have in support of Creation. His response was that evolution was eliminated from consideration and therefore he was not obligated to put forward positive evidence in favour of Creation, since there seemed to be no other alternative. Nevertheless, he referred to the argument from design. This was the fifth of St Thomas Aquinas's arguments for the existence of God, but Taylor was more familiar with William Paley's version of the design argument. In his *Natural Theology* (1802), Paley claimed that there was abundant evidence of intelligent design in nature, thus providing sound evidence for the existence of an omniscient Designer. However, Charles Darwin, who had studied Paley's treatise, claimed that natural selection, working in conjunction with genetic variation, could account for the appearance of design in nature.

Taylor chose Paley over Darwin, declaring himself to be an 'unreserved and wholehearted Paleyite'.[120]

In his final radio lecture Taylor maintained that there was 'a slight but perceptible movement away from the prevailing evolutionary faith: a growing scepticism of the Darwinian doctrine . . .' The merit of such an emerging trend was a movement away from materialism towards the acceptance of Creation. Taylor did not argue that Darwinism was in an advanced state of terminal illness but his reading of three recently published books gave him hope that an anti-evolutionary trend would gather momentum. The 'lightest' of the three volumes was *Butterfly Marvels and Mysteries* by Bernard Ackworth. The second book was *Is Evolution Proved?*, edited by Arnold Lunn and mainly comprised of a series of letters exchanged between H.S. Shelton, a supporter of evolutionary theory, and Douglas Dewar, an opponent of the theory. The third book, *Wonders of Nature* by E.L. Grant Watson, was presented as the best of the three volumes.[121] None of the figures referred to by Taylor were eminent in the life sciences. Ackworth was a retired British naval officer and an expert on submarine navigation. Lunn, an opponent of Darwinism, became a member of the Roman Catholic Church in 1933 and wrote in defence of his church. He trained as a lawyer and was a highly accomplished Alpine skier. Dewar had published extensively on ornithology while working in the Indian Civil Service, and was president of the Evolution Protest Movement founded in London in 1935. Watson had served as a tutor in biology at Cambridge.

Taylor was out of touch with developments in science. Darwinism was revised and gaining strength in the biological sciences. But it is highly probable that Taylor, disseminating his views over Radio Éireann and through the medium of the *Irish Monthly*, influenced many Catholic listeners and readers to believe that evolution was becoming increasingly untenable amongst professional scientists. Furthermore, by associating evolution with the twin evils of communism and materialism, he appealed to a prejudicial tendency which would evaluate evolutionary theory on grounds which were religious and political rather than scientific.

The concept of evolution was of central importance to the biological sciences. There was no realistic prospect of biologists discarding it because of unresolved difficulties such as those arising from the many imperfections of the fossil record. There was simply no scientific alternative to evolution. Tension between Roman Catholicism and science would continue to exist for as long as influential Roman Catholics expressed scepticism about the theory. If biology was seen as a source of discord between traditionalist Roman Catholicism and modern science, then it was relatively easy to see physics as a source of harmony – although physics was not without problems from a theological perspective.

From Discord to Harmony

In 1943 Henry V. Gill derived some satisfaction from the observation that James Hopwood Jeans and Arthur Stanley Eddington had taken cognisance of God in their philosophy of science. In his *New Pathways in Science* Eddington made the point that God could not be understood in terms of physics or mathematics. Free will or the supernatural could not be deduced from physics. A God deduced from science could be swept away when one scientific theory replaced another. Eddington's objective was to show that free will and the supernatural were still plausible when considered in the light of modern physics.[122] Gill did not express disagreement with Eddington on this point. Nevertheless, he asserted that the God sometimes upheld by physicists was not the God of Christianity. Gill was convinced that readers who lacked philosophical and scientific expertise would be confused about free will, determinism, and God's action in nature. All of these were of central importance to Christian doctrine. Therefore, Gill argued that these subjects should not receive attention in books intended for the popular market unless 'adequately' addressed.[123]

The interrelationship between free will and atomic physics continued to receive attention in the late 1940s. Rev. T. Crowley quoted Eddington's *The Nature of the Physical World* (1928) as follows: 'a particle may have position or it may have velocity but it cannot in any exact sense have both.'[124] Crowley believed that this could lead to ridiculous conclusions. An individual particle would be in a number of different positions at the same time and its motion would be at a number of different speeds at a given instant if Heisenberg was interpreted objectively. Objective indeterminacy was logically untenable.[125]

Crowley observed that a single cause did not always give the same effect. Other causes gave rise to irregularities in nature. The appropriate course of action was to search for these other causes. If this proved unsuccessful it did not indicate real indeterminacy but a failure in research.[126] Individual particles had 'a fixed mode of action' but scientists did not understand it. Thus, they had to settle for statistical averages and probability equations.[127]

Crowley observed that there was a resistance among physicists to the abandonment of causality in sub-atomic physics. There was considerable merit in this observation. Einstein had reaffirmed his belief in a universe subject to causal mechanisms. It was the purpose of science to discover and elaborate on these causes. Einstein was convinced that if more was known about the laws regulating sub-atomic particles, then a causal thesis of their behaviour could be constructed without being undermined by the very process of observation.[128]

Crowley reiterated a number of points which had already been made by Gill. The suggestion of a connection between indeterminacy and free will was due to confused thinking. And what was the source of this confusion? Crowley pointed to a lack of sound philosophical training, which in this instance was the scholastic philosophy endorsed by the Roman Catholic Church. Physicists failed to understand the methods and competencies of science. There was a tendency by a number of physicists to expand their disciplinary domain, to 'explain all things by the concepts of physical science'.[129] This led to conclusions which were illogical.

A dire consequence of linking free will to physics was that it created problems for upholding the concept of free will, which in turn had grave implications for moral philosophy and human freedom. The remedy, from a Catholic perspective, was to elevate mind above matter. Theoretical physics could not undermine, or support, belief in a freedom which was based on something which was 'immaterial'.[130]

Science had nothing to say about the 'immaterial' world, salvation or heaven – but it had much to say about the heavens. Its telescopes had penetrated far. The panorama of the night sky was potentially devastating to human aspirations. Michael Connolly (S.J.) observed that Copernicus had delivered the first blow. The earth was just another satellite orbiting the sun. The sun, although special to mankind, was just one among thousands of stars. And the status of mankind in the cosmos was to shrink much further. William Herschel (1738–1822) and John Herschel (1792–1871) – father and son – had surveyed far beyond the solar system, charting the positions of millions of stars. Any apprehension arising from an awareness of the spatial insignificance of mankind was likely to be intensified by geologists and palaeontologists as they extended the age of the Earth from a few thousand to 'millions of millions' of years.[131] Science had humbled mankind but Catholic philosophy would restore him to his former glory. Connolly understood that mainstream science supported the contention that the universe did not always exist. The only logical explanation of its origin was a First Cause – 'a Being Who is Himself uncaused, Who is His own supremely sufficient explanation and the ultimate explanation of everything else as well'. That being was called God.[132]

Science was relegated in the hierarchy of knowledge. Connolly asserted that philosophy, not science, revealed God to mankind. Scientists had failed to discern purpose in the universe. As Connolly set about elevating humankind to the pinnacle of creation, he conflated Catholic philosophy and theology. Although the universe was vast in terms of space and time, it was dying. Man, endowed with an immortal soul, would outlive it. The immensity of the universe testified to the immensity of God – a God who cared so deeply about mankind that the incarnate Word (or Son of God) had died for man's redemption. The Incarnation was 'far more astonishing' to Connolly than a galaxy measuring thousands of light years in diameter.[133]

Theoretical physics seemed increasingly supportive of theology, especially in the field of cosmology. The Belgian Catholic priest and cosmologist Georges Henri Lemaître (1894–1966) was a major contributor to the Big Bang thesis, which was worked out mainly by the Russian nuclear physicist George Gamow (1904–1968) in the late 1940s. According to this thesis the universe originated from a volume of matter at an incredibly high density and temperature at some moment in the finite past, exploding outwards to initiate cosmic expansion. From this it seemed that the universe began at a particular moment in time – something which was highly consistent with the doctrine of creation.

Sir Edmund Whittaker welcomed the theory of an expanding universe as very strongly supportive of what he understood to be St Thomas Aquinas's thesis that the demonstration of a finitely old universe was a very strong argument for God's existence.[134] Whittaker was a convert to Roman Catholicism and had entered the church in 1930. In June 1946 he delivered the Donnellan Lectures at Trinity College Dublin. His lectures were later published under the title of *Space and Spirit: Theories of the Universe and the Arguments for the Existence of God* (1946). Aodh de Blacam, writing in the *Irish Monthly*, expressed approval of Whittaker's lecture and declared *Space and Spirit* the 'most remarkable' book of his time. But de Blacam was concerned not to overrate Whittaker's book. The scholastic philosophy of St Thomas did not require confirmation from physicists, astronomers or mathematicians. Nevertheless, it was 'interesting and instructive' to see scientists following in the footsteps of Catholic philosophers. Whittaker had found St Thomas's arguments for the existence of God supported by the discoveries of science. The universe was of finite age; therefore, creation was 'an ascertained fact'; therefore, God existed.[135] There was some degree of optimism that scholastic philosophy, modern science and theology could be reintegrated.[136] This seemed all the more feasible in view of the perceived new awareness amongst scientists of the limited competencies of their discipline. Scientific theories were permeated by subjectivity, abstractions and uncertainties, and did not reveal the underlying nature of physical objects. Scientific experience could not claim primacy over religious, ethical and aesthetic forms of experience.[137]

Patrick McLaughlin, who was to become vice-president of St Patrick's College, Maynooth in 1951, acknowledged Edmund Whittaker as a first-class scientist in international terms and observed that he was a former Astronomer Royal of Ireland. Whittaker claimed, in opposition to conservative metaphysicians and theologians, that St Thomas's proofs were not purely metaphysical arguments, and were not completely independent of the natural sciences. The traditionalist stance against Whittaker saw St Thomas's arguments as immune to attack from any scientific findings if they were regarded as essentially metaphysical.[138] From a cautious and conservative theological point of view, there was little to be gained from associating physics with metaphysics. Physics was changing and unreliable. This was especially clear since the overthrow of the primacy of Newtonian physics.

From the viewpoint of natural theology the consonance between physics and the idea of Creation was important.[139] And yet it seemed to be overrated. Whittaker had thought far more in terms of physics than in metaphysics. Catholic philosophers were very unlikely to take Whittaker's observations and conclusions as an accurate exposition of St Thomas's metaphysical proofs and, therefore, unlikely to regard the points made by Whittaker as 'substantial additions' to St Thomas's arguments.[140] Isolation was the best policy, especially when the proposed bridge building was to be done by scientists. Even when science was friendly towards theology, it was still seen as potentially dangerous.

Science was also seen as dangerous in an earthly as distinct from a spiritual sense. T.S. Wheeler, Professor of Chemistry at University College Dublin, observed that science was now, apparently, out of control. The role of scientists was to discover. They were not in control of how their discoveries would be applied. The use of atomic weapons by the United States against Japan had indicated forcefully that science was likely to be used far more for destructive purposes than for enhancing the quality of life. In his concluding statements Wheeler raised the question of whether or not humankind would be better off if science had not been so energetically pursued.[141]

McLaughlin, writing in the March 1950 issue of *Studies*, expressed the view that the natural sciences seemed to command enormous influence and respect, in England and throughout much of Western Europe, out-shining both theology and philosophy in popular opinion. Scientists were widely regarded as 'prophets and oracles'. It is significant that MacLaughlin did not mention Ireland in this context. The prestige of science, he believed, was due to the success of its many applications rather than from the intellectual insights it offered. Science could never establish its own philosophical foundations. Therefore it was ultimately dependent on philosophy – which in this context meant Catholic philos-ophy – if it was to serve the best interests of humankind. Science could be 'integrated into the good life' if it was seen as only one of a number of approaches to exploring 'truth'. It was unable to address the moral and metaphysical issues which were of paramount importance.

McLaughlin believed that in recent decades there had been a resur-gence of Catholic participation in the natural sciences and especially in attempts to 'initiate a new synthesis of knowledge'. He pointed to the Pontifical Academy of Sciences in Italy. In France there were many out-standing contributions by Catholics, not only to the natural sciences but also to the history and philosophy of science, especially in the works of Pierre Duhem (1861–1916). Eminent Catholic scientists included the French physicist, Louis de Broglie (1892–1987), and Georges Lemaître. In England the contribution of Catholics to science was 'considerable'. MacLaughlin's list of names included those of two eminent scientists who had converted to Roman Catholicism in the 1930s and 1940s – Edmund Whittaker and F. Sherwood Taylor and some lesser-known figures such as J.K. Heydon and E.F. Caldin. He claimed that Ireland had also made 'worthwhile' contributions and in support of this he referred to Alfred O'Rahilly's *Electromagnetics* and Henry V. Gill's *Fact and Fiction in Modern Science*.[142] In this context MacLaughlin exaggerated the Irish Catholic contribution to science. O'Rahilly's work was of some value. Gill's volume, despite its 'big sales' in America, contributed nothing of significance to science.[143] In terms of scientific status, based on the quan-tity and quality of their output, O'Rahilly, and especially Gill, were nowhere near de Broglie, Lemaître or Whittaker.

One important aspect of the synthesis of knowledge referred to by MacLaughlin was the influence of modern cosmological theories on the doctrine of creation and arguments for God's existence. Although the Big Bang resonated well with the idea of an omnipotent and omniscient Creator, theologians were too distrustful of science to wholeheartedly embrace it. In the domain of cosmology they were justified to some extent. The Big Bang was not then on a sound theoretical footing and was challenged by the Cambridge professor Fred Hoyle and his colleagues Hermann Bondi and Thomas Gold. They proposed the Steady State model, which challenged the idea of creation associated with the Big Bang. However, this model did not seem consistent with the observations of Edwin Hubble's observations that galaxies were moving further and further apart – i.e. that the universe was expanding. To overcome this objection, Steady State theorists argued that just enough matter is continuously created to fill the extra space arising from the continuous expansion. Therefore, the appearance of the heavens would have remained constant throughout time. Determined to avoid a single creation event, with all its religious implications, Steady State theorists effectively proposed an infinite series of minuscule creation events to maintain an unchanging universe.

Hoyle expounded his views at length in *The Nature of the Universe* (1950). His book was reviewed by Richard E. Ingram, the Director of the Seismological Observatory at Rathfarnham Castle in Dublin. Hoyle's contention that matter simply emerged from nothing did not seem rational. Ingram observed that this aspect of the Steady State thesis could be accepted by Catholics because it was compatible with that article of faith which stated that God created the universe out of nothing. Hoyle, in refusing to admit the existence of a Creator, was unable to explain the source of the continuous emergence of matter.[144] It was, therefore, easy for Catholics to baptise the Steady State. If they chose to reject it, then the Big Bang seemed even more consonant with the doctrine of creation.[145] However, it was easy to exaggerate the significance of the Big Bang in the service of theology. Pope Pius XII, in his discourse to the Pontifical Academy of Sciences on 22 November 1951, had overstated the Big Bang as evidence for God's act of creation. It seems that, in 1952, Georges Lemaître influenced the pope to refrain from drawing theological conclusions from the 'primeval atom' and Big Bang hypotheses.[146]

Physics and cosmology were seen as of limited value to Catholic apologetics but at least the theological implications of theoretical developments in these major branches of science could be easily regarded as innocuous. The same could not be said for biology, where the theory of evolution was of central importance. There was a pressing need for the teaching authority of the church to clarify its position. Irish Catholics, generally, would humbly submit to whatever Rome pronounced on the issue.

8. Between Science and Dogma, 1950–mid-1970s

Humani Generis

The early years of Pope Pius XII's pontificate were characterised by innovative and progressive reforms. Pius had a deep interest in science and technology and endeavoured, more than any of his predecessors, to harmonise Catholic faith with new scientific and technological perspectives.[1] His encyclicals, allocutions and other pronouncements encouraged innovative thinking in Catholic theology. But Pius was by nature deeply conservative and in the late 1940s he became increasingly concerned about where the new theological trends might lead.[2] On 12 August 1950 he issued *Humani Generis*. The encyclical explicitly addressed the issue of evolution – this was unprecedented. Pius observed that evolution was not 'fully proved even in the domain of natural sciences'. Furthermore, he believed that evolutionary theory was used by communists to undermine belief in God so that they could more effectively gain support for their ideology of dialectical materialism. Evolution was associated with a range of unorthodox ideas, including monism, pantheism and existentialism.[3]

Pius maintained that some Catholic teachers were in danger of overstepping the mark in trying to reconcile theology and science, and were likely to lead others astray.[4] The pre-eminence of Thomism in Catholic philosophical studies was reaffirmed.[5] Some Catholic authors had expressed opinions which contradicted the doctrine of Original Sin.[6] This latter point was of central importance in determining the papal attitude towards evolution. Pius expressed his awareness of demands by many Catholics that theology should be revised 'as much as possible' to achieve harmony with the latest discoveries of science. Their stance was deemed commendable in the case of 'clearly proved facts' but evolution was in the realm of 'conjectural opinions'.[7] No concessions would be given to such opinions when they, directly or indirectly, contradicted revelation.

In paragraph 36 of the encyclical Pope Pius XII seemed to recognise the general theory of evolution as scientifically valid when he stated that the teaching authority of the church did not forbid research and dialogue about 'the doctrine of Evolution' amongst men who were professionally qualified in both theology and science. This liberty of discussion extended to the evolution of humans. But the pope sought to impose two conditions. Firstly, the immortal soul was to be excluded from the evolutionary scheme because it was held to be created directly and immediately by God. Secondly, it was not permissible to assume that evolution of the human body had certainly occurred 'as if there were nothing in the sources of Divine Revelation which demands the greatest moderation and caution in this'.

In paragraph 37, the thorny issue of polygenism was addressed. Before proceeding further it is necessary to examine what was meant by polygenism and monogenism. Conflicting opinions about human origins had emerged from anthropological discourse in the mid-nineteenth century against the background of slavery, British colonial expansion, and controversies about whether or not the various races of humanity were equal or not. Could the variety of human races all be seen as members of the same species, descended from a common ancestral stock (monogenism)? Or were the races different human species, descended from different ancestors (polygenism)?[8] Religious beliefs and anthropological ideas were frequently intertwined. Some Christians believed that all humans were descendants of Adam and Eve. A contrary idea was that the various races of humans were created separately, and that only the whites had descended from Adam and Eve. This latter idea was favoured by racially inspired anthropologists in the mid-nineteenth century.[9] There was a strong tendency amongst Roman Catholics to reject polygenism because it was seen as incompatible with the church's teachings on Original Sin and redemption.[10]

There were differences of opinion about the precise meanings of monogenism and polygenism. A Roman Catholic understanding of monogenism and polygenism, in the mid-twentieth century, will be given here with reference to Martin Brennan's essay 'Adam and the Biological Sciences', published in the *Irish Theological Quarterly* (April 1968). The Jesuit author used the term 'monophyletic' to mean human descent from a single animal population. 'Polyphyletic' meant human descent from more than one population, which was rejected in Catholic theology and not generally accepted in science. 'Monogenist' was understood as human descent from one couple. Brennan regarded it as erroneous to use 'monogenist' to indicate human descent from a single population. He acknowledged that evolutionary biologists thought in terms of population genetics – therefore science was 'polygenist'. He then stated that contemporary scientific thinking and *Humani Generis* were both monophyletic. However, science was polygenist, in contrast to *Humani Generis*, which was seen as monogenist.[11]

In *Humani Generis* the liberty of discussion granted for evolutionary theory in general would not be extended to polygenism. In the biological sciences, as indicated above, it was generally accepted that humankind originated from a population of hominoids, not from one hominoid couple such as Adam and Eve. But Pius XII declared that it was not permissible for loyal Catholics to believe that some men were not descended from Adam, and that Adam represented 'a certain number of first parents'. He reiterated the doctrine of Original Sin which stated that this sin was 'actually committed by an individual Adam and which through generation is passed on to all and is in everyone as his own'.[12] Therefore, 'it was in no way apparent' how the prevailing scientific theory of evolution, extended to humankind and based on population genetics, could be reconciled with Catholic doctrine.

An encyclical did not command assent on the strength of papal infallibility or dogma. Nevertheless, Pius maintained that once a pope passes judgement on an issue then it could no longer be regarded as a matter open to debate among theologians.[13] This prohibitive assertion was a formidable obstacle to any theologian who wished to move beyond the stifling confines of traditionalist thinking.

When Pope Pius XII was condemning a broad range of heterodox ideas he did not mention the names of those whom he had in mind. But there were widespread opinions in theological circles that liberal French theologians were his main target, although the ideas that were condemned also circulated in other countries, including Germany, Belgium, England, Italy and Spain.[14] A range of disciplinary measures were imposed against a number of theologians. Some were forbidden to teach or to publish. Action was taken against the French Dominicans Yves Congar and Marie-Dominique Chenu, and the Jesuits Henri de Lubac, Karl Rahner, Pierre Teilhard de Chardin (1881–1955), Jean Daniélou and John Courtney Murray. Censorship was imposed on Teilhard de Chardin – priest and palaeontologist – from the mid-1920s until his death in 1955 because his views on evolution and Original Sin had given rise to concerns about heterodoxy.[15] However, the campaign against heterodoxy did not reach anywhere near the same level of intensity as the campaign against modernism initiated during the pontificate of Pius X. There were two reasons for this. Firstly, Pius XII was not as reactionary as Pius X and kept the extreme elements of the curia in check.[16] Secondly, those theologians who were subjected to disciplinary measures had not constructed their ideas in clear violation of Catholic dogma and they had submitted to the authority of the papacy. It would not have been prudent of the Vatican to have accused them of heresy.[17] Nevertheless, *Humani Generis* raised fears that the excesses of anti-modernism would be revived. An extensive survey of commentaries about *Humani Generis* by the Jesuit author Gustave Weigel revealed a remarkably high level of concurrence with the encyclical.[18]

The Irish Catholic response to *Humani Generis* was cautious, and submissive, and was not rushed. Rev. Patrick J. Hamell of Maynooth, writing in the *Irish Ecclesiastical Record*, observed that Pope Pius XII had expressed dissatisfaction with new theological trends as far back as 1946 when he addressed an assembly of Jesuits in Rome. The pope's disapproval was clear when he stated that the 'new theology' was 'in a constant process of evolution, is supposed to be ever evolving, ever advancing, never reaching its term'.[19] The pope was worried that an evolutionary mindset, influenced by developments in the natural sciences, would become so strongly established in theology that dogmas and the unity of the faith would be undermined. Hamell's article, the only identifiable Irish Catholic contribution listed in Weigel's survey, was little more than an uncritical exposition of *Humani Generis*.

The main Irish Catholic response to *Humani Generis* was in the *Irish Theological Quarterly*. Rev. T. Crowley declared that the encyclical could not be regarded as unsympathetic to the modern age or to the notion of progress. Nevertheless, he indicated more than a hint of suppressed dissatisfaction when he discussed, at some length, frequent complaints that scholastic philosophy was grossly inadequate to the task of meeting the needs of contemporary scholarship, and, in the concluding paragraph of his article, stated that there were limits to the adaptability of scholasticism to modern intellectual trends. However, he was careful to make the point that he was not advocating the abandonment of scholasticism.[20]

Professor Gerard Mitchell of Maynooth observed that there was little awareness in Ireland of theological controversies in mainland Europe.[21] Mitchell regarded *Humani Generis* as a 'paternal warning' rather than a severe condemnation of new ideas.[22] But he also expressed his awareness of the difficulties and mitigating circumstances of those who had found themselves in trouble with the church authorities. There were concerns that theology had failed to keep up to date with the sciences and that there was a pressing need for revisions in theology.[23] Many Catholics were finding it 'increasingly difficult' to accept their church's teachings about human origins, especially in countries where evolutionary theory was taught as a 'scientific certainty' in the school system. They were worried about what seemed to be a conflict between Catholicism and the substantiated findings of science. They feared that the church was clinging to a position that was no longer tenable. Mitchell seems to have had some sympathy for their views but his outlook was primarily influenced by caution and obedience to ecclesiastical authority. The concerns of those Catholics who sought a greater measure of harmony between theology and science were judged to have arisen on the basis of a fundamental lack of understanding. The church did not feel under obligation to revise its theology for the purpose of reconciling it with the conjectures of science.[24]

In a later article Mitchell focused his attention on evolution and on the narrower but critical issue of polygenism. He observed that some writers in the popular press and in a number of non-scientific journals had harshly criticised the encyclical and had cited it in support of the contention that the church was hostile to the progress of science. Camille Muller, a professor of science at the University of Louvain, had written in his *L'Encyclique 'Humani Generis' et les Problèmes Scientifiques* (1951) that he had noticed among his 'more thoughtful Catholic brethren a certain feeling of embarrassment' arising from an anticipated negative reaction to the encyclical by non-Catholics who were otherwise well disposed towards the church. Although Muller stated his acceptance of the encyclical, he urged that the achievements and claims of scientists should receive due acknowledgement.[25]

Mitchell conceded that theologians were not competent to evaluate the merits of scientific arguments for evolution. To dismiss evolution as a mere thesis, as if there were serious doubts in mainstream science that it had occurred, was to misunderstand the position of the scientific profession on the matter. Mitchell referred to Muller's criticism of the encyclical in which it was suggested that the teaching authority of the church had not taken due cognisance of the attitude of 'certainty' by scientists towards evolution. And that 'certainty' seemed to extend to the evolution of humans. If the pope and his advisors had fully appreciated the scientific consensus for evolution then they would not have thought it necessary to urge a cautious attitude about its acceptance. Mitchell argued that such a criticism was not justified, maintaining that *Humani Generis* did not consider the 'problem' of evolution from a scientific perspective, nor did it pass judgement on the 'certainty' of evolution on a scientific basis. The encyclical was not addressed to scientists. It was issued as a directive for the benefit of 'ordinary people' so that distinctions could be made between evolution strictly as a scientific theory, and evolution with philosophical appendages which attempted 'to offer an ultimate explanation for all reality'.[26] Mitchell's moderate criticism of Muller seemed rather weak in view of paragraphs 5, and 35 to 37 of the encyclical, where it did seem that evolution, strictly as a scientific theory, was being called into question.

Mitchell relied heavily on Muller's work to convey his own views about *Humani Generis*, interpreting the encyclical to promote the maximum flexibility in harmonising science and theology while at the same time refraining from using intemperate language to criticise those who experienced difficulties in presenting their opinions in strict conformity with the heavy demands of Rome.

It was clearly not reasonable to see evolution and Genesis in complete isolation from each other. Scientists could pursue their research without concern for Catholic theology and the integrity of the scriptural narratives. They clearly had a professional right, and a professional duty, to do so. But theologians were not so fortunate. They could not ignore the implications of findings external to their own discipline and still maintain intellectual credibility. They were pressed by modern science to revise their ideas but were greatly restricted by the ecclesiastical authorities in doing so. Rev. John O'Flynn, who was appointed Professor of Scripture at Maynooth in 1932, pointed out that the teaching authority of the church was the supreme authority in determining the interpretation and meaning of scripture. The Bible was not to be treated in the same way as ordinary secular literature. Its divine authorship had to be recognised, which meant that it was to be regarded as infallible. It was to be studied 'with the eyes of Faith' – not in a purely rational way based on the methods of philology and literary-historical criticism.[27] In a second article on the subject O'Flynn maintained that *Humani Generis* was 'not purely negative in character' and was 'a magnificent defence of the claims of rational biblical exegesis'.[28] The opinions of O'Flynn and Mitchell are highly significant. As professors at Ireland's leading seminary, they were well placed to profoundly influence the intellectual formation of many priests.

A flexibility of theological thinking was required if a genuine attempt was to be made to overcome the persistent incompatibility between evolution and the doctrine of Original Sin. Catholic doctrine, as promulgated from Rome, did not permit the necessary latitude in thinking which was necessary for such a breakthrough. Irish Catholic apologists, like so many of their counterparts in the universal church, were probably so in awe of the authoritative weight of *Humani Generis* that they persuaded themselves that their opinions were the same as the pope's.[29] Thus, in the early 1950s they did little more than faithfully reiterate the restrictive conservatism enunciated by Pius XII.

Piety and Science

Humani Generis was unnecessarily restrictive on Catholic theologians and biblical scholars but it was not gratuitously offensive towards those whose views were censored, unlike *Pascendi Dominici Gregis* (1907) which had been issued by Pope Pius X at the height of the modernist crisis. Around this time also, the belligerent tone of Irish Catholic apologetics subsided. Irish Catholic opinions about science and religion became more nuanced, reflective and conciliatory.

In the 1950s there was still considerable scepticism of evolution despite the evidence that had accumulated in its favour. Michael A. MacConaill, Professor of Anatomy at University College Cork, claimed that the 'only proof' possible for evolution was in the fossil record.[30] This was not correct. The 'modern synthesis' had revived neo-Darwinism. The emergence of mathematical population genetics played a central role in this development. Neo-Darwinism became dominant in evolutionary biology and was underpinned by a convergence of data from genetics, biometrics, experimental laboratory work, field studies and palaeontology.[31] Nevertheless, MacConaill, failing to appreciate the strength of the evidence for evolution in general, and for neo-Darwinism in particular, maintained that there were so many discontinuities in the fossil record, and so much guesswork in filling the gaps, that evolution could only be regarded as a myth. Scientists could 'postulate Continuity, or Catastrophe, or Creation' – but only God knew the correct one to choose.[32] However, MacConaill was critical of writers who were less than professionally competent when challenging evolutionary theory. Thus he judged Vera Barclay's *Challenge to the Darwinians* (1951) as 'a gift of ammunition to the enemy'.[33] Barclay had been 'moved to wrath' by those who taught 'Darwinism as gospel' to schoolchildren.[34] Her efforts were directed in particular against Catholic evolutionists who were seen as the enemy within. MacConaill approved of her motives but he saw her means as hopelessly inadequate. In the last paragraph of his article he concluded with a point incidental to the main topic. Mindful that some scientists were implicated in the violation of human rights in Nazi Germany only several years previously, he urged his fellow Catholic scientists to pursue their research on the basis of ethical principles. There was still, he feared, 'a suspicion in Ireland that scientists are dangerous fellows – even if they go to Mass!'[35]

MacConaill believed that the poorly defined interdisciplinary terrain where science, philosophy and religion came into close contact was hazardous to the faith of most Irish Catholics. In his review of Anthony Standen's *Science Is a Sacred Cow* (1952), he concluded that the book was like some medicines – 'poisonous if administered to the wrong persons'. For this reason he advised that the book should not be freely distributed in Ireland. It was safe reading only for those who possessed 'some first-hand knowledge of a science coupled with a sense of proportion'. He was confident that those graduates of the National University of Ireland who were 'most likely to remain orthodox in religion when exposed to infidelity', were those who were 'thoroughly trained' in science. Theologians, who had 'the same rigid training in the use of reason', were judged to be well beyond the reach of infidelity.[36]

MacConaill continued to insist that evolution would be always in the realm of speculation. It could not be decisively confirmed or rejected. Having argued this point in the *Irish Theological Quarterly* he stated that the 'transformist hypothesis' was not a theological issue. But why had he chosen a theological journal to express his opinions? MacConaill's answer was that it was only in such a journal that he could have hoped for a 'dispassionate consideration' of the issue in question.[37] Apparently, scientific journals were not inclined to facilitate opinions from the outer non-conformist fringes of the scientific profession.

Although there was an element of uncertainty in science, especially in physics, scientists tended not to dwell on this when publishing their research data. There seemed to be, in other words, a diminished awareness of uncertainty among scientists relative to that of philosophers. MacConaill was a notable exception. Specialisation had led to fragmentation in the natural sciences. The majority of scientists had neither the time nor the leisure to address the broad philosophical foundations of their discipline which were in pressing need of revision. A comprehensive philosophy of science – a work of synthesis – was required.[38]

An essential element of any work of synthesis would have entailed defining the boundary between philosophy and science. Those who reflected on matters of science and religion frequently crossed from science to philosophy, sometimes without taking cognisance of such a disciplinary shift. Dr H.A. Brück, Director of the Dunsink Observatory, observed a tendency amongst Catholics to refer to Georges Henri Lemaître's concept of the expanding universe, and to Pope Pius XII's discourse to the Pontifical Academy of Sciences (22 November 1951), to make the point that there was direct scientific proof for the creation of the universe at a specific point in time. Brück maintained that such a tendency was based on a misunderstanding of both Lemaître and the pope. It was not within the domain of cosmological theory to identify the 'beginning' of the expansionary process of the universe with the moment of creation by God. Brück maintained that, for proof of God, one had to look to philosophy – specifically the arguments advanced by St Thomas Aquinas, which were not essentially changed by modern cosmology but were, nevertheless, strengthened by it.[39]

Another misuse of scientific theory was to be found in the 'God-of-the-gaps' approach. But there was some awareness in Irish Catholic circles that this argument for theism was philosophically indefensible. It was argued that those Christians who tried to fill the 'gaps' in science with God were committing a fundamental error of judgement. God was not to be found in Heisenberg's theory of indeterminacy or in parapsychology. The mistake of the Christian in this regard was analogous to that of an atheistic or sceptical scientist who proclaimed that he never detected God at the end of a telescope or in solving an equation.[40]

Misunderstandings about the disciplinary competencies of science, philosophy, and theology tended to feature in arguments about God's existence which were logically flawed. An appropriate response to such an unsatisfactory state of affairs would be to promote studies in the philosophy of science, as well as in science itself, and to extend such an educational enterprise to benefit the laity. There might then be less concern about the potentially harmful influences of such writers as Bertrand Russell and Julian Huxley. However, the merits of an educated laity were contemplated with considerable trepidation by Bishop William J. Philbin of Clonfert, whose opinions probably reflected those of the majority of his fellow prelates.[41] Philbin feared that 'mental culture' would endanger the faith as well as enriching it. Educated Catholics would not be as docile as their uneducated co-religionists – 'the occupational disease of intellectual pursuits is a craving for unbridled freedom of thought, that is, for an autonomy incompatible with the principles of faith and authority which form the bedrock of New Testament religion . . .' Philbin anticipated that the church would lose some of its most intellectually gifted members, although he conceded piety was not enough to protect the faith against a secular alternative to Christianity, which he believed was being propagated in Ireland.[42]

The danger envisaged by Philbin did not materialise. Jacques de Bivort de la Saudée, editor of *God, Man and the Universe* (1954), believed that the philosophical outlook most common in English-speaking countries was at least implicitly materialistic. This made these countries vulnerable, in the long term, to communism, which was associated with scientism and belief in a godless evolving universe. De la Saudée singled out Ireland as the notable exception.[43] There is no evidence to suggest that de la Saudée was wrong about Ireland. In the 1950s over 94% of the population of the Republic of Ireland was Roman Catholic. The country was far from unique in having such a large Catholic majority. What made it so unusual was the very high level of commitment of Catholics to the rituals and practices of their church.[44] There is no evidence to suggest that the published works of H.G. Wells, Bertrand Russell or Julian Huxley made any significant impact on the Catholic faith in Ireland, north or south. Piety, at least up to the late 1950s, seemed sufficient to sustain fidelity to Roman Catholicism. There were more pressing problems, such as high unemployment, high emigration, and low economic productivity. Concerns about whether or not human evolution could be reconciled with the doctrine of Original Sin were not uppermost in the minds of the vast majority of Irish Catholics. Discussions of controversial scientific topics which impinged on Catholic doctrine were confined mainly to the realm of periodicals of limited circulation, such as the *Irish Ecclesiastical Record*, *Studies* and the *Irish Theological Quarterly*. Irish Catholic authors were, essentially, doing little more than preaching to a relatively small number of their co-religionists who held similar views.

Harmonious Initiatives

In the last few years of his pontificate Pius XII became increasingly isolated and was surrounded by ultra-conservative advisors. He 'cultivated his role as Vatican oracle'. He was sure that he had something important to say about every topic, regardless of how specialised it was. It was, therefore, not unusual for him to lecture midwives about the most up-to-date gynaecological procedures, or to treat astronomers to a papal discourse on sunspots. The idea of pope as universal teacher was carried to extreme lengths.[45] When Patrick J. McLaughlin decided to write *The Church and Modern Science* (1957), he had an abundant source of documents to choose from. A large section of his book was comprised of discourses given by Pope Pius XII. An important objective of McLaughlin, with reference to Pius XII, was to help philosophers understand science and assist scientists in understanding philosophy. This meant, effectively, emphasising the inferior status of the natural sciences in the hierarchy of knowledge. The natural sciences, by their very nature, were limited to physical reality. It was asserted that there were other realities – metaphysical realities – beyond sensory perception.[46] Even within the realm of reason it seemed that the experimental sciences were not of paramount importance. Science was unable to penetrate to the heart of reality. Philosophy reigned supreme here because it, rather than science, studied the totality of being. Unifying ideas were essential and philosophy, not science, was able to address this need.[47]

One of the many scientific topics addressed by McLaughlin was biological evolution. He reiterated some of the old arguments against evolution and especially against natural selection. Natural selection, he claimed, lacked cogency and was widely regarded as weak. However, he acknowledged that the general theory of biological evolution was accepted by almost all biologists as 'the most satisfying and helpful interpretation of otherwise disparate facts' in a range of scientific disciplines – including comparative anatomy, palaeontology, biogeography, genetics and embryology.[48] McLaughlin referred extensively to *Humani Generis* in his exposition of the Catholic Church's stance on the matter.

The official Catholic position of scepticism towards evolution could only have given support to the idea that there was conflict between Roman Catholicism and the natural sciences. The Catholic priest and philosopher of science Ernan McMullin acknowledged that there had been conflict between theology and science to the detriment of both. Science had provoked antipathy towards theology and theology had often obstructed scientific progress. Errors of judgement had been made on both sides.[49] By the late 1950s a substantial subsidence of belligerent dogmatism had occurred. But there were still tensions between science and theology. Andrew Dickson White's book *A History of the Warfare of Science with Theology in Christendom* (1896) was republished in New York in 1955 and was, apparently, proving quite popular. However, the

polemical work of White could be easily refuted because of its poor standard of historical scholarship and its misplaced faith in 'the infallibility
of science'.[50]

McMullin believed that tensions, as distinct from conflict, still existed
between theology and science, and that these tensions existed at three
levels. Firstly, there seemed to be an incompatibility between scientific
and theological attitudes – between the sceptical and experimental
approach on the one hand, and the affinity for tradition and the transcendent on the other. Secondly, there seemed to be antipathy between
the mystical elements of traditional Christian theology and the scientific
outlook. Thirdly, Roman Catholicism was organised on authoritarian
principles and seemed to hold the 'temporal order' in low esteem. These
traits of Catholicism were frequently seen as sources of tension with the
scientific attitude.[51] All three sources of tension were unresolved.

McMullin's article in the *Irish Theological Quarterly* was based mainly
on a review of Dr E.L. Mascall's *Christian Theology and Natural Science*
(1956). Mascall, an Anglican and a lecturer in the philosophy of religion
at Oxford, was very much influenced by the philosophy of St Thomas
Aquinas. His adherence to Thomism won him admiration from Roman
Catholic readers. His book received complimentary reviews in Ireland.[52]
McMullin referred to Mascall's book to address themes of conflict and
harmony between theology and science. Conflict arose on the question of
human origins. Scientists spoke about the human species originating
from a population of hominoids; Catholic theology clung to the Genesis
account of Adam and Eve. Mascall's solution was to say that the Bible was
important only for its doctrinal teaching. Questions of history, including
natural history, were only of secondary importance. Mascall disagreed
with the papal intervention against polygenism in *Humani Generis*
because, he contended, it was mainly an issue of biological science.
McMullin disagreed, arguing that this would effectively 'divorce' theology
and (natural) history, which would be contrary to the traditional teaching
of the church. Theologians, as well as biologists, had something meaningful to say about human origins.[53]

There was broad agreement between McMullin and Mascall on the
idea of harmony between theology and science. Both disagreed with Pope
Pius XII's exaggeration of the significance of the Big Bang in the context of
arguing for the existence of an omnipotent Creator. McMullin was implicitly critical of Pius for ignoring the views of Lemaître and referring instead
to Sir Edmund Whittaker to make the point that the Big Bang could be

seen as the act of creation – although the pope had not absolutely ruled out the existence of the cosmos before the Big Bang. Lemaître, like Whittaker, was a member of the Pontifical Academy of Sciences and did not wish the Big Bang thesis to be used for purposes of natural theology. McMullin observed that the papal address 'caused a gasp of surprise' amongst Catholic philosophers, many of whom had criticised Whittaker's *Space and Spirit* (1946). It was widely known that St Thomas Aquinas, deeply influenced by Aristotle, disagreed with the idea that it was possible, through philosophy, to prove that the world had a beginning in time.[54]

Mascall was critical of using what he regarded as ephemeral scientific hypotheses to argue for God's existence. The Big Bang was not yet secure in cosmological thinking and Mascall was critical of Pius XII for arbitrarily rejecting the Steady State thesis. Even if the Big Bang did occur this could not simply be viewed as the beginning of the universe in time. Lemaître and Gamow speculated that the Big Bang might have been preceded by a period of contraction – Gamow's 'Big Squeeze'. All traces of a universe before the Big Bang would have been totally destroyed. Lemaître's thesis was consistent with the idea of an infinite series of contractions and expansions. The most that could be claimed for the Big Bang was that it made the temporal beginning of the universe more plausible, not certain. Both Mascall and McMullin believed that the Big Bang did not prove creation by God. Nevertheless, McMullin believed that the Big Bang was a very significant contribution to theology, making the argument for the existence of God more plausible. However, plausibility was not to be confused with 'rigorous demonstration'.[55]

McMullin praised Mascall's book as 'a fascinating store of information and a decided stimulus to thought'. Mascall had displayed 'wide competence', unlike so many other Christian authors.[56] Perhaps it is not reading too much into such generous praise for an Anglican author to say that it indicated a softening of antipathy towards Protestantism in Catholic Ireland.

McMullin's article was published in January 1959. In that month Pope John XXIII, only three months into his pontificate, announced that a general council was to be convened. This council – the Second Vatican Council – was to introduce widespread progressive reforms. The year 1959 also marked the centenary of Darwin's *Origin of Species*. Evolution was established beyond all reasonable doubt and the central position of natural selection in evolutionary biology also seemed secure. In reference to the status of evolutionary theory, Conor Reilly (S.J.) quoted the eminent geneticist Theodosius Dobzhansky to make the point that evolution was as well established as any series of events could be which were not directly observed. Reilly believed that Dobzhansky's opinion reflected the attitude most common amongst biologists and anthropologists.[57] Evolutionary theory could not simply be dismissed as mere conjecture, supported as it was by a large volume of scientific data. Reilly perceived some unease amongst Catholics about their church's position on the matter. The French priest M.M. Labourdette (O.P.) wrote in his *Le Péché Originel et les Origines de l'Homme* (1953) that many teachers of religion had been distressed at the reaction of adolescents to the teaching of the doctrine of Original Sin. According to Labourdette, students tended to regard the dogma of Original Sin as irreconcilable with the findings of science. It is significant that Reilly believed that Irish students probably were not so much influenced by the 'pronouncements of science' as to doubt the doctrine of Original Sin. But attitudes might change. There were difficulties in reconciling Adam and Eve's initial 'state of blessedness' with the theory of human evolution which described a process of development from primitive culture to highly civilised culture. If this apparent contradiction between Genesis and evolutionary theory was not addressed then it might lead adolescent students to conclude that there was a genuine incompatibility between faith and modern science.[58] Reilly discussed abstract theological ideas and human evolution in some detail and saw no contradiction between the scientific idea that early human culture was primitive and the theological idea that Adam was 'created in justice and sanctity'.[59] It is highly significant that, in seeking to reconcile science and theology, Reilly refrained from aggressively criticising scientists and evolutionary theory.

The Jesuit author John J. Moore, writing in the *Irish Theological Quarterly*, speculated in early 1959 that the centenary year of Darwin's *Origin of Species* would stimulate an outpouring of literature on evolutionary questions. He anticipated that this would revive the science-versus-religion conflict but he did not seem deeply concerned about it. He acknowledged the central role of evolutionary theory in enabling biologists to make sense of a vast volume of data. It bestowed coherence and unity to biology, which was splintering into a growing number of specialist disciplines. Furthermore, neo-Darwinism was the mechanism of evolutionary change now most widely accepted by biologists.[60]

Moore's observations suggest that it was becoming increasingly difficult to express scepticism of a scientific theory accepted by the vast majority of scientists while at the same time insisting that Catholic theology and science were compatible. The American Jesuit J. Franklin Ewing believed that evolution was taken for granted in modern society. Many Catholic theologians accepted evolutionary theory extended to human origins, some were 'more reserved', but none condemned it outright.[61] Ewing admitted that he did not base his understanding of Catholic theological opinions on a statistical study but, as a teacher of anthropology at Fordham University, he was probably well informed about contemporary trends in theology. Rémy Collin's *Evolution: Hypotheses and Problems* (1959) criticised evolutionary theory on a number of fronts but, nevertheless, conceded that the growing volume of fossil evidence justified the inclusion of humans in the evolutionary process. However, Collin was careful to state that such evidence did not constitute proof.[62] His volume was praised in the *Irish Ecclesiastical Record* as the best book on evolution published in English.[63]

John Moore moved beyond evolutionary theory to discuss broader issues in science which were of particular interest to theologians. He pointed to the epistemological developments arising from modern scientific theories such as relativity and quantum mechanics. Because of the awareness that scientific theories were subject to revision, and questions concerning the correlation between theoretical models and physical reality (concerning, for example, atomic structure), scientists had become less dogmatic, and generally were less inclined to draw grand philosophical conclusions from their scientific findings. However, the old dogmatic attitudes were not extinct and were still likely to be expressed through publications intended for popular as distinct from specialist readership.[64]

Moore's historical perspective on the conflict between theology and science was that errors had been committed by both theologians and scientists. To avoid such conflict in the future he advocated that theologians should examine with great care the all-important distinction between dogmatic and non-dogmatic elements of Catholic doctrine; and to repress any tendency to regard scientists as intellectually dishonest or stupid. Scientists were urged to cultivate diligence in taking cognisance of the 'epistemological deficiencies' of scientific theories.[65] In view of all this, how then were theologians to approach the subject of human evolution in the light of modern scientific developments? Moore observed that the evolution of the human species was no longer regarded as 'temerarious' by Catholic theologians, much to the 'immense relief' of Catholic biologists who were frequently embarrassed by enquiries from their more liberal-minded colleagues.[66] But there was still a reluctance to fully accept the evolution of humankind entirely on the basis of scientific explanation. Moore insisted on some degree of direct divine intervention in the emergence of humans from primitive hominoids. Furthermore, science could not decide whether or not all humans originated from one couple – this was not amenable to inductive generalisation and was, essentially, a historical question answerable only on the basis of testimony. The best that science could do was to declare that there was no insurmountable obstacle to all humans being descended from one couple.[67] This contention conveniently swept the thorny issue of polygenism aside.

By 1959 Catholic authors tended to focus increasingly on questioning how the evolutionary process occurred, not if it occurred, or if humankind was to be excluded from it. In *Darwin's Vision and Historical Perspectives* (1960), Alexander Wolsky, Professor of Experimental Embryology at Fordham University, addressed the question of whether or not neo-Darwinism was the only mechanism of evolution. Some scientists supported the contention that natural selection, acting on numerous micromutations (small hereditary changes), was unable to explain the vast range of species diversity by itself. Albert Dalcq (embryology), O.H. Schindewolf (palaeontology) and Richard Goldschmidt (genetics) pointed to a macroevolutionary mechanism. This meant that evolution proceeded occasionally by large steps. Schindewolf proposed that abrupt macroevolutionary changes were followed by long periods of microevolution. Wolsky, in examining the cumulative impact of Dalcq, Schindewolf and Goldschmidt on evolutionary theory, concluded that neo-Darwinism was still the leading concept in evolutionary biology and that the only question to be addressed was whether or not there was another mechanism, or mechanisms, of evolutionary change.[68]

Robert W. Gleason (S.J.), Chairman of the Departments of Theology and Religious Education at Fordham University, acknowledged that a number of ideas expressed in the book of Genesis were possibly erroneous in terms of science – although it was not these ideas that were being affirmed. The author of the narratives was simply using the contemporary understanding of nature to communicate a divine message. It was not the purpose of scripture to teach science. Gleason, writing in the same book as Wolsky, maintained that it was permissible for Roman Catholics to believe in the evolution of humankind. He speculated that God might have prepared the first human for 'infusion' of the human soul by directing a series of mutations.[69]

Darwin's Vision and Historical Perspectives was reviewed in the *Irish Theological Quarterly* by Ernan McMullin. He did not question the veracity of evolution or natural selection but agreed with Wolsky that debates about evolution were concerned with the causal factors of genetic change. Assessing the chapter by Gleason was more difficult. Catholic evolutionists believed that at some advanced stage in the human evolutionary process God infused 'the animal organism' with an immortal soul. However, God's *modus operandi* was not at all clear and McMullin concluded that it was obscured by 'some very dangerous philosophical quicksands'.[70] Gleason's theological speculation did not lift the veil of mystery about the final events leading to the emergence of humankind.

Evolution and Original Sin

In the less repressive atmosphere of Pope John XXIII's reign there seems to have been more scope for theological speculation than before. This facilitated tolerance for a less inhibited acceptance of evolutionary theory, including human evolution. This is reflected in a series of three articles in the *Irish Ecclesiastical Record* by Rev. Martin Brennan (S.J.) in 1961. He stated that although the proofs of evolution might not be 'absolutely compelling' they were sufficient to make the general theory 'incomparably more rational than any alternative'. He saw a convergence of evidence from a number of disciplines – biogeography, taxonomy, comparative anatomy, comparative physiology, embryology and palaeontology. Evidence from the fossil record was particularly strong – so strong that if species were created directly rather than through the medium of secondary causes then it would represent an act, or acts, of deliberate deception by God – which Brennan dismissed as ridiculous.[71]

In his second article Brennan addressed the subject of human evolution, pointing to an accumulation of fossil evidence. The main outline of human evolution was constructed from Oreopithecus, Australopithecus, Pithecanthropus and Cro-Magnon specimens. The gaps in the evidence were narrowing with new and frequent discoveries of fossil specimens. Experts disagreed on points of detail but not on the fact that humans had evolved from primitive hominoids. Brennan anticipated that theologians, 'under the guidance of the teaching magisterium of the Church', would 'naturally be slow to accept every latest claim as final truth'. Prudent theologians still found it necessary to exercise some caution when embracing the latest findings in science.[72]

Humani Generis stated that it was permissible for loyal Roman Catholics to believe in the evolution of the human body subject to certain conditions. Brennan saw an apparent contradiction between the church's doctrine of Original Sin and the polygenism of evolutionary biology. Biologists did not seriously consider the possibility that a new species could have originated from one couple. They viewed a species as an inter-breeding population of genetically similar individuals who evolved as a group. This seemed inconsistent with the Bible. And the problem was not just confined to the narratives of Genesis. Brennan pointed to Chapter 5 of St Paul's Epistle to the Romans where Adam was referred to as if he was a historical individual. The opposition between Catholic doctrine and science on the issue of monogenism versus polygenism was 'obvious'. But there was a loophole in *Humani Generis* which left some room for manoeuvre. The encyclical stated that it was not clear how the rejection of one individual Adam, as the father of all mankind, could be regarded as compatible with revelation and the doctrines of the church. This was seen as an inconclusive ruling. Catholic doctrine might yet evolve to enrich the knowledge of revelation. What might be deemed 'rash and dangerous' at one stage of development, and prohibited by the teaching authority of the church precisely because of the risk to the faith, might be permitted later on if the advance of knowledge eliminated the danger. Theologians might conclude that 'Tradition did not mean to teach formally that Original Sin can only be transmitted by descent.' Such a doctrinal change would occur only as a response to the remote possibility of science providing 'indis-putable proofs of polygenism'. Brennan concluded that, until then, aside from dialogue amongst theologians, Catholics were not free to advocate polygenism.[73] This claimed a greater freedom of opinion than that per-mitted by paragraph 20 of *Humani Generis*, which made specific reference to the prohibition of discussion among theologians on issues which had been pronounced upon by the pope.

If loyal and scientifically minded Catholics accepted that human evo-lution had occurred – including polygenism – then they were confronted with a conflict of loyalties. If one accepted the scientific explanation based on polygenism, this indicated a lack of due regard for the Catholic doctrine of Original Sin. But to insist on monogenism was to adopt an opinion incompatible with contemporary science. An apparently novel idea was to adopt an agnostic position on the issue. This was precisely what Michael MacConaill did. He had not changed his opinion about the epistemological status of evolutionary theory since he wrote on the subject a decade earlier. 'Thoughtful Christians', like himself, were non-evolutionists. By implication, Christians who were either anti-evolutionist or pro-evolutionist were consigned to the ranks of the intellectually lightweight.

MacConaill viewed the study of fossils as a branch of history. Like astronomy, it was outside the realm of the experimental sciences. He argued that it was 'a branch of exegesis, strictly comparable to theological exegesis', regardless of what palaeontologists thought. With particular reference to the Chou Kou Tien (near Peking, now Beijing) fossil finds in China, MacConaill argued that the evidence was 'purely scriptural' and subject to interpretation with due regard for 'tradition', somewhat analogous to the theological interpretation of scripture. MacConaill's stance probably gave a degree of reassurance to some readers of the *Irish Ecclesiastical Record* who were content to elevate the epistemological threshold for science but not for theology. Scepticism of evolution served to reinforce a smug complacency about the historicity of the early chapters of Genesis. However, there was a price to be paid for such theological bliss by Catholic authors who were practising scientists. Evidently, they were exposed, to some extent, to the caustic disapproval of their fellow scientists. MacConaill wrote of his own unpleasant experience:

> My ears as well as my eyes attest that the *odium scientificum* can be every whit as bitter as the *odium theologicum*. If you are known to be agnostic on the matter, to be a non-evolutionist, you are regarded by the influential groups of many learned societies as being even more eccentric than if you indulge in the abnormal sins.[74]

MacConaill drew no distinction between scientists at home and abroad. This suggests that the pro-evolutionist consensus among scientists in general was also true of scientists in Ireland. It is significant that MacConaill, like Alfred O'Rahilly before him, felt compelled to complain about the tribulations of scientists who dared to dissent.

The provocation of the *odium scientificum* was probably not offset by gestures of approval from theologians. Some theologians would not have been as dismissive of evolutionary theory as MacConaill. This is indicated by the sustained efforts of Catholic authors to reconcile evolution and Genesis. Fr Donal Flanagan, Professor of Dogmatic Theology at Maynooth, did not express scepticism of evolutionary theory and was satisfied that an evolutionary theory of human origins was reconcilable with the doctrine of creation if some problems were solved. However, rather than focusing on uncertainties in science, he focused on uncertainties in theology instead, and maintained that some biblical passages were 'notoriously difficult' to interpret.[75]

The perceived need to reconcile Genesis and evolution continued to agitate the minds of Catholic authors, especially concerning the doctrine of Original Sin and polygenism. In a paper read to the Irish Theological Association on 2 November 1966, J.P. Mackey pointed out that the question of polygenism and Original Sin was 'an extremely delicate one'. It seemed from an address by Pope Paul VI to an assembly of scientists and theologians in Rome, on 11 July 1966, that the church's attitude had hardened against polygenism. However, Mackey claimed that the pope had intended to condemn only some unspecified expositions of Original Sin and probably did not mean to rule out polygenism completely. Therefore, the Vatican's position had not changed substantially since the publication of *Humani Generis*.

Mackey believed that the obstacle to reconciling polygenism and Original Sin arose from two sources. Firstly, there was the 'apparent definiteness, not to say intransigence, of the Roman Catholic teaching authority'. Secondly, there was the 'contrasting indefiniteness' of empirical science.[76] Despite the lack of absolute proof of polygenism there was an 'escalation' of opinion amongst theologians about the need for change. Mackey maintained that it was clear from the works of scriptural scholars such as C. Hauret, J. de Fraine and A.M. Dubarle that such change did not mean the abandonment of the belief that monogenism was taught by scripture because these authors argued that monogenism was not clearly taught in the Bible to begin with.[77] According to Mackey, there was speculation in theological circles that the Vatican would not maintain its stricture on polygenism. But there was also strong resistance to change, and this resistance was to be found especially amongst dogmatic theologians.[78]

There was some awareness amongst theologians that scientists saw no reason why human origins should be singled out for explanation on the basis of monogenism while all other species were studied on the basis of polygenism. Monogenism was irrelevant to scientific discourse because genetics was essentially concerned with polygenism. It had, therefore, been naive of theologians to expect that empirical science would help them to solve any of their theological problems. Martin Brennan believed that the impact of the natural sciences on theology could only be negative. At its best it would assist in distinguishing revelation from its erroneous and obsolescent accretions, accumulated over time. Brennan observed that, in the nineteenth century, there had been a 'remarkable growth' in the numbers of theologians who accepted evolutionary theory. But their attempts to understand the origins of humans and Original Sin on the basis of an evolutionary theory circumscribed by monogenism had proved futile – 'the sands of the biological sciences ran through their sifting fingers and left them with a purely theological problem.'[79]

Attempts to integrate population genetics with the doctrine of Original Sin had not proved satisfactory. In this scheme it was postulated that Adam represented the first population of primates to reach human status. It was the collective sin of this population that resulted in their spiritual demise and that of their descendants. This, it was believed, raised more questions than it answered. For example, did the communal sin become effective only when the last person in the group sinned? What became of those who may have died before the last sin? Did it take effect when a sufficient number had sinned to make it morally a sin of the population? What became of those who did not sin? Brennan observed that it was this notion of Adam as a population and the idea of a collective sin that caused Pope Pius XII to issue *Humani Generis*.[80]

Theologians continued to pursue the elusive Adam but biological science was not able to present theology with any information about the first human being.[81] Brennan pointed out that such an expectation would have been unreasonable. In a process of very gradual evolutionary change there would not have been a clearly identifiable point when some primates became human. At some point there would have been a radically new development beyond the reach of scientific investigation. Two individuals in the evolutionary process would be fundamentally different in nature – one with an immortal soul, one without an immortal soul. The first human would have been sufficiently gifted with intellectual ability to make moral choices. But a single mutation would not have been sufficient to distinguish him fundamentally from his contemporaries. Explanations, based on a strange synthesis of speculative theology and population genetics, considered the role of macromutations and 'hybrid swarms'. However, these ideas were unsatisfactory because it seemed that they were not subject to verification and were based more on contrivance than on evidence.[82]

A radical shift in thinking was required if the tensions and incompatibilities between science and theology were to be satisfactorily dealt with. But this was not forthcoming. The failure of the papacy, and of the church, to revise its understanding of Catholic dogmas in the light of modern science may have contributed to a loss of faith amongst some educated Catholics and damaged the credibility of the church amongst non-Catholics.[83] The proceedings of the Second Vatican Council did not overcome the theological problems associated with the interpretation of Genesis. Bishop Michael Browne of Galway observed that exegetes and theologians were still searching for a solution to the unresolved difficulties arising from the creation narratives of the first two chapters. Non-Catholic authors had taken advantage of their ongoing dilemma to reject the doctrine of creation on the basis of textual analysis, historical criticism and evolutionary theory. Browne was satisfied that their claims were unsustainable, but religious teachers in secondary schools were nevertheless experiencing difficulties in addressing the apparent contradictions between scripture and the sciences (physical and historical).[84]

The Holy Ghost priest Maurice Curtin speculated that Original Sin might always remain somewhat shrouded in mystery. The lack of understanding about the origins of the human species and the complications that this created for the doctrine of Original Sin was not just an irritating problem for theologians and Biblical scholars. Fr Curtin, writing in *The Furrow* (1974), observed that it created difficulties for religious teachers and parents. He maintained that the church had not defined the nature of Original Sin, nor its mode of transmission, nor the existence of Adam and Eve as real historical figures. The Bible was neither a work of science nor of history. Curtin believed that it was possible to teach the doctrine of Original Sin without including Adam and Eve; but he did not regard it as 'advisable' for Ireland, considering 'all the circumstances'. There was a long-established practice in Ireland of teaching the doctrine of Original Sin on the basis of Adam and Eve. A new approach to the subject might not succeed if thorough training was not put in place. And yet the old approach was not satisfactory either. Curtin noted the objections of some teachers to the version of Original Sin presented to primary school pupils. Teachers were concerned that if Adam and Eve were regarded as real individuals in primary school, and not as real individuals in secondary school, then this would be 'teaching and unteaching' – a major pedagogical error. Teenagers might react angrily to what they perceived as lies in the primary system. In this context Curtin did not view two radically different versions of the same story as a U-turn in doctrine but as 'teaching and teaching more fully', i.e. as 'teaching and interpreting'.[85] A heavy dose of ambivalence was, apparently, just the remedy to quell any intellectual turmoil that might arise in youthful Irish minds.

Irish Catholic authors, especially theologians, had struggled to harmonise the doctrine of Original Sin with the population genetics of evolutionary theory. Like their counterparts abroad, they did not succeed in proposing a satisfactory remedy. However innovative theologians might be, they were only advisers to the teaching authority. They did not represent the official church position and could not independently determine the development or evolution of doctrine. That was the prerogative of the papacy – and the papacy had imposed restrictions which placed resolution beyond reach.[86]

9. The Elusive Master Narrative,[1] mid-1970s–2006

Dialogue or Isolation?

The soundness of Genesis had far-reaching implications for both Catholic theology and the Bible. The story of creation is not, and was not, limited to scientific and historical interest. Creation theology is inextricably connected to salvation and is therefore an essential element of Catholic doctrine. Nor was the Biblical account of creation confined to Genesis. Other accounts and references to creation are to be found elsewhere in the Bible; for example in Job 38, Psalms 74: 13–17, Proverbs 8: 22–31, and Romans 8: 19–23. If Genesis was totally discredited by the natural sciences this would do much harm, not only to the credibility of Catholic faith but also to the fundamental tenets of Christian belief. How were theologians to address controversial issues raised, not just by science but also by philosophy and the historical sciences? Firstly, they could cling rigidly to the old traditionalist positions, regardless of the adverse consequences for the credibility of Catholic theology. This would entail selectively rejecting some scientific theories or else pursuing a policy of maximum isolation where science and theology were seen as separate domains of knowledge with little or no overlap. Secondly, they could cautiously abandon some traditionalist stances to facilitate the harmonisation of theology with the physical and historical sciences. An obvious case in point here was the revision of Original Sin in line with polygenism. This would entail some risk taking, an extension of thinking beyond the stifling strictures of *Humani Generis*.

In the aftermath of the Second Vatican Council there was a more speculative, liberal and less dogmatic tone in Irish Catholic articles in the *Irish Theological Quarterly*, *The Furrow*, and *Doctrine and Life*. This is evident in, for example, P.J. McGrath's 'Believing in God' in the *Irish Theological Quarterly* (April 1975). McGrath conceded that there was a credibility deficit associated with the Five Ways of St Thomas Aquinas. Many Catholics had lost confidence in them as sound reasons for believing in God. If the Five Ways were no longer accepted as satisfactory, were there any alternative arguments to take their place? Were there any good arguments? If not, then how could one give a satisfactory explanation for one's belief in God? Could belief in God be regarded as intellectually respectable in the absence of arguments for God's existence? McGrath did not have a definitive answer to the above questions and stated that it was 'difficult to feel certain as to the answers to be given to them'. In adopting this position he consciously rejected the tenability of the anti-modernist oath imposed on the vast majority of priests from 1910 to 1967.[2] However, McGrath did maintain that there was still scope for arguments for God's existence. But these arguments would be modest. Such arguments would not be put forward as 'a complete justification of the religious outlook . . . but rather as providing some evidence for its validity'.[3] McGrath would probably have been condemned as a modernist in the early decades of the twentieth century.

In earlier decades, Martin Brennan would also have exposed himself to the risk of ecclesiastical censure for expressing approval of the visionary theology of Pierre Teilhard de Chardin. Writing in the *University Review*, Brennan stated that 'the overall reach' of Teilhard's thought was orthodox.[4] Teilhard's scheme of integrating evolutionary theory with theology had been banned by the church.[5] Shortly after Teilhard's death, his book *Le Phénomène Humain* (1955) was published in France. The English translation – *The Phenomenon of Man* – was published in 1959. Teilhard's posthumous publication stimulated much debate and influenced the outlook of many Catholics – although very few of them fully understood his abstruse work.

In Brennan's exposition of Teilhard's evolutionary scheme there is a continuous growth in the complexity of matter in the universe. Evolution leads to the emergence of life, to consciousness, and onwards to self-consciousness in the case of humans. Technological advances over time draw human beings closer together all over the world, in terms of communications, cultural interaction and interdependency. Humankind becomes more and more like a single vast organism developing in the womb of planet Earth. Simultaneously there is the growth of a spiritual dimension. Men are drawn together in love by God through the Mystical Body of Christ. This supernatural organism evolves to higher states of collective human consciousness and co-ordination so that human potentialities are developed to the maximum. The terminal point of this evolutionary process is the Omega Point, where humankind is blissfully reconciled with God. Teilhard's vision resonated well with evolutionary theory but it was excessively optimistic considering that the evils of war, oppression and poverty were causing so much suffering and were threatening the future of humankind.

Evolution was seen as a creative process. By the mid-1990s the future of creation had moved to a central position in theological discourse, against the background of the threat of nuclear weapons and the deterioration of various natural environments throughout the world. Fr Dermot Lane, a senior member of staff at the Mater Dei Institute in Dublin, expressed his views on the question in the Jesuit quarterly *Milltown Studies* (Autumn 1994). Lane's study was informed by the works of a wide range of authors, including Teilhard de Chardin, Edward Schillebeeckx, Elizabeth A. Johnson, Karl Rahner, Mary Midgley, John Polkinghorne and Ernan McMullin. He urged his fellow theologians to give careful consideration to the findings of science, especially in view of its immense influence.[6]

From a grand cosmological perspective, human beings constituted a tiny part of the cosmos that had become aware of itself – an outcome of billions of years of unbroken evolution. Because the human spirit subsisted in matter, the human person could not be understood without recourse to cosmogony. Christology also became creation-centred. Jesus Christ was seen as the summit of creation. When the Word (the second person of the Holy Trinity) became human, he (Jesus Christ) was like the rest of humanity – in physical terms. He too was made from stardust – from the elements formed inside the fiery furnaces of stars during the evolutionary process.[7] Like humans he became part of cosmic history, a child of the Earth, a child of the universe, and was sometimes referred to as 'the cosmic Christ'.[8] As a human his DNA may have linked him to an ancient lineage extending far beyond Adam, to primitive primordial life in the Earth's ancient oceans.[9] Christ was presented as the centre of creation: 'He is . . . first born of all creation. For in him all things in heaven and on earth were created. All things have been created through him and for him . . . In him all things hold together' (Colossians 1: 15–18).[10] Lane emphasised that questions about the future of creation would ultimately be answered by eschatology – that aspect of theology dealing with last things such as death, resurrection, judgement and eternal life. Eschatology, unlike evolution, pointed to some condition of finality some time in the future.[11] In this creation-centred Christology, theological connections were drawn between the incarnation, death, resurrection and Second Coming (the *Parousia*) of Jesus Christ, the salvation of humankind and the future transformation of the cosmos.[12] Christian salvation was not entirely confined to the spiritual domain. Revelation 21:1–5 prophesied the transformation of creation – the formation of 'a new heaven and a new earth'.

Lane cautioned his fellow theologians against the 'easy co-option' of scientific theories which, as history demonstrated, were vulnerable to change.[13] His work indicated a confidence in engaging with modern scientific theories. Evidently, he was not unduly restricted by traditionalist attitudes and was considerably flexible in adapting his thinking to new scientific concepts in the pursuit of constructive dialogue. Not all Catholic authors were at ease in the intellectual terrain jointly occupied by science and theology. Numerous attempts had been made to correlate the six days of creation in the first chapter of Genesis with scientific discoveries about natural history and had ended in failure.[14] The point was made that

> many philosophers, theologians, apologists and faithful believers have treated the Scriptures (and still do) as though they were intended to impart scientific and historical information rather than divine revelation. This attitude to Scripture is understandable since many books are presented as though they are factual accounts. That this is the wrong way to regard Scripture has only become clear gradually through advances in astronomy, palaeontology, archaeology, biology, textual analysis and suchlike sciences. Whatever about the historicity of scripture, it does not count for anything as science. Nor was it intended to . . .[15]

All of the above suggested that scripture could be isolated from the historical and natural sciences. A detached theology would have fewer problems to contend with. But a countervailing view in Catholic thought was that, because there was some overlap with other disciplines, there had to be some interaction. Theology had to enter into dialogue with science. Otherwise there was a danger that it might become isolated in a world deeply influenced by science.[16] It was argued that theology would be more credible if it resonated with the established findings of modern cosmology. Furthermore, science could help theology to explain God's mode of action in the world. Some degree of collaboration was seen as desirable in order to avoid a 'dehumanised' science and a 'ghettoized' theology.[17]

If science was elevated far above religion in terms of objectivity and its capacity to ascertain truth, then genuine dialogue would be extremely difficult, if not impossible, to initiate and sustain. There was a perception to be addressed, namely that science was a superior type of knowledge to theology in that it was strictly rational, objective and empirical. But the works of Werner Heisenberg, Kurt Gödel and Karl Popper had highlighted the uncertainties and tentative nature of many scientific and mathematical findings. The publication of Thomas S. Kuhn's *The Structure of Scientific Revolutions* (1962; 2nd ed., 1970) reinforced the sense of uncertainty about science which existed in some quarters. Kuhn argued that science was not a purely objective pursuit of truth. In reality, scientific methodology did not conform to an idealised process comprised of observation, experimentation, deduction and conclusion. Elements of chance and subjectivity influenced the beliefs of scientific communities. Kuhn's approach to the subject was that of an historian. He indicated that a particular paradigm or worldview dominated the practice of science, profoundly influencing the problems scientists regarded as important, the types of questions they asked, and the experimental procedures they carried out. Science progressed in cycles where paradigms were overthrown and replaced by new ones. Revolutionary changes were followed by periods of stability. Scientists were not unbiased seekers of truth.[18] External interests – religious, military and industrial – influenced or directed scientific activities. Kuhn's book profoundly influenced academic discourse in the philosophy of science.

James P. Mackey, writing in *The Irish Theological Quarterly*, observed that theologians were 'rejoicing that something akin to personal faith seemed to be emerging as a prerequisite for scientific research' shortly after the publication of Kuhn's book. It seemed, from the second edition of Kuhn's book (1970), that metaphysical assumptions about the nature of reality, and the mental faculty of imagination, both played key roles in the formation of scientific theories.[19] The demise of the mechanical model of the universe and its replacement by the relativistic space-time universe, and the counterintuitive findings of modern cosmology, all indicated the limited competency of the natural sciences and the uncertainty of its findings. It now seemed that scientists, metaphysicians and theologians were 'again back on even terms'.[20] Dermot Lane pointed to a 'post-empiricist' or 'post-modern' understanding of the natural sciences which had emerged over the previous thirty years. With particular reference to R.J. Bernstein's *Beyond Objectivism and Relativism: Science,*

Hermeneutics and Praxis (1983), he made four main points about the new philosophy of science. Firstly, there was no such thing as 'an absolute method' in the natural sciences which could be used to adjudicate on scientific theories and hypotheses. Secondly, there was a growing awareness that an objective and standardised basis for choosing the best arguments in scientific discourse did not exist. Thirdly, there was an increasing realisation of how historical and social circumstances influenced paradigms, theories and research programmes in science. Fourthly, the element of human judgement influenced the practice of science. Science was not pure unadulterated rationality. Subjectivity was clearly evident in how scientific findings were interpreted. Scientific data was not interpreted in a vacuum, devoid of theories and paradigms. There was a hermeneutical dimension to be considered.[21] Lane saw inspiring ideas in the works of Alfred North Whitehead and David Bohm which would greatly assist initiatives to construct a new metaphysics to address, from a Christian perspective, such pressing issues as the global threat of nuclear weapons and impending ecological crises throughout the world.[22]

A Concept of Four Dimensions

Thomas Corbett, Professor of Theology at Maynooth, referred to the work of Ian G. Barbour to discuss four elements in the relationship between religion and science, of which independence was one. The other three were dialogue, integration and conflict.[23] Barbour's work influenced, to a very considerable extent, literature on the relationship between religion and science.[24] In *Reconstructing Nature: The Engagement of Science and Religion* (1998), John Brooke and Geoffrey Cantor rejected the use of any 'master narrative' to advance 'a definitive historical account of how science and religion have been (and are) interrelated'. Both religion and science have persistently resisted precise objective definitions. This made a credible 'master narrative' extremely unlikely. Brooke and Cantor argued that, in this context, theses such as harmony, conflict, independence, dialogue and integration were all associated with 'a high degree of relativism', were biased in their use of evidence, and failed to take due cognisance of the complexity and diversity of opinions expressed in the past.[25] Cantor and Chris Kenny referred to the life history of St George Jackson Mivart to question the value of Barbour's taxonomic scheme. Mivart, depending on the particular circumstances, could be discussed under all four of Barbour's themes, depending on how science and religion were to be precisely defined. For example, Mivart's view of science was very different from that of the Darwinians, and his Catholicism was radically different from that of the reactionaries in Rome. Concepts of conflict, independence, dialogue and integration could only be usefully applied when specific aspects of both religion and science were identified.[26] Historians therefore referred to what is sometimes called the 'Complexity Thesis' to elucidate the relationship between science and religion.[27]

From the foregoing it is clear that the relationship between religion and science or, in this case, between Irish Catholicism and science cannot be defined in terms of a single theme. Corbett's essay will receive considerable attention here because of the broad scope of his discussion and the many points he raised. He observed that, historically, theology had some unpleasant encounters with science and that there was some inclination on the part of conservative theologians to adopt a policy of independence [would not 'isolation' be a more appropriate term?]. In this approach to the two disciplines, theology and science had their own different structures, subject matter, methods and purposes. On superficial examination, it seemed natural to keep them apart. But Corbett, concurring with Barbour, made the point that the different dimensions of life were, in reality, interconnected. Theologians had to develop a theology of nature to address ethical questions arising from scientific discoveries. Therefore they had to engage in dialogue with science.

Dialogue was not a problem from Corbett's perspective. Theologians would not be overawed by science – a 'certain humility *à la* Heisenberg' was 'demanded'.[28] Corbett believed that the desire for dialogue between religion and science was gaining more and more support. As evidence for this he pointed to *Physics, Philosophy and Theology: A Common Quest for Understanding*, published by the Vatican Observatory in 1988; and *Faith, Science and the Future* (1978), a collection of preparatory readings for the 1979 Conference of the World Council of Churches.[29] The desire for dialogue and collaboration was strong in the Vatican under Pope John Paul II. On 3 July 1981 the Pontifical Academy of Sciences set up an interdisciplinary commission to examine and report on the Galileo case, which still provoked occasional controversy in some academic and theological circles. The chairman of the commission was Bishop (later Cardinal) Paul Poupard. The primary purpose was to promote harmony between Roman Catholicism and science. The commission concluded its work on 31 October 1992 when it presented its findings to the pope. John Paul, in his address to the Pontifical Academy, found that Galileo was more perceptive than the theologians who disagreed with him. He urged theologians to keep themselves informed about developments in science and to determine whether or not changes in teaching were warranted by new developments. A greater understanding of the circumstances surrounding Galileo's condemnation would help to prevent misunderstandings and unnecessary conflicts in the future. It was crucially important to understand the distinction between scripture and the interpretation of scripture, and to comprehend the boundaries and limited competencies of theology and related disciplines such as philosophy and science.[30]

Pope John Paul's address and the findings of the Pontifical Academy of Sciences acknowledged the poor judgement of the Roman Catholic Church in the censorship of Galileo. Some Galilean scholars were disappointed and critical of the conclusions of the pope and the Galileo commission, especially concerning the excessive burden of proof placed on Galileo to prove the Copernican hypothesis, the placing of institutional guilt firmly on the shoulders of theologians, and the failure to criticise Cardinal Robert Bellarmine, Pope Paul V, the Roman Inquisition, the Congregation of the Index, and Pope Urban VIII.[31] Maurice A. Finocchiaro, Professor of Philosophy at the University of Nevada-Las Vegas, harshly criticised Cardinal Paul Poupard's chairmanship of the Vatican's interdisciplinary commission. He maintained that the pope's good intentions had been subverted by reactionaries and that Poupard was the 'main villain'.[32]

On 9 April 1995 Cardinal Poupard, then President of the Pontifical Council for Culture, addressed the Maynooth Bicentenary Conference on Faith and Culture. In his speech about 'Creation, Culture and Faith' he placed the error of the church in the context of 'the limitations of culture' prevailing at that time. Once again the theologians were blamed, and no reference was made to the culpability of the ecclesiastical authorities. After referring briefly to the Galileo case, Poupard next spoke fleetingly about Darwin and the 'initial panic' about his 'theories'. In his opinion there was now a 'mutual openness' between science and religion, largely because of the pope's initiatives in addressing the legacy of Galileo and the explicit acknowledgement of the 'rightful independence' of science by the Second Vatican Council in its document *Gaudium et Spes* (paragraph 36).[33]

The pope's address and the findings of the Galileo commission received very little attention in Ireland. Those responses which were published in Irish Catholic periodicals lacked originality and objectivity, and generally tried to minimise the institutional church's guilt while stressing Galileo's character defects and errors of judgement. Neil Porter, writing in *Doctrine and Life*, believed that the most important contributing factor to Galileo's 'downfall' was his habit of writing witty but offensive rhymes about his colleagues and opponents. The sentence imposed on him after his abjuration of the Copernican hypothesis in 1633 was 'lenient, by the standards of the time'. And 'the real sufferers were the Church, the people of God'.[34] This last statement underestimated the persecution of Galileo and the adverse effects of censorship imposed, not only on him but on other scientists and philosophers also – for example, René Descartes (1596–1650).[35]

The New York-based author George Sim Johnston expressed extreme views on the subject and was facilitated by the editors of *Position Papers* (Dublin), Rev. Charles Connolly and Rev. Patrick Gorevan. Johnston maintained that Galileo 'was intent on ramming Copernicus down the throat of Christendom', that his tactless and offensive manner alienated many potential supporters, that he left the ecclesiastical authorities with very little choice, that some of his scientific arguments were erroneous, that he could not prove the Copernican hypothesis, and that he insisted on introducing theology into the debate. Johnston did manage to acknowledge that the condemnation of Galileo was 'certainly unjust' but he quickly added that the error of the ecclesiastical authorities in this matter did not have any negative implications for the infallibility of Catholic dogma because no *ex cathedra* pronouncements had been issued. The Roman Catholic Church had 'little to apologise for in its relations with science'.[36] The views that were expressed in *Doctrine and Life* and in *Position Papers* about the Galileo affair were much more circumscribed by considerations of apologetics relative to those of Pope John Paul II.

John Paul continued to press for dialogue between Roman Catholicism and science and on 22 October 1996 he addressed the issue of evolutionary theory in a message to the Pontifical Academy of Sciences. He acknowledged that scientific evidence had continued to accumulate in favour of evolution since the publication of *Humani Generis*. In view of this, evolution could no longer be considered as 'a mere hypothesis'. Its implications for religious doctrine could not be ignored. Furthermore, the spiritual soul was to be excluded from the evolutionary process – it was 'immediately' created by God.[37]

The issue of reconciling polygenism with Original Sin was not resolved, at least not from a papal perspective. However, it seems that some Catholic authors did express opinions about how such harmony might be achieved. Augustine Kasujja, a future archbishop of Uganda, mindful of discoveries of fossil finds in east Africa (especially of *Homo habilis*), had proposed in 1986 that the understanding of Original Sin could be revised in harmony with the latest scientific discoveries if the transmission of Original Sin was understood on the basis of solidarity and not in terms of genetic descent.[38] Innovative theological ideas presented some opportunities to revise Catholic doctrine in harmony with what was firmly established in evolutionary biology. But the teaching authority of the church, in 1996, did not take advantage of such opportunities.

The papal statement received much attention in the international press. In Ireland it was rather misleadingly reported in *The Examiner* that the pope had lent his support to the theory of evolution.[39] Inaccurate reporting on this issue was probably not unusual.[40] Mary A. Vitoria, a biologist and philosopher living in Rome, wrote in *Position Paper 301* that a close reading of the papal address on evolution revealed an attitude that was very different from reports in most journals and newspapers. The papal address represented a shift in nuance arising from scientific developments, not a revision of doctrine. The pope's statements were made in a catechetical and theological context. Vitoria argued that the pope did not endorse Darwin's theory – for the simple reason that he was not in a position to dictate criteria for scientific research or for the evaluation of its empirical data. Vitoria believed that when the pope spoke of evolution as more than just a hypothesis he was merely acknowledging the consensus amongst scientists on the subject.[41]

Catholic teaching did not seem to be reconcilable with some versions of evolution. It was observed that evolution, 'as usually proposed' – that is, in its neo-Darwinian form – was not compatible with Catholic teaching about Original Sin. There was a tendency amongst preachers and teachers to avoid the doctrine of Original Sin because of their uncertainty about the subject.[42] There seemed to be a lack of interest amongst Irish Catholic authors in religious life in addressing the issue. This may have been for reasons of caution arising from the intransigence of the papacy on the subject. Silent dissent may have been regarded as the most prudent position to adopt. The notion of monogenism was so intellectually untenable in the light of science that it was probably regarded with some embarrassment by those theologians who were well informed about science. The predominant attitude amongst the Irish Catholic laity was probably one of indifference – if indeed there was any significant level of awareness of the formidable difficulty of reconciling evolutionary theory and the traditional stance of the church on Original Sin.

In July 2004 the institutional church took a major step in harmonising its teaching with evolutionary theory when the International Theological Commission in Rome, under the direction of Cardinal Joseph Ratzinger (the future Pope Benedict XVI), issued its *Communion and Stewardship: Human Persons Created in the Image of God*. In paragraph 63 of that document it was acknowledged that it was 'virtually certain' that biological evolution had occurred. Furthermore, the commission addressed the subject of human evolution, indicating that the institutional church was no longer expressing serious doubts about it:

> While the story of human origins is complex and subject to revision, physical anthropology and molecular biology combine to make a convincing case for the origin of the human species in Africa about 150,000 years ago in a humanoid population of common genetic lineage. However it is to be explained, the decisive factor in human origins was a continually increasing brain size, culminating in that of *homo sapiens*.[43]

This document was an important step in reducing discord between Catholic doctrine on Original Sin and evolutionary biology.[44]

The next element in the relationship between religion and science – that of integration – was seen to occur at two levels. Firstly, it was possible for scientific theories to contribute to the revision of theological ideas. Thomas Corbett pointed to the anthropic cosmological principle as an example.[45] There was some dissatisfaction with St Thomas Aquinas's five proofs for the existence of God and some Catholic authors looked to modern science for better arguments. The anthropic cosmological principle – the notion of a finely tuned universe for the emergence of intelligent life – was used to bolster the contention that the universe provided strong evidence of an intelligent designer. If the universe was not designed by an omniscient deity then it seemed incredibly coincidental that a number of physical constants – such as gravitational force, the speed of light, the weak and strong nuclear forces, the properties of subatomic particles (such as mass, charge and spin), and Planck's constant – were all precisely proportioned for the emergence of life. It was argued that any slight variation in one physical constant would have led to the development of an entirely different universe unsuitable for life (or at least life as we know it).[46]

Corbett saw integration occurring at a deeper level where theology relied heavily on the natural sciences for the construction of its new paradigms, as it had in the Middle Ages when it embraced Aristotelian philosophy. He quoted the author Stephen Toulmin to make the point that theology experienced severe difficulties when the scientific theories it was in close affinity with were 'radically questioned'. Therefore, he believed that the most theology should seek from science was 'a certain dialogue and consonance, or a certain compatibility'.[47]

The element of conflict requires little introduction here. Conflict took the form of inconsistencies, dissonance or contradictions between theology and the sciences. Conflict in another sense also occurred when individual scientists deliberately ventured beyond their disciplinary boundaries to attack religion, or sometimes only theology. In the last half of the twentieth century eminent scientists who expressed sceptical, agnostic or atheistic beliefs included Julian Huxley,[48] Jacques Monod (1910–1976),[49] Steven Weinberg,[50] Stephen Hawking[51] and Richard Dawkins.[52] Corbett acknowledged that the element of conflict still existed but believed that the discernment of chaos and random chance in nature did not exclude ordered purpose in the universe.[53]

The Conflict Thesis[54]

Conflict has frequently arisen when scientists and Catholic apologists ventured beyond their areas of professional competence. A clear case of scientists trespassing on religious ground is in the book *God and the New Physics* (1984) by Paul Davies, Professor of Natural Philosophy at the University of Adelaide. Davies expressed the opinion that 'science offers a surer path to God than religion'. He believed that it was becoming more widely accepted that developments in basic scientific research and theory formation would focus a more intense light on 'the deeper meaning of existence' than the insights offered by traditional religion. It would not be prudent for the upholders of religion to ignore advances in science.[55]

But was science a homogeneous entity *vis-à-vis* religion? Davies thought not! In the nineteenth century the mechanical model of the universe proposed by physics had gravitated towards materialism. Biologists, in contrast, had generally accorded a privileged status to the human mind in the hierarchy of nature. Now, in the late twentieth century, there was a reversal of trends. Biology had drifted towards materialism and physics had moved away from it. The two scientific disciplines were still travelling in different directions. Thomas Corbett referred extensively to

Davies to make the point that religious believers needed to take cognisance of what was happening in science.[56] Corbett saw a convergence of interests between science and theology with considerable scope for dialogue. However, some eminent scientists from both physics and biology, especially Hawking and Dawkins, continued to provoke criticism from those determined to write in defence of religious viewpoints.[57]

Dawkins, the Charles Simonyi Professor of the Public Understanding of Science at Oxford, was the best known and most vigorous exponent of the conflict thesis. In his international bestseller *The Selfish Gene*, first published in 1976, he attacked blind religious faith as being responsible for the repression of the intellect and for the propagation of violence in places as diverse as Belfast and Beirut.[58] Fr Enda McDonagh, formerly a Professor of Moral Theology at Maynooth, wrote in *The Irish Review* (2001) that the atheistic opinions of Dawkins had 'its own impact on Ireland'.[59] In quantitative terms this observation was prudently vague because it did not seem possible to state, with any reasonable degree of statistical confidence and precision, what the influence of Dawkins was in Ireland. The interaction between scientific and religious thought needed to be explored. McDonagh and his three co-editors of *The Irish Review* decided to make their own contribution to Irish intellectual discourse by inviting an eminent Irish geneticist, Professor David McConnell, and a leading Irish theologian, Fr Gabriel Daly, both of Trinity College Dublin, 'to continue their long running amicable dialogue' on the relationship between religion and science.

McConnell observed that the achievements of scientists in the twentieth century were not only extraordinary but unique in terms of cultural enterprise. Creativity in music, literature, art, philosophy and in other disciplines did not compare in relative terms. Unlike science, the achievements of professionals in these disciplines did not overshadow the achievements of previous centuries. Despite its shortcomings, science was 'in the intellectual driving seat'. The great strength of science was that it was constructed on the basis of a rational method of investigation and, in that sense, was internationally standardised. If a scientist's claims were to be sustained then they had to be independently verified by other professional scientists. Religion, on the other hand, was weakened by demands for evidence.

McConnell anticipated that as the people of Ireland became more educated in science they would become less religious. Although he hoped that scientific thinking would advance and proliferate, he was mindful of some potential problems arising from the concomitant demise of religion, such as the loss of comfort and support which some people find in religious belief. In a broader context, he recognised that the use of science needed to be regulated for the good of society, otherwise it might destroy humankind. But he was doubtful if religion could be reformed so that it could play a constructive role in moral guidance. His idea of reformed religion was one centred on 'a humanist God' – radically different from the God of Christianity.[60]

In his reply to McConnell, Gabriel Daly observed that the censorship of Galileo had damaged the relationship between religion and science but it is strange that he made no reference to the findings of the Vatican's interdisciplinary commission, or to papal pronouncements on the subject. It was as if the Vatican had nothing of importance to say about the troubled relationship between Roman Catholicism and science. In his concluding statement, Daly disagreed with McConnell on the replacement of a transcendent God by a humanist God, the basis of appeals to morality, and the idea of Jesus the man instead of the divine Jesus. This difference of opinion was moderately expressed. His disagreement with Dawkins was more vigorous. Dawkins was criticised for his assumptions about the non-existence of the supernatural, for the extension of reductionism beyond the domain of science, and for his refusal to recognise valid perspectives beyond the natural sciences.[61]

In 1998 Dawkins travelled to Ireland to promote his book *Unweaving the Rainbow*. In the course of a radio interview he asserted that science was eroding religious belief and that there was nothing to be learnt from religion. Professor William Reville of University College Cork expressed a contrary view through the medium of his regular science column in *The Irish Times*. He emphasised the limited competency of science. It could not answer fundamentally important questions such as whether or not there was a purpose to human existence, or if there was a supernatural realm. Even if religion was 'abolished', these questions would still persist.[62]

In a renewed attack on religion, Dawkins singled out the Roman Catholic Church for particularly harsh criticism. His opinions were published in the October 2002 issue of *The Dubliner* magazine. Dawkins was delighted that an Irish seminary had closed down due to a lack of religious vocations. He fervently hoped that the Roman Catholic Church would become extinct in Ireland and would 'not be replaced by some other idiotic superstition'. The church acted as a powerful instigator of evil, especially because of its influence over the minds of children – an influence derived from 'brilliant techniques in brain washing' refined to very high standards over centuries of practice. This had a strong and enduring effect. Many adults found it very difficult to liberate their minds from Roman Catholicism. Speaking more generally about religion, Dawkins claimed that belief in God obstructed the understanding of nature at all levels – the universe, planet Earth, and all life, including human life.[63]

Reville responded to Dawkins through the medium of *The Irish Times*. Firstly, he argued that the anti-religious opinions of Dawkins were not representative of scientists in general. Secondly, he made the point that the misuse of something, be it religion or science, cannot be reasonably put forward as justification to seek a cessation of practice. The errors of Christianity, such as eternal punishment in the fires of hell, the obsession with extreme codes of sexual morality, and Biblical literalism, had to be seen in a wider context where Christianity promoted social virtues. If Christianity was to be rejected for the evils it propagated or was implicated in, then it could be argued that science should be renounced for similar reasons. The role of science in eugenics contributed to the initiation of programmes of sterilisation in mental institutions in the United States and in other countries, and to the far greater evil of the Holocaust perpetrated by Nazi Germany.[64]

Dawkins continued his crusade against religion. In 2003 a collection of his essays was published under the title *A Devil's Chaplain*. One of these essays, 'The Great Convergence', was published in *The Irish Times* (17 February 2003). A radio interview with Marian Finucane gave Dawkins further valuable publicity for his book in Ireland. Dawkins argued trenchantly that there was no convergence between religion and science. Religion in this context was traditional, embracing such ideas as life after death, and a supreme being – the kind of God who answered prayers – in other words, religion in the traditional sense, religion as commonly understood. Dawkins castigated agnostic 'liberal intellectuals' whom he saw as advocating a policy of appeasement, dividing the intellectual terrain of religion and science by allocating 'how questions' to science and 'why questions' to religion. He conceded that there might be some important questions about the universe which would remain forever beyond the competence of science to answer. But he maintained that it was an error of judgement to think that religion could rise to the challenge of ultimate questions – there was simply no good reason to think that it could.[65]

Agnostic conciliation was unacceptable. Dawkins would settle for nothing less than conflict – scientific atheism versus theism. Agnosticism was an undesirable buffer between the two positions. Dawkins accepted the genuine difficulty of not being able to prove a negative in philosophical discourse. He also accepted that science could not disprove the existence of God. But he refused to accept that arguments for and against the existence of God were of equal merit. In support of such a contention he invoked Bertrand Russell's quirky notion of a celestial teapot. It is not possible, in an absolute philosophical sense, to disprove the preposterous idea of a china teapot in elliptical orbit around the sun. However, this does not mean that the possibility of an orbiting teapot is as strong as the probable absence of such a strange object.[66] Dawkins was confident that the arguments for God were no stronger than those for Russell's teapot – an assumption which dismissed the merits of the anthropic cosmological principle and assumed that there were overpowering arguments against theism in philosophy.

In his attack on religion Dawkins again singled out Roman Catholicism for special attention. Papal pronouncements about Galileo and evolution did not persuade him to adopt a conciliatory attitude towards the Roman Catholic Church. The notion that religion and science occupied separate 'magisteria' was dishonest because religion did make claims which were actually scientific claims. For Dawkins, miracles were 'blatant intrusions' into the domain of science. In this context he made specific reference to the Virgin Birth, the Resurrection, the raising of Lazarus, the apparitions of the Virgin Mary and the saints to Roman Catholics, and the Old Testament miracles. The doctrine of the Assumption, dogmatically defined by Pope Pius XII on 1 November 1950, was especially criticised because it seemed to imply that heaven was a physical place. Miracles were, effectively, scientific claims, and violated the normal functioning of the physical world. Dawkins maintained that religious apologists were very careful to respect the autonomy of science when speaking to intellectuals but adopted a different approach when talking to audiences of 'unsophisticates and children'. Miracles were used for purposes of religious propaganda and were very effective with the intellectually challenged and those of immature years. The claim by religious apologists that religion and science were converging was dismissed by Dawkins as a 'shallow, empty, hollow, spin-doctored sham'.[67]

William Reville, professedly Roman Catholic, was understandably stung by the contention that the Roman Catholic Church and other religious organisations used the idea of miracles to captivate impression-able adults and children. He conceded that miracles did 'run counter to scientific explanation'. But the acceptance of miracles played 'little or no role' in the lives of sensible Christians. Christian doctrine – 'ninety nine point nine percent' of it – was concerned with the moral teachings of Jesus Christ (surely an exaggeration?). Reville wrote in defence of 'thoughtful' Christianity, declaring that he had a practical reason for challenging the attack on religion by Dawkins, who did not represent scientists in general. He and others were endeavouring to stimulate a greater interest and engagement with science amongst the general public. Their task would be made much more difficult if they did nothing to counteract the idea that scientists who retained their religious faith were considered unreasonable by their colleagues.[68]

Reville's concerns about public opinion towards science, in the above context, were probably not well founded. As he stated in an earlier *Irish Times* article, Catholics and other Christians were not inclined to 'meekly' submit to 'backward rules' and were now inclined to form their own opinions.[69] But there was still reluctance by Irish Catholics to actively engage in debates about religion and science. Brian Trench, a lecturer at the School of Communications in Dublin City University, observed that Dawkins had stridently expressed his anti-religious opinions to an audience of about one thousand people in Dublin without provoking even 'a murmur of dissent'.[70] Presumably, there were theists of varying hues in the assembly, including Roman Catholics. And yet – no dissenting voices! Trench observed that there was relatively little discourse about science and religion in Ireland when cognisance was taken of international debates. This was particularly true of discussions at an advanced level. Letters to the editor of *The Irish Times* indicated that many people held strong views about religion and science. But these letters also indicated that the majority of such views lacked analytical rigour.[71]

In his book *The Minding of Planet Earth* (2004), Cardinal Cahal B. Daly acknowledged that the possibility of conflict between theological and scientific thinking could not be ruled out, but he sought to minimise it. It would be foolish of scientists to rule out the Virgin Birth of Jesus Christ because it was inconsistent with human reproductive biology. It would be foolish of Christians to hope for scientific proof of the Virgin Birth arising from research in genetics. The resurrection of the dead was not in accordance with the findings of science but Christians knew it to be true. A scientific examination of the consecrated bread of the

Eucharist would reveal nothing more than ordinary bread but this would not create a crisis of faith amongst Catholics who understood the doctrines of their church. The risen body of Jesus Christ was not amenable to scientific investigation. The essential articles of the Roman Catholic faith were simply beyond the reach of science.[72]

What Daly was trying to create was what Dawkins referred to as an 'epistemological Safe Zone' for religious belief, beyond the reach of rational scrutiny.[73] Dawkins did not refer specifically to Daly's book but it is clear that he challenged the isolationist strategy advocated by the cardinal. In his book *The God Delusion* (2006), he asserted that the existence of God, miracles such as the virgin birth of Jesus Christ and his resurrection, and the raising of Lazarus from the dead, were all scientific questions in principle. It was not likely that evidence would be discovered to answer such questions but if it was it would be scientific.[74] This claim for science – the expansion of its intellectual domain to address questions commonly regarded as theological – was not only unacceptable to theologians – it was also philosophically unsound and was extremely unlikely to gain the support of the majority of his fellow scientists.

Dawkins accepted that the non-existence of God cannot be proven with absolute certainty. But for him it was essentially a question of probability and improbability. He found that God's existence was extremely improbable – in the same category as Bertrand Russell's celestial teapot, the tooth fairy, and the Flying Spaghetti Monster. Natural selection demolished the idea of design in nature. Or did it? Dawkins acknowledged that some theologians believed that God used natural selection as a means of advancing his creation. He sought to manipulate this to his advantage. Natural selection would make the creative process efficient and easy, so easy that God would have very little to do – to the point that he could be dismissed as superfluous.[75] For Dawkins, natural selection was a better explanation of complexity in nature than God.

Dawkins took issue with a number of arguments for the existence of God, including St Thomas Aquinas's five proofs, the ontological argument, the argument from personal experience, Pascal's Wager, irreducible complexity, and the anthropic cosmological principle. There were some merits in the opinions he expressed, and some weaknesses. Although considerations of space do not permit an extensive critique of Dawkins here, a number of points will receive attention. Dawkins argued persuasively against the 'God of the Gaps' thinking underpinning intelligent design theory and dismissed it as lazy, defeatist and anti-scientific.[76] He rejected Pascal's Wager because it was inimical to an honest search for truth and encouraged insincere religious belief. Honest doubt was a virtue.[77] Tolerance and respect for those who were not atheists, and who were honest seekers of truth, was also a virtue. But this virtue did not feature prominently in Dawkins' work.

There was a tendency in *The God Delusion* to exaggerate the potency of arguments against the existence of God and to express assumptions and speculation as if they had the force of overpowering logic. Dawkins observed the apparent improbability of how the fundamental physical constants were interrelated. But he assumed that the existence of a God 'capable of calculating' these 'Goldilocks values' was at least as improbable. And there was the possibility that the constants were relatively invariable, like the ratio of a circle's diameter to its circumference.[78] The idea of a pluriverse or multiverse, sometimes postulated as a counterargument to the anthropic cosmological principle, was conveniently seen as less improbable than God.[79] Dawkins seems to have regarded this as an overpowering argument based on sound objective reasoning rather than as mere opinion founded on an amalgamation of scientific data, speculation and wishful thinking.

A key assumption in *The God Delusion* is the inverse relationship between probability and complexity, which is quite understandable in a physical or natural context. However, Dawkins simply extrapolated this reasoning into the supernatural domain, as if God could be reduced to a mere object of scientific enquiry. Thus, 'a designer God cannot be used to explain organised complexity because any God capable of designing anything would have to be complex enough to demand the same kind of explanation in his own right'.[80] Therefore, since Dawkins, or anyone else, cannot explain God then God – *ipso facto* – can be safely banished to the realm of extremely remote possibilities.

As stated earlier, Dawkins saw religious belief as a force for evil in the world, not least Roman Catholicism which, 'for all sorts of reasons', he disliked.[81] The primary reason, it seemed, was the psychological damage which had been inflicted on children arising from indoctrination about eternal punishment in hell. This, he contended, even surpassed the evil of the sexual abuse of children by priests (not all abusers, of course, were priests). Dawkins displayed an abysmal lack of sympathy and understanding for men and women who were still psychologically traumatised by distressing memories of their childhood experiences. It is indeed strange that, in this instance, Dawkins endeavoured to mitigate the evil deeds of those Roman Catholics who were most reactionary and morally bankrupt.[82] Underestimating the evil of the sexual abuse of children was inept and unnecessary in highlighting the terrible consequences of psychological abuse arising from religious indoctrination.

Irish Catholicism was singled out for special attention. Sexual abuse aside, the Roman Catholic Church in Ireland still had a case to answer. Dawkins referred to 'the sadistically cruel nuns who ran many of Ireland's girls' schools'. And the Christian Brothers, who had been entrusted with 'the education of a significant proportion of the male population of the country', had all too frequently acted in an extremely unchristian-like manner. Their 'brutality' was 'legendary'.[83] There is a very large volume of evidence in the public domain to support Dawkins on this point. All this of course does not seem very relevant to questions about the relationship between Catholicism and science. Nevertheless, it is important because the motivations of Dawkins can be seen in a broader context. He regarded religion as detrimental to the welfare of society and it was his mission to undermine its credibility as much as possible in the public interest. However, his book, and the conflict thesis which it promoted, seems to have received relatively little attention in Ireland. It seems that contradictions between religion and science, real or imaginary, have not caused Roman Catholics, and Christians in general, to cast aside their religious beliefs. This will be one of a number of topics discussed in the next chapter in an Irish context.

10. Science and Social Transformation

Science and the Decline of Irish Catholicism

In the early 1960s the institutional church in Ireland was authoritarian and highly centralised, and its stern authority over the laity went virtually unchallenged. It was untroubled by anticlericalism, and dissident intellectuals encountered little tolerance or support for their views. The virtues of authority, obedience and loyalty reigned supreme. The church in Ireland may have been even more right-wing than the papacy.[1] But radical changes were to occur in the last third of the twentieth century. Pope John Paul II seemed to be aware of the declining influence of the church when he visited Ireland in late September 1979. In an address at the Phoenix Park, Dublin, he told his audience that Irish Catholicism was not immune to dangers posed by competing ideologies and values transmitted through the mass media. Materialism, consumerism, self-indulgence and new ideas of morality proposed in the name of freedom were all listed as threats to Catholic morality.[2] At Galway he warned: 'The progress of science and technology seems inevitable and you may be enticed to look towards the technological society for the answers to all your problems.'[3]

Quantifying and analysing the decline or growth of religious beliefs and practices is extremely difficult and complicated.[4] Survey questions are of limited value in seeking to understand such complicated topics as the role of religion in society.[5] Nevertheless, it would be unreasonable to simply ignore data derived from surveys. There is strong evidence to indicate that the power and influence of the institutional church, and the practice of Catholicism, declined sharply in the years between the pope's visit and the dawn of the new millennium – especially in the 1990s.[6] Religious vocations had decreased consistently since the 1960s. The European Values Survey (1990) indicated that Irish Catholics had become more independent minded and were far less inclined to meekly submit to clerical directives on personal morality.[7] In December 1996 an *Irish Times*-MRBI poll indicated that 78% of Catholics followed their own consciences when making important moral decisions. Weekly attendance at Mass slumped from 85% in 1986 to 66% in 1996.[8] In February 1998 another survey showed that Mass attendance had fallen to 60% and that 40% of Catholics rarely or never went to confession.[9] National census figures revealed that the Roman Catholic sector of the population declined – not in terms of absolute figures but in proportionate terms – from 94.9% in 1961 to 88.4% in 2002. Nearly half of the percentage decrease occurred from 1991 to 2002.[10] The number of people who identified their status under the heading 'no religion' increased rapidly, from only 1,107 in 1961 to 66,270 in 1991. This sector of the population continued to grow strongly over the next eleven years to reach 138,264 (3.5%) in 2002.[11] Ireland was becoming less Catholic. However, it would be a mistake to assume that Irish Catholicism, or religion in general, is in terminal decline. But it can be argued with confidence that Irish Catholicism is now much weaker than it used to be. Did science play an important role in the declining role of Roman Catholicism in Irish society? Is science inherently inimical to religion?

It is easy to exaggerate the adverse effect of science on religion at the intellectual level. Religion was not overturned by coming into direct conflict with rational scientific thought. Very few people abandoned their faith because of a conviction that religion was irreconcilable with science. In the late nineteenth century John Tyndall wrote about the 'logical feebleness' of science in the context of reasoning with people who were obstinately superstitious. He envisaged that science would 'keep down the weed of superstition, not by logic but by slowly rendering the mental soil unfit for its cultivation'.[12] In the late twentieth century some authors have pointed to the subtle and corrosive effects of science on religion. Bill McSweeney, lecturer in social ethics at the Irish School of Ecumenics, argued that the findings of science did not contradict or support religious faith, although science had contradicted specific religious beliefs such as the earth's position in the cosmos, the origins of humankind, and the historicity of Biblical narratives. He maintained that the subject matter of science did not create difficulties in sustaining belief in a transcendent God. But this did not mean that science was neutral towards religion. McSweeney argued that science exerted a harmful effect on religion which was not obvious and direct but was, nevertheless, more damaging than the contradiction of specific articles of faith. Science tended to undermine faith by diminishing its status in the hierarchy of knowledge. It heightened an awareness of a distinction between knowledge which was testable and that which was not. Testable knowledge was rewarded with 'valued economic goods' and the consequence of this was the elevation of science above faith and ecclesiastical authority.[13] Richard Elliott Friedman, Professor of Hebrew and Comparative Literature at the University of California, maintained that the accumulation of scientific knowledge enhanced our understanding of the natural world and reduced our tendency to fill the gaps in our knowledge with the handiwork of the divine. Science and technology contributed to the feeling that humankind now had much greater control over its destiny, which, in turn, created the impression that God had disappeared.[14]

In 1996 Rev. Fachtna McCarthy, lecturer in theology at St Patrick's College, Drumcondra, Dublin, expressed concern about the apparent vulnerability of religious faith in a milieu of scientific rationality. He wrote:

> . . . there can be no denying which force is in the ascendancy. Scientific rationality to a great extent provides the theoretical base for what our culture accepts as knowledge . . . Popular culture has given science an almost sacred character, its practitioners held in awe as mediating the mysteries of the natural world to us. Science has transformed our map of the physical universe and dominates our daily lives by its amazing successful applications. How can we not have faith in science when it has produced the technology that underpins everything from our economy, our health and our lifestyles? . . . By comparison, religious faith seems outdated, vague and mythological; for many science has replaced religion as the primary source of authority and meaning. Hence Christian theology . . . appears to be in continuous retreat before a cumulative and infallible scientific method. Is it possible to take religion seriously in an age of science?[15]

Many people did continue to take their religion seriously.[16] McCarthy's outlook was not as pessimistic as the above quotation suggests and he proceeded to argue that a new and fruitful interaction was developing between religion and science in the final years of the twentieth century. From his perspective science and religion were highly compatible. If it is assumed that he was wrong about this – if looking at the world scientifically was lethal to religion – could this explain the weakened condition of Irish Catholicism in the mid-1990s? In response to this question it will be argued that science in Ireland was not widely appreciated, especially in terms of its intellectual value. Therefore, it was not in a strong position to overturn religious beliefs by itself. Under these circumstances it could only act as one influence amongst many. Scientific rationality was not so pervasive that it could act alone to undermine religious faith.

Sir George Porter, joint winner of the Nobel Prize in Chemistry with Manfred Eigen and Ronald Norrish in 1967, observed that if there is little public demand for the promotion of science then the government will not support it either, because the politicians in power depend on public opinion to retain their positions. Most politicians are not scientists and may share an attitude with the majority of their electorate in not appreciating the importance of adequately funding scientific education and research.[17] Insofar as interest was expressed in the Republic of Ireland, it was in the context of achieving economic and social objectives.[18] The Labour politician, university lecturer and future president of Ireland, Michael D. Higgins made the point that there was very little debate, both at academic level and in the popular media, about the uses of science and technology consistent with the preservation of the natural environment and the well-being of society. Because of the lack of interaction between the social and physical sciences, the world was not viewed from an interdisciplinary perspective. This fragmented vision stifled the possibility that a range of environmental and socio-economic problems could be satisfactorily addressed.[19]

The adverse economic conditions prevailing in Ireland held in check any enthusiasm there might be for the intellectual benefits of scientific knowledge. There was a lack of vision and commitment to investment in scientific research and this was perhaps nowhere more clearly expressed than in the National Science Council's report *Science Policy: Some Implications for Ireland* (January 1973). The Council stated that:

> Relatively limited national resources require that Irish science policy, because of urgent social and economic problems and opportunities, cannot be primarily concerned with pushing forward the frontiers of science or expanding the totality of man's knowledge of the universe or of gaining competitive advantages in spheres of 'big' science or technology such as high energy physics . . . Rather is it mainly concerned with demonstrating the uses of science and technology in defining and achieving the aims of public policy . . . Up to the present, science policy . . . has, as a rule, only incidentally been an intrinsic part of public policy in Ireland . . . [I]t has not yet informed or infused national policy as a whole in a unified way. It has not been given sufficient weight in existing economic and social policies.[20]

In the cultural domain science was also neglected. Andy Shearer, a contributor to *Technology Ireland*, observed that Ireland neglected to pay
tribute to its famous scientists. Political and literary figures were vener-
ated at the expense of scientists and technologists. Shearer observed that
'the memories and writing of Behan, Joyce, Swift and O'Casey live on
while the likes of Stoney, Tyndall, Joly and Grubb, and their work, remain
obscure. Yet it can be argued that their feats of creativity and imagination
are at least equally important.'[21] There was a strong tendency in broad-
ranging works on Irish cultural history to ignore the history of science
and its role in Irish society. Even when the economy was booming in the
'Celtic Tiger' years, contemporary cultural studies failed to give due
attention to the perceived importance of science and technology in
debates about the 'knowledge economy'.[22]

With the above observations in mind it would be remiss not to give
consideration to Dorinda Outram's 'Heavenly Bodies and Logical
Minds', originally published in the journal *Graph* in 1988 and republished in *Science and Irish Culture* in 2004. Outram wrote that science in
Ireland remained 'fixed in a culturally peripheral position', not only
because of insufficient expenditure by the state and 'the hostility of
bodies like the Church', but also because it remained 'locked in a colonial
mindset, identified willy-nilly with the "Protestant" moderniser rather
than the "Catholic" traditionalist'. This opinion lacked plausibility when
applied to late 1980s Ireland, and is conspicuously implausible for the
early years of the twenty-first century. The attitude of the Irish church
towards science from the 1980s onwards could not be correctly
described as one of hostility, notwithstanding its impoverished theology
of nature and its rejection of Enlightenment values. Those in positions
of influence in the church could hardly have failed to discern a certain
tension between the critical questioning attitude so essential for a sound
scientific outlook and the church's dogmatic insistence on the centrality
of faith and authority for sustaining religious belief. They would also
have known that scientific theories had compelled a revision of some
cherished doctrines of the church, and had been used in the service of
various ideologies in attempts to undermine religion. These considerations – collectively – probably dampened down enthusiasm for science
but did not lead to institutional hostility, at least not in any formal or
overt sense. It was more a case of indifference or avoidance, and sometimes indications of underlying concerns about the subversive effects of
science on faith.

Outram's point about the strong associations between science, colonialism and Protestantism were well founded for Ireland in the late nineteenth and early twentieth centuries. But these connections were probably long forgotten by 1988 (except by a few scholars) – along with Stoney, Tyndall, Joly and Grubb. Even if such associations lingered in the public consciousness, this would not have impeded the progress of science. The 'binary pairs of opposites' – Catholic versus Protestant, Celt Gaelic versus English, *et cetera* – had lost their potency well before 2004. Perceptions of the 'national heritage' had been radically transformed by such developments as membership of the European Union, the economic boom, and the legacy of the protracted conflict in Northern Ireland.[23] Furthermore, a radical change in government policy towards science, accompanied by a massive increase in investment, was well underway by 2004 – this will receive attention later in this chapter.

Up to the late 1990s government policies reflected the public's lack of interest in science. Successive Irish governments had failed to act upon a number of socio-economic reports that recommended investment in science and technology to enhance national competitive advantage.[24] State funding for scientific research was neither adequate nor sustained. Ireland was one of the lowest spenders in Europe on research and development when investment was calculated as a percentage of total government expenditure. The republic relied heavily on the Structural Funds of the European Community to support its scientific research in the 1980s and 1990s. However, economic growth in Ireland indicated that the state would receive a decreasing share of Cohesion and Structural Funds from the European Community. This had worrying implications for the future of Irish science.[25] In 1995 the Science, Technology and Innovation Advisory Council found that there was 'a passive approach' to science and technology in Ireland. Technical changes were mainly driven by imported products and especially through the attraction of foreign investment. It was clear to the council that stimulating the emergence of an innovation culture in science and technology was essential for industrial development.[26]

Science and its technological applications were of central importance to maintaining and enhancing the quality of life. People had over time become increasingly dependent on the fruits of scientific research and technological innovation, relying on such products as refrigerators, washing machines, televisions, telephones, motor cars, airplanes, computers, pharmaceuticals, *et cetera*. A number of contentious issues arose which required some degree of understanding of scientific and technical concepts – for example, renewable sources of energy as alternatives to fossil fuels, blood products contaminated with the human immunodeficiency virus (HIV), genetically modified foods, and bovine spongiform encephalopathy (BSE – 'mad cow' disease). And yet the council found that there was a poor public awareness of science and technology issues. There was an exceptionally low level of interest and expertise in science and technology amongst journalists and newspaper editors. Furthermore, scientists themselves made little effort to communicate the benefits of their work to the public. The Department of Education, although 'aware of the traditional bias in Irish education towards the arts and humanities for some time', had not yet remedied this imbalance.[27] *Science, Technology and Innovation: The White Paper* (October 1996) emphasised the need to promote public awareness of science and technology issues.[28] Ireland rated poorly when compared with thirteen other states – Canada, the United States, Japan, Belgium, the United Kingdom, Denmark, France, Germany, Greece, Italy, Netherlands, Portugal and Spain. This was evident from the report, *Science and Technology in the Public Eye* (1996), published by the Organization for Economic Cooperation and Development (OECD). Irish interest in new scientific discoveries, new medical discoveries, new inventions and technologies, and environmental pollution was considerably less relative to most of the countries listed above. Attentiveness to science and technology issues was also relatively weak in Ireland.[29]

It seems that science, occupying a relatively low position in matters of public concern, was not a major contributor to the decline of Roman Catholicism in Ireland. What role did science play at the professional level? There is some evidence to indicate that science at the professional level did contribute to the decline of religious belief (including Roman Catholicism) in the Republic of Ireland. The national census of April 2002 revealed that there were 51,151 workers categorised under the heading of scientific and technical occupations. Of these, 4,019 (7.9%) stated that they had 'no religion'. This was substantially higher than the national average of 3.5%. The total workforce for all occupational groups was 1,641,587, with 78,084 (4.8%) stating 'no religion'.[30] The vast majority of scientists and technicians were still religious to some extent. Of these, 42,911 (83.9%) were Roman Catholic – a slight under-representation given that 88.4% of the population was Roman Catholic.[31] This differential of 4.5% could be seen as an indicator that a small minority of Roman

Catholics do experience difficulties in reconciling their religion with a scientific outlook.

It might be expected that the sceptical and questioning attitude appropriate to science would be detrimental to religious belief to a far greater extent, where, in the religious sphere, faith is put forward as a virtue. However, the tendency to subject religious belief to intellectual scrutiny, influenced by scientific methodology, was probably counterbalanced extensively by the high level of specialisation in modern science. Many scientists were probably not well-read in the philosophy of science. Generally, they were narrowly focused in their research interests and this is likely to have counteracted, to a large extent, any sceptical, agnostic or atheistic tendencies which might otherwise have emerged from their work.

Catholicism in the Cultural Market

Many intellectual, religious, cultural, political and economic factors have been identified with the decline of Roman Catholicism in Ireland. These include: the failure to respond adequately to the decrees and proclamations of the Second Vatican Council, the widespread rejection of the papal encyclical on contraception (*Humanae Vitae*, 1968) which provoked many Catholics to question the validity of their church's teaching in a broader sense, economic prosperity, industrialisation, urbanisation, technological thinking, the influx of new ideas and information through the media (especially television), travel, ideological pluralism, the pervasiveness of rationality and a functional outlook, the declining numbers of priests and members of religious orders in the education system, a highly educated and more independent-minded laity, the growing influence of Anglo-American music and culture over Irish youth, liberalisation, consumer culture, the decline of certitudes, the weakness of social Catholicism, the legal and social changes brought about by Ireland's entry into the European community, the feminist movement, boredom with dull conformity, individualism, apathy, clerical scandals, the failure of the church to respond positively and adequately to the needs of a rapidly changing society, and the misrepresentation of Jesus Christ's teaching from within the church itself.[32]

Fr Michael Paul Gallagher (S.J.), whose dialogue with students at University College Dublin stimulated him to take a particular interest in religious unbelief, argued that it was far less due to ideologies, such as atheistic communism, and was much more associated with culture. By the 1990s it seemed that there had been a shift from a conscious and deliberate denial of God amongst unbelievers to a vague disengagement from religious faith. Unbelief was based more on scepticism about big ideas rather than on a deliberate rejection of God. Religious faith was 'not so much denied as sensed to be unreal'.[33] Indifference to religion rather than overt intellectual opposition seemed to present the greatest challenge to Christian faith.[34]

The role of the education system in the decline of Roman Catholicism in Ireland may seem strange when cognisance is taken of the control exerted over it by the church. However, it is probable that the church's influence has been overestimated. In second-level schools relatively little time was given to the study of religious values. The concepts and principles associated with many subjects – for example, physics, chemistry, biology, technical drawing, business organisation, accountancy, and economics – have very little in common with Catholic or Christian values. In some instances these subjects may even propose values and influence attitudes that contradict, or are difficult to reconcile with, religious beliefs. For example, in economics the maximisation of profits may not be entirely in agreement with the Christian commandment to love one's neighbour because it is frequently based on assumptions of exploitation. Pupils are taught the importance of seeking, and critically evaluating, evidence in the context of assessing the plausibility of an alleged fact or theory when studying science. This is a radically different approach to what is demanded by religious faith where the emphasis is on belief without proof. These contradictory values in the school curriculum counteract, to some extent, a firm and uncritical adherence to the Roman Catholic faith.[35]

From the above it will be seen that science is one of a number of inter-related factors in the decline of Roman Catholicism in Ireland. In his *Science and Religion: Some Historical Perspectives* (1991), John Hedley Brooke maintained that scientific and technological advances acted as powerful forces in facilitating the secularisation of Western society but these developments did not, by themselves, bring about the proliferation of secular attitudes. The reduced influence of the main Christian churches was due to a broad and complex range of social, economic and political changes that await further exploration and analysis. Science and technical applications contributed to a diminished role for religion in society but there are many other factors to be considered.[36]

In considering the impact of science on religion, Paul Davies argued that the greatest effect on the masses was at the practical level – through

technology rather than at the intellectual level.[37] Applied science empowered humankind to exert much more control over its environment. This
in turn gave rise to greater confidence and an accompanying diminished
reliance on supernatural intervention. It seemed that technology was
more reliable than religion. In his book *God Save Ulster: The Religion and
Politics of Paisleyism* (1986), Steve Bruce vividly exemplified this point in
the context of Ulster Protestantism:

> Prayer can save one's cattle from ringworm but chemicals are more
> reliable. The religious farmer may begin by combining prayer and
> chemicals and gradually reduce the range of things which he 'takes to
> the Lord in prayer' as technical solutions are found. Technical
> advances gradually remove areas of uncertainty and unpredictability
> and, by so doing, shrink the regions of life for which religion is still
> thought to offer the best explanations and remedies.[38]

Advances in technology occurred with increasing frequency. At the
beginning of the twenty-first century plans were in progress at government level to ensure that science and technology would play increasingly
important roles in economic development.[39] It was anticipated that
IR£560 million would be spent to enable Ireland to become a world-class
leader in two areas of scientific research – biotechnology and computer
technology. This was a key element of a planned IR£1.9 billion investment in science and was an essential part of the National Development
Plan for 2000–2006.[40] On 27 July 2000 the Tánaiste,[41] Mary Harney, and
Noel Treacy, Minister of State for Science, Technology and Commerce,
officially launched Science Foundation Ireland to oversee the spending of
over £500 million (€634 million) on scientific research.[42] As scientific
research in Ireland went from strength to strength, a report in the *New
Scientist* (September 2003) stated: 'Irish researchers are spending like
never before. They are awash with cash thanks to research spending programmes that will pump €2.54 billion of state funding into research
between now and 2006 . . . With such government largesse, Ireland must
look like a researcher's El Dorado.' Some curtailment of funding had
occurred due to a slowdown in economic growth, and concerns were
expressed about financial security in the long term, but 'the good times'
were 'still rolling – if a bit more slowly'.[43] And yet – as observed by Brian
Trench – the massive spending programme for science was put together
with very little public involvement and almost no formal debate at political level. There was still a need to stimulate a greater public awareness of

science, to cultivate a vision beyond economic considerations, extending to the intellectual dimension and quality-of-life issues.[44]

Dick Ahlstrom's *Flashes of Brilliance: The Cutting Edge of Irish Science* (2006) evokes an appreciation of the dynamic nature of Irish science, and the great diversity of its research projects, in the first decade of the new millennium.[45] The increasing importance of science and technology in the economic sphere, and in everyday life, raises the question of whether or not religious belief will be adversely affected to a greater extent in future years. The Irish Jesuit theologian Dr James Corkery pointed to what he saw as a tendency of technology to work against transcendence. The technological mindset was focused on competency, efficiency, production, consumption and profit to such an extent that it was prioritised over other human qualities, such as the aesthetic, artistic, poetic and religious aspects of life.[46] It was clear to him that the 'logic' of Christianity was incompatible with the 'logic' of technological culture. The Christian outlook was 'ex-centric, self-emptying, other-directed . . .'. The technological way of looking at the world was 'I-centred, focused on my rights and possibilities, basically ego-centric'.[47] Technological development gave rise to 'a McDonaldised culture'[48] which infiltrated the church too so that it became bureaucratic, rationalised and coldly impersonal. People were treated as consumers rather than as persons. They were 'handled and processed . . . managed, controlled – but not greatly appreciated, listened to or loved'. Apparently, the 'McDonaldised system' had won – technology had triumphed.[49] A fundamental error of judgement here is that Corkery confused a capitalist-driven consumerist culture with the advances of technology. Technological innovations, generated optimally in capitalist environments, have merely facilitated a multiplicity of changes, some of which indirectly affected Catholic beliefs and practices – for example, in a way similar to that described by Steve Bruce above. The attitudes described by Corkery seem characteristic of *laissez-faire* capitalist ideology and consumerism rather than of technological thinking *per se*.

Corkery's analysis was bleak but he was not despondent. There were signs of hope. He saw in contemporary Irish culture an intense desire for meaning and a quest for spiritual experience.[50] Such a finding is consistent with the rational choice theory of religion expounded by Rodney Stark and William Sims Bainbridge. The Stark-Bainbridge theory of religion offers no judgement about the truths or falsehoods of religion. It challenges the notion that secularisation is an irreversible process of modernisation. It is contended that people will naturally tend to seek the meaning of life and enlightenment within a framework of belief in the supernatural and will always desire immortality. Adherence to religion can be viewed in terms of rewards and costs. People resort to the super-natural domain to obtain rewards when no cheaper or more efficient alternatives are on offer. A reward is defined as something which is desired, a cost as something which is avoided. It is assumed, quite rea-sonably, that humans are reward-seeking by nature.

According to rational choice theory, people try to make choices that maximise rewards and minimise costs. This applies to religion as well as to other aspects of life. People enter exchange relationships with gods, believing that supernatural beings also have desires which humans can satisfy. Gods make demands upon humans and offer rewards in exchange. Some rewards are otherworldly and are based entirely on faith. In a world beset by gross injustice, suffering and the inevitability of death, religion offers comforting assurances and gives meaning to life.[51]

If it is accepted that individuals choose their faith, and their level of commitment to it, on the basis of cost-benefit assessment,[52] then it is also reasonable to argue that they choose to interpret their religion in the light of such considerations, conveniently ignoring or misinterpreting doctrine which they feel would make excessive demands on their loyalty. This would help to explain why Catholics adopt Catholicism *à la carte*, move to the outer margins, and, in some cases, leave the church. In the competitive marketplaces of Western societies religions will invariably compete with each other. Those which are most able to 'satisfy their customers' will prosper; those which are not will decline, even to the point of extinction.[53]

Roman Catholicism is in no immediate danger of extinction. Neither is its dominance, or even its survival, assured simply on the basis that it has weathered the storms of two millennia.[54] In the long term, the domi-nance of Roman Catholicism in the religious marketplace of Ireland will be determined by its ability to reform itself, so that it can adapt to a rapidly changing cultural milieu.[55] Scientific ways of looking at the world will not single-handedly prove lethal to the Roman Catholic faith in Ireland or elsewhere. Modern science is 'godless' in the sense that it rig-orously excludes God from explanations of nature. God and the supernatural are, by definition, beyond nature, and, therefore, beyond scientific explanation. Religion will continue to find sanctuary in the non-scientific aspects of culture and will prove remarkably resilient, even in scientifically advanced societies.[56]

Notes and References

INTRODUCTION

1 Janet Browne, 'Noah's Flood, the Ark and the Shaping of Early Modern Natural History', in David C. Lindberg and Ronald L. Numbers (eds), *When Science and Christianity Meet* (Chicago: The University of Chicago Press, 2003), pp. 111–138.

2 Tess Cosslett, 'Introductory Essay', in idem (ed.), *Science and Religion in the Nineteenth Century* (Cambridge: Cambridge University Press, 1984), pp. 12–14.

3 Alvar Ellegård, *Darwin and the General Reader: The Reception of Darwin's Theory of Evolution in the British Periodical Press, 1859–1872*, foreword by David L. Hull (Chicago: The University of Chicago Press, 1990), pp. 98–100, 155.

4 These observations were made by William J. Astore about American Catholics. It is very likely that the attitudes of Irish Catholics were similar to their American counterparts. See William J. Astore, 'Gentle Skeptics? American Catholic Encounters with Polygenism, Geology and Evolutionary Theories from 1845 to 1875', *The Catholic Historical Review*, vol. 82, no. 1 (January 1996), pp. 71–73.

5 See Andrew R. Holmes, 'Presbyterians and Science in the North of Ireland before 1874', *The British Journal for the History of Science*, vol. 41, no. 151 (December 2008), p. 561; in reference to J.R. Moore, '1859 and All That: Remaking the Story of Evolution and Religion', in R.G. Chapman and C.T. Duval (eds), *Charles Darwin, 1809-1882: A Centennial Commemorative* (Wellington, NZ: Nova Pacifica, 1982), pp. 167–194. We are informed by R.B. McDowell and D.A. Webb, in their history of Trinity College Dublin, that from 1860 to about 1890, academic interests focused mainly on physics, mathematics and classics. These subjects were almost entirely free from controversies at the time. Very few scholars were interested in geology, biology, philosophy, or literary criticism. Biblical criticism attracted little attention. R.B. McDowell and D.A. Webb, *Trinity College Dublin, 1592-1952: An Academic History* (Dublin: Trinity College Dublin Press in association with Environmental Publications, 2004), pp. 240–241. Samuel Haughton (1821–1897) – mathematician, geologist, anatomist, physiologist and a Church of Ireland minister – has been identified as Darwin's first critic in Ireland. See Miguel DeArce, 'Darwin's Irish Correspondence', *Biology and Environment: Proceedings of the Royal Irish Academy*, vol. 108B, no. 1 (2008), p. 48.

6 L. Perry Curtis Jr., *Apes and Angels: The Irishman in Victorian Caricature*, revised ed. (Washington, DC: Smithsonian Institution Press, 1997), p. 104. See also Aodhán Kelly, 'The Darwin Debate in Dublin, 1859-1908' (M. Litt. thesis, National University of Ireland, Maynooth, 2009), pp 15–56.

7   Sean Lysaght, 'Themes in the Irish History of Science', *The Irish Review*, vol. 19 (Spring-Summer 1996), pp. 87–97; Philip McGuinness, 'The Hue and Cry of Heresy: John Toland, Isaac Newton & the Social Context of Scientists', *History Ireland*, vol. 4, no. 4 (Winter 1996), pp. 22–27; 'Editors' Introduction', in Peter J. Bowler and Nicholas Whyte (eds), *Science and Society in Ireland: The Social Context of Science and Technology in Ireland, 1800–1950* (Belfast: The Institute of Irish Studies, The Queen's University of Belfast, 1997), p. vii.

8   David N. Livingstone, 'Science, Region and Religion: The Reception of Darwinism in Princeton, Belfast and Edinburgh', in Ronald L. Numbers and John Stenhouse (eds), *Disseminating Darwinism: The Role of Place, Race, Religion and Gender* (Cambridge: Cambridge University Press, 1999), pp. 7–38.

9   See Dorinda Outram, 'The History of Natural History: Grand Narrative or Local Lore?', in John Wilson Foster and Helena C.G. Chesney (eds), *Nature in Ireland: A Scientific and Cultural History* (Dublin: The Lilliput Press, 1997), p. 468; and John Wilson Foster, 'Natural History in Modern Irish Culture', in Bowler and Whyte (eds), *Science and Society in Ireland*, p. 127.

10 See Owen Chadwick, *The Secularization of the European Mind in the Nineteenth Century* (Cambridge: Cambridge University Press, 1975), pp. 164–165, 168–169, 172–173; and Martin Conway, *Catholic Politics in Europe, 1918–1945* (London: Routledge, 1997), p. 12. Historian Jon H. Roberts, writing about the responses of religious authors in Britain and the United States to Darwinism, observed that public opinion polls were not undertaken until after 1920. Thus, 'we know very little about what views, if any, the vast majority of people held about Darwinism.' Jon H. Roberts, 'Religious Reactions to Darwin', in Peter Harrison (ed.), *The Cambridge Companion to Science and Religion* (Cambridge: Cambridge University Press, 2010), p. 82.

11 See Ellegård, *Darwin and the General Reader*, pp. 20–23.

12 David Mathew, *Lord Acton and His Times* (London: Eyre & Spottiswoode, 1968), p. 201. Bishop Verot of St Augustine, Florida, strongly opposed to papal infallibility, made the statement against the background of heated debates on the issue.

13 Emmet Larkin, *The Historical Dimensions of Irish Catholicism* (Washington, DC: The Catholic University of America Press; and Dublin: Four Courts Press, 1984), p. 9. See also Kenneth Scott Latourette, *Christianity in a Revolutionary Age: A History of Christainity in the Nineteenth and Twentieth Centuries*, vol. 1 of *The Nineteenth Century in Europe: Background and the Roman Catholic Phase* (London: Eyre & Spottiswoode, 1959), p. 451; Patrick Corish, *The Irish Catholic Experience: A Historical Survey* (Dublin: Gill & Macmillan, 1985), p. 215; and William L. Smith, '*Euntes Docete Omnes Gentes*: Emigrant Irish Secular Priests in America', *History Ireland*, vol. 8, no. 3 (Autumn 2000), pp. 39–43.

14 See, for example, Gordon L. Herries Davies, 'Irish Thought in Science', in Richard Kearney (ed.), *The Irish Mind: Exploring Intellectual Traditions* (Dublin: Wolfhound Press, 1985), pp. 294–310; Charles Mollan, William Davis and Brendan Finucane (eds), *Irish Innovators in Science and Technology* (Dublin: Royal Irish Academy, 2002); Mary Mulvihill, *Ingenious Ireland: A County-by-County Exploration of Irish Mysteries and Marvels* (Dublin: Townhouse, 2002).

15 Don O'Leary, *Roman Catholicism and Modern Science: A History* (New York: Continuum, 2006), pp. 31–39; and idem, 'From the *Origin* to *Humani Generis*: Ireland as a Case Study', in Louis Caruana (ed.), *Darwin and Catholicism: The Past and Present Dynamics of a Cultural Encounter* (London: T&T Clark, 2009), pp. 13–26.

16 Some of these topics are referred to by Patrick J. McLaughlin in his 'A Century of Science in the IER: Monsignor Molloy and Father Gill', *The Irish Ecclesiastical Record*, 5th series, vol. 102 (1964), p. 254 and were published under the series heading of 'Science and Ourselves'.

17 Thomas Dillon, 'Iodine and Potash from Irish Seaweed', *Studies*, vol. 19 (June 1930), pp. 267–278; Henry Kennedy, 'Winter Fodder and a New Discovery', *Studies*, vol. 20 (September 1931), pp. 389–394; H.V. Gill, 'The Constitution of Matter, II', *The Irish Ecclesiastical Record*, 5th series, vol. 48 (August 1936), pp. 161–169; Pius Walsh, 'The Meson: Ultimate Bond', *The Irish Ecclesiastical Record*, 5th series, vol. 75 (February 1951), pp. 140–148.

18 Work is in progress on a manuscript about artificial contraception, *in vitro* fertilisation and stem cell research – all of which have given rise to controversies amongst Irish Catholics.

1. POLITICS, RELIGION AND SCIENCE, 1840s–1874

1 Gordon L. Herries Davies, 'Irish Thought in Science', in Richard Kearney (ed.), *The Irish Mind: Exploring Intellectual Traditions* (Dublin: Wolfhound Press, 1985), pp. 305–306.

2 James Bennett, 'Science and Social Policy in Ireland in the Mid-Nineteenth Century', in Peter J. Bowler and Nicholas Whyte (eds), *Science and Society in Ireland: The Social Context of Science and Technology in Ireland, 1800–1950* (Belfast: The Institute of Irish Studies, The Queen's University of Belfast, 1997), p. 38.

3 Those who were disadvantaged in science included not only Catholics, but also women and people in the lower-income sector of society (John Wilson Foster, 'Natural Science and Irish Culture', *Éire-Ireland*, vol. 26, no. 2 [1991], p. 101).

4 See Greta Jones, 'Catholicism, Nationalism and Science', *The Irish Review*, no. 20 (Spring 1997), pp. 47, 49.

5 Juliana Adelman, *Communities of Science in Nineteenth-Century Ireland* (London: Pickering & Chatto, 2009), p. 168. For the marginal status of science in Irish nationalism, see pp. 131–159.

6 See Brian B. Kelham, 'The Royal College of Science for Ireland (1867–1926)', *Studies*, vol. 56 (Autumn 1967), p. 307; and Terry Eagleton, *Scholars and Rebels in Nineteenth-Century Ireland* (Oxford: Blackwell Publishers, 1999), p. 91.

7 Kelham, 'The Royal College of Science for Ireland', pp. 300–301, 306–307.

8 This is inferred from Donal Synnott, 'Botany in Ireland', in John Wilson Foster and Helena C.G. Chesney (eds), *Nature in Ireland: A Scientific and Cultural History* (Dublin: The Lilliput Press, 1997), pp. 172–173.

9 John Wilson Foster, 'Nature and Nation in the Nineteenth Century', in Foster and Chesney (eds), *Nature in Ireland*, p. 425.

10 Steven Yearley, 'Colonial Science and Dependent Development: The Case of the Irish Experience', *Sociological Review*, vol. 37 (1989), p. 314.

11 Davies, 'Irish Thought in Science', pp. 305–306.

12 Nicholas Whyte, *Science, Colonialism and Ireland* (Cork: Cork University Press, 1999), p. 155.

13 The status of the University of Dublin was very unclear. It had no formal charter, and an attempt to obtain such a charter failed. Its supposed existence was ignored constantly in Letters Patent and Acts of Parliament. In the Letters Patent of 1857 a formal incorporation of the university was intentionally avoided. R.B. McDowell and D.A. Webb, *Trinity College Dublin 1592–1952: An Academic History* (Dublin:

Trinity College Dublin Press in association with Environmental Publications, 2004), p. 548, note 9.

14 Whyte, *Science, Colonialism and Ireland*, pp. 21–24, 42–43, 59–62, 68–69, 152.

15 See Foster, 'Nature and Nation', pp. 417, 424; and Dorinda Outram, 'The History of Natural History: Grand Narrative or Local Lore?', p. 468; both in Foster and Chesney (eds), *Nature in Ireland*. There was a similar antipathy amongst Irish Catholics towards technical education. See Jim Cooke, 'Dublin Corporation and the Development of Technical Education in Ireland', in Norman McMillan (ed.), *Prometheus's Fire: A History of Scientific and Technological Education in Ireland* (n.p.: Tyndall Publications, 2000), p. 426.

16 Richard A. Jarrell, 'The Department of Science and Art and Control of Irish Science, 1853–1905', *Irish Historical Studies*, vol. 23, no. 92 (November 1983), pp. 330–347; and Yearley, 'Colonial Science', p. 316.

17 See Tom Garvin, 'Introduction', in Walter McDonald, *Some Ethical Questions of Peace and War with Special Reference to Ireland* (London: Burns, Oates & Washbourne, 1920; republished, Dublin: University College Dublin Press, 1998), p. xiv, in reference to McDonald's *Reminiscences of a Maynooth Professor* (London: Jonathan Cape, 1925), p. 127.

18 Eagleton, *Scholars and Rebels*, pp. 28–29.

19 Desmond Clarke, 'An Outline of the History of Science in Ireland', *Studies*, vol. 62 (Autumn-Winter 1973), pp. 298–299; Charles Mollan, 'Elements of Irish Science: An Historical Sketch', in idem (ed.), *Science and Ireland: Value for Society* (Dublin: The Royal Dublin Society, 2005), pp. 46–47; and Michael T. Casey, 'Nicholas Callan: Physicist', in Charles Mollan, William Davis, and Brendan Finucane (eds), *Irish Innovators in Science and Technology* (Dublin: Royal Irish Academy, 2002), pp. 79–80.

20 Its full name was the Museum of Irish Industry and Government School of Science Applied to Mining and the Arts.

21 Sir Robert Kane served on Peel's Commission, which was set up to carry out research on potato blight in Ireland (1845). A number of other important appointments included the Commissioner of National Education (1873), President of the Royal Irish Academy (1877) and the Vice-Chancellor of the Royal University (1880). For details of his contribution to chemical research, see William J. Davis, 'Robert Kane: Chemist and Educationalist', in Mollan, Davis and Finucane (eds), *Irish Innovators in Science and Technology*, pp. 100–101.

22 Clara Cullen, 'The Museum of Irish Industry, Robert Kane and Education for All in the Dublin of the 1850s and 1860s', *History of Education*, vol. 38, no. 1 (January 2009), pp. 102, 104, 110–111.

23 Kelham, 'The Royal College of Science for Ireland', p. 300; and Cullen, 'The Museum of Irish Industry', pp. 109–110.

24 See, for example, Ruth Bayles, 'Understanding Local Science: The Belfast Natural History Society in the Mid-Nineteenth Century', in David Attis and Charles Mollan (eds), *Science and Irish Culture: Why the History of Science Matters in Ireland* (Dublin: Royal Dublin Society, 2004), pp. 139–169; and Elizabeth Neswald, 'Science, Sociability and the Improvement of Ireland: The Galway Mechanics' Institute, 1826–51', *The British Journal for the History of Science*, vol. 39, no. 143 (December 2006), pp. 503–534.

25 Enda Leaney, 'Phrenology in Nineteenth-Century Ireland', *New Hibernia Review*, vol. 10, no. 3 (Autumn 2006), pp. 24–25.

26 For the above points, see Neswald, 'Science, Sociability and the Improvement of

Ireland', pp. 515, 519, 531–534; Enda Leaney, 'Missionaries of Science: Provincial Lectures in Nineteenth-Century Ireland', *Irish Historical Studies*, vol. 34, no. 135 (May 2005), pp. 266, 273–274; and idem, 'Science and Conflict in Nineteenth-Century Ireland', in Neil Garnham and Keith Jeffery (eds), *Culture, Place and Identity* (Dublin: University College Dublin Press, 2005), pp. 66–77. For details of Catholic participation in scientific societies, see Adelman, *Communities of Science*, pp 25–26, 38–40.

27   Bennett, 'Science and Social Policy in Ireland', in Bowler and Whyte (eds), *Science and Society in Ireland*, pp. 37–47; and Jim Bennett, 'Why the History of Science Matters in Ireland', in Attis and Mollan (eds), *Science and Irish Culture*, pp. 5–6

28   Anthony J. Mioni (ed.), *Syllabus of Errors*, in *The Popes against Modern Errors: 16 Papal Documents* (Rockford, Illinois: Tan Books, 1999), pp. 27–39.

29   The general reaction to the *Syllabus of Errors* is discussed in detail in E.E.Y. Hales, *Pio Nono: A Study in European Politics and Religion in the Nineteenth Century* (London: Eyre Spottiswoode, 1954), pp. 255–262.

30   Roger Aubert, 'Internal Catholic Controversies in Connection with Liberalism', in Hubert Jedin and John Dolan (eds), *History of the Church: The Church in the Age of Liberalism* (London: Burns & Oates, 1981), vol. 8, p. 297.

31   Richard L. Camp, *The Papal Ideology of Social Reform* (Leiden, The Netherlands: E.J. Brill, 1969), pp. 8–9.

32   In 1849 and again in 1859–1860, Irish public opinion about the Risorgimento was sharply divided along a Catholic-Protestant fault-line, with Catholics – predictably enough – supporting the papacy and Protestants supporting the Italian movement for independence and unification. See Jennifer O'Brien, 'Irish Public Opinion and the Risorgimento, 1859–60', *Irish Historical Studies*, vol. 34, no. 135 (May 2005), pp. 289–305.

33   Walter L. Arnstein, 'Victorian Prejudice Reexamined', *Victorian Studies*, vol. 12 (1968–1969), p. 454.

34   Hugh McLeod, *Secularisation in Western Europe, 1848–1914* (Basingstoke, UK: Macmillan Press, 2000), p. 226.

35   J.P. Parry, *Democracy and Religion: Gladstone and the Liberal Party, 1867–1875* (Cambridge: Cambridge University Press, 1986), p. 43. The British statesman William Gladstone, leader of the Liberal Party and four times prime minister between 1868 and 1894, was outraged by the Vatican decrees. His polemical campaign was deeply resented by Irish Catholics. E.R. Norman, *Anti-Catholicism in Victorian England* (London: George Allen & Unwin, 1968), pp. 212–221; and Walter L. Arnstein, *Protestant versus Catholic in Mid-Victorian England: Mr. Newdegate and the Nuns* (Columbia: University of Missouri Press, 1982), pp. 190–192. See also F.S.L. Lyons, *Ireland since the Famine* (London: Fontana Press, 1985), p. 152.

36   Joseph Lee, *The Modernisation of Irish Society, 1848–1918* (Dublin: Gill & Macmillan, 1989), pp. 42–49.

37   The appropriateness of the term 'devotional revolution', is disputed by some scholars. See David M. Miller, 'Religious History', in Laurence M. Geary and Margaret Kelleher (eds), *Nineteenth-Century Ireland: A Guide to Recent Research* (Dublin: University College Dublin Press, 2005), pp. 66–70.

38   Donal McCartney, *The Dawning of Democracy: Ireland, 1800–1870* (Dublin: Helicon, 1987), p. 35; and Patrick Corish, *The Irish Catholic Experience: A Historical Survey* (Dublin: Gill & Macmillan, 1985), p. 232.

39   Terence Brown, *Ireland: A Social and Cultural History, 1922–1985* (London: Fontana Press, 1985), pp. 27, 30.

40 See Thomas Duddy, *A History of Irish Thought* (London: Routledge, 2002), pp. 250–251.

41 Parry, *Democracy and Religion*, see pp. 43, 195–196, 314–315, 344, 371–372. See also Jeffrey Paul von Arx, *Progress and Pessimism: Religion, Politics and History in Late-Nineteenth-Century Britain* (Cambridge, Massachussetts: Harvard University Press, 1985), pp. 8, 203–205. The wealthy landowning sector of English Catholicism ('the Upper Ten Thousand') was staunchly opposed to Home Rule. Representatives of these Catholics, such as Sir George Bowyer and Lord Robert Montague, were highly influential at the Vatican. For an account of the interaction between English Catholicism and Irish nationalism, see Jacqueline Clais-Girard, 'The English Catholics and Irish Nationalism, 1865–1890: A Tragedy in Five Acts', *Victorian Literature and Culture*, vol. 32, no. 1 (2004), pp. 177–189.

42 Alice Tracey, 'Professor John Tyndall', *Carloviana*, vol. 1, no. 3 (January 1949), p. 142.

43 Leonard Huxley, *Life and Letters of Thomas Henry Huxley* (London: Macmillan, 1903), vol. 2, pp. 326, 438–441; vol. 3, pp. 181, 207.

44 J.V. Jensen, 'The X Club: Fraternity of Victorian Scientists', *The British Journal for the History of Science*, vol. 5, no. 17 (1970), pp. 70–71. See also Roy M. MacLeod, 'The X-Club: A Social Network of Science in Late-Victorian England', *Notes and Records of the Royal Society of London*, vol. 24, no. 2 (April 1970), p. 314.

45 James R. Moore, *The Post-Darwinian Controversies: A Study of the Protestant Struggle to Come to Terms with Darwin in Great Britain and America, 1870–1900* (Cambridge: Cambridge University Press, 1979), p. 65.

46 See Greta Jones, 'Scientists against Home Rule', in D. George Boyce and Alan O'Day (eds), *Defenders of the Union: A Survey of British and Irish Unionism since 1801* (London: Routledge, 2001), pp. 188, 193. See also Michael D. Gordin, 'Points Critical: Russia, Ireland, and Science at the Boundary', *Osiris*, vol. 24 (2009), pp. 116–117.

47 Colin Barr, 'University Education, History, and the Hierarchy', in Lawrence W. McBride (ed.), *Reading Irish Histories: Texts, Contexts, and Memory in Modern Ireland* (Dublin: Four Courts Press, 2003), pp. 62–79.

48 Anon., 'Catholic Education – Disendowment of the Protestant Establishment', *The Irish Ecclesiastical Record*, vol. 1 (1865), p. 229.

49 Barr, 'University Education', p. 63; and Fergal McGrath, *Newman's University: Idea and Reality* (Dublin: Browne Nolan, 1951), pp. 45, 58.

50 'Extract from a Memorandum by Mr. Wilfrid Ward on some Aspects of the Religious Difficulty', in *Royal Commission on University Education in Ireland: Appendix to the Final Report*, Cd. 1484 (Dublin: His Majesty's Stationery Office, 1903), p. 6.

51 Harry W. Paul, 'Science and the Catholic Institutes in Nineteenth-Century France', *Societas: a Review of Social History*, vol. 1, no. 4 (1971), pp. 271–285.

52 William J. Schoenl, *The Intellectual Crisis in English Catholicism: Liberal Catholics, Modernists, and the Vatican in the Late Nineteenth and Early Twentieth Centuries* (New York: Garland Publishing, 1982), pp. 56–57.

53 John Coolahan, *Irish Education: Its History and Structure* (Dublin: Institute of Public Administration, 1981), p. 122; and J.H. Whyte, *Church and State in Modern Ireland, 1923–1979*, 2nd ed. (Dublin: Gill % Macmillan, 1984), p. 343.

54 McGrath, *Newman's University*, p. 44.

55 Ibid., pp. 84, 88–89.

56 See Louis McRedmond, *Thrown among Strangers: John Henry Newman in Ireland* (Dublin: Veritas, 1990), pp. 183–184.

57 Charles Stephen Dessain (ed.), *The Letters and Diaries of John Henry Newman* (London: Nelson, 1967), vol. 17, p. 385.

58 John Henry Newman, *The Idea of a University*, ed. with introduction and notes by I.T. Ker (Oxford: Clarendon Press, 1976), pp. 190, 346–348, 360–361. Words in quotation marks are from p. 346.

59 Ibid., p. 354.

60 Ibid., p. 376.

61 Ibid., pp. 349–351.

62 Ibid., p. 381.

63 *Report of the Dean and Faculty of Science of the Catholic University of Ireland: Session 1857–1858* (Dublin: 1858), p. 11; MS 7668, Thomas Aiskew Larcom papers, The National Library of Ireland, Dublin (hereafter NLI). This document first came to my attention in Juliana Adelman's 'Communities of Science: the Queen's Colleges and Scientific Culture in Provincial Ireland, 1845–75' (PhD thesis, National University of Ireland, Galway, 2007), p. 47.

64 *Report of the Dean and Faculty of Science*, pp. 11–13, 19.

65 Adelman, 'Communities of Science' (2007), p. 47; in reference to E. Leaney, '"The Property of All": Public Access to Scientific Education in Nineteenth-Century Ireland' (PhD thesis, University of Oxford, 2002), p. 248.

66 'Pastoral Address of the Roman Catholic Archbishops and Bishops, to the Catholic Clergy and People of Ireland, on the Catholic University', newspaper clipping 'Post' 22 November 1859, MS 7672, Thomas Aiskew Larcom papers, NLI.

67 Anon., 'Claims of the Catholics of Ireland to Independent University Education', *The Irish Ecclesiastical Record*, vol. 2 (1866), pp. 320–331.

68 Anon., 'Lord Mayo and the Catholic University of Ireland', *The Irish Ecclesiastical Record*, vol. 4 (1868), p. 488.

69 Barth. Woodlock, 'University Education in Ireland', *The Irish Ecclesiastical Record*, vol. 4 (1868), p. 440.

70 J.W. Burrow, *The Crisis of Reason: European Thought, 1848–1914* (New Haven: Yale University Press, 2000), pp. 197–200.

71 Claude Welch, 'Dispelling Some Myths about the Split between Theology and Science in the Nineteenth Century', in W. Mark Richardson and Wesley J. Wildman (eds), *Religion and Science: History, Method, Dialogue* (New York: Routledge, 1996), p. 34.

72 Jones, 'Catholicism, Nationalism and Science', pp. 49–51; and idem, 'Darwinism in Ireland', in Attis and Mollan (eds), *Science and Irish Culture*, p. 131.

73 McLeod, *Secularisation in Western Europe*, p. 155

74 Owen Chadwick, *The Secularization of the European Mind in the Nineteenth Century* (Cambridge: Cambridge University Press, 1975), pp. 165, 169.

75 See Sander Gliboff, 'Evolution, Revolution, and Reform in Vienna: Franz Unger's Ideas on Descent and Their Post-1848 Reception', *Journal of the History of Biology*, vol. 31 (1998), pp. 204–205.

76 Anon., 'The Revival of Atheism', *The Irish Ecclesiastical Record*, vol. 3 (1867), pp. 500–509. Words in quotation marks are from pp. 507–508.

77 Chadwick, *The Secularization of the European Mind*, p. 165.

78 [Molloy, Gerald], 'Geology and Revelation', parts 1–9, *The Irish Ecclesiastical Record*, vol. 3 (1867), pp. 121–134, 241–261, 358–374, 448–467; vol. 4 (1868), pp. 49–66, 169–187, 326–341, 373–385; vol. 5 (1869), pp. 49–73, 193–223.

79 For discussions of Molloy's *Geology and Revelation*, see: (1) Duddy's *A History of Irish Thought*, pp. 257–259; (2) my *Roman Catholicism and Modern Science: A History* (New York: Continuum, 2006), pp. 11–15; and (3) Aodhán Kelly's 'The Darwin Debate in Dublin, 1859–1908' (M. Litt. thesis, National University of Ireland, Maynooth, 2009), pp. 40–49.

80 Copy of the 'Memorial', published under the title of 'The Catholic University', paper cutting, dated 10 December 1873, MS 7674, Thomas Aiskew Larcom papers, NLI.

81 Ibid.

82 *The Atlantis*, no. 6 (January 1862), inserted typed note.

83 The other four Catholic members of the Royal Irish Academy were given as Mr John T. Gilbert, Dr C.W. Russell, Dr Casey and Mr O'Looney.

84 Copy of the 'Memorial'.

85 Ibid.

86 Press cuttings, December 1873, MS 7674, Thomas Aiskew Larcom papers, NLI; and 'Science at the Catholic University', *The Times*, 2 December 1873, p. 7.

87 'Irish University Education', newspaper cutting dated 19 November 1872, MS 7662, Thomas Aiskew Larcom papers, NLI.

88 Newspaper cutting, 'Times', dated 20 October 1873, MS 7674, Thomas Aiskew Larcom papers, NLI.

89 Sullivan to Monsell, 15 May 1873, MS 8318 (6), William Monsell papers, NLI.

90 John A. Murphy, *The College: A History of Queen's/University College Cork* (Cork: Cork University Press, 1995), pp. 99–100.

91 Adelman, *Communities of Science* (2009), pp. 45–47.

92 Adelman, 'Communities of Science' (2007), pp. 53–54; and idem, *Communities of Science* (2009), pp. 64–70.

93 Adelman, *Communities of Science* (2009), pp. 67–68.

94 Barr, 'University Education', pp. 72, 79; and idem, 'The Failure of Newman's Catholic University of Ireland', *Archivium Hibernicum*, vol. 55 (2001), pp. 126–139.

95 Thomas J. Morrissey, *Towards a National University: William Delany SJ (1835–1924): An Era of Initiative in Irish Education* (Dublin: Wolfhound Press; Atlantic Highlands, New Jersey: Humanities Press, 1983), pp. 47–48.

96 Barr, 'University Education', pp. 72–73, 79.

97 Senia Pašeta, 'The Catholic Hierarchy and the Irish University Question, 1880–1908', *History*, vol. 85, no. 278 (April 2000), p. 271.

98 Murphy, *The College*, p. 120.

99 Jeremiah Molony, 'The Catholic Education Question', *The Irish Ecclesiastical Record*, new series, vol. 8 (August 1872), p. 491, quoting Newman's 'Lectures on Education', *Catholic University Gazette*.

100 See Frank M. Turner, 'John Tyndall and Victorian Scientific Naturalism', in W.H. Brock, N.D. McMillan and R.C. Mollan (eds), *John Tyndall: Essays on a Natural Philosopher* (Dublin: Royal Dublin Society, 1981), p. 169.

101 Frank Turner, *Contesting Cultural Authority: Essays in Victorian Intellectual Life* (Cambridge: Cambridge University Press, 1993), pp. 157–158.

102 Bernard Lightman, 'Victorian Sciences and Religions: Discordant Harmonies', in John Hedley Brooke, Margaret J. Osler and Jitse M. van der Meer (eds), *Science in Theistic Contexts: Cognitive Dimensions*, vol. 16 of *Osiris* (2001), pp. 346–347.

103 David N. Livingstone, 'Re-placing Darwinism and Christianity', in David C. Lindberg and Ronald N. Numbers (eds), *When Science and Christianity Meet* (Chicago: The University of Chicago Press, 2003), p. 194.

104 Frank Miller Turner, *Between Science and Religion: The Reaction to Scientific Naturalism in Late Victorian England* (New Haven: Yale University Press, 1974), pp. 13–14.

105 Martin Fichman, 'Science in Theistic Contexts: A Case Study of Alfred Russel Wallace on Human Evolution', in Brooke, Osler and van der Meer (eds), *Science in Theistic Contexts*, pp. 227–250.

106 Lightman, 'Victorian Sciences and Religions', pp. 351–354, 366.

107 Cyril Bibby (ed.), *T.H. Huxley on Education: A Selection from His Writings* (Cambridge: Cambridge University Press, 1971), pp. 24, 113–115.

108 Frank Turner, 'The Victorian Crisis of Faith and the Faith That Was Lost', in Richard J. Helmstadter and Bernard Lightman (eds), *Victorian Faith in Crisis: Essays on Continuity and Change in Nineteenth-Century Religious Belief* (Stanford, California: Stanford University Press, 1990), p. 18; and Turner, *Contesting Cultural Authority*, pp. 195–196.

109 See Adrian Desmond, *Huxley: From Devil's Disciple to Evolution's High Priest* (London: Penguin Books, 1998), pp. 340–341.

110 Wilfrid Ward, *Problems and Persons* (London: Longmans, Green & Co., 1903), pp. 234–235.

111 Desmond, *Huxley*, p. 407; see also p. 331.

112 Huxley, *Life and Letters*, vol. 1, p. 443.

113 Desmond, *Huxley*, p. 341; and Moore, *The Post-Darwinian Controversies*, p. 63.

114 *The Nation*, 4 November 1871.

115 For a comprehensive exposition of the social, religious and political context of the conflict thesis, see Frank M. Turner, 'The late Victorian conflict of science and religion as an event in nineteenth-century intellectual and cultural history', in Thomas Dixon, Geoffrey Cantor and Stephen Pumfrey (eds), *Science and Religion: New Historical Perspectives* (Cambridge: Cambridge University Press, 2010), pp. 87–110.

116 Welch, 'Dispelling Some Myths', pp. 29–30.

117 Official census figures showed that, in 1841, 53 per cent of people over five years of age could not read or write. By 1901 this illiteracy figure had fallen to 14 per cent (Coolahan, *Irish Education*, p. 7).

118 See Adelman, *Communities of Science* (2009), pp. 133–146.

119 'Pastoral Letter of the Archbishops and Bishops of Ireland', 22 January 1873, published in *The Irish Ecclesiastical Record*, new series, vol. 9 (1873), p. 195.

120 Ibid.

121 Quotations from Norman P. Tanner (ed.), *Decrees of the Ecumenical Councils: Trent to Vatican II* (London: Sheed & Ward; Washington, DC: Georgetown University Press, 1990), vol. 2, pp. 809–810.

122 Anon., 'The Church and Modern Thought – I', *The Irish Ecclesiastical Record*, new series, vol. 9 (1873), pp. 496–497, 499–501.

123 Anon., 'The Church and Modern Thought – II', *The Irish Ecclesiastical Record*, new series, vol. 9 (1873), pp. 533–543.

124 *Syllabus of Errors*, proposition 12, in Mioni (ed.), *The Popes against Modern Errors*, p. 29.

125 Anon., 'The Church and Modern Thought – III', *The Irish Ecclesiastical Record*, new series, vol. 10 (1874), pp. 56–62.

126 Anon., 'The Church and Modern Thought – IV', *The Irish Ecclesiastical Record*, new series, vol. 10 (1874), p. 102; quoting Huxley, *Lay Sermons*, p. 68.

127 Anon., 'The Church and Modern Thought – IV', pp. 104–105. The author of the

article referred to the second edition of *Fragments of Science*, p. 448.

128 John Tyndall, 'Reflections on Prayer and Natural Law' (1861), in idem, *Fragments of Science: A Series of Detached Essays, Addresses, and Reviews* (New York: D. Appleton & Co., 1896), vol. 2, pp. 5–7. See also Turner, 'John Tyndall and Victorian Scientific Naturalism', pp. 174–177.

129 Victorian debates about prayer, acts of providence and miracles, in the context of discussing the relationship between science and religion, are examined in detail by Robert Bruce Mullin, 'Science, Miracles and the Prayer-Gauge Debate', in Lindberg and Numbers (eds), *When Science and Christianity Meet*, pp. 203–224; see especially pp. 207–210.

130 Anon., 'The Church and Modern Thought –V', *The Irish Ecclesiastical Record*, new series, vol. 10 (1874), pp. 239, 241, 243.

131 Ibid., pp. 237–239.

132 Joe Burchfield, 'John Tyndall – A Biographical Sketch', in Brock, McMillan and Mollan (eds), *John Tyndall*, p. 9.

133 See Tyndall, 'Apology for the Belfast Address' (1874), in idem, *Fragments of Science*, pp. 210–214.

134 Tyndall, 'The Belfast Address' (19 August 1874), in idem, *Fragments of Science*, p. 197.

135 Ibid., p. 143.

136 Ibid., pp. 191, 194.

137 A.S. Eve and C.H. Creasey, *Life and Work of John Tyndall* (London: Macmillan, 1945), pp. 186–187.

138 See Ruth Barton, 'John Tyndall, Pantheist: A Rereading of the Belfast Address', *Osiris*, 2nd series, vol. 3 (1987), p. 121. For additional insights into the background of Tyndall's Belfast Address, see Matthew Brown, 'Darwin at Church: John Tyndall's Belfast Address', in James H. Murphy (ed.), *Evangelicals and Catholics in Nineteenth-Century Ireland* (Dublin: Four Courts Press, 2005), pp. 235–246.

139 See Tess Cosslett, introduction to 'John Tyndall, "The Belfast Address," Nature, 20 August 1874', in idem (ed.), *Science and Religion in the Nineteenth Century* (Cambridge: Cambridge University Press, 1984), p. 172.

140 'Pastoral Address of the Archbishops and Bishops of Ireland to their Flocks' (14 October 1874), in Patrick Francis Moran (ed.), *Pastoral Letters and Other Writings of Cardinal Cullen* (Dublin: Browne Nolan, 1882), vol. 3, pp. 596–598.

141 Ibid., p. 599.

142 John Wilson Foster, *Recoveries: Neglected Episodes in Irish Cultural History, 1860–1912* (Dublin: University College Dublin Press, 2002), pp. 7–48.

143 An editorial in *The Times* (31 October 1874) expressed admiration of the shrewdness of the Catholic bishops in taking advantage of Tyndall's address. In the light of this, James H. Murphy wrote: 'Tyndall emerges from this as a naïve blunderer who was playing into the bishops' hands'. There is no denying the astuteness of the bishops, but Murphy's harsh assessment of Tyndall on this point is unsound. It is very likely that Tyndall was appealing to anti-Catholic opinion in Britain for his own interests. Murphy conceded this probability when he wrote that: 'Tyndall's allusion to the university may have been his attempt to garner political advantage with British opinion, just as his attack on Catholicism in general certainly represented an embrace of the widespread international hostility to Catholicism at the time . . .' James H. Murphy, 'The Irish-Catholics-in-Science debate: John Tyndall, Cardinal Cullen and the Uses of Science at Castleknock College in the Nineteenth Century', in Juliana Adelman and Éadaoin Agnew (eds),

Science and Technology in Nineteenth-Century Ireland (Dublin: Four Courts Press, 2011), pp. 129, 130.

144 'Pastoral Address', see especially pp. 595–596, 604–608.

145 See Murphy, *The College*, pp. 44–46, 99–101; and Cullen, 'The Museum of Irish Industry', p. 104.

146 Murphy, *The College*, pp. 44–46; and Louis McRedmond, 'Could Newman Have Succeeded in Ireland?' in *Proceedings of the John Henry Newman Centenary Symposium* (Cork: Department of Education, University College Cork, November 1990), pp. 1–17.

147 Tyndall, 'Apology for the Belfast Address', in *Fragments of Science*, pp. 213–214.

2. FAITH AND EVOLUTION, 1860S–1880S

1 Charles Darwin, *The Origin of Species by Means of Natural Selection, or the Preservation of Favoured Races in the Struggle for Life*, ed. and introduction by J.W. Burrow (London: John Murray, 1859; republished, London: Penguin Books, 1985), p. 142, Chapter 9 and p. 453.

2 Ibid., Chapter 6: 'Difficulties on Theory', pp. 205–233. See also pp. 291–292, 435, 440,

3 Sources here for the scientific objections to Darwin's theory of evolution are: Peter J. Bowler, *Charles Darwin: The Man and His Influence* (Cambridge: Cambridge University Press, 1990), pp. 133–134, 154–155, 163–164; and idem, *The Eclipse of Darwinism: Anti-Darwinian Evolution Theories in the Decades around 1900* (Baltimore: The Johns Hopkins University Press, 1983), pp. 22–26 and 229, note 8; David N. Livingstone, *Darwin's Forgotten Defenders: The Encounter between Evangelical Theology and Evolutionary Thought* (Grand Rapids, Michigan: William B. Eerdmans; Edinburgh: Scottish Academic Press, 1987), pp. 52–53.

4 John Tyler Bonner and Robert M. May, 'Introduction', to Charles Darwin, *The Descent of Man and Selection in Relation to Sex* (London: John Murray, 1871; republished, Princeton, New Jersey: Princeton University Press, 1981), vol. 1, pp. xvii-xxi.

5 Alvar Ellegård, *Darwin and the General Reader: The Reception of Darwin's Theory of Evolution in the British Periodical Press, 1859–1872*, foreword by David L. Hull (Chicago: The University of Chicago Press, 1990), pp. 174–175, 189–190.

6 John Hedley Brooke, *Science and Religion: Some Historical Perspectives* (Cambridge: Cambridge University Press, 1991), pp. 286–287.

7 Bowler, *Charles Darwin*, pp. 130–132, 138, 160, 166.

8 For a detailed discussion of Roman Catholic apologetics relating to science and to Darwinism in particular, for the period 1859–1872, see Tord Simonsson's *Logical and Semantic Structures in Christian Discourses*, trans. Agnes George (Oslo: Universitetsforlaget, 1971), pp. 15–47.

9 Peter J. Bowler, *Evolution: The History of an Idea*, 3rd ed. (Berkeley: University of California Press, 2003), pp. 208–210.

10 Irish naturalists published much of their work in *Proceedings of the Royal Irish Academy* and in the journals of the Royal Dublin Society. Miguel DeArce's survey of these publications found no articles concerning Darwin's theory. One footnote by the Catholic engineer and scientist Henry Hennessy (1826–1901), in the *Proceedings of the Royal Irish Academy* referred to Darwin's *Origin of Species*. Miguel DeArce, 'Darwin's Irish Correspondence', *Biology and Environment: Proceedings of the Royal Irish Academy*, vol. 108B, no. 1 (2008), 43–56.

11 Thomas Duddy, 'The Irish Response to Darwinism', in Juliana Adelman and

Éadaoin Agnew (eds), *Science and Technology in Nineteenth-Century Ireland* (Dublin: Four Courts Press, 2011), p. 18.

12 J.G.C., 'Darwinism', *The Irish Ecclesiastical Record*, new series, vol. 9 (1873), pp. 349–350.

13 Ibid., p. 339.

14 Ibid., p. 361.

15 Ibid., p. 360.

16 Patrick Allitt, *Catholic Converts: British and American Intellectuals Turn to Rome* (Ithaca, New York: Cornell University Press, 1997), p. 33.

17 See H.E.D., 'Revelation, Geology, The Antiquity of Man', *The Irish Ecclesiastical Record*, 3rd series, vol. 1 (1880), p. 271.

18 See Mariano Artigas, Thomas F. Glick and Rafael A. Martínez, *Negotiating Darwin: The Vatican Confronts Evolution, 1877–1902* (Baltimore: The John Hopkins University Press, 2006), p. 281; and Jon H. Roberts, 'Religious Reactions to Darwin', in Peter Harrison (ed.), *The Cambridge Companion to Science and Religion* (Cambridge: Cambridge University Press, 2010), pp. 82–84.

19 J.G.C., 'Darwinism', p. 361.

20 Ronald L. Numbers, 'Science without God: Natural Laws and Christian Beliefs', in David C. Lindberg and Ronald L. Numbers (eds.), *When Science and Christianity Meet* (Chicago: The University of Chicago Press, 2003), pp. 280–281.

21 Finlay cultivated a wide range of interests and was gifted with corresponding abilities. He served, sequentially, as professor of classics, philosophy and economics. He was the author of many educational texts and served on a number of boards and commissions and was a co-founder of the Irish Co-operative Movement. He was editor of the *Irish Homestead*, the journal of the Irish Co-operative Movement and of the *New Ireland Review* (1894–1911), the forerunner of *Studies*. He was popular, both as a lecturer and a preacher. Thomas J. Morrissey, *William J. Walsh, Archbishop of Dublin, 1841–1921: No Uncertain Voice* (Dublin: Four Courts Press, 2000), p. 165.

22 T.F., 'Mr Tyndall at Belfast', *The Irish Monthly*, vol. 2 (October 1874), pp. 563–564.

23 Ibid., pp. 574–575.

24 Gowan Dawson, *Darwin, Literature and Victorian Respectability* (Cambridge: Cambridge University Press, 2007).

25 T.F., 'The Aggressions of Science', *The Irish Monthly*, vol. 4 (December 1875), pp. 16–19.

26 J.V. Jensen, 'The X Club: Fraternity of Victorian Scientists', *The British Journal for the History of Science*, vol. 5, no. 17 (1970), p. 63; Ruth Barton, '"An Influential Set of Chaps": The X-Club and Royal Society Politics, 1864–1885', *The British Journal for the History of Science*, vol. 23, no. 76 (March 1990), p. 57; and Roy M. MacLeod, 'The X-Club: A Social Network of Science in Late-Victorian England', *Notes and Records of the Royal Society of London*, vol. 24, no. 2 (April 1970), p. 311.

27 Adrian Desmond, *Huxley: From Devil's Disciple to Evolution's High Priest* (London: Penguin Books, 1998), p. 341, p. 688, note 3.

28 Greta Jones, 'Scientists against Home Rule', in D. George Boyce and Alan O'Day (eds), *Defenders of the Union: A Survey of British and Irish Unionism since 1801* (London: Routledge, 2001), p. 193. In the case of Haddon, see also Greta Jones, 'Contested Territories: Alfred Cort Haddon, Progressive Evolutionism and Ireland', *History of European Ideas*, vol. 24, no. 3 (1998), p. 197.

29 T.A.F., 'The Royal Irish University and the Catholic Irish Faith', *The Irish Ecclesiastical Record*, 3rd series, vol. 1 (1880), p. 143; see also pp. 147–148.

30 Emma Wedgwood, shortly before her marriage to Charles Darwin, wrote to him expressing concerns that the critical questioning attitude, so essential for the practice of science, might encourage doubts about Christian faith (John Hedley Brooke, 'Revisiting Darwin on Order and Design', in Niels Henrik Gregersen and Ulf Görman (eds), *Design and Disorder: Perspectives from Science and Theology* [London: T&T Clark, 2002], p. 40).

31 Senia Pašeta, *Before the Revolution: Nationalism, Social Change and Ireland's Catholic Élite, 1879–1922* (Cork: Cork University Press, 1999), p. 36.

32 See, for example, Anon., 'The Genesis, According to Scripture and Science', *The Catholic Record*, vol. 4, no. 23 (March 1873), pp. 307–308.

33 T.F., 'The Aggressions of Science', p. 16.

34 'Pastoral Address of the Archbishops and Bishops of Ireland to their Flocks' (14 October 1874), in Patrick Francis Moran (ed.), *Pastoral Letters and Other Writings of Cardinal Cullen* (Dublin: Browne Nolan, 1882), vol. 3, see pp. 593–594.

35 Darwin was known to be an agnostic and was frequently accused of being an atheist. His supporters emphasised not only his intellectual achievements and dedication to the pursuit of truth, but also a number of social and personal virtues such as his industriousness, moral rectitude, wisdom, the tranquillity of his domestic life and his modesty. See Janet Browne, 'Presidential Address: Commemorating Darwin', *The British Journal for the History of Science*, vol. 38, no. 138 (September 2005), pp. 251–274.

36 J. FitzGerald, 'Life and Letters of Charles Darwin', *The Irish Ecclesiastical Record*, 3rd series, vol. 9 (July 1888), pp. 606–607. FitzGerald gave two reasons for the favourable reception of the three-volume work of *Life and Letters of Charles Darwin* (London: Murray, 1887): (1) 'the sweet and gentle nature of the man, the elevation of character, the love of home and family, the persevering industry and self-sacrifice in the pursuit of what he thought true' and (2) the popularity of his work.

37 Jacob W. Gruber, *A Conscience in Conflict: The Life of St George Jackson Mivart* (Westport, Connecticut: Greenwood Press, 1960), pp. 53–56.

38 St George Mivart, *The Genesis of Species*, 2nd ed. (London: Macmillan, 1871), pp. 302–305, 317.

39 Gruber, *Conscience in Conflict*, pp. 87, 92.

40 J. Derek Holmes, 'Newman and Mivart – Two Attitudes to a Nineteenth-Century Problem', *Clergy Review*, new series, vol. 50, no. 11 (November 1965), p. 854.

41 See John Gerard Lysaght, 'Robert Lloyd Praeger and the Culture of Science in Ireland, 1865–1953' (Ph.D. thesis, St Patrick's College, Maynooth, 1996), p. 7. For an historical study of the Belfast Natural History Society, see Ruth Bayles, 'Understanding Local Science: The Belfast Natural History Society in the Mid-Nineteenth Century', in David Attis and Charles Mollan (eds), *Science and Irish Culture: Why the History of Science Matters in Ireland* (Dublin: Royal Dublin Society, 2004), pp. 139–169.

42 Michael Viney, 'Introduction', in Robert Lloyd Praeger, *The Way That I Went* (Cork: The Collins Press, 1997), p. ii. See also Gordon L. Herries Davies, 'Irish Thought in Science', in Richard Kearney (ed.), *The Irish Mind: Exploring Intellectual Traditions* (Dublin: Wolfhound Press, 1985), p. 308.

43 Several annual meetings of the British Association for the Advancement of Science were held in Ireland, as follows: Dublin (1835, 1857, 1878, 1930), Cork (1843), Belfast (1852, 1874, 1902). Charles Withers, Rebekah Higgitt and Diarmid Finnegan, 'Historical Geographies of Provincial Science: Themes in the Setting

and Reception of the British Association for the Advancement of Science in Britain and Ireland, 1831–c. 1939', *The British Journal for the History of Science*, vol. 41, no. 150 (September 2008), p. 391.

44   H.E.D., 'Revelation, Geology, the Antiquity of Man', *The Irish Ecclesiastical Record*, 3rd series, vol. 1 (1880), p. 187. Canon Dennehy is identified from a list of contributors' initials published in *The Irish Ecclesiastical Record*, 5th series, vol. 102 (July-December 1964), pp. 277–278. The list was originally published in the IER in the January 1881 issue.

45   For a similar pessimistic opinion about the decline of both Catholicism and the 'apostate Churches' in western Europe, see Anon., 'Catholicity and the Spirit of the Age', *The Irish Monthly*, vol. 1, no. 1 (July 1873), p. 25.

46   H.E.D., 'Revelation, Geology, the Antiquity of Man', pp. 186–187.

47   See Roger Aubert, 'The Backwardness of Religious Studies and the Controversy about the "German Theologians"', in Hubert Jedin and John Dolan (eds), *History of the Church: The Church in the Age of Liberalism* (London: Burns & Oates, 1981), vol. 8, pp. 228–247.

48   Walter McDonald, *Reminiscences of a Maynooth Professor*, edited with a memoir by Denis Gwynn (London: Jonathan Cape, 1925; republished, Cork: Mercier Press, 1967), p. 66.

49   Ibid., p. 74.

50   Ibid., pp. 92-93.

51   Ibid., p. 78.

52   See Patrick J. McLaughlin, 'A Century of Science in the IER: Monsignor Molloy and Father Gill', *The Irish Ecclesiastical Record*, 5th series, vol. 102 (July-December 1964), p. 253.

53   Gruber, *Conscience in Conflict*, pp. 156, 163–164; and Holmes, 'Newman and Mivart', pp. 861–862.

54   Allitt, *Catholic Converts*, pp. ix, 1–3; and Walter L. Arnstein, *Protestant versus Catholic in Mid-Victorian England: Mr Newdegate and the Nuns* (Columbia and London: University of Missouri Press, 1982), pp. 42–43.

55   James Tunstead Burtchaell, 'The Biblical Question and the English Catholics', *The Review of Politics*, vol. 31, no. 1 (January 1969), pp. 108–109.

56   Gruber, *Conscience in Conflict*, p. 243, note 35.

57   For the state of affairs in England, see John D. Root, 'English Catholic Modernism and Science: The Case of George Tyrrell', *Heythrop Journal*, vol. 18 (July 1977), p. 274.

58   See William J. Astore, 'Gentle Skeptics? American Catholic Encounters with Polygenism, Geology, and Evolutionary Theories from 1845 to 1875', *The Catholic Historical Review*, vol. 82 (January 1996), pp. 40, 45–46; and John Rickards Betts, 'Darwinism, Evolution, and American Catholic Thought, 1860–1900', *The Catholic Historical Review*, vol. 45 (April 1959–January 1960), p. 162.

59   Constance Areson Clark, '"You Are Here": Missing Links, Chains of Being, and the Language of Cartoons', *Isis*, vol. 100, no. 3 (September 2009), p. 580. For a detailed account of the simianized Irish in Victorian caricature, see L. Perry Curtis Jr., *Apes and Angels: The Irishman in Victorian Caricature*, revised ed. (Washington DC: Smithsonian Institution Press, 1997).

60   See Don O'Leary, *Roman Catholicism and Modern Science: A History* (New York: Continuum, 2006), pp. 63–65.

61   James Tunstead Burtchaell, *Catholic Theories of Biblical Inspiration since 1810: A Review and Critique* (London: Cambridge University Press, 1969), pp. 74–78.

62 H.J.T. Johnson, 'Leo XIII, Cardinal Newman and the Inerrancy of Scripture', *The Downside Review*, vol. 69 (1951), p. 420.

63 For a study of the social, economic and political background to Jeremiah Murphy's opposition to evolutionary theory, see Miguel DeArce's 'The Multi-Faceted Anti-Darwinism of Fr Jeremiah Murphy (1840-1915)', *Cork Historical and Archaeological Journal*, vol. 115 (2010), pp. 87–108.

64 J. Murphy, 'Darwinism', *The Irish Ecclesiastical Record*, 3rd series, vol. 5 (1884), p. 586.

65 Ibid., p. 589.

66 Ibid., p. 586.

67 Ibid., pp. 591–592.

68 Robert E. Stebbins, 'France', in Thomas F. Glick (ed.), *The Comparative Reception of Darwinism* (Chicago: The University of Chicago Press, 1988), p. 157.

69 See Stebbins, 'France', pp. 157–158.

70 Charles Darwin, *Descent of Man*, vol. 1, pp. 65-68, 104–106; and vol. 2, pp. 385–405.

71 Ibid., vol. 1, pp. 32–33.

72 Murphy, 'Darwinism', p. 594.

73 J. Murphy, 'The Case of Galileo', *The Nineteenth Century*, vol. 19 (May 1886), pp. 722–723.

74 The Provincial Council of Cologne (1860) had issued a declaration against the idea of a process of 'spontaneous transformation' giving rise to the first humans. Non-teleological evolution was definitely rejected, but human evolution was not completely ruled out. Furthermore, no other provincial ecclesiastical council reiterated the above decree, nor was it endorsed by Rome. See O'Leary, *Roman Catholicism and Modern Science*, p. 47; in reference to Ernest C. Messenger, *Evolution and Theology: The Problem of Man's Origin* (London: Burns, Oates & Washbourne, 1931), pp. 226–227. See also Artigas, Glick and Martínez, *Negotiating Darwin*, pp. 21–23. Fr Raffaello Caverni, in his *New Studies of Philosophy: Lectures to a Young Student* (1877), argued for the harmonisation of Christianity and evolution but he omitted humans from the evolutionary scheme. Nevertheless, his book was placed on the Vatican's Index of Prohibited Books in July 1878. However, the decree of the Congregation of the Index did not give the reasons for the prohibition. There was no reference to evolution in the title and the prohibition received little attention. Furthermore, the treatment of evolutionary theory seems not to be the main reason for the prohibition. Artigas, Glick and Martínez, *Negotiating Darwin*, Chapter 2 and pp. 278–279.

75 J. Murphy, 'Evolution and Faith', *The Irish Ecclesiastical Record*, 3rd series, vol. 5 (1884), p. 766.

76 Ibid., p. 759.

77 Ibid., p. 760.

78 Murphy quoted the text in Latin (p. 760). The English version was obtained from Norman P. Tanner (ed.), *Decrees of the Ecumenical Councils: Trent to Vatican II* (London: Sheed & Ward; Washington, DC: Georgetown University Press, 1990), vol. 2, p. 807.

79 Quotation from the text of the *Syllabus of Errors*, in Raymond Corrigan, *The Church and the Nineteenth Century* (Milwaukee, Wisconsin: The Bruce Publishing Company, 1938), p. 291.

80 Murphy, 'Evolution and Faith', p. 761. Scriptural passages quoted in this context were (1) Genesis 2:7, 'And the Lord God formed man out of the slime of the earth';

(2) Job 10:8, 'Thy hands have made me, and fashioned me'.

81   J. Murphy, 'Faith and Evolution', *The Irish Ecclesiastical Record*, 3rd series, vol. 6 (1885), p. 487.

82   Murphy, 'Evolution and Faith', pp. 762–763.

83   Murphy, 'Faith and Evolution', pp. 490–491.

84   Murphy, 'Evolution and Faith', see pp. 766–767.

85   John S. Vaughan identified himself as an Englishman in his article 'Bishop Clifford's Theory of the Days of Creation', *The Dublin Review*, 3rd series, vol. 9 (January 1883), p. 45. The debate between Murphy and Vaughan also receives attention in John Privilege's *Michael Logue and the Catholic Church in Ireland, 1879–1925* (Manchester: Manchester University Press, 2009), pp. 56–58. Vaughan became bishop of Salford in 1908 (p. 57).

86   John S. Vaughan, 'Faith and Evolution: A Further Consideration on the Question', *The Irish Ecclesiastical Record*, 3rd series, vol. 6 (1885), pp. 413–424.

87   John S. Vaughan, 'Faith and Evolution – a Reply', *The Irish Ecclesiastical Record*, 3rd series, vol. 6 (1885), pp. 654, 657–658.

88   Vaughan gave the examples of the heliocentric hypothesis contradicting Joshua 10: 13 and the impossibility of a global deluge in the light of modern geology. The observation of stellar parallax by the German astronomer and mathematician, Friedrich Wilhelm Bessel (1784–1846) in 1838 and the experiments of the French physicist, Jean Foucault (1819–1868) eliminated any residue of doubt may have lingered about the veracity of the Copernican system which contradicted a literal interpretation of some Old Testament verses. See Jerome J. Langford, *Galileo, Science and the Church*, 3rd ed. (Ann Arbor: The University of Michigan Press, 1992), p. 134.

89   Vaughan, 'Faith and Evolution – a Reply', p. 663.

90   Ibid., p. 652.

91   Vaughan, 'Faith and Evolution: A Further Consideration on the Question', p. 424.

92   Murphy, 'Faith and Evolution', p. 491.

93   J. Murphy, 'Faith and Evolution', *The Irish Ecclesiastical Record*, 3rd series, vol. 6 (1885), p. 725.

94   Ibid., p. 736.

95   Patrick Corish, *The Irish Catholic Experience: A Historical Survey* (Dublin: Gill & Macmillan, 1985), p. 210.

96   T.J.C., 'Introductory', *The Irish Ecclesiastical Record*, 3rd series, vol. 1 (1880), p. 1.

97   McLaughlin, 'A Century of Science in the IER', pp. 251–252.

98   See Ruth Fleischmann, *Catholic Nationalism in the Irish Revival: A Study of Canon Sheehan, 1852–1913* (London: Macmillan Press, 1997), pp. 40, 87–88, 97.

99   Murphy, 'Faith and Evolution', p. 481.

100 Vaughan invoked such writers as Padre José Mendive, Professor of Metaphysics at the University of Madrid and John Gmeiner, professor at the Theological Seminary at St Francis, Milwaukee (Vaughan, 'A Further Consideration on the Question', pp. 420–421). Murphy's authors included Matthias Joseph Scheeben (1835–1888); Camillo Mazzella, S.J. (1833–1900), Professor of the Gregorian University in Rome and a cardinal prefect of the Congregation of the Index (1889–1893); and Giovanni Perrone, S.J. (1794–1876). Murphy, 'Faith and Evolution', pp. 734–735.

101 See Artigas, Glick and Martínez, *Negotiating Darwin*, pp. 19, 23 and p. 291, note 54, in relation to the last endnote above.

102 See John D. Root, 'The Final Apostasy of St George Jackson Mivart', *The Catholic*

Historical Review, vol. 71, no. 1 (January 1985), p. 4.

103 St George Mivart, 'Modern Catholics and Scientific Freedom', *The Nineteenth Century*, vol. 18 (July 1885), pp. 30–47. Quotation from p. 35.

104 J. Murphy, 'The Case of Galileo', *The Nineteenth Century*, vol. 19 (May 1886), pp. 723, 736.

105 St George Mivart, 'Letter from Dr. Mivart on the Bishop of Newport's Article in Our Last Number', *The Dublin Review*, 3rd series, vol. 19 (January–April 1888), pp. 181–182.

106 Artigas, Glick and Martínez, *Negotiating Darwin*, pp. 244–248.

107 For an account of Mivart's opposition to Darwinism, see Adrian Desmond and James Moore, *Darwin* (London: Penguin Books, 1992), pp. 568–571, 577, 582–592.

108 St George Mivart, 'Roman Congregations and Modern Thought', *The North American Review*, vol. 170 (April 1900), p. 565. See also Sister Mary Frederick, *Religion and Evolution since 1859* (Chicago: Loyola University Press, 1935), p. 69.

109 Gruber, *Conscience in Conflict*, p. 196.

110 St George Mivart, 'The Catholic Church and Biblical Criticism', *The Nineteenth Century*, vol. 22 (July 1887), p. 31

111 John S. Vaughan, 'Man or Monkey?' *The Irish Ecclesiastical Record*, 3rd series, vol. 10 (1889), p. 2.

112 See Darwin, *The Descent of Man*, vol. 1, p. 105.

113 Vaughan, 'Man or Monkey?', pp. 4, 11.

114 Ibid., pp. 2, 11.

115 Ibid., pp. 7, 10.

116 Ibid., p. 10.

117 Ibid., pp. 2-3.

118 Gerald Molloy, 'On the Philosophy of a Candle', *The Irish Monthly*, vol. 4 (1876), pp. 529–538. The quotation is from p. 538. Molloy lectured on this subject to St Mary's Branch of the Catholic Union.

119 Anon., review of J.B. Kavanagh, *Solar Physics: A Lecture* (Dublin: Dollard, 1877) in *The Irish Monthly*, vol. 5 (1877), pp. 235, 237. Secchi was a pioneer of astronomical spectroscopy. He was the author of *Le Soleil* (1875), an illustrated popular book.

120 Anon., review of J.B. Kavanagh, *Comets and Meteors: A Lecture* (Dublin: Dollard, 1877), in *The Irish Monthly*, vol. 5 (September 1877), p. 594.

121 Anon., 'Scientific Notices: Afternoon Scientific Lectures', *The Irish Ecclesiastical Record*, 3rd series, vol. 2 (May 1881), pp. 284-293. Quotations are from pp. 285–286.

122 Henry Bedford, 'Scientific Gossip', *The Irish Monthly*, vol. 7 (1879), pp. 32–45. Words in quotation marks are from p. 42. For further discussion on Bedford's articles on scientific subjects, see Juliana Adelman, *Communities of Science in Nineteenth-Century Ireland* (London: Pickering & Chatto, 2009), pp. 149–150, 155–156.

123 Henry Bedford, 'Scientific Gossip 2: The Uses of the Sun', *The Irish Monthly*, vol. 7 (1879), pp. 80–81.

124 Henry Bedford, 'Scientific Gossip 4, Part 1: The Telephone', *The Irish Monthly*, vol. 7 (July 1879), p. 344.

125 See Bedford, 'Scientific Gossip 4', pp. 342–344; and idem, 'Scientific Gossip 5: Heat, Part 1, What Is It?' *The Irish Monthly*, vol. 8 (January 1880), pp. 29–32. Bedford praised the work of Charles Darwin's son, George, who was at the time showing promise as a mathematical astronomer. He expressed the mildest criticism of Charles, merely stating that his theory was open to question. See Henry Bedford, 'The History of the Earth and Moon', *The Irish Ecclesiastical Record*, 3rd series, vol. 3 (January 1882), pp. 1–11.

126 F. Lennon, review of Gerald Molloy's *Gleanings in Science* (London: Macmillan, 1888), *The Irish Ecclesiastical Record*, 3rd series, vol. 10 (June 1889), pp. 61–69.

127 Canon Sheehan, 'The Two Civilisations', in idem, *Early Essays and Lectures* (London: Longmans, Green & Co., 1917), p. 239. (This essay was first published in *The Irish Monthly*, vol. 18 [June-July 1890], pp. 293–301, 358–367.)

128 Ibid., pp. 240-241; see also pp. 242–243.

129 Another debatable issue which arose in the harmonising of science and scripture was whether or not the Flood narrated in Genesis was local or universal. See F. Cane, 'The Physics of the Flood', *The Irish Ecclesiastical Record*, 3rd series, vol. 10 (October 1889), pp. 901–906. However, the question about whether or not a local or universal flood had occurred proved to be far less contentious and received far less attention than human evolution.

3. Catholicism and Science, 1890s–1903

1 Barry Brundell, 'Catholic Church Politics and Evolution Theory, 1894–1902', *The British Journal for the History of Science*, vol. 34 (2001), pp. 90–91; and Ernest C. Messenger, *Evolution and Theology: The Problem of Man's Origin* (London: Burns, Oates & Washbourne, 1931), pp. 232–233.

2 Messenger, *Evolution and Theology*, p. 234.

3 Ibid., pp. 235–236.

4 Mariano Artigas, Thomas F. Glick and Rafael A. Martínez, *Negotiating Darwin: The Vatican Confronts Evolution, 1877–1902* (Baltimore: The Johns Hopkins University Press, 2006), pp. 29–30.

5 Ibid., pp. 29, 68.

6 Ibid., pp. 29–30, 278–279.

7 Brundell, 'Catholic Church Politics', p. 91, note 38.

8 Letter from T.H. Huxley to Arthur Bennett, *The Irish Times*, 1 August 1891.

9 John Tyndall, 'Mr Gladstone and the English Girondins', in *Professor Tyndall's Belfast Speech (28th January, 1890) and Correspondence with Mr Gladstone* (Dublin: The Irish Loyal and Patriotic Union, 1890). Tyndall's speech was also published in the *Dublin Daily Express*, 29 January 1890.

10 See J.F.H, review of Leonard Huxley (ed.), *The Life and Letters of Thomas Henry Huxley*, in *The Irish Ecclesiastical Record*, 4th series, vol. 8 (July–December 1900), p. 570.

11 T.E. Judge, 'The Spirit of Modern Science', *The Irish Ecclesiastical Record*, 3rd series, vol. 13 (1892), pp. 1094, 1095.

12 Tyndall exerted little influence in Ireland. Norman McMillan and Martin Nevin, 'Tyndall of Leighlin', in W.H. Brock, N.D. McMillan and R.C. Mollan (eds), *John Tyndall: Essays on a Natural Philosopher* (Dublin: Royal Dublin Society, 1981), pp. 30–34. For the little support Tyndall did receive in Ireland, see Greta Jones, 'Scientists against Home Rule', in D. George Boyce and Alan O'Day (eds), *Defenders of the Union: A Survey of British and Irish Unionism since 1801* (London: Routledge, 2001), p. 190.

13 E. Gaynor, 'Sir Robert S. Ball on Evolution', *The Irish Ecclesiastical Record*, 4th series, vol. 1 (1897), pp. 243–260.

14 E. Gaynor continued his critical commentary on evolution in 'Darwinism: Sensation', *The Irish Ecclesiastical Record*, 4th series, vol. 6 (1899), pp. 147–166.

15 See Peter J. Bowler, *Evolution: The History of an Idea*, 3rd ed. (Berkeley: University of California Press, 2003), pp. 216–217, 322–323.

16 George Sigerson, 'Genesis and Evolution II', *The New Ireland Review*, vol. 1, no. 2 (April 1894), p. 88.

17 John Hedley Brooke, *Science and Religion: Some Historical Perspectives* (Cambridge: Cambridge University Press, 1991), p. 299.

18 John L. Morrison, 'William Seton – a Catholic Darwinist', *The Review of Politics*, vol. 21, no. 3 (1959), pp. 582–583.

19 Brundell, 'Catholic Church Politics', p. 93.

20 Greta Jones, 'Darwinism in Ireland', in David Attis and Charles Mollan (eds), *Science and Irish Culture: Why the History of Science Matters in Ireland* (Dublin: Royal Dublin Society, 2004), pp. 130–131.

21 See John Stenhouse, 'Catholicism, Science, and Modernity: The Case of William Miles Maskell', *The Journal of Religious History*, vol. 22, no. 1 (February 1998), pp. 59–82. See especially pp. 65–67, 70, 80–81.

22 Morrison, 'William Seton', pp. 574–575.

23 See Harry W. Paul, 'Religion and Darwinism', in Thomas F. Glick (ed.), *The Comparative Reception of Darwinism* (Chicago: The University of Chicago Press, 1988), p. 430.

24 The best example is Galileo's 'Letter to the Grand Duchess Christina'. For an English translation of this document, see Maurice A. Finocchiaro (ed. and trans.), *The Galileo Affair: A Documentary History* (Berkeley: University of California Press, 1989), pp. 87–118, especially pp. 104–105, 109–113.

25 John Augustine Zahm, *Evolution and Dogma*, introduction by Thomas J. Schlereth (Chicago: D.H. McBride, 1896; republished, New York: Arno Press, 1978), pp. 71, 283.

26 Philip Burton, 'Was St Augustine an Evolutionist?' *The Irish Ecclesiastical Record*, 4th series, vol. 5 (February 1899), pp. 102–110. Quotations are from pp. 106–107.

27 The source of the quotation is given as Huxley, *Darwiniana*, p. 147.

28 Patrick F. Coakley, 'Was St Augustine an Evolutionist?' *The Irish Ecclesiastical Record*, 4th series, vol. 5 (April 1899), pp. 346–347, 357–358.

29 Philip Burton, 'St Augustine and the Missing Link', *The Irish Ecclesiastical Record*, 4th series, vol. 5 (May 1899), pp. 451, 455, 457. Burton referred to *The Tablet* (6 March 1897), p. 379, in reference to Leroy's retraction.

30 Of the four articles expressing differences of opinion between Burton and Coakley, only the second article was by Coakley. Burton had the last word in 'Was St Augustine an Evolutionist?' *The Irish Ecclesiastical Record*, 4th series, vol. 5 (June 1899), pp. 521–530. The debate between Burton and Coakley receives attention in John Privilege's *Michael Logue and the Catholic Church in Ireland, 1879–1925* (Manchester: Manchester University Press, 2009), pp. 58–59.

31 M. Barrett, 'The Origin and Conservation of Motion', *The Irish Ecclesiastical Record*, 4th series, vol. 3 (1898), p. 62.

32 Walter McDonald, *Reminiscences of a Maynooth Professor*, edited with a memoir by Denis Gwynn (London: Jonathan Cape, 1925; republished, Cork: Mercier Press, 1967), pp. 104–105.

33 See Jacob W. Gruber, *A Conscience in Conflict: The Life of St George Jackson Mivart* (Westport, Connecticut: Greenwood Press, 1960), Chapter 11.

34 McDonald, *Reminiscences*, pp. 116–118.

35 Walter McDonald, 'The Kinetic Theory of Activity', *The Irish Ecclesiastical Record*, 4th series, vol. 2 (October 1897), p. 292.

36 Nicholas Whyte, *Science, Colonialism and Ireland* (Cork: Cork University Press, 1999), p. 160; and Privilege, *Michael Logue and the Catholic Church*, p. 61.

37 For more detailed accounts, see the biographical memoir by Denis Gwynn in McDonald's *Reminiscences*, pp. 30–38; Patrick J. Corish, *Maynooth College, 1795–1995* (Dublin: Gill & Macmillan, 1995), pp. 252–255; Louise Fuller, 'Walter McDonald's Window on Maynooth, 1870–1920', in James H. Murphy (ed.), *Evangelicals and Catholics in Nineteenth-Century Ireland* (Dublin: Four Courts Press, 2005), pp. 146–148; and Privilege, *Michael Logue and the Catholic Church*, pp. 60–64.

38 McDonald, *Reminiscences*, pp. 32, 180.

39 See Michael J. Crowe, 'Astronomy and Religion (1780–1915): Four Case Studies Involving Ideas of Extraterrestrial Life', in John Hedley Brooke, Margaret J. Osler and Jitse M. van der Meer (eds), *Science in Theistic Contexts: Cognitive Dimensions*, vol. 16 of *Osiris* (2001), pp. 211–212, 217–218.

40 Robert Ball was a lecturer and an author of popular books on astronomy, including *The Story of the Heavens* (1885), *In Starry Realms* (1892), *The Story of the Sun* (1893) and *In the High Heavens* (1893). Charles Mollan, 'Elements of Irish Science: An Historical Sketch', in idem (ed.), *Science and Ireland: alue for Society* (Dublin: The Royal Dublin Society, 2005), p. 25.

41 E.A. Selley, 'Is Our Earth Alone Inhabited?' *The Irish Ecclesiastical Record*, 4th series, vol. 12 (1902), see pp. 435–436, 439, 441.

42 M.F.H., 'Is Our Earth Alone Inhabited?' *The Irish Ecclesiastical Record*, 4th series, vol. 13 (1903), pp. 167–169.

43 J.S. Vaughan, 'Is Our Earth Alone Inhabited? A Friendly Comment upon Rev. E.A. Selley's Essay', *The Irish Ecclesiastical Record*, 4th series, vol. 13 (1903), p. 143.

44 This is indicated by E.A. Selley's 'The Nebular Theory and Divine Revelation I', *The Irish Ecclesiastical Record*, 4th series, vol. 13 (1903), p. 335.

45 E.A. Selley, 'The Nebular Theory and Divine Revelation: II', *The Irish Ecclesiastical Record*, 4th series, vol. 13 (1903), pp. 418–429. Quotations are from pp. 421, 427–428.

46 John Meehan, 'Haeckel and the Existence of God', *The Irish Ecclesiastical Record*, 4th series, vol. 14 (July–December 1903), p. 148.

47 Artigas, Glick and Martínez, *Negotiating Darwin*, pp. 5–6, 281–282.

48 See Jones, 'Scientists against Home Rule', p. 192.

49 Ibid., p. 193; Jones, 'Darwinism in Ireland', pp. 134–135; and idem, 'Catholicism, Nationalism and Science', *The Irish Review*, no. 20 (Winter/Spring 1997), p. 50.

50 Maurice A. Finocchiaro, 'Galileo as a "Bad Theologian": A Formative Myth about Galileo's Trial', *Studies in History and Philosophy of Science*, vol. 33A, no. 4 (December 2002), pp. 776–777.

51 St George Mivart, 'Some Recent Catholic Apologists', *Fortnightly Review*, vol. 67 (1900), p. 33.

52 John M. Harty, 'The Church and Science', *The Irish Ecclesiastical Record*, 4th series, vol. 7 (1900), pp. 168–171.

53 David C. Lindberg, 'Galileo, the Church, and the Cosmos', in David C. Lindberg and Ronald L. Numbers (eds), *When Science and Christianity Meet* (Chicago: The University of Chicago Press, 2003), pp. 33–60.

54 John M. Harty, 'Galileo and the Roman Congregations', *The Irish Ecclesiastical Record*, 4th series, vol. 7 (1900), p. 311. Harty's point about civil tribunals was also made by Cardinal Herbert Vaughan and his fellow bishops in the province of Westminster in their joint pastoral letter against liberal Catholicism issued on 29 December 1900. See 'Text of the Joint Pastoral Letter, by the Cardinal Archbishop and the Bishops of the Province of Westminster', Appendix B in George Tyrrell,

Letters from a 'Modernist': The Letters of George Tyrrell to Wilfrid Ward, 1893–1908, introduced and annotated by Mary Jo Weaver (Shepherdstown, West Virginia: Patmos Press; London: Sheed & Ward, 1981), p. 152. The pastoral letter condemned, in particular, ideas that had been expressed by Mivart. Edward Norman, *The English Catholic Church in the Nineteenth Century* (Oxford: Clarendon Press, 1984), p. 334.

55 John William Draper, *History of the Conflict between Religion and Science*, 10th ed. (London: Henry S. King & Co., 1877), pp. 168, 171–172.

56 W.P.C., 'Draper's "Conflict between Science and Religion"', *The New Ireland Review*, vol. 9 (1898), p. 373. The list given by W.P.C. is more extensive.

57 In late-nineteenth-century France this argument had lost much of its persuasive power. Only a few of the great scientists who were Catholic were contemporary and most of these did not rise to the defence of Christianity against irreligious activists such as Jean Macé and the *Ligue de l'Enseignement* who used science as an ideological weapon. A remedy adopted by French Catholics was the foundation of Catholic institutes of higher education in Paris, Lille, Angers, Lyon and Toulouse. One of their important functions was to train Catholic scientists who would be motivated to work in harmony with the Catholic faith. See Harry W. Paul, 'Science and the Catholic Institutes in Nineteenth-Century France', *Societas – a Review of Social History*, vol. 1, no. 4 (1971), pp. 271–273.

58 Peter Coffey, 'The Hexahemeron and Science: I', *The Irish Ecclesiastical Record*, 4th series, vol. 12 (August 1902), pp. 141–162. See especially pp. 141–144.

59 Ibid., p. 158; in reference to *The Nineteenth Century* (November 1885–February 1886).

60 See Peter Coffey, 'The Hexahemeron and Science: II', *The Irish Ecclesiastical Record*, 4th series, vol. 12 (1902), pp. 269–270.

61 Anon., 'Preliminary Steps', *Record of the Maynooth Union* (1895–1896), pp. 7–8.

62 Walter McDonald, 'A Maynooth Union, as a Social and Academic Memorial of the Centenary', *Record of the Maynooth Union* (1895–1896), pp. 17–18.

63 The well-known English Roman Catholic Wilfrid Ward (1856–1916) wrote in *The Nineteenth Century* (December 1895) that the struggle between Catholicism and Protestantism had been superseded by the conflict between religion and infidelity. See Paschal Scotti, 'Wilfrid Ward: A Religious Fabius Maximus', *The Catholic Historical Review*, vol. 88, no. 1 (January 2002), p. 51.

64 McDonald, 'A Maynooth Union', 19. See also Patrick Corish, *The Irish Catholic Experience: A Historical Survey* (Dublin: Gill & Macmillan, 1985), p. 209.

65 See Ruth Fleischmann, *Catholic Nationalism in the Irish Revival: A Study of Canon Sheehan, 1852–1913* (London: Macmillan Press, 1997), pp. 23, 40–41, 97.

66 M.J. Murphy, in response to Very Rev. Fr. Carbery, 'Higher Education Our Hope for the Future', *Record of the Maynooth Union* (1895–1896), pp. 45–46.

67 Coghlan in response to Carbery, 'Higher Education', pp. 46–47.

68 M.P. Hickey, 'The Old Order Changeth', *Record of the Maynooth Union* (1897–1898), pp. 17–23. Quotations are from p. 17.

69 M. O'Riordan, 'A Catholic Truth Society for Ireland', *Record of the Maynooth Union* (1898–1899), p. 44.

70 Peter C. Yorke, 'Concerning Certain Aspects of Clerical Education', *Record of the Maynooth Union* (1898–1899), p. 49.

71 E.A. Dalton, 'A Plea for Irish History', *Record of the Maynooth Union* (1899–1900), p. 78.

72 See Hugh McLeod, *Religion and the People of Western Europe, 1789–1970* (Oxford: Oxford University Press, 1981), pp. 113–114.

73 See Dorinda Outram, 'The History of Natural History: Grand Narrative or Local Lore?' in John Wilson Foster and Helena C.G. Chesney (eds), *Nature in Ireland: A Scientific and Cultural History* (Dublin: The Lilliput Press, 1997), pp. 468–469; and Nicholas Whyte, 'Lords of Ether and of Light: The Irish Astronomical Tradition of the Nineteenth Century', *The Irish Review*, nos.17–18 (Winter 1995), p. 127.

74 Eve Patten, 'Ireland's "Two Cultures" Debate: Victorian Science and the Literary Revival', *Irish University Review*, vol. 33, no. 1 (Spring/Summer 2003), pp. 8–9.

75 See Juliana Adelman, 'Evolution on Display: Promoting Irish Natural History and Darwinism at the Dublin Science and Art Museum', *The British Journal for the History of Science*, vol. 38, no. 139 (December 2005), pp. 416–417, 435.

76 J.M. O'Reilly, 'The Threatening Metempsychosis of a Nation', *Record of the Maynooth Union* (1899–1900), p. 51.

77 P.J. Dowling, 'Save the Child: A Suggestion to Clerical Managers', *The Irish Ecclesiastical Record*, 4th series, vol. 14 (December 1903), p. 521.

78 Ibid., pp. 521–522.

79 Ibid., p. 521; and Seán MacCartáin, 'The Department of Agriculture and Technical Instruction, 1899–1930', in Norman McMillan (ed.), *Prometheus's Fire: A History of Scientific and Technological Education in Ireland* (n.p.: Tyndall Publications, 2000), pp. 213, 219.

80 Dowling, 'Save the Child', p. 522. In a later article Dowling praised Germany and Switzerland and was sharply critical of Britain, especially with reference to what he saw as the inefficiencies and wasteful expenditures pertaining to the Department of Science and Art and the Royal College of Science in Ireland. P.J. Dowling, 'Technical Education – Some Queries and Replies', *The Irish Ecclesiastical Record*, 4th series, vol. 15 (1904), p. 415.

81 George F. Fleming, 'The Case of Ireland against the Science and Art Department', *The Irish Ecclesiastical Record*, 4th series, vol. 15 (February 1904), pp. 128–141.

82 G. Molloy, 'On the Teaching of Experimental and Practical Science in the Secondary Schools of Ireland', *The Irish Ecclesiastical Record*, 4th series, vol. 16 (October 1904), pp. 289–297, a paper read at a meeting of the British Association for the Advancement of Science in Cambridge in August 1904.

83 McDonald, *Reminiscences*, p. 75.

84 Adelman, 'Evolution on Display', pp. 427–428.

85 Huxley coined the term 'agnostic' in 1869 but it was not until 1883 that knowledge of this entered the public domain (Bernard Lightman, 'Huxley and Scientific Agnosticism: The Strange History of a Failed Rhetorical Strategy', *The British Journal for the History of Science*, vol. 35 [2002], pp. 271–289).

86 Bernard Lightman, *The Origins of Agnosticism: Victorian Unbelief and the Limits of Knowledge* (Baltimore: The Johns Hopkins University Press, 1987).

87 See Harry W. Paul, *The Edge of Contingency: French Catholic Reaction to Scientific Change from Darwin to Duhem* (Gainesville: University Presses of Florida, 1979), pp. 183–185.

88 See E. Gaynor, 'Modern Scientific Materialism: A Necessity of Thought', *The Irish Ecclesiastical Record*, 4th series, vol. 3 (March 1898), pp. 193–215.

89 M. O'Riordan, 'Scientific Dogma v. Dogmatic Science', *The New Ireland Review*, vol. 9, no. 6 (August 1898), pp. 322–323, 328.

90 P. Coffey, 'Agnosticism: A General Sketch', *The Irish Ecclesiastical Record*, 4th series, vol. 10 (October 1901), p. 296.

91 Ibid., p. 294.

92 Ibid., pp. 294–295.

93 Ibid., p. 299.
94 Ibid., p. 297.
95 Ibid., p. 310.
96 Peter Coffey, 'Agnosticism: A Special Study', *The Irish Ecclesiastical Record*, 4th series, vol. 10 (1901), p. 514.
97 Ibid., p. 539.
98 W.P.C., 'Drapers "Conflict,"', p. 371.

4. COMMISSIONS OF ENQUIRY, 1901–1907

1 *Royal Commission on University Education in Ireland: Appendix to the First Report: Minutes of Evidence*, Cd. 826 (Dublin: His Majesty's Stationery Office, 1901), p. 35. His Majesty's Stationery Office is hereafter given as HMSO.
2 Ibid., p. 56.
3 Ibid.
4 Ibid., p. 17.
5 Ibid., p. 99.
6 Ibid., p. 85.
7 This point is made in R.B. McDowell and D.A. Webb, *Trinity College Dublin, 1592–1952: An Academic History* (Dublin: Trinity College Dublin Press in association with Environmental Publications, 2004), p. 365.
8 *Appendix to the First Report*, p. 85.
9 Ibid. Words in quotation marks are from p. 85.
10 Ibid., p. 92; and Rev. William Delany, 'Further Letter to the Secretary of the Commission', p. 338.
11 *Appendix to the First Report*, p. 88.
12 Ibid., pp. 88–89.
13 Ibid., p. 90.
14 Greta Jones, 'Catholicism, Nationalism and Science', *The Irish Review*, no. 20 (Winter/ Spring 1997), p. 50.
15 *Appendix to the First Report*, p. 92.
16 Ibid., p. 92; and Jones, 'Catholicism, Nationalism and Science', p. 50.
17 *Appendix to the First Report*, p. 92.
18 T.W. Moody, 'The Irish University Question of the Nineteenth Century', *History*, vol. 43, no. 148 (June 1958), p. 104; and 'Statement of the Roman Catholic Hierarchy, June 1897', in *Appendix to the First Report*, pp. 387–388.
19 *Royal Commission on University Education in Ireland: Appendix to the Third Report: Minutes of Evidence*, Cd. 1229 (Dublin: HMSO, 1902), p. 287.
20 Ibid., p. 294.
21 Delany, 'Further Letter to the Secretary', p. 338.
22 *Appendix to the Third Report*, p. 361.
23 Ibid., p. 192; evidence of Rev. Brother Connolly, Superior of the Presentation Brothers' College, Cork.
24 Ibid., pp. 187, 297: based on the evidence of Rev. Brother J.D. Burke (Superior, Christian Brothers' Schools, Cork) and Bishop Thomas O'Dea.
25 Ibid., p. 187.
26 *Appendix to the First Report*, pp. 24–25
27 *Appendix to the Third Report*, p. 362.
28 Ibid., p. 361.
29 Peter J. Bowler, *Evolution: The History of an Idea*, 3rd ed. (Berkeley: University of California Press, 2003), p. 257; and Daniel J. Kevles, 'From Eugenics to Patents:

Genetics, Law and Human Rights, *Annals of Human Genetics*, vol. 75 (2011), p. 326.

30 Greta Jones, 'Eugenics in Ireland: The Belfast Eugenics Society, 1911–15', *Irish Historical Studies*, vol. 28, no. 109 (May 1992), pp. 81–95. Jones observed that 'Eugenics came to Ireland, officially at least, in 1911. In August of that year the National Public Health Congress was held in Dublin' (p. 83). Eugenics gained very little support in Catholic Ireland because some aspects of it were incompatible with Catholic doctrine concerning marriage and family life. Furthermore, the conservative social policies of the Irish Free State made the emergence of a eugenics movement even more highly improbable.

31 *Royal Commission on University Education in Ireland: Appendix to the Second Report: Minutes of Evidence*, Cd. 900 (Dublin: HMSO, 1902), p. 195.

32 *Royal Commission on University Education in Ireland: Final Report of the Commissioners*, Cd. 1483 (Dublin: HMSO, 1903), p. 27.

33 Ibid., p. 29.

34 Ibid., p. 30.

35 Ibid., pp. 34–35.

36 Ibid., p. 29.

37 Ibid., p. 41.

38 Ibid., p. 58.

39 Ibid., pp. 33–34.

40 Ibid., p. 59.

41 Moody, 'The Irish University Question', p. 105.

42 Ibid.

43 Nicholas Whyte, *Science, Colonialism and Ireland* (Cork: Cork University Press, 1999), p. 43.

44 John Coolahan, *Irish Education: History and Structure* (Dublin: Institute of Public Administration, 1981), p. 122.

45 *Royal Commission on Trinity College, Dublin, and the University of Dublin: Appendix to the First Report: Statements and Returns*, Cd. 3176 (Dublin: HMSO, 1906), p. 81.

46 Ibid., p. 82.

47 *Royal Commission on Trinity College, Dublin, and the University of Dublin: Appendix to the Final Report: Minutes of Evidence and Documents*, Cd. 3312 (Dublin: HMSO, 1907), pp. 271, 273.

48 Ibid., pp. 272–273.

49 Ibid., p. 273.

50 Ibid., p. 276.

51 Ibid.

52 Ibid., p. 277.

53 Letter from Walsh to Sir Anthony MacDonnell, 20 October 1906, published in *Appendix to the Final Report* (1907), pp. 421–422. The letter was received by Sir Edward Fry from McDonnell with 'an intimation' that Walsh approved of it being published by the commission.

54 Joly was acknowledged in the table of contents of the *Appendix to the Final Report* (1907) as 'representing the Signatories to Joint Statements IV., V., VI.', in pp. 25–35 of the *Appendix to the First Report*.

55 *Appendix to the Final Report* (1907), p. 52.

56 Ibid.

57 Statement submitted by John Joly, published in *Appendix to the Final Report* (1907), p. 355.

58 Ibid., p. 356.

59 Ibid.

60 Ibid., pp. 359–360.

61 'The Royal Commission on Trinity College, Dublin, and the University of Dublin: Suggested legislation towards rendering Trinity College more acceptable to Roman Catholics: Memorandum submitted by J. Joly, Sc.D., F.R.S', dated 1906, MS 2304/ 8, John Joly papers, Trinity College Dublin.

62 *Royal Commission on Trinity College, Dublin, and the University of Dublin: Final Report of the Commissioners*, Cd. 3311 (Dublin: HMSO, 1907), p. 28.

63 'Irish university question', *The Irish Times*, 26 January 1907.

64 Daniel Coghlan, 'The Church and the Universities in Countries of Mixed Religions', *Appendix to the Final Report* (1907), p. 415. Coghlan's essay was originally published in *The Irish Ecclesiastical Record* (October 1906). The above quotation is also in Whyte, *Science, Colonialism and Ireland*, p. 45; in reference to: [E.P. Culverwell], *Mr Bryce's Speech on the Proposed Reconstruction of the University of Dublin: Annotated Edition Issued by the Dublin University Defence Committee* (1907), p. 27.

65 Whyte, *Science, Colonialism and Ireland*, pp. 44–45.

66 'Statement of the Defence Committee: A reply to Mr. Bryce', *The Irish Times*, 11 March 1907. The above statement is quoted in (1) Whyte, *Science, Colonialism and Ireland*, pp. 45–46, in reference to the Dublin University Defence Committee, 'Trinity College, Dublin, and the Proposed University Legislation for Ireland', published in the *Freeman's Journal*, 11 March 1907; and (2) Greta Jones, 'Scientists against Home Rule', in D. George Boyce and Alan O'Day (eds), *Defenders of the Union: A Survey of British and Irish Unionism since 1801* (London: Routledge, 2001), p. 199.

67 Draft for speech by Joly, 'probably for deputation to Augustine Birrell', objecting to the Bryce proposals, dated November 1905, MS 2304/ 4, John Joly papers, Trinity College, Dublin. The date of November 1905 seems to be an error. Joly's opinions in this document were probably expressed after Bryce's proposals were published on 26 January 1907. See Jones, 'Scientists against Home Rule', p. 198; and p. 206, note 57.

68 John Joly, *An Epitome of the Irish University Question* (Dublin: Hodges, Figgis & Co. [1907]), pp. 44–45. The handwritten date on the cover is 16 May 1907 (MS 2304/ 17, John Joly papers, Trinity College Dublin). In a footnote to this quotation, Joly referred to an essay by Huxley, under the title of 'Method and Results', p. 47; and to Tyndall's 'The Scientific Use of the Imagination', in *Fragments of Science*, vol. 2, p. 101.

69 Joly, *An Epitome of the Irish University Question*, pp. 48–49.

70 Ibid., p. 49.

71 Report by J. Joly, 'ordered to be printed and circulated among Members of the Committee', marked 'strictly confidential', and dated 9 July (MS 2304/ 11, John Joly papers, Trinity College Dublin).

72 Moody, 'The Irish University Question', pp. 106–108.

73 Jones, 'Scientists against Home Rule', p. 200.

74 John A. Murphy, *The College: A History of Queen's/University College Cork* (Cork: Cork University Press, 1995), p. 163.

75 Jones, 'Scientists against Home Rule', pp. 199–200.

5. ANTI-MODERNISM, 1907–1920S

1   Peter J. Bowler, *Reconciling Science and Religion: The Debate in Early-Twentieth-Century Britain* (Chicago: The University of Chicago Press, 2001).

2   Owen Chadwick, *A History of the Popes, 1830–1914* (Oxford: Oxford University Press, 2003), pp. 346–359.

3   See Harry W. Paul, *The Edge of Contingency: French Catholic Reaction to Scientific Change from Darwin to Duhem* (Gainesville: University Presses of Florida, 1979), p. 189.

4   Alec R. Vidler, *The Modernist Movement in the Roman Church: Its Origins and Outcome* (London: Cambridge University Press, 1934), pp. 57–58.

5   Kenneth Scott Latourette, *Christianity in a Revolutionary Age: A History of Christianity in the Nineteenth and Twentieth Centuries*, vol. 1 of *The Nineteenth Century in Europe: Background and the Roman Catholic Phase* (London: Eyre & Spottiswoode, 1959), p. 317.

6   Frank J. Coppa, *The Modern Papacy since 1789* (London: Longman, 1998), pp. 141–147.

7   A *motu proprio* is a document issued directly from the pope's office concerning administrative and pastoral matters.

8   English translations of the texts of *Lamentabili Sane Exitu*, *Pascendi Dominic Gregis* and the anti-modernist oath are re-published in Anthony J. Mioni (ed.), *The Popes against Modern Errors:16 Papal Documents* (Rockford, Illinois: Tan Books, 1999), pp. 171–179, 180–241 and 270–272 respectively.

9   *Pascendi Dominic Gregis*; see paragraphs 6, 17, 45, 52.

10 See Vidler, *The Modernist Movement*, pp. 232–233.

11 See Patrick J. Corish, *Maynooth College, 1795–1995* (Dublin: Gill & Macmillan, 1995), pp. 251–257.

12 Daniel Coghlan, 'Evolution: Kant and the Loisy Theory of the Evolution of Christianity-II', *The Irish Ecclesiastical Record*, 4th series, vol. 21 (1907), pp. 60, 62, 75.

13 Daniel Coghlan, 'Evolution: Darwin and the Abbé Loisy-I', *The Irish Ecclesiastical Record*, 4th series, vol. 19 (June 1906), p. 481. T. Slater (S.J.) pointed to what he saw as a tendency of anthropologists, historians and philologists to present religion, including Christianity, as a feature of human culture – in terms of natural selection (T. Slater, 'The Evolution of Religion', *The Irish Ecclesiastical Record*, 5th series, vol. 17 [June 1921], pp. 561, 563).

14 Coghlan, 'Evolution: Darwin and the Abbé Loisy-I', pp. 485–487, 491–495.

15 Four additional articles on modernism by Professor Daniel Coghlan were published in *The Irish Ecclesiastical Record*, 4th series, under the title 'The Decree "Lamentabili Sane Exitu" and Modernism', in four parts: vol. 22 (October 1907), pp. 337–348; vol. 22 (November 1907), pp. 486–499; vol. 23 (January 1908), pp. 61–74; vol. 23 (May 1908), pp. 498–509. See also T. Slater, 'Evolution in Doctrine and Progress in Theology', *The Irish Ecclesiastical Record*, 4th series, vol. 14 (July-December 1903), pp. 506–507.

16 James MacCaffrey, 'The Papal Encyclical on Modernism', *The Irish Ecclesiastical Record*, 4th series, vol. 22 (December 1907), pp. 561–575; P.J. Toner, 'The Encyclical on Modernism', *The Irish Theological Quarterly*, vol. 3 (January 1908), pp. 1–21; John Shine, 'The Place of Modernism as a Philosophy of Religion', *The Irish Theological Quarterly*, vol. 3 (January 1908), pp. 22–31; E. Maguire, 'Anglicanism versus Modernism', *The Irish Theological Quarterly*, vol. 12 (April

1917), pp. 124–145; W. Moran, 'An Echo of the Modernist Crisis', *The Irish Ecclesiastical Record*, 5th series, vol. 37 (1931), pp. 249–263.

17 T.J. Walshe, 'Botanical Evolution in Theory and in Fact', *The Irish Theological Quarterly*, vol. 4 (January 1909), p. 81.

18 Tom Garvin, introduction to Walter McDonald's *Some Ethical Questions of Peace and War* (London: Burns, Oates & Washbourne, 1920; republished, Dublin: University College Dublin Press, 1998), pp. xii–xiii.

19 Walter McDonald, *Reminiscences of a Maynooth Professor*, edited by Denis Gwynn (London: Jonathan Cape, 1925; republished, Cork: Mercier, 1967), pp. 104–105.

20 James Tunstead Burtchaell, *Catholic Theories of Biblical Inspiration Since 1810: A Review and Critique* (London: Cambridge University Press, 1969), pp. 3–4.

21 McDonald, *Reminiscences*, pp. 195–196.

22 Ibid., p. 201.

23 Ibid., p. 208.

24 Ibid., pp. 208–209.

25 Ibid., pp. 38–40, 180–181, 209–210.

26 Ibid., pp. 265–269.

27 For a more detailed study of Walter McDonald's opinions and the reaction of the ecclesiastical authorities, see Louise Fuller, 'Walter McDonald's Window on Maynooth, 1870–1920', in James H. Murphy (ed.), *Evangelicals and Catholics in Nineteenth-Century Ireland* (Dublin: Four Courts Press, 2005), pp. 142–153.

28 For a summary of these arguments, see Alister E. McGrath, *Christian Theology: An Introduction*, 2nd ed. (Cambridge, Massachusetts: Blackwell Publishers, 1997), pp. 160–161.

29 See Alister E. McGrath, *Science and Religion: An Introduction* (Oxford: Blackwell Publishers, 1999), p.102, for a summary of Hume's main criticisms of the argument from design.

30 Bill McSweeney, *Roman Catholicism: The Search for Relevance* (Oxford: Basil Blackwell, 1980), pp. 73–74.

31 Karl Otmar von Aretin, *The Papacy and the Modern World* (London: Weidenfeld & Nicolson, 1970), p. 138.

32 See John Meehan, 'Haeckel and the Existence of God', *The Irish Ecclesiastical Record*, 4th series, vol. 14 (July–December 1903), pp. 157–158.

33 For a brief account of Emil du Bois-Reymond's role in the materialistic movement in nineteenth-century German science, see Peter J. Bowler and Iwan Rhys Morus, *Making Modern Science: A Historical Survey* (Chicago: The University of Chicago Press, 2005), pp. 95–96, 177–178.

34 W. McDonald, 'Some Tendencies of Modern Apologetics: Proof of Theism', *The Irish Theological Quarterly*, vol. 1 (January 1907), pp. 1–14. Words in quotation are from p. 4.

35 R. Fullerton, 'The Evolution of Mind – I', *The Irish Ecclesiastical Record*, 4th series, vol. 26 (1909), p. 261.

36 McDonald, 'Some Tendencies of Modern Apologetics', p. 8.

37 P. Coffey, 'Philosophy and the Sciences: I', *The Irish Ecclesiastical Record*, 4th series, vol. 17 (1905), pp. 25–29.

38 P. Coffey, 'Philosophy and the Sciences: II', *The Irish Ecclesiastical Record*, 4th series, vol. 17 (1905), p. 174. See also P. Coffey, 'The New Knowledge and Its Limitations – III', *The Irish Ecclesiastical Record*, 4th series, vol. 26 (1909), p. 586.

39 Coffey, 'Philosophy and the Sciences – II', pp. 163, 165.

40   See P. Coffey, 'Scholasticism and Modern Thought', *The Irish Theological Quarterly*, vol. 4 (1909), p. 472.

41   Coffey, 'The New Knowledge and its Limitations – III', p. 586.

42   Coffey, 'Scholasticism and Modern Thought', p. 472.

43   Coffey, 'Philosophy and the Sciences – II', p. 173.

44   P. Coffey, 'The New Knowledge and its Limitations – I', *The Irish Ecclesiastical Record*, 4th series, vol. 26 (October 1909), p. 337.

45   Coffey, 'Philosophy and the Sciences – II', pp. 173–174.

46   P. Coffey, 'Some Questionable Tendencies in the Logic of Scientific Method', *The Irish Ecclesiastical Record*, 4th series, vol. 28 (July 1910), pp. 2, 10.

47   See Wilfrid Ryan, 'The Charter of Science', *The Irish Ecclesiastical Record*, 5th series, vol. 1 (1913), pp. 253–254.

48   Coffey, 'The New Knowledge and its Limitations – I', pp. 337–339.

49   Alfred J. Rahilly, 'The Scientific Standpoint', *Studies*, vol. 2 (June 1913), pp. 60–61.

50   J. Rickaby, 'Faith versus Freethinking', *The Irish Theological Quarterly*, vol. 16 (1921), pp. 22, 27.

51   See John A. Murphy, *The College: A History of Queen's/University College Cork, 1845–1995* (Cork: Cork University Press, 1995), pp. 165, 204–207.

52   Monica Taylor, *Sir Bertram Windle: A Memoir* (London: Longmans, Green & Co., 1932), p. 52.

53   Patrick Allitt, *Catholic Converts: British and American Intellectuals Turn to Rome* (Ithaca, New York: Cornell University Press, 1997), p. 169.

54   Taylor, *Sir Bertram Windle*, pp. 233–234.

55   Charles Darwin is a case in point. He gradually distanced himself from his Anglican faith and became an agnostic, although afterwards he did occasionally return, momentarily, to theism. His scientific studies were a major contributor to his loss of faith. Shortly before his marriage, Emma Wedgwood, his future wife, expressed concern that the critical and sceptical attitude so essential for a professional life in science might provoke doubts about the truths of Christian faith. See John Hedley Brooke, 'Revisiting Darwin on Order and Design', in Niels Henrik Gregersen and Ulf Görman (eds), *Design and Disorder: Perspectives from Science and Theology* (London: T&T Clark, 2002), pp. 39–41. See also Owen Chadwick, *The Secularization of the European Mind in the Nineteenth Century* (Cambridge: Cambridge University Press, 1975), p. 187; in reference to Francis Darwin, *The Life and Letters of Charles Darwin*, 3rd ed. (1887), vol. I, p. 307.

56   Taylor, *Sir Bertram Windle*, pp. 234–235. See also Ann Keogh and Dermot Keogh, *Bertram Windle: The Honan Bequest and the Modernisation of University College Cork, 1904–1919* (Cork: Cork University Press, 2010), pp. 150–153.

57   For a more detailed discussion of vitalism and neo-vitalism see Bowler, *Reconciling Science and Religion*, especially pp. 161, 166–171.

58   See, for example, Charles Gelderd, 'The Regeneration of Lost Parts in Animals and the Theory of Matter and Form', *The Irish Ecclesiastical Record*, 4th series, vol. 25 (1909), pp. 50–51; and James Kelly, 'The Idea of Life: Aristotle's Theory v. Modern Science', *The Irish Ecclesiastical Record*, 4th series, vol. 14 (October 1903), pp. 317–324.

59   Windle regarded vitalism and neo-vitalism as essentially the same (Bertram C.A. Windle, *What Is Life? A Study of Vitalism and Neo-Vitalism* [London: Sands & Co., 1908], pp. 139, 143).

60   Bertram C.A. Windle, *The Church and Science* (London: Catholic Truth Society, 1920), pp. 305–315. For a supportive opinion, see E. Maguire, 'Facts and

Theories of Life III: Vitalism', *The Irish Theological Quarterly*, vol. 14 (1919), pp. 122–123.

61 R. Fullerton, 'Evolution of Mind – Materialism – II', *The Irish Ecclesiastical Record*, 4th series, vol. 26 (July-December 1909), pp. 390–392.

62 Windle, *What Is Life?* p. 8; see also, pp. 142–143.

63 Greta Jones, 'Darwinism in Ireland', in David Attis and Charles Mollan (eds), *Science and Irish Culture: Why the History of Science Matters in Ireland* (Dublin: Royal Dublin Society, 2004), pp. 121–122, 127–129; and Bowler, *Reconciling Science and Religion*, pp. 257–260.

64 Windle, *The Church and Science*, pp. 386–387.

65 R. Fullerton, 'Basis of Monism – Evolution', *The Irish Ecclesiastical Record*, 4th series, vol. 28 (1910), p. 161.

66 Words in quotation marks from Fullerton, 'Basis of Monism – Evolution', p. 172. Fullerton, like Walter McDonald, pointed to the discontinuities of scientific explanations of nature with reference to Emil Heinrich du Bois-Reymond (pp. 168–169).

67 Charles Gelderd, 'Modern Ideas on Darwinism', *The Irish Ecclesiastical Record*, 4th series, vol. 32 (July 1912), p. 2.

68 Garrett Pierse, 'The Apostacy of "Science"', *The Catholic Bulletin*, vol. 2 (February 1912), p. 56.

69 W.P. Ryan, *The Pope's Green Island* (London: James Nisbet & Co., 1912), p. 206.

70 Ibid., p. 224.

71 See Garrett Pierse, 'The Apostacy of "Science"', pp. 57–58; and Canon Sheehan, 'Irish Youth and High Ideals' and 'The Limitations and Possibilities of Catholic Literature', both in *Early Essays and Lectures* (London: Longmans Green & Co., 1917), pp. 226–227, 337, 345–346.

72 David Thomson, *Europe since Napoleon*, revised ed. (London: Penguin Books, 1966), p. 435. See also Steven Weinberg, 'The Great Reduction: Physics in the Twentieth Century', in Michael Howard and W. Roger Louis (eds), *The Oxford History of the Twentieth Century* (Oxford: Oxford University Press, 1998), p. 22.

73 J.W. Burrow, *The Crisis of Reason: European Thought, 1848–1914* (New Haven, Connecticut: Yale University Press, 2000), pp. 59–60, 62, 67.

74 P.A. Sheehan, 'The Dawn of the Century', in idem, *Literary Life, Essays, Poems* (Dublin: The Phoenix Publishing Company, n.d.), p. 123. This essay was the text of an address to Maynooth students on 1 December 1903.

75 Tom Garvin, 'Priests and Patriots: Irish Separatism and Fear of the Modern, 1890–1914', *Irish Historical Studies*, vol. 25, no. 97 (May 1986), p. 70.

76 See James Joll, *Europe since 1870: An International History*, 4th ed. (London: Penguin Books, 1990), pp. 102–103, 164, 332; and Michael Howard, 'The Dawn of the Century', in Howard and Louis (eds), *The Oxford History of the Twentieth Century*, pp. 6–7.

77 See P.J. Connolly, 'Darwinism and History: A Dialogue-I', *The Irish Ecclesiastical Record*, 4th series, vol. 28 (November 1910), p. 463.

78 Fullerton, 'Evolution of Mind – Materialism – II', pp. 388–389.

79 Greta Jones, 'Contested Territories: Alfred Cort Haddon, Progressive Evolutionism and Ireland', *History of European Ideas*, vol. 24, no. 3 (1998), pp. 195–196.

80 Peter J. Bowler, *Charles Darwin: The Man and His Influence* (Cambridge: Cambridge University Press, 1990), p. 219.

81 David Young, *The Discovery of Evolution* (Cambridge: Cambridge University Press, 1992), p. 175.

82   Peter J. Bowler, *The Eclipse of Darwinism: Anti-Darwinian Evolution Theories in the Decades around 1900* (Baltimore, Maryland: The Johns Hopkins University Press, 1983), p. 4. Eberhart Dennert's *Von Sterbelager des Darwinismus* was translated from German to English. For claims about the death of Darwinism in the early twentieth century, see also Tord Simonsson's *Logical and Semantic Structures in Christian Discourses*, trans. Agnes George (Oslo: Universitetsforlaget, 1971), pp. 48–49.

83   See Gelderd, 'Modern Ideas on Darwinism', pp. 7, 9.

84   D.J. Coffey, 'The Origin of Life: Its Physical Basis and Definition', *The Irish Theological Quarterly*, vol. 1 (October 1907), p. 424.

85   Ryan, 'The Charter of Science', pp. 255–256.

86   Windle, *The Church and Science*, p. 317.

87   Ibid., p. 322.

88   See Windle, *The Church and Science*, p. 321; and J. O'Mahony, 'On Some Difficulties Recently Raised against the Argument from Design for the Existence of God', *The Irish Theological Quarterly*, vol. 3 (1908), p. 303.

89   Windle, *The Church and Science*, p. 322.

90   Alfred J. Rahilly, 'The Meaning of Evolution', *Studies*, vol. 1 (March 1912), pp. 40–41, 43.

91   E. Maguire, 'Facts and Theories of Life: I – Facts Historical and Biological', *The Irish Theological Quarterly*, vol. 12 (October 1917), pp. 333–334; and idem, 'Facts and Theories of Life: II – The Development Hypothesis', *The Irish Theological Quarterly*, vol. 13 (1918), p. 202.

92   Maguire, 'Facts and Theories of Life: III – Vitalism', p. 114.

93   Fullerton, 'The Evolution of Mind – I', p. 267.

94   See, for example, W. Leo Moore, 'Insect Life and the Argument from Design', *The Irish Theological Quarterly*, vol. 9 (1914), p. 144; Thomas J. Agius, 'Genesis and Evolution', *The Irish Ecclesiastical Record*, 5th series, vol. 13 (June 1919), pp. 444–445.

95   Windle, *The Church and Science*, pp. 387–388.

96   Fullerton, 'Basis of Monism – Evolution', p. 163.

97   'On the historical character of the first three chapters of Genesis', in *Rome and the Study of Scripture: A Collection of Papal Enactments on the Study of Holy Scripture Together with the Decisions of the Biblical Commission*, 7th ed. (St Meinrad, Indiana: Abbey Press, 1964), pp. 123–124.

98   John A. O'Brien, *Evolution and Religion: A Study of the Bearing of Evolution upon the Philosophy of Religion* (New York: The Century Co., 1932), p. 25.

99   Canon Dorlodot, *Darwinism and Catholic Thought* (New York: Benziger Brothers, 1925), pp. 2–3.

100   Reference is made to the findings of the Pontifical Biblical Commission in the following articles: Leo O'Hea, 'The Days of Genesis', *The Irish Ecclesiastical Record*, 5th series, vol. 9 (March 1917), pp. 204–205; and Agius, 'Genesis and Evolution', pp. 452–453. Alfred O'Rahilly, writing for the Irish Jesuit journal *Studies* in 1912, referred to the Council of Cologne (1860) and the condemnation of Père Marie Dalmace Leroy's book (*L'Évolution Restreinte aux Espèces Organiques* ['Evolution Restricted to Organic Species'], 1891) in *La Civiltà Cattolica* to bolster his contention that the notion of human evolution was 'theologically temerarious'. O'Rahilly did not mention the later work of John A. Zahm which was more widely circulated in the English-speaking world, nor did he refer to the Pontifical Biblical Commission, which was more authoritative than *La Civiltà Cattolica* (Rahilly, 'The

Meaning of Evolution', p. 41). Windle, as observed earlier, referred to Vatican disapproval of evolutionary theory extending to humankind (Windle, *The Church and Science*, pp. 386–387).

101 O'Hea, 'The Days of Genesis', pp. 200–201.

102 Ibid., p. 203.

103 Gordon L. Herries Davies, 'Irish Thought in Science', in Richard Kearney (ed.), *The Irish Mind: Exploring Intellectual Traditions* (Dublin: Wolfhound Press, 1985), pp. 297, 306–309.

104 See J.H. Whyte, *Church and State in Modern Ireland, 1923–1979*, 2nd ed. (Dublin: Gill & Macmillan, 1984), pp. 3–8; Tom Inglis, *Moral Monopoly: The Rise and Fall of the Catholic Church in Modern Ireland*, 2nd ed. (Dublin: University College Dublin Press, 1998); and Sean Farren, *The Politics of Irish Education, 1920–1965* (Belfast: The Institute of Irish Studies, The Queen's University of Belfast, 1995), p. 235.

105 See, for example, Michael J.F. McCarthy, *Priests and People in Ireland* (Dublin: Hodges and Figgis & Co.; London: Simpkin, Marshall, Hamilton, Kent & Co., 1903).

106 Filson Young, *Ireland at the Cross Roads: An Essay in Explanation* (London: Grant Richards, 1903), pp. 62, 67.

107 L. Paul-Dubois, *Contemporary Ireland* (Dublin: Maunsel, 1911), p. 496.

108 See: Terence Brown, *Ireland: A Social and Cultural History, 1922–1985* (London: Fontana Press, 1985), pp. 30–32; Tom Garvin, 'Priests and Patriots', pp. 71–72; and Patrick Corish, *The Irish Catholic Experience: A Historical Survey* (Dublin: Gill & Macmillan, 1985), pp. 230–231.

109 This point is made by Brian Fallon in *An Age of Innocence: Irish Culture, 1930–1960* (Dublin: Gill & Macmillan, 1999), p. 196.

110 Horace Plunkett, *Ireland in the New Century: With an Epilogue in Answer to Some Critics*, 3rd ed. (New York: E.P. Dutton & Co., 1908), p. 102.

111 Ibid., pp. 107–108.

112 Ibid., p. 132.

113 Plunkett, *Ireland in the New Century*, pp. 267–272; and Seán MacCartáin, 'The Department of Agriculture and Technical Instruction, 1899–1930', in Norman McMillan (ed.), *Prometheus's Fire: A History of Scientific and Technological Education in Ireland* (n.p.: Tyndall Publications, 2000), p. 213.

114 Fr P.J. Dowling (C.M.), Honorary Secretary of the Irish Technical Instruction Association, maintained that there was anecdotal evidence to indicate that German Catholics were even more willing than German Protestants to use new technology. The conclusion he drew from this was that 'this little fact is an awkward one for those who ascribe industrial and economic short-sightedness to the influence of the Catholic Church' (P.J. Dowling, 'Technical Education – Some Queries and Replies', *The Irish Ecclesiastical Record*, 4th series, vol. 15 [1904], p. 415).

115 M. O'Riordan, *Catholicity and Progress in Ireland*, 2nd ed. (London: Kegan Paul, Trench, Trübner & Co.; St Louis: B. Herder, 1906), pp. 495–496.

116 Dorinda Outram, 'Heavenly Bodies and Logical Minds', *Graph: Irish Literary Review*, no. 4 (Spring 1988), pp. 10–11.

117 H.V. Gill, 'The Need of Scientific Training in Ireland', *The Irish Ecclesiastical Record*, 5th series, vol. 14 (1919), pp. 115, 122.

118 John Corkery, 'Ecclesiastical Learning', in *A History of Irish Catholicism: The Church since Emancipation* (Dublin: Gill & Macmillan, 1970), vol. 5, pp. 32–33.

119   Dorinda Outram, 'The History of Natural History: Grand Narrative or Local Lore?' in John Wilson Foster and Helena C.G. Chesney (eds), *Nature in Ireland: A Scientific and Cultural History* (Dublin: The Lilliput Press, 1997), p. 469.

6. Evolution, Entropy and Electro-Magnetics, 1920s–1930s

1   Nicholas Whyte, *Science, Colonialism and Ireland* (Cork: Cork University Press, 1999), p. 172.

2   Greta Jones, 'Catholicism, Nationalism and Science', *The Irish Review*, no. 20 (Winter–Spring 1997), p. 52; Nicholas Allen, 'States of Mind: Science, Culture and the Irish Intellectual Revival, 1900–30', *Irish University Review*, vol. 33, no. 1 (Spring/Summer 2003), pp. 152–153.

3   Gordon L. Herries Davies, 'Irish Thought in Science', in Richard Kearney (ed.), *The Irish Mind: Exploring Intellectual Traditions* (Dublin: Wolfhound Press, 1985), pp. 308–310.

4   In a later essay Davies elaborated on the point that politically motivated violence and the threat of such violence, were detrimental to scientific endeavour in Ireland. See Gordon L. Herries Davies, 'Before a Blood-Stained Tapestry: Irish Political Violence and Irish Science', in David Attis and Charles Mollan (eds), *Science and Irish Culture: Why the History of Science Matters in Ireland* (Dublin: The Royal Dublin Society, 2004), pp. 33–50.

5   Davies, 'Irish Thought in Science', pp. 309–310.

6   Richard Kearney, *Postnationalist Ireland: Politics, Culture, Philosophy* (London: Routledge, 1997), pp. 170–173.

7   Steven Yearley, 'Colonial Science and Dependent Development: the Case of the Irish Experience', *Sociological Review*, vol. 37 (1989), pp. 324–327; Sean Lysaght, 'Themes in the Irish History of Science', *The Irish Review*, no. 19 (Spring-Summer 1996), p. 95; and John Gerard Lysaght, 'Robert Lloyd Praeger and the Culture of Science in Ireland, 1865–1953' (PhD thesis, St Patrick's College, Maynooth, 1996), p. 191.

8   Don Thornhill, 'Developing a Research Culture', in Charles Mollan (ed.), *Science and Ireland – Value for Society* (Dublin: Royal Dublin Society, 2005), p. 77.

9   Vox Clamantis in Deserto, 'Science in Secondary Schools', *The Irish Monthly*, vol. 58, no. 679 (January 1930), p. 23; Senia Pašeta, *Before the Revolution: Nationalism, Social Change and Ireland's Catholic Élite, 1879–1922* (Cork: Cork University Press, 1999), p. 122; and J.J. Lee, *Ireland, 1912–1985: Politics and Society* (Cambridge: Cambridge University Press, 1989), p. 131.

10   T.S. Wheeler, 'Newman and Science', *Studies*, vol. 42 (Summer 1953), pp. 185–186.

11   Sean Farren, *The Politics of Irish Education, 1920–65* (Belfast: Institute of Irish Studies, The Queen's University Belfast, 1995), p. 235.

12   T. Corcoran, 'Mathematical and Technical Studies in Ireland', *The Irish Monthly*, vol. 54, no. 632 (February 1926), pp. 734–737.

13   T. Corcoran, 'The Rural District Continuation School', *The Irish Monthly*, vol. 51 (September 1923), p. 460; and idem, 'Rural Continuation Schools', *The Irish Monthly*, vol. 53 (January 1925), p. 11.

14   T. Corcoran, 'Types of Agricultural Education: The "Farmer-Worker"', *The Irish Monthly*, vol. 53 (March 1925), pp. 123–126.

15   Work on the Shannon Scheme was started in August 1925 and it was completed in 1929. The construction of the hydroelectric dam was a central element of the initial phase of the electrification project in the Irish Free State. For details of the Drumm battery and state support for the project, see Tony Scott, 'James Drumm:

Chemist and Industrial Technologist', in Charles Mollan, William Davis and Brendan Finucane (eds), *Irish Innovators in Science and Technology* (Dublin: Royal Irish Academy, 2002), pp. 228–229.

16 Patrick J. McLaughlin, 'A Century of Science in the IER: Monsignor Molloy and Father Gill', *The Irish Ecclesiastical Record*, 5th series, vol. 102 (1964), p.260.

17 Henry V. Gill, 'Science in Our Schools', *Studies*, vol. 21 (September 1932), pp. 461–470. Quotations are from p. 466 and p. 470.

18 T. Wibberley, 'Agricultural Education', *Studies*, vol. 8 (September 1919), pp. 424–433; idem, 'The Irish Climate and Tillage Farming', *Studies*, vol. 8 (December 1919), pp. 590–597 and *Studies*, vol. 9 (June 1920), pp. 281–290; Henry Kennedy, 'The Winter Dairying Problem', *Studies*, vol. 19 (December 1930), pp. 537–548; idem, 'Winter Fodder and a New Discovery', *Studies*, vol. 20 (September 1931), pp. 389–394; idem, 'Some Problems of Our Agriculture', *Studies*, vol. 27 (June 1938), pp. 240–246.

19 James L. O'Donovan, 'Experimental Research in University College, Dublin', *Studies*, vol. 10 (March 1921), pp. 109–122; W.J. Williams, 'The Shannon Scheme and the Teaching of Science: A Plea for Realism in Education', with comments by Edward Leen, John J. Nolan and Hugh Ryan, *Studies*, vol. 15 (June 1926), pp. 177–192; Thomas J. Nolan, 'Science and Manufacture', *Studies*, vol. 15 (June 1926), pp. 255–273; Thomas Dillon, 'The Application of Electricity to Chemical Industry', *Studies*, vol. 16 (June 1927), pp. 291–305; idem, 'Iodine and Potash from Irish Seaweed', *Studies*, vol. 19 (June 1930), pp. 267–278; and Joseph Reilly, 'Essential Oils and Medicinal Herbs: Suggested Industries for Ireland', *Studies*, vol. 22 (September 1933), pp. 373–388.

20 Edward Leen, Comments on 'The Shannon Scheme and the Teaching of Science', by W.J. Williams, pp. 187–189. See previous endnote.

21 Hugh Ryan, Comments on 'The Shannon Scheme and the Teaching of Science', by W.J. Williams, p. 192.

22 Thomas Dillon, 'Chemistry in the Service of Man', *Studies*, vol. 28 (March 1939), pp. 49–62. See especially pp. 58–62.

23 Thomas Dillon, 'The Relation of Chemical Research to the Development of Our Industries', *Studies*, vol. 32 (March 1943), pp. 55–56.

24 Dorinda Outram, 'Heavenly Bodies and Logical Minds', *Graph: Irish Literary Review*, no. 4 (Spring 1988), pp. 10–11.

25 Dorinda Outram's 'Heavenly Bodies and Logical Minds' was republished in Attis and Mollan (eds), *Science and Irish Culture*, pp. 19–25.

26 Whyte, *Science, Colonialism and Ireland*, pp. 180–181.

27 Ibid., pp. 159, 181.

28 Ibid., p. 181.

29 J.H. Whyte, *Church and State in Modern Ireland, 1923–1979*, 2nd ed. (Dublin: Gill & Macmillan, 1984), pp. 16–21.

30 Greta Jones, 'Scientists against Home Rule', in D. George Boyce and Alan O'Day (eds), *Defenders of the Union: A Survey of British and Irish Unionism since 1801* (London: Routledge, 2001), pp. 200–202.

31 D.T. Barry, 'Descent and Selection: A Query', *The Irish Ecclesiastical Record*, 5th series, vol. 15 (January 1920), pp. 43–46.

32 See Thomas J. Agius, 'Genesis and Evolution', *The Irish Ecclesiastical Record*, 5th series, vol. 13 (June 1919). The quotation is from p. 452, not p. 445 as stated by Barry.

33 Barry, 'Descent and Selection', p. 53.

34   Garrett Pierse, 'Evolution and Creation: A New Argument for the Latter', *The Irish Theological Quarterly*, vol. 15 (July 1920), pp. 227–238. Pierse reiterated the compatibility between theism and evolution in a subsequent article; see idem, 'The Ideal as Furnishing a Proof for the Existence of God', *The Irish Theological Quarterly*, vol. 16 (1921), pp. 156–166.

35   For a detailed account of the 'Dorlodot Affair', see Raf De Bont's 'Rome and Theistic Evolutionism: The Hidden Strategies behind the "Dorlodot Affair", 1920–1926', *Annals of Science*, vol. 62, no. 4 (October 2005), pp. 457–478.

36   H.V. Gill, 'Catholics and Evolution Theories', *The Irish Ecclesiastical Record*, 5th series, vol. 19 (June 1922), pp. 614–624. Quotations are from pp. 614, 621 and 624.

37   For a brief discussion of Thomson's book, see Peter J. Bowler, *Reconciling Science and Religion: The Debate in Early-Twentieth-Century Britain* (Chicago: The University of Chicago Press, 2001), pp. 138–139.

38   John Ashton, 'Modern Science and the Theory of Continuity', *The Dublin Review*, vol. 178, no. 356 (January–March 1926), pp. 92–93.

39   Ibid., pp. 99, 104.

40   Michael Browne, 'Modern Theories of Evolution I: Stellar and Planetary Evolution', *The Irish Ecclesiastical Record*, 5th series, vol. 27 (June 1926), pp. 567–570.

41   Michael Browne, 'Modern Theories of Evolution II: Evolution of the Chemical Elements', *The Irish Ecclesiastical Record*, 5th series, vol. 28 (July 1926), pp. 35–43.

42   Michael Browne, 'Modern Theories of Evolution III: The Evolution of Life', *The Irish Ecclesiastical Record*, 5th series, vol. 28 (August 1926), pp. 131–132.

43   Ibid., p. 129. For another article, critical of the idea that living organisms could have developed from inanimate matter, see William Robert Fearon, 'Spontaneous Generation', *Studies*, vol. 17 (March 1928), pp. 72–81.

44   Michael Browne, 'Modern Theories of Evolution IV: The Evolution of Organisms', *The Irish Ecclesiastical Record*, 5th series, vol. 28 (December 1926), pp. 564–565, 582.

45   Patrick Allitt, *Catholic Converts: British and American Intellectuals Turn to Rome* (Ithaca, New York: Cornell University Press, 1997), pp. 164–165.

46   Ann Keogh and Dermot Keogh, *Bertram Windle: The Honan Bequest and the Modernisation of University College Cork, 1904–1919* (Cork: Cork University Press, 2010), pp. 24–25, 150–153.

47   Bertram C.A. Windle, *The Catholic Church and Its Reactions with Science* (London: Burns, Oates & Washbourne, 1927), pp. 125–126.

48   Bertram C.A. Windle, *The Evolutionary Problem as It Is Today* (New York: Joseph F. Wagner, 1927), pp. 58–59, 62–65.

49   Patrick J. Gannon, 'The Conflict between Religion and Science', *Studies*, vol. 15 (September 1926), pp. 464–479. Quotations are from pp. 467–468.

50   Carroll Stuhlmueller, 'Catholic Biblical Scholarship and College Theology', *The Thomist*, vol. 23, no. 4 (October 1960), pp. 540–541.

51   See Louis McRedmond, *To the Greater Glory: A History of the Irish Jesuits* (Dublin: Gill & Macmillan, 1991), pp. 279–281.

52   Bowler, *Reconciling Science and Religion*, p. 66.

53   Patrick J. Gannon, 'Evolution and Catholic Doctrine', *Studies*, vol. 17 (June 1928), pp. 271–281. Quotations are from pp. 271, 273.

54   John Hedley Brooke, 'Revisiting Darwin on Order and Design', in Niels Henrik Gregersen and Ulf Görman (eds), *Design and Disorder: Perspectives from Science and Theology* (Edinburgh: T&T Clark, 2002), p. 42; in reference to Francis Darwin, *The Life and Letters of Charles Darwin* (London: Murray, 1887), vol. 1, p. 313.

55 Gannon, 'Evolution and Catholic Doctrine', pp. 276–280.

56 Ibid., p. 281.

57 Shortly after the Scopes trial two states, Mississippi and Arkansas, passed legislation against the propagation of evolutionary theory similar to that of the Tennessee law. Attempts to enact similar legislation in Minnesota and Rhode Island failed. Edward J. Larson, 'The Scopes Trial in History and Legend', in David C. Lindberg and Ronald L. Numbers (eds), *When Science and Christianity Meet* (Chicago: The University of Chicago Press, 2003), p. 263.

58 Ronald L. Numbers, 'The Creationists', in David C. Lindberg and Ronald L. Numbers (eds), *God and Nature: Historical Essays on the Encounter between Christianity and Science* (Berkeley, California: University of California Press, 1986), pp. 402–404.

59 Messenger's book was published under the imprimatur of the Bishop of Northampton, Dudley Charles Cary-Elwes. Two Catholic theologians wrote laudatory prefaces. These were Fr Cuthbert Lattey S.J., who acted as *censor deputatus* and was Professor of Fundamental Theology at Heythrop College and Very Rev. Dr Charles Souvay C.M., who was President of Kenrick Seminary in the United States. For another indication of the growing Catholic acceptance of evolutionary theory (including that of humankind), see John A. O'Brien, *Evolution and Religion: A Study of the Bearing of Evolution upon the Philosophy of Religion* (New York: The Century Co., 1932). Charles Souvay wrote the introduction to O'Brien's book which was published under the imprimatur of Bishop Joseph H. Schlarman.

60 Ernest C. Messenger, *Evolution and Theology: The Problem of Man's Origin* (London: Burns, Oates & Washbourne, 1931), pp. 224–225, 250–251, 275.

61 In the early 1930s the American Catholic author Sister Mary Frederick wrote that the majority of Catholics who expressed an opinion on evolutionary theory disagreed with it, but not aggressively. She believed that opinions amongst Catholic 'leaders' were shifting at least towards tolerance, if not acceptance. Sister Mary Frederick, *Religion and Evolution since 1859: Some Effects of the Theory of Evolution on the Philosophy of Religion* (Chicago: Loyola University Press, 1935), pp. 169–170.

62 Michael Browne, 'Evolution and Theology: Another Opinion', in E.C. Messenger (ed.), *Theology and Evolution: A Sequel to Evolution and Theology* (London: Sands & Co., 1951), pp. 67–71. Quotations are from pp. 68, 71. Browne's article was originally published in *The Irish Ecclesiastical Record* (May 1932).

63 Stephen J. Lee, *The European Dictatorships, 1918–1945* (London: Methuen, 1987), pp. 18–23.

64 Don O'Leary, *Vocationalism and Social Catholicism in Twentieth-Century Ireland: The Search for a Christian Social Order* (Dublin: Irish Academic Press, 2000).

65 E.J. Coyne, 'First Lecture: The Historical Background to Rerum Novarum' (typescript of a lecture delivered at Ruskin College, Oxford, 30 July [1934]), Document no. 19, p. 8, Edward J. Coyne papers, The Jesuit Archives, Dublin. The year 1934 was ascertained from the periodical article 'Unemployed and Professors Discuss Papal Encyclicals at the C.S.G. Summer School', *The Universe*, 3 August 1934; also in the Coyne papers. The article gave a brief account of Coyne's lecture.

66 Coyne, 'First Lecture', p. 13.

67 Ibid., p. 12.

68 Dermot Keogh, *Twentieth-Century Ireland: Nation and State* (Dublin: Gill & Macmillan, 1994), pp. 54–55, 59–60, 79–80; Fearghal McGarry, 'General O'Duffy,

the National Corporate Party and the Irish Brigade', in Joost Augusteijn (ed.), *Ireland in the 1930s: New Perspectives* (Dublin: Four Courts Press, 1999), pp. 123–133.

69 See Donal Ó Drisceoil, *Censorship in Ireland, 1939–1945: Neutrality, Politics and Society* (Cork: Cork University Press, 1996).

70 Terence Brown, *Ireland: A Social and Cultural History, 1922–1985* (London: Fontana Press, 1985), p. 149.

71 Bertrand Russell, *The Scientific Outlook*, 2nd ed. (London: George Allen & Unwin, 1949), pp. 33–34. The first edition of *The Scientific Outlook* was published in 1931. In the prefatory note to the second edition (1949), Russell stated that 'no important changes' had been made. He took the opportunity to correct 'topical allusions' which had become out of date.

72 G.C. Heseltine, 'Science and Pseudo-Science', *The Irish Monthly*, vol. 60 (December 1932), pp. 756–766. Quotations are from pp. 757, 760, 766 and 765.

73 For an article entirely concerned with this, see Leonora Power, 'Catholics Who Gave Their Names to Science', *The Irish Monthly*, vol. 75 (April 1947), pp. 168–173.

74 Erwin N. Hiebert, 'Modern Physics and Christian Faith', in Lindberg and Numbers (eds), *God and Nature*, pp. 424–427. There was some awareness of the theory of the 'heat death' of the universe in late-nineteenth-century Ireland, but it probably caused little concern because it was seen as evidence of the 'Prime Worker'. See F. Lennon, 'The Future of the Earth (Viewed from a Physicist's Standpoint)', *The Irish Ecclesiastical Record*, 3rd. series, vol. 9 (April 1888), p. 319; and John Gerard, 'The Mainspring of the Universe', *The Irish Monthly*, vol. 16 (June 1888), pp. 329–331.

75 Helge S. Kragh, *Entropic Creation: Religious Contexts of Thermodynamics and Cosmology* (Aldershot, England: Ashgate, 2008), pp. 5, 47, 193.

76 On that occasion he did not address the issue of biological evolution. See Pope Pius XII's discourse to the Pontifical Academy of Sciences, 22 November 1951, in Paul Haffner (ed.), *Discourses of the Popes from Pius XI to John Paul II to the Pontifical Academy of Sciences, 1936–1986* (Vatican City: Pontificia Academia Scientiarum, 1986), p. 79.

77 For a succinct account of St Thomas's five arguments, see Alister E. McGrath, *Christian Theology: An Introduction*, 2nd ed. (Cambridge, Massachusetts: Blackwell Publishers, 1997), pp. 160–161.

78 See Cyril Barrett, 'Secular Theologians of Science', *Milltown Studies*, vol. 36 (Autumn 1995), p. 15, note 3, for some points about Bonaventure's arguments for a universe of finite age.

79 Francis J. McGarrigle, 'Could the World Have Had No Beginning?' *The Irish Ecclesiastical Record*, 5th series, vol. 41 (January 1933), pp. 1–12. McGarrigle was not the first Irish Catholic writer to refer to thermodynamics as a proof of God's existence. See R. Fullerton, 'Basis of Monism – Evolution', *The Irish Ecclesiastical Record*, 4th series, vol. 28 (July–December 1910), pp. 166–167.

80 Henry V. Gill, 'Entropy, Life and Evolution', *Studies*, vol. 22 (March 1933). Quotations are from pp. 135 and 138.

81 Stephen G. Brush, 'The Nebular Hypothesis and the Evolutionary Worldview', *History of Science*, vol. 25, no. 3 (1987), pp. 263–264.

82 Kragh, *Entropic Creation*, pp. 79–80.

83 Ibid., p. 215.

84 Ibid., p. 205. It was argued that the universe was created – regardless of whether it was finite or infinite in time (pp. 210–211, 214–216). There were a number of other contentious points in the debate which made it less than straightforward. The

universal validity of the second law of thermodynamics was called into question (p. 218). It was argued that if the universe was infinite in terms of space and matter then the quantity of energy would also be infinite and would therefore take an infinite amount of time to dissipate to the level of bound heat energy (p. 219). Hypotheses were put forward that envisaged regeneration processes at work to counterbalance the ongoing dispersal of energy in the universe.

85 Peter J. Bowler and Iwan Rhys Morus, *Making Modern Science: A Historical Survey* (Chicago: The University of Chicago Press, 2005), p. 363.

86 See John Hedley Brooke, *Science and Religion: Some Historical Perspectives* (Cambridge: Cambridge University Press, 1991), pp. 326–334.

87 Hiebert, 'Modern Physics and Christian Faith', pp. 429–434.

88 Russell, *The Scientific Outlook*, pp. 108–113. The quotation is from p. 111.

89 Ibid., p. 115.

90 Arthur Stanley Eddington, Presidential Address to the Mathematical Association on 'The Decline of Determinism', 4 January 1932, published in *Nature* (13 February 1932), quoted by Henry V. Gill. See H.V. Gill, 'Physics and Free Will', *The Irish Ecclesiastical Record*, 5th series, vol. 40 (August 1932), p. 151 and idem, 'Facts and Fancies: Physics and Philosophy', *Studies*, vol. 32 (March 1943), p. 92.

91 Gill, 'Physics and Free Will', p. 151.

92 Bowler and Morus, *Making Modern Science*, p. 363.

93 Brooke, *Science and Religion*, p. 331.

94 Gill, 'Physics and Free Will', p. 152.

95 In an earlier article Gill elaborated on how little scientists knew about life, energy and matter; and on the provisional and mutable nature of scientific theories (H.V. Gill, 'A Puzzle of Modern Science', *The Irish Ecclesiastical Record*, 5th series, vol. 18 [December 1921], pp. 593–601).

96 Gill, 'Physics and Free Will', pp. 153–154.

97 Bowler and Morus, *Making Modern Science*, p. 268.

98 Gill, 'Physics and Free Will', p. 150.

99 Ibid., see pp. 146, 152.

100 Ibid., p. 152.

101 Ibid., p. 151.

102 F.R. Hoare, 'Physical Determinism and Free Will', *The Irish Ecclesiastical Record*, 5th series, vol. 43 (January 1934), pp. 30–34. The quotation is from p. 30. Hoare sourced Eddington's opinions from: (1) *The Nature of the Physical World* (1928), especially Chapter 14; (2) Presidential Address to the Mathematical Association on 'The Decline of Determinism', 4 January 1932; (3) A lecture on 'Physics and Philosophy', 15 November 1932, published in *Philosophy* (January 1933).

103 Hoare, 'Physical Determinism and Free Will', p. 28.

104 Ibid., pp. 33–34.

105 Ibid., p. 35.

106 See Peter J. Bowler, *Evolution: The History of an Idea*, 3rd ed. (Berkeley: University of California Press, 2003), pp. 335–336.

107 P. Sexton, 'Science and Religion', *The Capuchin Annual* (1933), p. 190.

108 Jerome J. Langford, *Galileo, Science and the Church*, 3rd ed. (N.p.: Ann Arbor Paperbacks: The University of Michigan Press, 1992), p. 134.

109 Gordon McOuat and Mary P. Winsor, 'J.B.S. Haldane's Darwinism in Its Religious Context', *The British Journal for the History of Science*, vol. 28, no. 97 (June 1995), pp. 227–231.

110 Bowler, *Reconciling Science and Religion*, pp. 359–360, 395–398. H.G. Wells, Julian

Huxley and G.P. Wells wrote in their *Evolution – Fact and Theory* that natural selection explained the evolutionary process 'with a completeness approached by no other explanation'. Furthermore, they stated that evolution itself, contrary to the assertions of 'dishonest Creationists, narrow fanatics and muddle-headed people', was 'proven up to the hilt'. This book was written for readers who were not professionally qualified in the life sciences. H.G. Wells, Julian Huxley and G.P. Wells, *Evolution – Fact and Theory* (London: Cassell, 1934), see pp. v–vi, 4 and 196.

111   Sexton, 'Science and Religion', pp. 192–198.

112   John A. Murphy, *The College: A History of Queen's/University College Cork, 1845–1995* (Cork: Cork University Press, 1995), pp. 262–263.

113   G.B. Marini-Bettòlo, *Outlines of the Activity of the Pontifical Academy of Sciences, 1936–1986* (Vatican City: Pontificia Academia Scientiarum, 1986), p. 6.

114   Haffner, *Discourses of the Popes*, p. ix.

115   For details of the opposition of both church and state to artificial means of contraception, see Sandra L. McAvoy, 'The Regulation of Sexuality in the Irish Free State, 1929–1935', in Elizabeth Malcolm and Greta Jones (eds), *Medicine, Disease and the State in Ireland, 1650–1940* (Cork: Cork University Press, 1999), pp. 253–266.

116   H.V. Gill, 'The Popes and Natural Science', *The Irish Ecclesiastical Record*, 5th series, vol. 50 (July 1937), pp. 15–24. Quotations are from pp. 17, 19, 21.

117   Alfred O'Rahilly, *Electromagnetics: A Discussion of Fundamentals* (London: Longmans, Green & Co.; Cork: Cork University Press, 1938). Quotation is from the preface, p. vii. See also p. 848.

118   For example, in the preface (p. viii) he arrogantly states that, in the light of his radical treatment of the question pertaining to units and dimensions, 'there is no further excuse for electrotechnologists to continue talking nonsense'. In p. 443 he wrote about Einstein's 'tasteless exhibition of pedantry'. In an extensive endnote (note 45) to pp. 851–852, he drew attention to 'the most absurd' statement of Eddington and was also harshly critical of Jeans.

119   For a detailed account of O'Rahilly's dissenting views on scientific issues, see J. Anthony Gaughan, *Alfred O'Rahilly I: Academic* (Dublin: Kingdom Books, 1986), pp. 171–184. Amongst those who wrote approvingly of O'Rahilly's book were Professor Becker of Göttingen University (review in *Die Naturwissenschaften*); Professor P.W. Bridgman of Harvard University (review in the *Journal of the American Chemical Society*); Professor C.V. Drysdale (review in *Nature*); and William H. McCrea, Professor of Mathematics at Queen's University Belfast. *Electromagnetics* was praised in the Irish Jesuit journal *Studies* by P.J. McLaughlin, Professor of Mathematics and Experimental Physics at St Patrick's College, Maynooth. See P.J. McLaughlin, 'Fundamentals of Physical Science', *Studies*, vol. 27 (1938), pp. 656–666.

7. FROM DE VALERA'S INSTITUTE TO THE BIG BANG, 1939–1950

1   *Seanad Éireann Parliamentary Debates*, vol. 24, col. 1293 (8 May 1940) and col. 1574 (22 May 1940).

2   Walter Moore, *Schrödinger: Life and Thought* (Cambridge: Cambridge University Press, 1992), p. 353.

3   Sir William McCrea, 'Eamon de Valera, Erwin Schrödinger and the Dublin Institute', in C.W. Kilmister (ed.), *Schrödinger: Centenary Celebration of a Polymath* (Cambridge: Cambridge University Press, 1997), p. 124.

4   Tim Pat Coogan, *De Valera: Long Fellow, Long Shadow* (London: Hutchinson, 1993), pp. 699–700, 736, note 17. Schrödinger was also a member of the Pontifical

Academy of Sciences. Edmund Taylor Whittaker and Arthur W. Conway (Professor of Mathematics at University College Dublin) were members of both institutes. E.J. Conway, 'Pope Pius XII and Science', *University Review*, vol. 3, no. 5/6 (1964), p. 19. This article was originally published in *The Furrow*, March 1957.

5 Schrödinger wrote in his 'Autobiographical Sketches' that he had a 'wonderful time' in the 'remote and beautiful' island of Ireland, safe from the Nazis and untouched by the war raging in Europe. He was offered a professorship in Austria in 1946 but was advised by de Valera not to accept it because of the adverse political conditions prevailing in central Europe at the time. Schrödinger spent ten more years in Dublin, which was of 'great value' to him. Erwin Schrödinger, *What Is Life? With Mind and Matter and Autobiographical Sketches*, Canto ed. (Cambridge: Cambridge University Press, 1992), pp. 182–183.

6 *Dáil Éireann Parliamentary Debates*, vol. 79, col. 1082 (10 April 1940).

7 Ibid., col. 1862 (25 April 1940).

8 Ibid., col. 1862; and vol. 76, cols. 1969–1970 (6 July 1939).

9 Ibid., vol. 76, col. 1970; vol. 79, col. 1081.

10 Ibid., vol. 79, cols. 1093–1094 (10 April 1940) and *Seanad Éireann Parliamentary Debates*, vol. 24, cols. 1381–1382 (15 May 1940).

11 See *Seanad Éireann Parliamentary Debates*, vol. 24, cols. 1400–1402 (15 May 1940).

12 See *Seanad Éireann Parliamentary Debates*, vol. 24, cols. 1366, 1376 (15 May 1940) and col. 1671 (22 May 1940).

13 David Kennedy (MSc, HDip.Ed.), writing in *Studies*, pointed to a lack of sound understanding at official level concerning the methods and aims of teaching science, especially at second level. What were the priorities in teaching science? Was the primary purpose of science in secondary schools to prepare pupils for university courses or to teach them the social importance of science? Or was 'the scientific method' to serve mainly as 'an intellectual discipline'? What was the role of practical work in the teaching of scientific courses? Course content would be determined by answers to these questions. David Kennedy, 'Dr. D.B. Reid and the Teaching of Chemistry', *Studies*, vol. 31 (September 1942), p. 350.

14 Thomas Dillon, 'The Relation of Chemical Research to the Development of Our Industries', *Studies*, vol. 32 (March 1943), pp. 53–57.

15 Ibid., pp. 51–52.

16 *Commission on Vocational Organisation Report* (Dublin: The Stationery Office, dated 1943 but published 1944), par. 226; see also par. 536.

17 Ibid., pars 226 and 538.

18 See James J. Byrne, 'Investment and Research in Irish Agriculture', *Studies*, vol. 44 (Summer 1955), pp. 197–199, 206; Robert O'Connor, 'A Living from the Land', *Studies*, vol. 44 (Winter 1955), pp. 405, 407; John J. Scully, 'Education for Agriculture', *Studies*, vol. 57 (Autumn 1968), pp. 252–260. Byrne was a lecturer in economics at University College Dublin, O'Connor was an agricultural scientist and Scully was the Western Regional Officer in the Department of Agriculture and Fisheries.

19 *Commission on Vocational Organisation Report*, par. 351 and par. 357.

20 Thomas Garvin, *Preventing the Future: Why Was Ireland So Poor for So Long?* (Dublin: Gill & Macmillan, 2004), pp. 158–160.

21 In *The Irish Ecclesiastical Record* Canice Mooney (O.F.M.) expressed the opinion that all Ireland had to offer to the world, in an economic sense, was '. . . the export of a certain amount of useful agricultural produce, the loan of healthy, brawny men as workers and soldiers and of strong, quick-witted, practical girls as governesses and nurses and maids'. In matters of the intellect, Ireland had a very

good reputation abroad in the realm of literature and drama but generally lagged behind in 'the sphere of higher learning', including science. Mooney disagreed with those critics of the Dublin Institute for Advanced Studies who argued that it should not be used to support the work of foreigners when it was funded by Irish taxpayers. He maintained that, because of the absence of Irishmen 'of sufficiently high qualifications', it would enhance the intellectual reputation of Ireland by attracting scholars of high international standing and would benefit the most promising of Irish students by bringing them into contact with the best minds the world could offer. Canice Mooney, 'The Dublin Institute for Advanced Studies', *The Irish Ecclesiastical Record*, 5th series, vol. 64 (1944), pp. 187, 189.

22 Norman MacKenzie and Jeanne MacKenzie, *The Time Traveller: The Life of H.G. Wells* (London: Weidenfeld & Nicolson, 1973), p. 57.

23 Ibid., pp. 324, 347–348, 394, 428–429, 431, 434–436, 439–442.

24 H.G. Wells, *The Fate of Homo Sapiens: An Unemotional Statement of the Things That Are Happening to Him Now, and of the Immediate Possibilities Confronting Him* (London: Secker & Warburg, 1939), p. 11.

25 Ibid., p. 150.

26 Ibid., p. 151.

27 Ibid., p. 161.

28 Ibid., p. 153.

29 Ibid., p. 154.

30 Ibid., p. 155.

31 Ibid., pp. 157–158.

32 Ibid., p. 165.

33 Ibid., p. 166.

34 Ibid., pp. 166–167.

35 J.J. Lee, *Ireland, 1912–1985: Politics and Society* (Cambridge: Cambridge University Press, 1989), p. 220.

36 Wells, *The Fate of Homo Sapiens*, p. 168.

37 For a detailed account of O'Rahilly versus Wells, see J. Anthony Gaughan, *Alfred O'Rahilly III: Controversialist, Part II: Catholic Apologist* (Dublin: Kingdom Books, 1993), pp. 53–55; and Appendix 2 (pp. 224–283) for the text of the articles in *The Standard*.

38 F. O'Reilly to Alfred O'Rahilly, 16 December 1939, Alfred O'Rahilly papers, Archives of Blackrock College, Dublin.

39 J.H. Whyte, *Church and State in Modern Ireland, 1923–1979*, 2nd ed. (Dublin: Gill & Macmillan, 1984), p. 71.

40 Gaughan, *Alfred O'Rahilly III: Controversialist*, p. 54.

41 'Mr Wells and Eire: The Catholic Irish', *The Standard*, 9 February 1940; in vol. 3, 'Reply to Wells 1940', Alfred O'Rahilly papers, Archives of Blackrock College, Dublin. All subsequent references to *The Standard* newspaper are from paper clippings in this archival collection.

42 'Further Libels of Mr Wells', *The Standard*, 2 February 1940.

43 'Mr Wells and Catholic Priests, Explorers, Scientists, Scholars…', *The Standard*, 19 January 1940.

44 Ibid.

45 J. Anthony Gaughan, *Alfred O'Rahilly I: Academic* (Dublin: Kingdom Books, 1986), p. 183.

46 Nicholas Whyte, *Science, Colonialism and Ireland* (Cork: Cork University Press, 1999), pp. 177–178.

47 Alfred O'Rahilly, *Religion and Science: Broadcast Talks* (Dublin: The Standard, 1948), pp. 41–48.

48 Ibid., p. 53.

49 Ibid., pp. 10, 11, 66.

50 Ibid., p. 14.

51 Ibid., pp. 18–19.

52 Ibid., p. 16.

53 Ibid., p. 25.

54 Ibid., p. 24.

55 Ibid., p. 30.

56 Ibid., pp. 32–33.

57 Ibid., p. 14.

58 Ibid., p. 53.

59 Ibid., pp. 63–65.

60 Ibid., p. 32.

61 Daniel J. Kevles, 'From Eugenics to Patents: Genetics, Law, and Human Rights', *Annals of Human Genetics*, vol. 75 (2011), pp. 326–333.

62 In the early years of the twentieth century there was some limited Catholic support for eugenics which called for steps to be taken to improve the physical and mental traits of human populations. However, a number of methods advocated for use in pursuit of such objectives, such as sterilisation, were deemed morally unacceptable by the church. The publication of *Casti Connubii* (31 December 1930) decisively ruled out compatibility between eugenic policies and Catholic doctrine. See Greta Jones, 'Eugenics in Ireland: the Belfast Eugenics Society, 1911–15', *Irish Historical Studies*, vol. 28, no. 109 (May 1992), pp. 91–95.

63 O'Rahilly, *Religion and Science*, p. 65.

64 See David C. Lindberg, 'Galileo, the Church, and the Cosmos', in David C. Lindberg and Ronald L. Numbers (eds), *When Science and Christianity Meet* (Chicago: The University of Chicago Press, 2003), pp. 45, 50.

65 Stephen J. Lee, *The European Dictatorships, 1918–1945* (London: Methuen, 1987), p. xi.

66 Don O'Leary, *Vocationalism and Social Catholicism in Twentieth-Century Ireland: The Search for a Christian Social Order* (Dublin: Irish Academic Press, 2000).

67 O'Rahilly *Religion and Science*, p. 34.

68 Ibid., p. 36.

69 Ibid., p. 39.

70 Ibid., pp. 39–40.

71 Greta Jones, 'Catholicism, Nationalism and Science', *The Irish Review*, no. 97 (Winter–Spring 1997), p. 53.

72 For a critical evaluation of Schrödinger's book, see M.F. Perutz, 'Erwin Schrödinger's *What Is Life?* and Molecular Biology', in Kilmister (ed.), *Schrödinger: Centenary Celebration*, pp. 234–251. For a positive appraisal see Fionn Murtagh, 'Irish Contributions to International Science', in Charles Mollan (ed.), *Science and Ireland : Value for Society* (Dublin: Royal Dublin Society, 2005), p. 263.

73 Gaughan, *Alfred O'Rahilly III: Controversialist*, pp. 76–79.

74 'Professor O'Rahilly Refutes a Scholar', *The Catholic Herald*, 12 March 1945, in Scrapbook no. 5, Alfred O'Rahilly papers, Archives of Blackrock College, Dublin.

75 'A unique broadcaster', *The Irish Times*, 28 February 1946, in Scrapbook no. 5, Alfred O'Rahilly papers, Archives of Blackrock College, Dublin.

76 Patrick J. McLaughlin, 'A Century of Science in the IER: Monsignor Molloy and Father Gill', *The Irish Ecclesiastical Record*, 5th series, vol. 102 (July–December 1964), p. 260.

77 Henry V. Gill, *Fact and Fiction in Modern Science*, 2nd ed. (Dublin: M.H. Gill & Son, 1943), pp. 15–29. The note to the second edition states that the only changes made were 'one or two trifling corrections', the addition of an index of subjects and a short list of authors quoted.

78 Ibid., p. 59.

79 Ibid., pp. 60–61.

80 Ibid., pp. 66–67, 83–85, 95–98.

81 Ibid., p. 68.

82 Bohr's contribution to theoretical physics and his concept of complementarity, are discussed in John Hedley Brooke, *Science and Religion: Some Historical Perspectives* (Cambridge: Cambridge University Press, 1991), pp. 327–333.

83 Gill, *Fact and Fiction*, pp. 73–74, 98.

84 Ibid., p. 75.

85 For the above points see also H.V. Gill, 'Logic and Modern Science', *The Irish Ecclesiastical Record*, 5th series, vol. 44 (August 1934), pp. 113–122.

86 Gill, *Fact and Fiction*, pp. 70–72.

87 Ibid., p. 58.

88 Ibid., pp. 150–151.

89 Ibid., p. 158.

90 Ibid., p. 159.

91 Ibid., p. 161.

92 For Gill's misunderstanding about the ether see Gill, *Fact and Fiction*, p. 183; and Erwin N. Hiebert, 'Modern Physics and Christian Faith', in David C. Lindberg and Ronald L. Numbers (eds), *God and Nature: Historical Essays on the Encounter between Christianity and Science* (Berkeley: University of California Press, 1986), p. 429. Scientific considerations aside, the notion of the ether was seen by some religiously minded scientists, such as John William Strutt (Lord Rayleigh) and J.J. Thomson, as more aligned to theology than materialism by facilitating a view of the universe which was unified and interconnected. See Peter J. Bowler and Iwan Rhy Morus, *Making Modern Science: A Historical Survey* (Chicago: The University of Chicago Press, 2005), pp. 362–363.

93 W.A. Hauber, 'Evolution and Catholic Thought', *The Ecclesiastical Review*, vol. 106, no. 3 (March 1942), p. 161.

94 Gill, *Fact and Fiction*, p. 178.

95 Ibid., p. 182.

96 See Tom Inglis, *Moral Monopoly: The Rise and Fall of the Catholic Church in Modern Ireland* (Dublin: University College Dublin Press, 1998).

97 P.J. McLaughlin, 'Science, Philosophy and Religion', *The Irish Ecclesiastical Record*, 5th series, vol. 63 (January 1944), pp. 1–6. The quotation is from p. 4.

98 Bernal abandoned his Catholic faith in 1921, declaring himself an atheist. His reasons for doing so were mainly due to his political views. Science, it seems, was not a significant contributing factor. See Ann Synge, 'Early Years and Influences', pp. 12–13; and Fred Steward, 'Political Formation', pp. 40–41, 44–45; both in Brenda Swann and Francis Aprahamian (eds), *J.D. Bernal: A Life in Science and Politics* (London: Verso, 1999).

99 Peter J. Bowler, *Reconciling Science and Religion: The Debate in Early-Twentieth-Century Britain* (Chicago: The University of Chicago Press, 2001), 75 *et sequens*.

100 McLaughlin, 'Science, Philosophy and Religion', p. 4.
101 Alfred O'Rahilly, 'A Jesuit on Science', volume 4, Alfred O'Rahilly papers, Archives of Blackrock College, Dublin. The title of the newspaper is not identified in the paper clipping. No date for the paper clipping was given.
102 See Louis McRedmond, *To the Greater Glory: A History of the Irish Jesuits* (Dublin: Gill & Macmillan, 1991), pp. 278–281.
103 Hermann Sasse, 'Rome and the Inspiration of Scripture', *The Reformed Theological Review*, vol. 22, no. 2 (June 1963), pp. 41–43.
104 Raymond E. Brown, 'The Contribution of Historical Biblical Criticism to Ecumenical Church Discussion', in Richard John Neuhaus (ed.), *Biblical Interpretation in Crisis: The Ratzinger Conference on Bible and Church* (Grand Rapids, Michigan: William B. Eerdmans, 1989), p. 36.
105 Eamon Duffy, *Saints and Sinners: A History of the Popes* (New Haven: Yale University Press, 1997), pp. 265–266.
106 John A. O'Flynn, '"Divino Afflante Spiritu": The New Encyclical on the Scriptures', *The Irish Ecclesiastical Record*, 5th series, vol. 63 (May 1944), p. 300.
107 Liam Brophy, 'In Search of *Homo Perfectus*', *The Irish Ecclesiastical Record*, 5th series, vol. 68 (December 1946), pp. 396–397.
108 Ibid., p. 399, in reference to Gerard Heard's *The Third Morality*. See also John Durant, 'Darwinism and Divinity: A Century of Debate', in idem (ed.), *Darwinism and Divinity: Essays on Evolution and Religious Belief* (Oxford: Basil Blackwell, 1985), pp. 9, 36; in reference to James Strachey (ed.), *The Standard Edition of the Complete Psychological Works of Sigmund Freud* (London: Hogarth Press, 1959–1974), vol. 17, pp. 140–143.
109 Brophy, '*Homo Perfectus*', p. 401.
110 Ibid., pp. 401–402; and Bertrand Russell, 'A Free Man's Worship', in Robert E. Egner and Lester E. Denonn (eds), *The Basic Writings of Bertrand Russell, 1903–1959* (London: George Allen & Unwin, 1961), p. 67.
111 Wells, *The Fate of Homo Sapiens*, Chapter 26: 'Decadent World', 296–312.
112 Liam Brophy, 'Scientific Humanism', *The Irish Monthly*, vol. 75, no. 887 (May 1947), pp. 195–200.
113 MacKenzie and MacKenzie, *The Time Traveller*, p. 440.
114 Liam Brophy, 'Will Men Be Like Gears?' *The Irish Monthly*, vol. 75, no. 888 (June 1947), pp. 261–265.
115 Liam Brophy, 'Science – Bane or Blessing?' *The Irish Monthly*, vol. 75 (September 1947), pp. 391–396. Quotations are from p. 391.
116 Bertrand Russell, 'What I Believe: The Faith of a Rationalist', *The Listener*, 29 May 1947, pp. 826, 836. This paper was based on a BBC Home Service broadcast, 20 May 1947; information from Garrett FitzGerald's article (see next note).
117 Garrett FitzGerald, 'The Faith of the Infidel', *The Irish Monthly*, vol. 75 (October 1947), pp. 441–445. Quotations are from pp. 443, 445.
118 Geoffrey Taylor, 'Evidence and Evolution – I', *The Irish Monthly*, vol. 76 (March 1948), pp. 117–123. Quotations are from p. 117. Taylor's second radio lecture was published as 'Evidence and Evolution – II: Contemporary Life', *The Irish Monthly*, vol. 76 (April 1948), pp. 157–164. The first three radio lectures were given in January 1948, the fourth was given in April and the last lecture was broadcasted in May.
119 Geoffrey Taylor, 'Evidence and Evolution III – the Record of the Rocks', *The Irish Monthly*, vol. 76 (1948), pp. 221–227. The quotation is from p. 226.
120 Geoffrey Taylor, 'Evidence and Evolution: IV – Primitive Plants', *The Irish Monthly*, vol. 76 (September 1948), pp. 407–413. The quotation is from p. 413.

121   Geoffrey Taylor, 'Evidence and Evolution – V: Notes on Some Recent Books', *The Irish Monthly*, vol. 76 (October 1948), pp. 464–471. The quotation is from p. 464.

122   Henry V. Gill, 'Facts and Fancies: Physics and Philosophy', *Studies*, vol. 32 (March 1943), p. 99; in reference to Arthur Stanley Eddington, *New Pathways in Science* (Cambridge: Cambridge University Press, 1934), pp. 306–307. See also Bowler, *Reconciling Science and Religion*, pp. 107–108, in reference to Eddington's *The Nature of the Physical World* (1928), pp. 338, 350, 353.

123   Gill, 'Facts and Fancies', p. 100.

124   T. Crowley, 'Some Philosophical Aspects of Physical Indeterminacy', *The Irish Ecclesiastical Record*, 5th series, vol. 70 (1948), p. 789; in reference to Arthur Eddington, *The Nature of the Physical World*, p. 220.

125   Ibid., p. 793.

126   Ibid., p. 792.

127   Ibid., p. 794.

128   Brooke, *Science and Religion*, p. 329.

129   Crowley, 'Some Philosophical Aspects of Physical Indeterminacy', p. 798.

130   Ibid., pp. 797–798.

131   Michael Connolly, 'The Expanded Universe', *The Irish Monthly*, vol. 74 (September 1946), pp. 367–370.

132   Ibid., p. 372.

133   Ibid., pp. 372–375.

134   Bowler, *Reconciling Science and Religion*, pp. 42, 120.

135   Aodh de Blacam, 'The Re-Discovery of God: Two Notable Books', *The Irish Monthly*, vol. 75 (August 1947), pp. 363–364.

136   J.A. Teegan, 'Thomism and Modern Science', *Studies*, vol. 36 (June 1947), p. 193.

137   James A. Teegan, 'Science and Reality', *Studies*, vol. 37 (June 1948), pp. 203–211

138   P.J. McLaughlin, 'Modern Science and the Five Ways', *The Irish Ecclesiastical Record*, 5th series, vol. 69 (April 1947), pp. 274–275.

139   Ibid., p. 284.

140   Ibid., pp. 288–289.

141   T.S. Wheeler, 'From Atom to Atomic Bomb: The Chemist through the Ages', *Studies*, vol. 39 (March 1950), p. 13.

142   P.J. MacLaughlin, 'Philosophy and Science: The Place of Science in Human Affairs', *Studies*, vol. 39 (March 1950), pp. 100–102.

143   Words in quotation marks from MacLaughlin, 'Philosophy and Science', p. 100.

144   Richard E. Ingram, 'A New Cosmology', *Studies*, vol. 39 (December 1950), pp. 450–452.

145   H.A. Brück, Director of Dunsink Observatory, wrote that 'continuous creation would be no more "difficult" than creation at a specific moment' for an all-powerful creator, who not only created the universe but also sustained it (H.A. Brück, 'Astronomical Cosmology, Part 2: Theoretical Investigations', *Studies*, vol. 43 [Spring 1954], p. 49).

146   George V. Coyne, 'Evolution and the Human Person: The Pope in Dialogue', in Robert John Russell, William R. Stoeger and Francisco J. Ayala (eds), *Evolutionary and Molecular Biology: Scientific Perspectives on Divine Action* (Vatican City State: Vatican Observatory Publications; Berkeley, California: Center for Theology and the Natural Sciences, 1998), p. 13.

8. BETWEEN SCIENCE AND DOGMA, 1950–MID-1970S

1 Frank J. Coppa, *The Modern Papacy since 1789* (London: Longman, 1998), pp. 204–206.

2 Eamon Duffy, *Saints and Sinners: A History of the Popes* (New Haven: Yale University Press, 1997), p. 266; and Richard P. McBrien, *Lives of the Popes: The Pontiffs from St Peter to John Paul II* (New York: Harper Collins, 2000), p. 365.

3 Pius XII, *Humani Generis* (1950), pars 5–6, in Anthony J. Mioni (ed.), *The Popes against Modern Errors: 16 Papal Documents* (Rockford, Illinois: Tan Books, 1999).

4 Ibid., par. 10.

5 Ibid., par. 31.

6 Ibid., par. 26.

7 Ibid., par. 35.

8 See Robert Kenny, 'From the Curse of Ham to the Curse of Nature: The Influence of Natural Selection on the Debate on Human Unity before the Publication of *The Descent of Man*', *The British Journal for the History of Science*, vol. 40, part 3 (September 2007), p. 367.

9 Peter J. Bowler, *Evolution: The History of an Idea*, 3rd ed. (Berkeley: University of California Press, 2003), pp. 294–295.

10 William J. Astore, 'Gentle Skeptics? American Catholic Encounters with Polygenism, Geology, and Evolutionary Theories from 1845 to 1875', *The Catholic Historical Review*, vol. 82 (January 1996), pp. 40–76; and David L. Livingstone, *Adam's Ancestors: Race, Religion and the Politics of Human Origins* (Baltimore: The Johns Hopkins University Press, 2008), pp. 128–131, 163–164.

11 Martin Brennan, 'Adam and the Biological Sciences', *The Irish Theological Quarterly*, vol. 35, no. 2 (April 1968), pp. 152–153.

12 *Humani Generis*, par. 37; in reference to Romans 5: 12–19 and the Council of Trent, session V, canons 1–4.

13 Ibid., par. 20.

14 Cyril Vollert, '*Humani Generis* and the Limits of Theology', *Theological Studies*, vol. 12 (March 1951), p. 3.

15 Ursula King, *Spirit of Fire: The Life and Vision of Teilhard de Chardin* (Maryknoll, New York: Orbis Books, 1996), pp. 106–109, 190–198; Amir D. Aczel, *The Jesuit and the Skull: Teilhard de Chardin, Evolution and the Search for Peking Man* (New York: Riverhead Books, 2007), pp. 82–85, 100–103, 211–213; Mark Schoof, *A Survey of Catholic Theology, 1800–1970* (Paramus, New Jersey: Paulist Newman Press, 1970), p. 117; and Stanley J. Grenz and Roger E. Olson, *20th-Century Theology: God and the World in a Transitional Age* (Milton Keynes, UK: Paternoster Press, 1992), p. 132.

16 Karl Otmar von Aretin, *The Papacy and the Modern World* (London: Weidenfeld & Nicolson, 1970), p. 226.

17 Bill McSweeney, *Roman Catholicism: The Search for Relevance* (Oxford: Basil Blackwell, 1980), pp. 114–115.

18 Weigel's list of ninety-six articles was mostly categorised on the basis of language – English, French, German, Italian, Spanish, Portuguese, Latin, Dutch and Polish. Five articles were listed under the heading of non-Catholic, four in German and one in English. The only critical voices were those of C. Sejournas – a Catholic 'non-theologian' and the five non-Catholics – four of whom were German-speaking Protestants. Gustave Weigel, 'Gleanings from the Commentaries of *Humani Generis*', *Theological Studies*, vol. 12 (1951), pp. 520–527. For further

information on Catholic responses to *Humani Generis*, see Livingstone, *Adam's Ancestors*, pp. 208–212.

19 Patrick J. Hamell, '"Humani Generis": Its Significance and Teaching', *The Irish Ecclesiastical Record*, 5th series, vol. 75 (April 1951), p. 289. The allocution referred to by Hamell is quoted extensively in Vollert, '*Humani Generis* and the Limits of Theology', p. 18.

20 T. Crowley, '"Humani Generis" and Philosophy', *The Irish Theological Quarterly*, vol. 19, no. 1 (January 1952), pp. 25–32.

21 Gerard Mitchell, '"Humani Generis" and Theology', *The Irish Theological Quarterly*, vol. 19, no. 1 (January 1952), p. 1.

22 Ibid., p. 15.

23 Ibid., pp. 1–2.

24 Ibid., p. 12.

25 Gerard Mitchell, 'Evolution and Polygenism', *The Irish Theological Quarterly*, vol. 19, no. 3 (July 1952), p. 280.

26 Ibid., pp. 281–283.

27 John A. O'Flynn, '"Humani Generis" and Sacred Scripture', *The Irish Theological Quarterly*, vol. 19, no. 1 (January 1952), pp. 23–24.

28 John A. O'Flynn, '"Humani Generis" and Sacred Scripture', *The Irish Theological Quarterly*, vol. 19, no. 2 (April 1952), p. 174.

29 For evidence of this tendency, see Tord Simonsson's *Logical and Semantic Structures in Christian Discourses*, trans. Agnes George (Oslo: Universitetsforlaget, 1971), p. 52.

30 Michael A. MacConaill, 'Evolution and Enthusiasm', *Studies*, vol. 41 (September-December 1952), p. 355.

31 Peter J. Bowler, *The Eclipse of Darwinism: Anti-Darwinian Evolution Theories in the Decades around 1900* (Baltimore: The Johns Hopkins University Press, 1983), pp. 216–217.

32 MacConaill, 'Evolution and Enthusiasm', p. 356.

33 Ibid., p. 359.

34 Ibid., p. 358.

35 Ibid., p. 361.

36 M.A. MacConaill, review of Anthony Standen, *Science Is a Sacred Cow*, in *Studies*, vol. 42 (March 1953), pp. 105–106.

37 M.A. MacConaill, 'The Evolutionary Dilemma', *The Irish Theological Quarterly*, vol. 20, no. 4 (October 1953), p. 415.

38 John J. Moore (S.J.), review of William H. Kane, John D. Corcoran, Benedict M. Ashley and Raymond J. Nogar, *Science in Synthesis: A Dialectical Approach to the Integration of the Physical and Natural Sciences*, in *Studies*, vol. 44 (Summer 1955), pp. 247–249.

39 H.A. Brück, 'Astronomical Cosmology: Theoretical Investigations', *Studies*, vol. 43 (Spring 1954), p. 49.

40 Kevin Smyth, review of C.A. Coulson, *Science and Christian Belief*, in *Studies*, vol. 44 (Winter 1955), p. 483.

41 See Brian Fallon, *An Age of Innocence: Irish Culture, 1930–1960* (Dublin: Gill & Macmillan, 1999), p. 191.

42 William J. Philbin, 'New Directions for the Maynooth Union', *The Irish Theological Quarterly*, vol. 22, no. 4 (October 1955), p. 292. This paper was read at the Maynooth Union on 21 June 1955, on the occasion of its diamond jubilee.

43 Jacques de Bivort de la Saudée, 'Introduction', in idem (ed.), *God, Man and the*

Universe: A Christian Answer to Modern Materialism (London: Burns & Oates, 1954), p. vi.

44 J.H. Whyte, *Church and State in Modern Ireland, 1923–1979*, 2nd ed. (Dublin: Gill & Macmillan, 1984), pp. 3–8. For a detailed account of Irish Catholic devotional practices in the 1950s, see Louise Fuller, *Irish Catholicism since 1950: The Undoing of a Culture* (Dublin: Gill & Macmillan, 2002), pp. 19–36.

45 Duffy, *Saints and Sinners*, p. 268.

46 Extract from a papal address to students and professors of Studium Urbis, 15 June 1952, on 'Responsibilities of Students', in P.J. McLaughlin, *The Church and Modern Science* (Dublin: Clonmore & Reynolds; London: Burns, Oates & Washbourne, 1957), p. 245.

47 McLaughlin, *Church and Modern Science*, pp. 122–124.

48 Ibid., pp. 261–264. Quotation is from p. 261.

49 Ernan McMullin, 'Natural Science and Christian Thought', *The Irish Theological Quarterly*, vol. 26, no. 1 (January 1959), pp. 1, 7.

50 Ibid., p. 3.

51 Ibid., p. 2.

52 *Dublin Magazine*, new series, vol. 31, no. 4 (October–December 1956), pp. 64–65; and review by Richard E. Ingram, *Studies*, vol. 45 (Winter 1956), pp. 473–475. Ingram disagreed with some of Mascall's opinions but, nevertheless, believed that such opinions were 'well worth hearing' because of Mascall's advanced understanding of Thomistic philosophy and his extensive knowledge of the natural sciences.

53 McMullin, 'Natural Science and Christian Thought', pp. 7–8.

54 Ibid., pp. 10–11.

55 Ibid., p. 11.

56 Ibid., p. 22.

57 Conor Reilly, 'Adam and Primitive Man', *The Irish Theological Quarterly*, vol. 26 (1959), pp. 334–335. Bibliographical details for Dobzhansky are as follows: *Science*, vol. 127 (1958), pp. 1091–1098.

58 Ibid., p. 331.

59 Ibid., pp. 344–345.

60 John J. Moore, 'The Darwin Centenary and the Theologian: A Survey of Modern Approaches to Evolution', *The Irish Theological Quarterly*, vol. 26, no. 2 (April 1959), pp. 117–119.

61 J. Franklin Ewing, 'Darwin Today', *America* (21 March 1959), p. 711.

62 Rémy Collin, *Evolution: Hypotheses and Problems* (London: Burns & Oates, 1959), p. 137.

63 T.C., review of Rémy Collin, *Evolution: Hypotheses and Problems*, in *The Irish Ecclesiastical Record*, 5th series, vol. 94 (July–December 1960), p. 127.

64 Moore, 'The Darwin Centenary and the Theologian', pp. 120–121.

65 Ibid., p. 127.

66 Ibid., pp. 128–129.

67 Ibid., p. 129.

68 Alexander Wolsky, 'A Hundred Years of Darwinism in Biology', in Walter J. Ong (ed.), *Darwin's Vision and Christian Perspectives* (New York: The Macmillan Company, 1960), pp. 21–32.

69 Robert W. Gleason, 'A Note on Theology and Evolution', in Ong (ed.), *Darwin's Vision*, p. 109.

70 Ernan McMullin, review of Ong (ed.), *Darwin's Vision*, in *The Irish Theological Quarterly*, vol. 28 (April 1961), p. 164.

71 M. Brennan, 'Evolution – I', *The Irish Ecclesiastical Record*, 5th series, vol. 95 (1961), pp. 327–329.

72 M. Brennan, 'Evolution – II: The Origin of Man', *The Irish Ecclesiastical Record*, 5th series, vol. 95 (1961), p. 402.

73 M. Brennan, 'Evolution – III: Philosophical and Theological Implications', *The Irish Ecclesiastical Record*, 5th series, vol. 96 (1961), pp. 43–49. Quotations are from pp. 46–47.

74 M.A. MacConaill, 'Piltdown and Peking: An Essay on Evidence', *The Irish Ecclesiastical Record*, 5th series, vol. 102 (July–December 1964), pp. 367–374. Quotations are from pp. 367, 371 and 372.

75 Donal Flanagan, 'Some Theological Implications of Evolution', *The Irish Theological Quarterly*, vol. 33, no. 3 (July 1966), p. 269.

76 J.P. Mackey, 'Original Sin and Polygenism: The State of the Question', *The Irish Theological Quarterly*, vol. 34, no. 2 (April 1967), pp. 99–100.

77 Ibid., p. 101. Mackey referred to: C. Hauret, *Beginnings: Genesis and Modern Science*, 2nd revised ed. (Dubuque, Iowa: Priory Press, 1964), pp. 134 ff.; J. de Fraine, *The Bible and the Origin of Man* (New York: Tournai, 1962), p. 82; and A.M. Dubarle, *The Biblical Doctrine of Original Sin* (London: Chapman, 1964), pp. 221 ff.

78 Ibid., p. 103.

79 Brennan, 'Adam and the Biological Sciences', p. 141.

80 Ibid., p. 151.

81 Ibid., pp. 153, 164.

82 Ibid., pp. 157–164.

83 See Francis Xavier Murphy, *The Papacy Today* (London: Weidenfeld & Nicolson, 1981), p. 22.

84 Michael Browne, 'Genesis 1 and 2', *The Furrow*, vol. 21, no. 6 (June 1970), pp. 344–346.

85 Maurice Curtin, 'Adam & Eve: A Problem for the Religion Teacher', *The Furrow*, vol. 25, no. 7 (July 1974), pp. 363–368. Quotations are from pp. 367, 368.

86 Earlier in this chapter it was observed that Pope Pius XII asserted in paragraph 20 of *Humani Generis* that once a pope passes judgement on an issue then it can no longer be regarded as a matter open to debate among theologians. This restriction was not retracted by the Second Vatican Council. In *Lumen Gentium* (*Dogmatic Constitution on the Church*, 21 November 1964), par. 25, the Council asserted that '. . . loyal submission of the will and intellect must be given, in a special way, to the authentic teaching authority of the Roman Pontiff, even when he does not speak *ex cathedra* . . .'. The published source here is Austin Flannery (general ed.), *Vatican Council II: The Conciliar and Post Conciliar Documents*, New revised ed. (Dublin: Dominican Publications, 1992).

9. The Elusive Master Narrative, mid-1970s–2006

1 There is a longstanding consensus amongst historians that simple theses of conflict, harmony, dialogue, independence and integration are not adequate to the task of writing satisfactory historical narratives of the relationship between scientific theories and religious beliefs. There is no 'master narrative'. This is discussed under the sub-heading of 'A Concept of Four Dimensions' in this chapter.

2 P.J. McGrath, 'Believing in God', *The Irish Theological Quarterly*, vol. 42, no. 2 (April 1975), pp. 87–88. On 1 September 1910 Pope Pius X issued 'The Oath

against Modernism' obliging all clergymen to take it, except in Germany where resistance to it was particularly strong. Those who swore the oath gave their assent to a number of articles of faith. The first article declared that the existence of God 'can be known with certainty' and that his existence can be 'demonstrated' from the application of reason to the 'visible works of creation'. See 'The Oath against Modernism', in Anthony J. Mioni (ed.), *The Popes against Modern Errors: 16 Papal Documents* (Rockford, Illinois: Tan Books, 1999), p. 270. The anti-modernist oath was rescinded by the Congregation for the Doctrine of the Faith in July 1967.

3   McGrath, 'Believing in God', p. 96.
4   Martin Brennan, 'From Matter to Man: The Evolutionism of Teilhard de Chardin', *University Review*, vol. 5, no. 2 (Summer 1968), pp. 223–233. The words in quotation marks are from p. 232.
5   Ursula King, *Spirit of Fire: The Life and Vision of Teilhard de Chardin* (Maryknoll, New York: Orbis Books, 1996), pp. 106–109, 190–198; Amir D. Aczel, *The Jesuit and the Skull: Teilhard de Chardin, Evolution and the Search for Peking Man* (New York: Riverhead Books, 2007), pp. 82–85, 100–103, 211–213.
6   Dermot A. Lane, 'The Future of Creation', *Milltown Studies*, vol. 34 (Autumn 1994), p. 95.
7   Ibid., pp. 102–103.
8   Ibid., p. 104.
9   Ibid., p. 108.
10 Ibid., p. 105.
11 Ibid., pp. 106–107.
12 Ibid., pp. 108–113.
13 Ibid., p. 95.
14 Céline Mangan, 'Creation Theology in the Bible', *Doctrine and Life*, vol. 45, no. 2 (February 1995), p. 168. See also Philip E. Devine, 'Creation and Evolution', *Religious Studies*, vol. 32, no. 3 (September 1996), pp. 328–329.
15 Cyril Barrett, 'Secular Theologians of Science', *Milltown Studies*, no. 36 (Autumn 1995), p. 13.
16 Dermot Lane, 'Theology and Science in Dialogue', *The Irish Theological Quarterly*, vol. 52 (1986), pp. 31–32. See also Denis Carroll, 'The God of Life: "Back Here" and "Out There"', *Doctrine and Life*, vol. 39, no. 4 (April 1989), p. 179; and Charles Barclay, 'When I See the Heavens . . .', *The Furrow*, vol. 45, no. 11 (November 1994), pp. 614–624.
17 Thomas Corbett, 'Science and Religion', *The Irish Theological Quarterly*, vol. 56, no. 2 (1990), p. 111.
18 Thomas S. Kuhn, *The Structure of Scientific Revolutions*, 2nd ed. (Chicago: The University of Chicago Press, 1970).
19 James P. Mackey, 'Theology, Science and the Imagination: Exploring the Issues', *The Irish Theological Quarterly*, new series, vol. 52 (1986), p. 4.
20 John G. Burr, 'Black Holes and the Creation of the Universe', *Doctrine and Life*, vol. 38, no. 1 (January 1988), pp. 41–45. Quotation is from p. 45.
21 Lane, 'Theology and Science in Dialogue', pp. 39–40.
22 Ibid., p. 51.
23 Corbett, 'Science and Religion', pp. 107–113. For Ian G. Barbour's ways of relating science and religion, see his *Religion and Science: Historical and Contemporary Issues*, revised ed. (London: SCM Press, 1998), Chapter 4. Corbett's reference to Ian G. Barbour is as follows: Ian G. Barbour, 'Ways of Relating Science and

Theology', in Robert John Russell *et al.* (eds), *Physics, Philosophy and Theology* (Vatican City State: Vatican Observatory, 1988), pp. 22–45.

24 Preface to John Hedley Brooke, Margaret J. Osler and Jitse M. van der Meer (eds), *Science in Theistic Contexts: Cognitive Dimensions*, vol. 16 of *Osiris* (2001), p. vii.

25 John Brooke and Geoffrey Cantor, *Reconstructing Nature: The Engagement of Science and Religion* (Edinburgh: T&T Clark, 1998), pp. xi, 20–21, 66. See also Bernard Lightman, 'Victorian Sciences and Religions: Discordant Harmonies', in Brooke, Osler and van der Meer (eds), *Science in Theistic Contexts*, p. 344.

26 Geoffrey Cantor and Chris Kenny, 'Barbour's Fourfold Way: Problems with His Taxonomy of Science–Religion Relationships', *Zygon*, vol. 36, no. 4 (December 2001), pp. 777–778.

27 Geoffrey Cantor, 'What Shall We Do with the "Conflict Thesis"?' in Thomas Dixon, Geoffrey Cantor and Stephen Pumfrey (eds), *Science and Religion: New Historical Perspectives* (Cambridge: Cambridge University Press, 2010), p. 286. See also 'Introduction', in David C. Lindberg and Ronald L. Numbers (eds), *God and Nature: Historical Essays on the Encounter between Christianity and Science* (Berkeley: University of California Press, 1986), pp. 10–14; and 'Introduction', in David C. Lindberg and Ronald L. Numbers (eds), *When Science and Christianity Meet* (Chicago: The University of Chicago Press, 2003), pp. 1–5. Cantor (p. 297, note 11) questioned the appropriateness of the word 'thesis' when he wrote: 'I'm not sure whether the recognition of historical complexity deserves to be called a thesis; the claim that we see "complexity" in history sheds little light on the specific question of how science and religion interrelate. Moreover, the discovery of "complexity" is not confined to the historical study of science and religion. In every branch of history with which I am familiar historians have forsaken Whiggish narratives and instead pursued contextualism by examining closely the primary sources and have found that master-narratives are inadequate and that the situation turns out to be far more complex.'

28 Corbett, 'Science and Religion', p. 107.

29 Ibid., p. 108.

30 Pope John Paul II, 'Faith can never conflict with reason', address to the Pontifical Academy of Sciences, 31 October 1992; *L'Osservatore Romano*, vol. 44, no. 1264 (4 November 1992), p. 2.

31 See Maurice A. Finocchiaro, 'Science, Religion and the Historiography of the Galileo Affair: On the Undesirability of Oversimplification', in Brooke, Osler and van der Meer (eds), *Science in Theistic Contexts*, p. 122, note 30; and idem, 'Galileo as a "Bad Theologian": A Formative Myth about Galileo's Trial', *Studies in History and Philosophy of Science*, vol. 33A, no. 4 (2002), pp. 762, 780–781; idem, 'The Galileo Affair from John Milton to John Paul II: Problems and Prospects', *Science and Education*, vol. 8 (1999), pp. 202–203; Michael Segre, 'Critiques and Contentions: Light on the Galileo Case?' *Isis*, 88 (1997), pp. 497–498; Michael Sharratt, *Galileo: Decisive Innovator* (Cambridge: Cambridge University Press, 1996), pp. 214–222; James Reston, *Galileo: A Life* (London: Cassell Publishers, 1994), pp. 284–286; George V. Coyne, 'The Church in Dialogue with Science: The Wojtyla Years', in *New Catholic Encyclopedia; Jubilee Volume: The Wojtyla Years* (Detroit, Michigan: Gale Group, 2001), pp. 103–104.

32 Finocchiaro, 'The Galileo Affair from John Milton to John Paul II', pp. 202–203. For further criticism of Poupard, see Reston, *Galileo: A Life*, pp. 285–286; Segre, 'Light on the Galileo Case?' pp. 488–498. For criticisms of the institutional church in relation to Galileo, see George V. Coyne, 'The Church's Most Recent Attempt to

Dispel the Galileo Myth', in Ernan McMullin (ed.), *The Church and Galileo* (Notre Dame, Indiana: University of Notre Dame Press, 2005), Chapter 13.

33 Paul Poupard, 'Creation, Culture and Faith', *The Furrow*, vol. 46, no. 5 (May 1995), pp. 277–278.

34 Neil Porter, 'Galileo and the Inquisition', *Doctrine and Life*, vol. 43, no. 6 (July–August 1993), pp. 349, 356–357.

35 See William B. Ashworth, Jr., 'Catholicism and Early Modern Science', in Lindberg and Numbers (eds), *God and Nature*, pp. 150–154; Lewis Pyenson and Susan Sheets-Pyenson, *Servants of Nature: A History of Scientific Institutions, Enterprises and Sensibilities* (London: Fontana Press, 1999), p. 217; and John Hedley Brooke, *Science and Religion: Some Historical Perspectives* (Cambridge: Cambridge University Press, 1991), pp. 100–101.

36 George S. Johnston, 'The Galileo Affair', *Position Paper 250* (October 1994), pp. 320–321, 325–326. *Position Papers* were at this time published by Four Courts Press (Dublin). Robert P. Lockwood argued in mitigation of the church's position, but his opinions were moderate, unlike those of Johnston. See his article 'The Galileo Affair', in *Position Paper 324* (December 2000), pp. 339–342. This article was republished with minor amendments in *Position Paper 329* (May 2001), pp. 159–162.

37 Quotations are from 'Message to the Pontifical Academy of Sciences', published in Robert John Russell, William R. Stoeger and Francisco J. Ayala (eds), *Evolutionary and Molecular Biology: Scientific Perspectives on Divine Action* (Vatican City State: Vatican Observatory Publications; Berkeley, California: Center for Theology and the Natural Sciences, 1998), pp. 4, 6. This is a slightly altered version of 'Magisterium is concerned with question of evolution, for it concerns conception of man' message to the Pontifical Academy of Sciences, 22 October 1996, *L'Osservatore Romano*, vol. 44, no. 1464 (30 October 1996), p. 7.

38 David L. Livingstone, *Adam's Ancestors: Race, Religion and the Politics of Human Origins* (Baltimore: The Johns Hopkins University Press, 2008), pp. 211–212.

39 Anon., 'Pontiff lends his support to theory of evolution', *The Examiner*, 25 October 1996, p. 10.

40 Don O'Leary, *Roman Catholicism and Modern Science: A History* (New York: Continuum, 2006), p. 206.

41 Mary A. Vitoria, 'The Mystery of Life: Evolution Is Not Enough', *Position Paper 301* (January 1999), pp. 30–34.

42 John Young, 'Original Sin – a Controverted Teaching', *Position Paper 320/321* (August–September 2000), pp. 245, 252.

43 The International Theological Commission, *Communion and Stewardship: Human Persons Created in the Image of God* (23 July 2004), par. 63, http://www.vatican.va/roman_curia/congregations/cfaith/cti_documents/rc_con_cfaith_doc_20040723_communion-stewardship_en.html#t (accessed on 9 November 2011).

44 *Communion and Stewardship: Human Persons Created in the Image of God* is studied at greater length in O'Leary, *Roman Catholicism and Modern Science*, pp. 211–212.

45 Corbett, 'Science and Religion', p. 111. For the argument of God's existence based on the anthropic cosmological principle, see also Richard Swinburne, 'Arguments for the Existence of God', *Milltown Studies*, vol. 33 (Spring 1994), p. 32.

46 For explanations of the anthropic cosmological principle, see John Houghton's *The Search for God: Can Science Help?* (Oxford: Lion Publishing, 1995), Chapter 3; Stephen T. Davis, *God, Reason and Theistic Proofs* (Edinburgh: Edinburgh

University Press, 1997), pp. 107–115; Mark Wynn, 'Design Arguments', in Brian Davies (ed.), *Philosophy of Religion: A Guide to the Subject* (London: Cassell, 1998), pp. 59–63; and J.J.C. Smart and J.J. Haldane, *Atheism and Theism*, 2nd ed. (Malden, Massachusetts: Blackwell Publishing, 2003), especially Smart's 'Atheism and Theism', pp. 15–26.

47   Corbett, 'Science and Religion', pp. 111–112.

48   Extract from Julian Huxley's *New Bottles for New Wine* (1957), in Connie Barlow (ed.), *Evolution Extended: Biological Debates on the Meaning of Life* (Cambridge, Massachusetts: The MIT Press, 1995), pp. 166–175.

49   Jacques Monod, *Chance and Necessity: An Essay on the Natural Philosophy of Modern Biology* (New York: Vintage Books, 1972), p. 180.

50   Steven Weinberg, *The First Three Minutes: A Modern View of the Origin of the Universe* (London: Andre Deutch, 1977), p. 154.

51   Stephen Hawking, *A Brief History of Time: From the Big Bang to Black Holes* (London: Bantam Books, 1995), pp. 156–157.

52   Richard Dawkins, *The Selfish Gene*, new ed. (Oxford: Oxford University Press, 1989), pp. 198, 330–331; and idem, *River out of Eden: A Darwinian View of Life* (London: Phoenix, 1996), see especially pp. 107, 155.

53   For an examination of the coexistence and interrelationship of order and chance in nature, see Niels Henrik Gregersen and Ulf Görman (eds), *Design and Disorder: Perspectives from Science and Theology* (Edinburgh: T&T Clark, 2002).

54   '. . . however much the conflict may be qualified and contextualized, there is no question that . . . conflict did occur and involved writers of considerable ability and professional standing on both sides'. Frank M. Turner, 'The late Victorian conflict of science and religion as an event in nineteenth-century intellectual and cultural history', in Dixon, Cantor and Pumfrey (eds), *Science and Religion*, p. 88. Historian Colin Russell has suggested four categories for the analysis of conflict between science and religion. Conflict may originate from different world views (referred to as epistemological), or it may be methodological. It may be based on different values – especially in relation to the applied sciences and medicine – or it may be social, that is, occurring between different social groups, such as the scientific naturalists versus the Anglican Church in Victorian Britain. Russell has stressed the contingency of conflict rather than its inevitability – regardless of what form it takes. Cantor, 'What Shall We Do with the "Conflict Thesis"?' in Dixon, Cantor and Pumfrey (eds), *Science and Religion*, pp. 284–285; in reference to Colin A. Russell, 'The Conflict of Science and Religion', in Gary B. Ferngren *et al.* (eds), *The History of Science and Religion in the Western Tradition: An Encyclopedia* (New York and London: Garland, 2000), pp. 12–16.

55   Paul Davies, *God and the New Physics* (London: Penguin Books, 1990), pp. ix, 8.

56   Ibid., p. 8; and Corbett, 'Science and Religion', pp. 104–105.

57   Cyril Barrett, 'Secular Theologians of Science', *Milltown Studies*, vol. 36 (Autumn 1995), pp. 5–16.

58   Dawkins, *The Selfish Gene*, pp. 198, 330–331.

59   Enda McDonagh, 'A Post-Christian Ireland? An Introduction', *The Irish Review*, vol. 27 (Summer 2001), p. 4.

60   David McConnell, 'Science and Post-Christian Ireland', *The Irish Review*, vol. 27 (Summer 2001), pp. 40–47. Quotations are from pp. 43, 47.

61   Gabriel Daly, 'Science, Religion and Scientism', *The Irish Review*, vol. 27 (Summer 2001), pp. 48–54.

62   William Reville, 'Is Science Replacing Religion?' http://understandingscience.

ucc.ie/naturalworld/science_replacing_religion.pdf (accessed on 9 November 2011; article first published in the *The Irish Times* [7 December 1998]).

63 Richard Dawkins in conversation with Emily Hourican, 'The God Shaped Hole', *The Dubliner* (October 2002).

64 William Reville, 'Is religion the people's opium?' *The Irish Times* (7 November 2002), p. 10. See also idem, 'Prof Dawkins should target PC rather than religion', *The Irish Times* (4 January 2007), p. 13.

65 Richard Dawkins, *A Devil's Chaplain*, 2nd ed. (London: Phoenix, 2004), pp. 176–177; and idem, 'The great convergence', *The Irish Times* (17 February 2003).

66 Dawkins, *A Devil's Chaplain*, pp. 177–178.

67 Ibid., pp. 178–179.

68 William Reville, 'God knows, Richard Dawkins is wrong', *The Irish Times* (13 March 2003), p. 15.

69 Reville, 'Is religion the people's opium?' It seems that Reville was determined to respond to every provocation by Dawkins, believing that the Oxford professor particularly enjoyed attacking religion in Ireland. See William Reville, 'A little knowledge leads away from God, much . . . leads towards Him', *The Irish Times* (3 March 2005), p. 15.

70 Brian Trench, 'Science, Culture and Religion in Contemporary Ireland', in Joseph McCann (ed.), *Religion and Science: Education, Ethics and Public Policy* (Drumcondra, Dublin: St Patrick's College, 2003), pp. 34.

71 Ibid., pp. 37–38.

72 Cardinal Cahal B. Daly, *The Minding of Planet Earth* (Dublin: Veritas, 2004), pp. 89–90.

73 See Richard Dawkins, *The God Delusion* (London: Bantam Press, 2006), p. 154.

74 Ibid., pp. 58–59.

75 Ibid., p. 118.

76 Ibid., pp. 119–134.

77 Ibid., pp. 103–105.

78 Ibid., pp. 143–144.

79 Ibid., pp. 146–147.

80 Ibid., p. 109. See also pp. 120–121, 125, 143, 147.

81 Ibid., p. 316.

82 Dawkins placed heavy emphasis on the work of psychologist Elizabeth Loftus to make the point that there was a tendency for people to 'concoct' false memories which seemed to the victim to be as real as if the imagined events actually happened. Juries were easily influenced by sincere but false testimonies (p. 316). Many of those who were burdened with a dysfunctional imaginative faculty were manipulated by avaricious solicitors. Hence Dawkins' cynical comment – 'there's gold in them thar [*sic*] long-gone fumbles in the vestry . . .'. Incredibly, Dawkins even thought that the Roman Catholic Church, especially in America and Ireland, might have been 'unfairly demonized' on the issue of the sexual abuse of children (pp. 316–318).

83 Ibid., pp. 316–317.

10. SCIENCE AND SOCIAL TRANSFORMATION

1 See Fergal Tobin, *The Best of Decades: Ireland in the Nineteen Sixties* (Dublin: Gill & Macmillan, 1984), p. 44.

2 'The Faith of the Irish', *The Pope Teaches*, vol. 2, no. 3 (July–September 1979), pp. 385–386.

3   'To the Youth of Ireland', *The Pope Teaches*, vol. 2, no. 3 (July–September 1979), p. 404.

4   Malcolm B. Hamilton, *The Sociology of Religion: Theoretical and Comparative Perspectives* (London: Routledge, 1995), p. 169; Andrew M. Greeley, 'Are the Irish Really Losing the Faith?' *Doctrine and Life*, vol. 44, no. 3 (March 1994), pp. 132–142.

5   Michael Breen, 'Ask Me Another: An Evaluation of Issues Arising from the European Values Survey in Relation to Questions Concerning Technology and Transcendence', in Michael Breen, Eamonn Conway and Barry McMillan (eds), *Technology and Transcendence* (Dublin: The Columba Press, 2003), p. 141.

6   Marguerite Corish, 'Aspects of the Secularisation of Irish Society, 1958–1996', in Eoin G. Cassidy (ed.), *Faith and Culture in the Irish Context* (Dublin: Veritas, 1996), p. 168.

7   Michael P. Hornsby-Smith and Christopher T. Whelan, 'Religious and Moral Values', in Christopher T. Whelan (ed.), *Values and Social Change in Ireland* (Dublin: Gill & Macmillan, 1994), p. 44.

8   Andy Pollak, '78% of Catholics follow own consciences in making moral decisions, survey shows' and 'Poll shows church's moral authority in decline', *The Irish Times* (16 December 1996), pp. 1, 5.

9   Kevin O'Sullivan, 'Attendance at Mass has fallen from 77% to 60% in past four years, survey on Catholic attitudes finds', *The Irish Times* (4 February 1998), p. 3.

10   These percentages are calculated from the national census figures of April 2002. Publication details are as follows: Central Statistics Office, *Census 2002: Religion* (Dublin: The Stationery Office, April 2004), vol. 12, table 1. The following details were given for year, total population, numbers of Roman Catholics, followed by my calculated percentage, given to the nearest figure right of the decimal point:

YEAR	TOTAL POPULATION	ROMAN CATHOLIC	ROMAN CATHOLIC PERCENTAGE
1961	2,818,341	2,673,473	94.9
1971	2,978,248	2,795,666	93.9
1981	3,443,405	3,204,476	93.1
1991	3,525,719	3,228,327	91.6
2002	3,917,203	3,462,606	88.4

11   Central Statistics Office, *Census 2002: Religion*, vol. 12, table 1.

12   John Tyndall, *Fragments of Science*, 6th ed. (London: Longmans, Green & Co., 1879), vol. 2, pp. 503–504. See also his 'Apology for the Belfast Address' in *Fragments of Science* (New York: D. Appleton & Co., 1896), vol. 2, p. 205.

13   Bill McSweeney, *Roman Catholicism: The Search for Relevance* (Oxford: Basil Blackwell, 1980), p. 55.

14   Richard Elliott Friedman, *The Disappearance of God: A Divine Mystery* (Boston: Little, Brown & Co., 1995), pp. 202–203.

15   Fachtna McCarthy, 'The Mind of God: Science and Theology Today', in Cassidy (ed.), *Faith and Culture in the Irish Context*, pp. 35–36.

16   Neil Spurway, Professor of Exercise Physiology at the University of Glasgow, claimed that the erosive effect of science on faith had not only stopped but had been reversed. He believed that if faith continued to decline it would be for other reasons. Neil Spurway, 'The Erosion of Faith and Its Consequences', *Studies*, vol. 86, no. 344 (Winter 1997), p. 342.

17   George Porter, 'What Science Is For', *New Scientist*, vol. 112, no. 1535 (20 November 1986), p. 32.

18   See, for example, Tom Garvin, *Preventing the Future: Why Was Ireland So Poor for So Long?* (Dublin: Gill & Macmillan, 2004), p. 143.

19 Michael D. Higgins, 'Science and Society – Principles of Error?' *Technology Ireland* (April 1990), p. 21.

20 National Science Council, *Science Policy: Some Implications for Ireland* (Dublin: National Science Council, January 1973), p. 8.

21 Andy Shearer, 'What's Cultural about Science & Technology?' *Technology Ireland* (March 1991), p. 17.

22 Brian Trench, 'Science, Culture and Public Affairs', *The Republic*, no. 3 (July 2003), pp. 56–57.

23 Quotations from Dorinda Outram, 'Heavenly Bodies and Logical Minds', *Graph: Irish Literary Review* (Spring 1988), pp. 10–11; and idem, republished in David Attis and Charles Mollan (eds), *Science and Irish Culture: Why the History of Science Matters in Ireland* (Dublin: The Royal Dublin Society, 2004), pp. 22–23.

24 The Science, Technology and Innovation Advisory Council, *Making Knowledge Work for Us* (Dublin: The Stationery Office, 1995), vol. 2, pp. 9, 43.

25 T.P. Hardiman and E.P. O'Neill, 'The Role of Science and Innovation', in Fionán Ó Muircheartaigh (ed.), *Ireland in the Coming Times: Essays to Celebrate T.K. Whitaker's 80 Years* (Dublin: Institute of Public Administration, 1997), pp. 267–269.

26 The Science, Technology and Innovation Advisory Council, *Making Knowledge Work for Us* (Dublin: The Stationery Office, 1995), vol. 1, p. 23.

27 Ibid., pp. 149–154.

28 Office of Science and Technology, Department of Enterprise and Employment, *Science, Technology and Innovation: The White Paper* (Dublin: The Stationery Office, October 1996), pp. i–iii, 130–131.

29 Group on the Science System of the OECD Committee for Scientific and Technological Policy, *Science and Technology in the Public Eye* (n.p.: OECD [Organization for Economic Cooperation and Development], January 1997), pp. 9, 11.

30 Central Statistics Office, *Census 2002: Religion*, vol. 12, table 17A.

31 Percentages are calculated from CSO figures to the nearest figure one place right of the decimal point.

32 Sources are as follows: David Regan, 'Is Irish Catholicism Dying?' *Doctrine and Life*, vol. 34, no. 8 (October 1984), pp. 472–473; Kevin Hegarty, 'Is Irish Catholicism Dying?' *The Furrow*, vol. 36, no. 1 (January 1985), pp. 44–45; Michael Paul Gallagher, 'Secularization and New Forms of Faith', *Studies*, vol. 74 (Spring 1985), p. 16; Ursula Coleman, 'Secularisation: A Healing Process?' *Studies*, vol. 74 (Spring 1985), pp. 33–34; David Regan, 'Ireland, a Church in Need of Conversion', parts 1 & 2, *Doctrine and Life*, vol. 34, nos 13 and 14 (April & May–June 1985), pp. 202–205, 266; Tim Lynch, 'Secularisation in Ireland', *The Furrow*, vol. 36, no. 8 (August 1985), pp. 506–507; Louis McRedmond, 'A Brawling Church: The Malaise of Irish Catholicism', *Doctrine and Life*, vol. 34, no. 7 (September 1985), pp. 377–383; Paul Bowe, 'Ireland, a Church in Need of Conversion, Comment on Father Regan's Article', *Doctrine and Life*, vol. 34, no. 7 (September 1985), pp. 387, 389–390; Ray Brady, 'Will Our Children Believe and Belong?' *The Furrow*, vol. 41, no. 1 (January 1990), pp. 4–5; Colm Kilcoyne, 'Church to blame for the shift from religion', *Sunday Tribune* (22 February 1998), p. 19; John Waters, *An Intelligent Person's Guide to Modern Ireland* (London: Duckworth, 1998), Chapter 7: 'On How God Has Been Kidnapped and Held to Ransom;' Willie Walsh (Bishop of Killaloe), 'The Church in the New Millennium', in Denis Carroll (ed.), *Religion in Ireland: Past, Present and Future* (Dublin: The Columba Press, 1999), pp. 165–174; Tom Inglis, 'A Religious Frenzy?' in Michael Peillon and Eamonn Slater (eds), *Encounters with Modern*

Ireland: A Sociological Chronicle, 1995–1996 (Dublin: Institute of Public Administration, 1998), pp. 73–79; and Jean-Christophe Penet, 'Closer to Brussels Than to Rome? The EU as the New External Referent for a Secularised Irish Society and a Redefined Catholic Identity', *Études Irlandaises*, vol. 34, no. 1 (2009), pp. 53–66.

Television provoked a few alarmist and extreme comments; for example: 'television . . . can tend to become an intruder and can dominate family life . . . The TV is not an innocent piece of furniture; it almost has a life of its own' (Jorge Yarce, 'Television and Family Life', *Position Papers 170* (January 1988), p. 58). Although useful as an instrument of information, recreation and the propagation of cultural values, it was also seen as a conduit of immoral values, especially pertaining to sex and violence. This, it was claimed, led to altered behavioural patterns which in turn caused serious social problems. Furthermore, television 'addiction' was blamed for making children passive, less inclined to work and reluctant to give service to others. Adults too were seen to have succumbed to the 'psychological coercion' of television, suffering symptoms similar to those of children, becoming introverted and less intellectually active (p. 59). The greatest calamity, from this Catholic point of view, was that television would replace Christ at the centre of family life. See C. John McCloskey, '12 Step TV Recovery Program', *Position Paper 255* (March 1995), pp. 97–99. Catholic apologists of course did not claim that there was something intrinsically evil about television. They maintained that, like any other technological device, it could be used for good or evil.

33 Michael Paul Gallagher, 'The New Agenda of Unbelief and Faith', in Dermot A. Lane (ed.), *Religion and Culture in Dialogue: A Challenge for the Next Millennium* (Dublin: The Columba Press, 1993), pp. 134–135.

34 See Andrew Pierce, 'Christianity – a Credible Presence?' p. 11; and Dermot A. Lane, 'Reconstructing Faith for a New Century and a New Society', pp. 169–170; both in Dermot A. Lane (ed.), *New Century, New Society* (Dublin: The Columba Press, 1999).

35 See Sheelagh Drudy and Kathleen Lynch, *Schools and Society in Ireland* (Dublin: Gill & Macmillan, 1993), pp. 82, 85–87.

36 John Hedley Brooke, *Science and Religion: Some Historical Perspectives* (Cambridge: Cambridge University Press, 1991), p. 340. See also idem, 'Science and Secularization', in Peter Harrison (ed.), *The Cambridge Companion to Science and Religion* (Cambridge: Cambridge University Press, 2010), pp. 103–123. Brooke pointed to evidence that indicated that 'science barely featured at all' as a reason for the unbelief of secularists (p. 111).

37 Paul Davies, *God and the New Physics* (London: Penguin Books, 1990), pp. 1–3. This observation by Davies is not original. In 1950 the Maynooth professor P.J. MacLaughlin observed that the prestige and influence enjoyed by scientists was due mainly to the success of scientific applications rather than to an understanding of science itself (P.J. MacLaughlin, 'Philosophy and Science: The Place of Science in Human Affairs', *Studies*, vol. 39 (1950), p. 100).

38 Steve Bruce, *God Save Ulster: The Religion and Politics of Paisleyism* (Oxford: Oxford University Press, 1986), pp. 236–237.

39 For a detailed account of government policies towards science in the Republic of Ireland, see Don Thornhill, 'Developing a Research Culture', in Charles Mollan (ed.), *Science and Ireland – Value for Society* (Dublin: The Royal Dublin Society, 2005), pp. 75–100.

40 Dick Ahlstrom, 'Scientists fight for full share of Tiger droppings', *The Irish Times* (15 February 2000), Education & Living supplement; p. 2. Further discussion and

speculation about the government's spending plans for scientific research are to be found in p. 3 of the same *The Irish Times* supplement: Yvonne Healy, 'Colleges could lose cutting edge if institutes approved' and Dick Ahlstrom, 'The battle for a half-billion: Some arguments in focus'.

41 The tánaiste is second in command to the taoiseach (prime minister) and undertakes the responsibilities of prime minister when he/she is absent.

42 Dick Ahlstrom, '£500 million put up for research', *The Irish Times* (28 July 2000), 'Business This Week 1' supplement, p. 2.

43 Dick Ahlstrom, 'The Insider: Focus on Ireland: Spend, Spend, Spend', *New Scientist*, vol. 179, no. 2412 (13 September 2003), pp. 54–55. The figure of €2.54 billion allocated for scientific research for the period 2000–2006 indicated a radical change in government policy. Only the equivalent of about €500 million was spent in the period 1994–1999. See Terence Brown, *Ireland: A Social and Cultural History, 1922–2002* (London: Harper Perennial, 2004), pp. 424–425. In terms of expenditure on scientific research in the OECD (26 countries), Ireland moved from nineteenth position in 2002 to sixteenth position in 2004. Maurice Dagg, 'Building a Research Culture: The Public Investment', *Technology Ireland*, vol. 37, issue 6 (January–February 2007), p. 22. In June 2006 the Fianna Fáil–Progressive Democrat coalition government published plans to spend at least €3.8 billion on scientific research over the seven-year period up to 2013 (Dick Ahlstrom, 'Scientific R&D to receive €3.8bn over next 7 years', *The Irish Times* [19 June 2006]), p. 1. See also, in the same issue, by Ahlstrom: 'Government hopes science will supply formula to spur growth', 'Range of research to be widened in future' and 'Investment by State to be 2.5% of GDP' (p. 5).

44 Trench, 'Science, Culture and Public Affairs', pp. 58–59. See also idem, 'Paradoxes of Irish Scientific Culture', *The Irish Review*, no. 43 (Summer 2011), pp. 1–13.

45 Dick Ahlstrom, *Flashes of Brilliance: The Cutting Edge of Irish Science* (Dublin: Royal Irish Academy, 2006).

46 Jim Corkery, 'Does Technology Squeeze out Transcendence – or What?' in Breen, Conway and McMillan (eds), *Technology and Transcendence*, pp. 11–12. Corkery's essay was republished under the same title in *The Furrow*, vol. 55, no. 2 (February 2004), pp. 97–106.

47 Corkery, 'Does Technology Squeeze out Transcendence – or What?' in Breen, Conway and McMillan (eds), *Technology and Transcendence*, p. 18.

48 Ibid., p. 15.

49 Ibid., pp. 19–20.

50 Ibid., pp. 16–17.

51 Sources studied for the rational choice theory of religion, developed by Rodney Stark and William Sims Bainbridge, include Alan Aldridge, *Religion in the Contemporary World: A Sociological Introduction* (Cambridge: Polity Press, 2000), pp. 94–106; Malcolm B. Hamilton, *The Sociology of Religion: Theoretical and Comparative Perspectives* (London: Routledge, 1995), pp. 183–192; Rodney Stark and Roger Finke, *Acts of Faith: Explaining the Human Side of Religion* (Berkeley, California: University of California Press, 2000), pp. 83–113.

52 See Aldridge, *Religion in the Contemporary World*, p. 97.

53 Ibid., pp. 103–104.

54 In Ireland the power of the institutional church over the Roman Catholic laity decreased but relatively few Irish Catholics left the church completely. However, there was a greater reliance on private judgement, religious belief was more lukewarm and religious practice was less frequent (Tony Fahey, Bernadette C.

Hayes and Richard Sinnott, *Conflict and Consensus: A Study of Values and Attitudes in the Republic of Ireland and Northern Ireland* [Dublin: Institute of Public Administration, 2005], pp. 55–56, 219). For additional information and opinions about the above points and more, see Caroline O'Doherty, 'Losing our religion', *Irish Examiner* (20 March 2008), p. 1; and articles in 'Religion and Ireland' supplement in the same newspaper, pp. 2–8.

55 Reform in the Catholic Church is not an option. Diminishing numbers in religious life is just one powerful driving force for change. Numbers of diocesan priests will continue to decline to the point where many parishes will not have a resident priest. Over the next ten years active diocesan priests in Ireland may decline by as much as 40 per cent – from 2,800 to about 1,700. It seems inevitable that members of the laity will undertake some church duties previously carried out by priests (Caroline O'Doherty, 'A life of mistrust . . . and sacrifice', *Irish Examiner* [24 June 2011], pp. 10–11).

56 A case in point is the United States. Ronald L. Numbers, Professor of the History of Science and Medicine at the University of Wisconsin-Madison, pointed to a survey of American opinion in the 1990s which indicated that religious belief and science, to a large extent, still coexisted side by side. Nearly 40 per cent of American scientists maintained belief in a personal God. Despite the powerful influence of 'naturalistic science', a very large majority of Americans sustained an active belief in the supernatural. Seventy-seven per cent believed that God occasionally intervened to cure those who suffered from serious illness. Ronald L. Numbers, 'Science without God: Natural Laws and Christian Beliefs', in David C. Lindberg and Ronald L. Numbers (eds), *When Science and Christianity Meet* (Chicago: The University of Chicago Press, 2003), pp. 284–285.

Bibliography

Primary Sources

OFFICIAL PUBLICATIONS

Central Statistics Office, *Census 2002: Religion* (Dublin: The Stationery Office, April 2004), vol. 12.

Cooper, Charles, and Noel Whelan, *Science, Technology and Industry in Ireland: Report to the National Science Council* (Dublin: The Stationery Office: January 1973).

Commission on Vocational Organisation Report (Dublin: The Stationery Office, dated 1943, published 1944).

Dáil Éireann Parliamentary Debates.

Group on the Science System of the OECD Committee for Scientific and Technological Policy, *Science and Technology in the Public Eye* (n.p.: OECD [Organization for Economic Cooperation and Development], January 1997).

Office of Science and Technology, Department of Enterprise and Employment, *Science, Technology and Innovation: The White Paper* (Dublin: The Stationery Office, October 1996).

Royal Commission on the University of Dublin (Trinity College), Report of the Commissioners, Cd. 1078 (Dublin: His Majesty's Stationery Office, 1920). His Majesty's Stationery Office is hereafter HMSO.

Royal Commission on Trinity College, Dublin, and the University of Dublin: First Report of the Commissioners, Cd. 3174 (Dublin: HMSO, 1906).

Royal Commission on Trinity College, Dublin, and the University of Dublin: Appendix to the First Report: Statements and Returns, Cd. 3176 (Dublin: HMSO, 1906).

Royal Commission on Trinity College, Dublin, and the University of Dublin: Final Report of the Commissioners, Cd. 3311 (Dublin: HMSO, 1907).

Royal Commission on Trinity College, Dublin, and the University of Dublin: Appendix to the Final Report: Minutes of Evidence and Documents, Cd. 3312 (Dublin: HMSO, 1907).

Royal Commission on University Education in Ireland: First Report of the Commissioners, Cd. 825 (Dublin: HMSO, 1901).

Royal Commission on University Education in Ireland: Appendix to the First Report: Minutes of Evidence, Cd. 826 (Dublin: HMSO, 1901).

Royal Commission on University Education in Ireland: Second Report of the Commissioners, Cd. 899 (Dublin: HMSO, 1901).

Royal Commission on University Education in Ireland: Appendix to the Second Report: Minutes of Evidence, Cd. 900 (Dublin: HMSO, 1902).

Royal Commission on University Education in Ireland: Third Report of the Commissioners, Cd. 1228 (Dublin: HMSO, 1902).

Royal Commission on University Education in Ireland: Appendix to the Third Report: Minutes of Evidence, Cd. 1229 (Dublin: HMSO, 1902).

Royal Commission on University Education in Ireland: Final Report of the Commissioners, Cd. 1483 (Dublin: HMSO, 1903).

Royal Commission on University Education in Ireland: Final Report of the Commissioners: Documents, Cd. 1484 (Dublin: HMSO, 1903).

Seanad Éireann Parliamentary Debates

Science, Technology, and Innovation Advisory Council, Making Knowledge Work for Us (Dublin: The Stationery Office, 1995), vols 1–3.

The National Science Council, Science Policy Formulation and Resource Allocation (Dublin: The Stationery Office, August 1972).

The National Science Council, Progress Report, 1969–71 (Dublin: The Stationery Office, November 1972).

The National Science Council, Science Policy: Some Implications for Ireland (Dublin: National Science Council, January 1973).

ARCHIVAL DOCUMENTS:

Edward J. Coyne papers, Irish Jesuit Archives, Dublin.
John Joly papers, Trinity College Dublin.
Thomas Aiskew Larcom papers, The National Library of Ireland, Dublin.
William Monsell papers, The National Library of Ireland, Dublin.
Alfred O'Rahilly papers, Archives of Blackrock College, Dublin.

BOOKS, JOURNALS AND NEWSPAPERS:

Bibby, Cyril (ed.), T.H. Huxley on Education: A Selection from His Writings (London: Cambridge University Press, 1971).

Cosslett, Tess (ed.), Science and Religion in the Nineteenth Century (Cambridge: Cambridge University Press, 1984).

Dessain, Charles Stephen (ed.), The Letters and Diaries of John Henry Newman (London: Nelson, 1967), vol. 17.

Finocchiaro, Maurice A. (ed. and trans.), The Galileo Affair: A Documentary History (Berkeley: University of California Press, 1989).

Flannery, Austin (general ed.), Vatican Council II: More Postconciliar Documents. (Collegeville, Minnesota: The Liturgical Press, 1982).

Flannery, Austin (general ed.), Vatican Council II: The Conciliar and Post Conciliar Documents. New revised ed. (Dublin: Dominican Publications, 1992).

Huxley, Leonard, Life and Letters of Thomas Henry Huxley. 3 vols (London: Macmillan, 1903).

John Paul II (Pope), 'The Faith of the Irish', *The Pope Teaches*, vol. 2, no. 3 (July–September 1979), pp. 384–389.

John Paul II (Pope), 'To the Youth of Ireland', *The Pope Teaches*, vol. 2, no. 3 (July–September 1979), pp. 403–406.

John Paul II (Pope), 'Faith Can Never Conflict with Reason' (address to the Pontifical Academy of Sciences, 31 October 1992), *L'Osservatore Romano*, no. 1264 (4 November 1992), pp. 1–2.

Mioni, Anthony J. (ed.), *The Popes against Modern Errors: 16 Papal Documents* (Rockford, Illinois: Tan Books, 1999).

Rome and the Study of Scripture: A Collection of Papal Enactments on the Study of Holy Scripture together with the Decisions of the Biblical Commission. 7th ed. (St Meinrad, Indiana: Abbey Press, 1964).

Tanner, Norman P. (ed.), *Decrees of the Ecumenical Councils: Trent to Vatican II* (London: Sheed & Ward; Washington, DC: Georgetown University Press, 1990), vol. 2.

The Archbishops and Bishops of Ireland, 'Pastoral Letter of the Archbishops and Bishops of Ireland' (22 January 1873), *The Irish Ecclesiastical Record*, new series, vol. 9 (1873), pp. 193–207.

The Archbishops and Bishops of Ireland, 'Pastoral Address of the Archbishops and Bishops of Ireland to their Flocks' (14 October 1874), in Patrick Francis Moran (ed.), *Pastoral Letters and Other Writings of Cardinal Cullen* (Dublin: Browne & Nolan, 1882), vol. 3, pp. 587–614.

Tyrrell, George, *Letters from a 'Modernist': The Letters of George Tyrrell to Wilfrid Ward, 1893–1908*, introduced and annotated by Mary Jo Weaver (Shepherdstown, West Virginia: Patmos Press; London: Sheed & Ward, 1981).

Ward, Wilfrid, *The Life of John Henry Cardinal Newman: Based on his Private Journals and Correspondence* (London: Longman's, Green & Co., 1921), vol. 1.

Secondary Sources

Aczel, Amir D., *The Jesuit and the Skull: Teilhard de Chardin, Evolution and the Search for Peking Man* (New York: Riverhead Books, 2007).

Adelman, Juliana, 'Evolution on Display: Promoting Irish Natural History and Darwinism at the Dublin Science and Art Museum', *British Journal for the History of Science*, vol. 38, no. 139 (December 2005), pp. 411–436.

Adelman, Juliana, 'Communities of Science: The Queen's Colleges and Scientific Culture in Provincial Ireland, 1845–75' (PhD thesis, National University of Ireland, Galway, 2007).

Adelman, Juliana, *Communities of Science in Nineteenth-Century Ireland* (London: Pickering & Chatto, 2009).

Adelman, Juliana, and Éadaoin Agnew (eds), *Science and Technology in Nineteenth-Century Ireland* (Dublin: Four Courts Press, 2011).

Agius, Thomas J., 'Genesis and Evolution', *The Irish Ecclesiastical Record*, 5th series, vol. 13 (June 1919), pp. 441–453.

Ahlstrom, Dick, 'Scientists fight for full share of Tiger droppings', and 'The battle for a half-billion: Some arguments in focus', *The Irish Times* (15 February 2000), Education & Living supplement, pp. 2–3.

Ahlstrom, Dick, '£500 million put up for research', *The Irish Times* (28 July 2000), 'Business This Week 1' supplement, p. 2.

Ahlstrom, Dick, 'The Insider: Focus on Ireland: Spend, Spend, Spend', *New Scientist*, vol. 179, no. 2412 (13 September 2003), pp. 54–55.

Ahlstrom, Dick, 'Scientific R & D to receive €3.8bn over next 7 years', *The Irish Times* (19 June 2006), p. 1.

Ahlstrom, Dick, 'Government hopes science will supply formula to spur growth', 'Range of research to be widened in future', and 'Investment by State to be 2.5% of GDP', *The Irish Times* (19 June 2006), p. 5.

Ahlstrom, Dick, *Flashes of Brilliance: The Cutting Edge of Irish Science* (Dublin: Royal Irish Academy, 2006).

Aldridge, Alan, *Religion in the Contemporary World: A Sociological Introduction* (Cambridge: Polity Press, 2000).

Allen, Nicholas, 'States of Mind: Science, Culture and the Irish Intellectual Revival, 1900–30', *Irish University Review*, vol. 33, no. 1 (Spring/Summer 2003), pp. 150–164.

Allitt, Patrick, *Catholic Converts: British and American Intellectuals Turn to Rome* (Ithaca and London: Cornell University Press, 1997).

Anon., 'Catholic Education – Disendowment of the Protestant Establishment', *The Irish Ecclesiastical Record*, vol. 1 (1865), pp. 227–238.

Anon., 'Catholicity and the Spirit of the Age', *The Irish Monthly*, vol. 1, no. 1 (July 1873), pp. 24–30.

Anon., 'Claims of the Catholics of Ireland to Independent University Education', *The Irish Ecclesiastical Record*, vol. 2 (1866), pp. 320–331.

Anon., 'Lord Mayo and the Catholic University of Ireland', *The Irish Ecclesiastical Record*, vol. 4 (1868), pp. 483–494.

Anon., 'Preliminary Steps', *Record of the Maynooth Union* (1895–1896), pp. 5–8.

Anon., 'Pontiff lends his support to theory of evolution', *The Examiner* (25 October 1996), p. 10.

Anon., review of J.B. Kavanagh, *Solar Physics: A Lecture* (Dublin: Dollard, 1877) in *The Irish Monthly*, vol. 5 (1877), pp. 234–237.

Anon., review of J.B. Kavanagh, *Comets and Meteors: A Lecture* (Dublin: Dollard, 1877), in *The Irish Monthly*, vol. 5 (September 1877), pp. 593–595.

Anon., 'Scientific Notices: Afternoon Scientific Lectures', *The Irish Ecclesiastical Record*, 3rd series, vol. 2 (May 1881), pp. 284–293.

Anon., 'The Church and Modern Thought', parts 1–2, *The Irish Ecclesiastical Record*, new series, vol. 9 (1873), pp. 494–502, 533–543.

Anon., 'The Church and Modern Thought', parts 3–5, *The Irish Ecclesiastical Record*, new series, vol. 10 (1874), pp. 56–62, 102–109, 237–245.

Anon., 'The Genesis, According to Scripture and Science', *The Catholic Record*, vol. 4, no. 23 (March 1873), pp. 306–310.

Anon., 'The Revival of Atheism', *The Irish Ecclesiastical Record*, vol. 3 (1867), pp. 500–509.

Arnstein, Walter L., 'Victorian Prejudice Reexamined', *Victorian Studies*, vol. 12 (June 1969), pp. 452–457.

Arnstein, Walter L., *Protestant versus Catholic in Mid-Victorian England: Mr. Newdegate and the Nuns* (Columbia: University of Missouri Press, 1982).

Artigas, Mariano, Thomas F. Glick, and Rafael A. Martínez, *Negotiating Darwin: The Vatican Confronts Evolution, 1877-1902* (Baltimore: The Johns Hopkins University Press, 2006).

Ashton, John, 'Modern Science and the Theory of Continuity', *The Dublin Review*, vol. 178, no. 356 (January–March 1926), pp. 89–107.

Astore, William J, 'Gentle Skeptics? American Catholic Encounters with Polygenism, Geology, and Evolutionary Theories from 1845 to 1875', *The Catholic Historical Review*, vol. 82 (January 1996), pp. 40–76.

Attis, David, and Charles Mollan (eds), *Science and Irish Culture: Why the History of Science Matters in Ireland* (Dublin: The Royal Dublin Society, 2004).

Augusteijn, Joost (ed.), *Ireland in the 1930s: New Perspectives* (Dublin: Four Courts Press, 1999).

Barbour, Ian G., *Religion and Science: Historical and Contemporary Issues* (London: SCM Press, 1998).

Barclay, Charles, 'When I See the Heavens...', *The Furrow*, vol. 45, no. 11 (November 1994), pp. 614–624.

Barlow, Connie (ed.), *Evolution Extended: Biological Debates on the Meaning of Life* (Cambridge, Massachusetts: The MIT Press, 1995).

Barr, Colin, 'The Failure of Newman's Catholic University of Ireland', *Archivium Hibernicum*, vol. 55 (2001), pp. 126–139.

Barr, Colin, 'University Education, History, and the Hierarchy', in Lawrence W. McBride (ed.), *Reading Irish Histories: Texts, Contexts, and Memory in Modern Ireland* (Dublin: Four Courts Press, 2003), pp. 62–79.

Barrett, Cyril, 'Secular Theologians of Science', *Milltown Studies*, vol. 36 (Autumn 1995), pp. 5–16.

Barrett, M., 'The Origin and Conservation of Motion', *The Irish Ecclesiastical Record*, 4th series, vol. 3 (1898), pp. 60–69.

Barry, D.T., 'Descent and Selection: A Query', *The Irish Ecclesiastical Record*, 5th series, vol. 15 (January 1920), pp. 43–55.

Barton, Ruth, 'John Tyndall, Pantheist: A Rereading of the Belfast Address', *Osiris*, 2nd series, vol. 3 (1987), pp. 111–134.

Barton, Ruth, '"An Influential Set of Chaps": The X-Club and Royal Society Politics, 1864-85', *The British Journal for the History of Science*, vol. 23, no. 76 (March 1990), pp. 53–81.

Bedford, Henry, 'Scientific Gossip', *The Irish Monthly*, vol. 7 (1879), pp. 32–45.

Bedford, Henry, 'Scientific Gossip 2: The Uses of the Sun', *The Irish Monthly*, vol. 7 (1879), pp. 69–81.

Bedford, Henry, 'Scientific Gossip 3: Recent Additions to the Solar System', *The Irish Monthly*, vol. 7 (1879), pp. 141–149.

Bedford, Henry, 'Scientific Gossip 4: The Telephone, Part 1', *The Irish Monthly*, vol. 7 (July 1879), pp. 337–345.

Bedford, Henry, 'Scientific Gossip 4: The Telephone, Part 2', *The Irish Monthly*, vol. 7 (1879), pp. 406–413.

Bedford, Henry, 'Scientific Gossip 5: Heat, Part 1, What Is It?' *The Irish Monthly*, vol. 8 (January 1880), pp. 24–32.

Bedford, Henry, 'Scientific Gossip 5: Heat, Part 2, How Heat Is Communicated from One Body to Another', *The Irish Monthly*, vol. 8 (March 1880), pp. 139–146.

Bedford, Henry, 'Scientific Gossip 6: Radiant Matter', *The Irish Monthly*, vol. 8 (June 1880), pp. 306–313.

Bedford, Henry, 'The History of the Earth and Moon', *The Irish Ecclesiastical Record*, 3rd series, vol. 3 (January 1882), pp. 1–11.

Betts, John Rickards, 'Darwinism, Evolution, and American Catholic Thought, 1860–1900', *The Catholic Historical Review*, vol. 45 (April 1959–January 1960), pp. 161–185.

Boland, Vivian, 'New Developments in Human Reproduction', *Doctrine and Life*, vol. 35, no. 8 (October 1985), pp. 464–468.

Bowe, Paul, 'Ireland, a Church in Need of Conversion, Comment on Father Regan's Article', *Doctrine and Life*, vol. 34, no. 7 (September 1985), pp. 384–391.

Bowler, Peter J., *The Eclipse of Darwinism: Anti-Darwinian Evolution Theories in the Decades around 1900* (Baltimore: The Johns Hopkins University Press, 1983).

Bowler, Peter J., *Charles Darwin: The Man and His Influence* (Cambridge: Cambridge University Press, 1996).

Bowler, Peter J., *Reconciling Science and Religion: The Debate in Early-Twentieth-Century Britain* (Chicago: The University of Chicago Press, 2001).

Bowler, Peter J., *Evolution: The History of an Idea*, 3rd ed. (Berkeley: University of California Press, 2003).

Bowler, Peter J., and Nicholas Whyte (eds), *Science and Society in Ireland: The Social Context of Science and Technology in Ireland, 1800–1950* (Belfast: The Institute of Irish Studies, The Queen's University of Belfast, 1997).

Bowler, Peter J., and Iwan Rhys Morus, *Making Modern Science: A Historical Survey* (Chicago: The University of Chicago Press, 2005).

Brady, Ray, 'Will Our Children Believe and Belong?' *The Furrow*, vol. 41, no. 1 (January 1990), pp. 3–8.

Breen, Michael, Eamonn Conway and Barry McMillan (eds), *Technology and Transcendence* (Dublin: The Columba Press, 2003).

Brennan, M. 'Evolution – I', *The Irish Ecclesiastical Record*, 5th series, vol. 95 (1961), pp. 327–329.

Brennan, M., 'Evolution – II: The Origin of Man', *The Irish Ecclesiastical Record*, 5th series, vol. 95 (1961), pp. 396–402.

Brennan, M., 'Evolution – III: Philosophical and Theological Implications', *The Irish Ecclesiastical Record*, 5th series, vol. 96 (1961), pp. 43–49.

Brennan, Martin, 'Adam and the Biological Sciences', *The Irish Theological Quarterly*, new series, vol. 35, no. 2 (April 1968), pp. 141–165.

Brennan, Martin, 'From Matter to Man: The Evolutionism of Teilhard de Chardin', *University Review*, vol. 5, no. 2 (Summer 1968), pp. 223–233.

Brock, W.H., N.D. McMillan and R.C. Mollan (eds), *John Tyndall: Essays on a Natural Philosopher* (Dublin: Royal Dublin Society, 1981).

Brooke, John Hedley, *Science and Religion: Some Historical Perspectives* (Cambridge: Cambridge University Press, 1991).

Brooke, John, and Geoffrey Cantor, *Reconstructing Nature: The Engagement of Science and Religion* (Edinburgh: T&T Clark, 1998).

Brooke, John Hedley, Margaret J. Osler and Jitse M. van der Meer (eds), *Science in Theistic Contexts: Cognitive Dimensions*, vol. 16 of *Osiris* (2001).

Brophy, Liam, 'In Search of *Homo Perfectus*', *The Irish Ecclesiastical Record*, 5th series, vol. 68 (December 1946), pp. 395–403.

Brophy, Liam, 'Scientific Humanism', *The Irish Monthly*, vol. 75, no. 887 (May 1947), pp. 195–200.

Brophy, Liam, 'Will Men Be Like Gears?' *The Irish Monthly*, vol. 75, no. 888 (June 1947), pp. 261–265.

Brophy, Liam, 'Science – Bane or Blessing?' *The Irish Monthly*, vol. 75 (September 1947), pp. 391–396.

Brown, Terence, *Ireland: A Social and Cultural History, 1922–1985* (London: Fontana Press, 1985).

Brown, Terence, *Ireland: A Social and Cultural History, 1922–2002* (London: Harper Perennial, 2004).

Browne, Janet, 'Presidential Address: Commemorating Darwin', *The British Journal for the History of Science*, vol. 38, no. 138 (September 2005), pp. 251–274.

Browne, Michael, 'Modern Theories of Evolution: I – Stellar and Planetary Evolution', *The Irish Ecclesiastical Record*, 5th series, vol. 27 (June 1926), pp. 561–570.

Browne, Michael, 'Modern Theories of Evolution: II – Evolution of the Chemical Elements', *The Irish Ecclesiastical Record*, 5th series, vol. 28 (July 1926), pp. 35–43.

Browne, Michael, 'Modern Theories of Evolution: III – the Evolution of Life', *The Irish Ecclesiastical Record*, 5th series, vol. 28 (August 1926), pp. 124–132.

Browne, Michael, 'Modern Theories of Evolution: IV – the Evolution of Organisms', *The Irish Ecclesiastical Record*, 5th series, vol. 28 (December 1926), pp. 561–582.

Browne, Michael, 'Genesis 1 and 2', *The Furrow*, vol. 21, no. 6 (June 1970), pp. 344–346.

Bruce, Steve, *God Save Ulster: The Religion and Politics of Paisleyism* (Oxford: Oxford University Press, 1986).

Brück, H.A., 'Astronomical Cosmology: The Observational Evidence', *Studies*, vol. 42 (Winter 1953), pp. 361–380.

Brück, H.A., 'Astronomical Cosmology, Part 2: Theoretical Investigations', *Studies*, vol. 43 (Spring 1954), pp. 31–50.

Brundell, Barry, 'Catholic Church Politics and Evolution Theory, 1894–1902', *The British Journal for the History of Science*, vol. 34 (2001), pp. 81–95.

Brush, Stephen G., 'The Nebular Hypothesis and the Evolutionary Worldview', *History of Science*, vol. 25, no. 3 (1987), pp. 245–278.

Burke, Mary, 'Evolutionary Theory and the Search for Lost Innocence in the Writings of J.M. Synge', *Canadian Journal of Irish Studies*, vol. 30, no. 1 (Spring 2004), pp. 48–54.

Burr, John G., 'Black Holes and the Creation of the Universe', *Doctrine and Life*, vol. 38, no. 1 (January 1988), pp. 41–45.

Burrow, J.W., *The Crisis of Reason: European Thought, 1848–1914* (New Haven: Yale University Press, 2000).

Burtchaell, James Tunstead, 'The Biblical Question and the English Liberal Catholics', *The Review of Politics*, vol. 31, no. 1 (January 1969), pp. 108–120.

Burtchaell, James Tunstead, *Catholic Theories of Biblical Inspiration since 1810: A Review and Critique* (London: Cambridge University Press, 1969).

Burton, Philip, 'Was St. Augustine an Evolutionist?' *The Irish Ecclesiastical Record*, 4th series, vol. 5 (February and June 1899), pp. 102–110, 521–530.

Burton, Philip, 'St. Augustine and the Missing Link', *The Irish Ecclesiastical Record*, 4th series, vol. 5 (May 1899), pp. 450–459.

Byrne, James J., 'Investment and Research in Irish Agriculture', *Studies*, vol. 44 (Summer 1955), pp. 193–206.

C., J.G., 'Darwinism', *The Irish Ecclesiastical Record*, new series, vol. 9 (1873), pp. 337–361.

C., T., review of Rémy Collin, *Evolution: Hypotheses and Problems*, in *The Irish Ecclesiastical Record*, 5th series, vol. 94 (July–December 1960), p. 127.

C., T.J., 'Introductory', *The Irish Ecclesiastical Record*, 3rd series, vol. 1 (1880), pp. 1–2.

C., W.P., 'Draper's "Conflict Between Science and Religion"', *New Ireland Review*, vol. 9 (1898), pp. 371–373.

Camp, Richard L., *The Papal Ideology of Social Reform* (Leiden, The Netherlands: E.J. Brill, 1969).

Cane, F., 'The Physics of the Flood', *The Irish Ecclesiastical Record*, 3rd series, vol. 10 (October 1889), pp. 901–906.

Cantor, Geoffrey, and Chris Kenny, 'Barbour's Fourfold Way: Problems with his Taxonomy of Science–Religion Relationships', *Zygon*, vol. 36, no. 4 (December 2001), pp. 765–781.

Carroll, Denis, 'The God of Life: "Back Here" and "Out There"', *Doctrine and Life*, vol. 39, no. 4 (April 1989), pp. 176–180.

Carroll, Denis (ed.), *Religion in Ireland: Past, Present and Future* (Dublin: The Columba Press, 1999).

Cassidy, Eoin G. (ed.), *Faith and Culture in the Irish Context* (Dublin: Veritas, 1996).

Chadwick, Owen, *The Secularization of the European Mind in the Nineteenth Century* (Cambridge: Cambridge University Press, 1975).

Chadwick, Owen, *A History of the Popes, 1830–1914* (Oxford: Oxford University Press, 2003).

Clais-Girard, Jacqueline, 'The English Catholics and Irish Nationalism, 1865–1890: A Tragedy in Five Acts', *Victorian Literature and Culture*, vol. 32, no. 1 (2004), pp. 177–189.

Clark, Constance Areson, '"You Are Here": Missing Links, Chains of Being, and the Language of Cartoons', *Isis*, vol. 100, no. 3 (September 2009), pp. 571–589.

Clarke, Desmond, 'An Outline of the History of Science in Ireland', *Studies*, vol. 62 (Autumn–Winter 1973), pp. 287–302.

Coakley, Patrick F., 'Was St. Augustine an Evolutionist?' *The Irish Ecclesiastical Record*, 4th series, vol. 5 (April 1899), pp. 342–358.

Coffey, D.J., 'The Origin of Life: Its Physical Basis and Definition', *The Irish Theological Quarterly*, vol. 1 (October 1907), pp. 423–434.

Coffey, P., 'Agnosticism: A General Sketch', *The Irish Ecclesiastical Record*, 4th series, vol. 10 (October 1901), pp. 289–310.

Coffey, P., 'Philosophy and the Sciences: I', *The Irish Ecclesiastical Record*, 4th series, vol. 17 (1905), pp. 25–43.

Coffey, P., 'Philosophy and the Sciences: II', *The Irish Ecclesiastical Record*, 4th series, vol. 17 (1905), pp. 156–176.

Coffey, P., 'The New Knowledge and Its Limitations', parts I–III, *The Irish Ecclesiastical Record*, 4th series, vol. 26 (1909), pp. 337–351, 461–474, 571–586.

Coffey, P., 'The New Knowledge and Its Limitations', part IV, *The Irish Ecclesiastical Record*, 4th series, vol. 27 (1910), pp. 17–35.

Coffey, P., 'Scholasticism and Modern Thought', *The Irish Theological Quarterly*, vol. 4 (1909), pp. 457–473.

Coffey, P., 'Some Questionable Tendencies in the Logic of Scientific Method', *The Irish Ecclesiastical Record*, 4th series, vol. 28 (July 1910), pp. 1–10.

Coffey, P., 'Some Principles Underlying "Scientific Explanation"', *The Irish Ecclesiastical Record*, 4th series, vol. 28 (August 1910), pp. 130–149.

Coffey, P., 'The Principle of the "Uniformity of Nature": Its Relations to Induction and to Deduction', *The Irish Ecclesiastical Record*, 4th series, vol. 28 (September 1910), pp. 228–248.

Coffey, Peter, 'Agnosticism: A Special Study', *The Irish Ecclesiastical Record*, 4th series, vol. 10 (1901), pp. 513–539.

Coffey, Peter, 'The Hexahemeron and Science', parts I and II, *The Irish Ecclesiastical Record*, 4th series, vol. 12 (1902), pp. 141–162, 249–271.

Coghlan, Daniel, 'Evolution: Darwin and the Abbé Loisy–I', *The Irish Ecclesiastical Record*, 4th series, vol. 19 (June 1906), pp. 481–496.

Coghlan, Daniel, 'Evolution: Kant and the Loisy Theory of the Evolution of Christianity – II', *The Irish Ecclesiastical Record*, 4th series, vol. 21 (1907), pp. 60–77.

Coghlan, Daniel, 'The Decree "Lamentabili Sane Exitu" and Modernism', parts I–II, *The Irish Ecclesiastical Record*, 4th series, vol. 22 (1907), pp. 337–348, 486–499.

Coghlan, Daniel, 'The Decree "Lamentabili Sane Exitu" and Modernism', parts III–IV, *The Irish Ecclesiastical Record*, 4th series, vol. 23 (1908), pp. 61–74, 498–509.

Coleman, Ursula, 'Secularisation: A Healing Process?' *Studies*, vol. 74 (Spring 1985), pp. 26–36.

Collin, Rémy, *Evolution: Hypotheses and Problems* (London: Burns & Oates, 1959).

Connolly, Michael, 'The Expanded Universe', *The Irish Monthly*, vol. 74 (September 1946), pp. 367–375.

Connolly, P.J., 'Darwinism and History: A Dialogue', parts I–II, *The Irish Ecclesiastical Record*, 4th series, vol. 28 (1910), pp. 449–469, 590–610.

Conway, E.J., 'Pope Pius XII and Science', *University Review*, vol. 3, nos 5/6 (1964), pp. 19–24.

Conway, Martin, *Catholic Politics in Europe, 1918–1945* (London: Routledge, 1997).

Coogan, Tim Pat, *De Valera: Long Fellow, Long Shadow* (London: Hutchinson, 1993).

Coolahan, John, *Irish Education: Its History and Structure* (Dublin: Institute of Public Administration, 1981).

Coppa, Frank J., *The Modern Papacy since 1789* (London: Longman, 1998).

Corbett, Thomas, 'Science and Religion', *The Irish Theological Quarterly*, new series, vol. 56, no. 2 (1990), pp. 102–113.

Corcoran, T., 'The Rural District Continuation School', *The Irish Monthly*, vol. 51 (September 1923), pp. 459–462.

Corcoran, T., 'Rural Continuation Schools', *The Irish Monthly*, vol. 53 (January 1925), pp. 9–11.

Corcoran, T., 'Types of Agricultural Education: The "Farmer-Worker"', *The Irish Monthly*, vol. 53 (March 1925), pp. 123–126.

Corcoran, T., 'Mathematical and Technical Studies in Ireland', *The Irish Monthly*, vol. 54, no. 632 (February 1926), pp. 734–737.

Corkery, Jim, 'Does Technology Squeeze Out Transcendence – or What?' *The Furrow*, vol. 55, no. 2 (February 2004), pp. 97–106.

Corkery, John, 'Ecclesiastical Learning', in *A History of Irish Catholicism: The Church since Emancipation* (Dublin: Gill & Macmillan, 1970), vol. 5, pp. 1–33.

Corish, Patrick, *The Irish Catholic Experience: A Historical Survey* (Dublin: Gill & Macmillan, 1985).

Corish, Patrick J., *Maynooth College, 1795–1995* (Dublin: Gill & Macmillan, 1995).

Corrigan, Raymond, *The Church and the Nineteenth Century* (Milwaukee, Wisconsin: The Bruce Publishing Company, 1938).

Coyne, George V., 'The Church in Dialogue with Science: The Wojtyla Years', in *New Catholic Encyclopedia; Jubilee Volume: The Wojtyla Years* (Detroit, Michigan: Gale Group, 2001), pp. 101–107.

Crowe, M.B., 'Some Recent Trends in Soviet Science and Philosophy', *Studies*, vol. 46 (Winter 1957), pp. 421–430.

Crowe, M.B., 'Huxley and Humanism', *Studies*, vol. 49 (Autumn 1960), pp. 249–260.

Crowley. T., 'Some Philosophical Aspects of Physical Indeterminacy', *The Irish Ecclesiastical Record*, 5th series, vol. 70 (1948), pp. 785–799.

Crowley. T., '"Humani Generis" and Philosophy', *The Irish Theological Quarterly*, vol. 19, no. 1 (January 1952), pp. 25–32.

Cullen, Clara, 'The Museum of Irish Industry, Robert Kane and Education for All in the Dublin of the 1850s and 1860s', *History of Education*, vol. 38, no. 1 (January 2009), pp. 99–113.

Curtin, Maurice, 'Adam & Eve: A Problem for the Religion Teacher', *The Furrow*, vol. 25, no. 7 (July 1974), pp. 363–368.

Curtis Jr., Perry, *Apes and Angels: The Irishman in Victorian Caricature*, revised ed. (Washington, DC: Smithsonian Institution Press, 1997).

D., H.E., 'Revelation, Geology, the Antiquity of Man', *The Irish Ecclesiastical Record*, 3rd series, vol. 1 (1880), pp. 185–193, 260–272.

Dagg, Maurice, 'Building a Research Culture: The Public Investment', *Technology Ireland*, vol. 37, no. 6 (January–February 2007), pp. 20–23.

Dalton, E.A., 'A Plea for Irish History', *Record of the Maynooth Union* (1899–1900), pp. 75–79.

Daly, Cahal. B., 'Man and Cosmos', *The Irish Ecclesiastical Record*, 5th series, vol. 104 (1965), pp. 202–232.

Daly, Cardinal Cahal B., *The Minding of Planet Earth* (Dublin: Veritas, 2004).

Daly, Gabriel, 'Science, Religion and Scientism', *The Irish Review*, vol. 27 (Summer 2001), pp. 48–54.

Darwin, Charles, *The Origin of Species by Means of Natural Selection, or the Preservation of Favoured Races in the Struggle for Life*, ed. and introduction by J.W. Burrow (London: John Murray, 1859; republished, London: Penguin Books, 1985).

Darwin, Charles, *The Descent of Man, and Selection in Relation to Sex*, introduction by John Tyler Bonner and Robert M. May, 2 vols (London: John Murray, 1871; republished, Princeton, New Jersey: Princeton University Press, 1981).

Davies, Brian (ed.), *Philosophy of Religion: A Guide to the Subject* (London: Cassell, 1998).

Davies, Gordon L. Herries, 'Irish Thought in Science', in Richard Kearney (ed.), *The Irish Mind: Exploring Intellectual Traditions* (Dublin: Wolfhound Press, 1985), pp. 294–310.

Davies, Paul, *God and the New Physics* (London: Penguin Books, 1990).

Davis, Stephen T., *God, Reason and Theistic Proofs* (Edinburgh: Edinburgh University Press, 1997).

Dawkins, Richard, *The Selfish Gene*. New ed. (Oxford: Oxford University Press, 1989).

Dawkins, Richard, *River out of Eden* (London: Phoenix, 1996).

Dawkins, Richard, 'The God Shaped Hole', in conversation with Emily Hourican, *The Dubliner*, October 2002.

Dawkins, Richard, 'The great convergence', *The Irish Times* (17 February 2003).

Dawkins, Richard, *A Devil's Chaplain*, 2nd ed. (London: Phoenix, 2004).

Dawkins, Richard, *The God Delusion* (London: Bantam Press, 2006).

Dawson, Gowan, *Darwin, Literature and Victorian Respectability* (Cambridge: Cambridge University Press, 2007).

DeArce, Miguel, 'Darwin's Irish Correspondence', *Biology and Environment: Proceedings of the Royal Irish Academy*, vol. 108B, no. 1 (2008), pp. 43–56.

DeArce, Miguel, 'The Multi-Faceted Anti-Darwinism of Fr Jeremiah Murphy (1840–1915)', *Cork Historical and Archaeological Journal*, vol. 115 (2010), pp. 87–108.

De Bivort de la Saudée, Jacques (ed.), *God, Man and the Universe: A Christian Answer to Modern Materialism* (London: Burns & Oates, 1954).

De Blacam, Aodh, 'The Re-Discovery of God: Two Notable Books', *The Irish Monthly*, vol. 75 (August 1947), pp. 363–366.

De Bont, Raf, 'Rome and Theistic Evolutionism: The Hidden Strategies behind the "Dorlodot Affair", 1920–1926', *Annals of Science*, vol. 62, no. 4 (October 2005), pp. 457–478.

De Duve, Christian, 'Prelude to a Cell: Life Began with a Primitive Metabolism in the Primeval Soup', *The Sciences* (November–December 1990), pp. 22–28.

Desmond, Adrian, *Huxley: From Devil's Disciple to Evolution's High Priest* (London: Penguin Books, 1998).

Desmond, Adrian, and James Moore, *Darwin* (London: Penguin Books, 1992).

Devine, Philip E. 'Creation and Evolution', *Religious Studies*, vol. 32, no. 3 (September 1996), pp. 325–337.

Dillon, Thomas, 'The Application of Electricity to Chemical Industry', *Studies*, vol. 16 (June 1927), pp. 291–305.

Dillon, Thomas, 'Iodine and Potash from Irish Seaweed', *Studies*, vol. 19 (June 1930), pp. 267–278.

Dillon, Thomas, 'Chemistry in the Service of Man', *Studies*, vol. 28 (March 1939), pp. 49–62.

Dillon, Thomas, 'The Relation of Chemical Research to the Development of Our Industries', *Studies*, vol. 32 (March 1943), pp. 45–57.

Dixon, Thomas, Geoffrey Cantor and Stephen Pumfrey (eds), *Science and Religion: New Historical Perspectives* (Cambridge: Cambridge University Press, 2010).

Dorlodot, Canon, *Darwinism and Catholic Thought*, trans. Ernest Messenger (New York: Benziger Brothers, 1925).

Dowling, P.J., 'Save the Child: A Suggestion to Clerical Managers', *The Irish Ecclesiastical Record*, 4th series, vol. 14 (December 1903), pp. 520–526.

Dowling, P.J., 'Technical Education – Some Queries and Replies', *The Irish Ecclesiastical Record*, 4th series, vol. 15 (1904), pp. 412–418.

Draper, John William, *History of the Conflict Between Religion and Science*. 10th ed. (London: Henry S. King & Co., 1877).

Drudy, Sheelagh, and Kathleen Lynch, *Schools and Society in Ireland* (Dublin: Gill & Macmillan, 1993).

Duddy, Thomas, *A History of Irish Thought* (London: Routledge, 2002).

Duffy, Eamon, *Saints and Sinners: A History of the Popes* (New Haven: Yale University Press and S4C, 1997).

Durant, John (ed.), *Darwinism and Divinity: Essays on Evolution and Religious Belief* (Oxford: Basil Blackwell, 1985).

Eagleton, Terry, *Scholars and Rebels in Nineteenth-Century Ireland* (Oxford: Blackwell, 1999).

Egner, Robert E., and Lester E. Denonn, *The Basic Writings of Bertrand Russell, 1903–1959* (London: George Allen & Unwin, 1961).

Ellegård, Alvar, *Darwin and the General Reader: The Reception of Darwin's Theory of Evolution in the British Periodical Press, 1859–1872*, foreword by David L. Hull (Chicago: The University of Chicago Press, 1990).

Eve, A.S., and C.H. Creasey, *Life and Work of John Tyndall* (London: Macmillan, 1945).

Ewing, J. Franklin, 'Darwin Today', *America* (21 March 1959), pp. 709–711.

F., T., 'Mr. Tyndall at Belfast', *The Irish Monthly*, vol. 2 (October 1874), pp. 563–578.

F., T., 'The Aggressions of Science', *The Irish Monthly*, vol. 4 (December 1875), pp. 16–19.

F., T.A., 'The Royal Irish University and the Catholic Irish Faith', *The Irish Ecclesiastical Record*, 3rd series, vol. 1 (1880), pp. 140–149.

Finlay, Thomas A., 'Science and Scepticism', *The Irish Monthly*, vol. 8 (July 1880), pp. 349–360.

Fahey, Tony, Bernadette C. Hayes, and Richard Sinnott, *Conflict and Consensus: A Study of Values and Attitudes in the Republic of Ireland and Northern Ireland* (Dublin: Institute of Public Administration, 2005).

Fallon, Brian, *An Age of Innocence: Irish Culture, 1930–1960* (Dublin: Gill & Macmillan, 1999).

Farren, Sean, *The Politics of Irish Education, 1920–1965* (Belfast: The Institute of Irish Studies, The Queen's University of Belfast, 1995).

Fearon, William Robert, 'Spontaneous Generation', *Studies*, vol. 17 (March 1928), pp. 72–81.

Ferriter, Diarmaid, 'Breaking with the past', *The Irish Examiner* (20 March 2008), 'Religion and Ireland' supplement, p. 8.

Finocchiaro, Maurice A., 'The Galileo Affair from John Milton to John Paul II: Problems and Prospects', *Science & Education*, vol. 8 (1999), pp. 189–209.

Finocchiaro, Maurice A., 'Galileo as a "Bad Theologian": A Formative Myth about Galileo's Trial', *Studies in History and Philosophy of Science*, vol. 33A, no. 4 (December 2002), pp. 753–791.

FitzGerald, Garrett, 'The Faith of the Infidel', *The Irish Monthly*, vol. 75 (October 1947), pp. 441–445

FitzGerald, J., 'Life and Letters of Charles Darwin', *The Irish Ecclesiastical Record*, 3rd series, vol. 9 (July 1888), pp. 606–618.

Flanagan, Donal, 'Some Theological Implications of Evolution', *The Irish Theological Quarterly*, vol. 33, no. 3 (July 1966), pp. 265–270.

Fleischmann, Ruth, *Catholic Nationalism in the Irish Revival: A Study of Canon Sheehan, 1852–1913* (London: Macmillan Press, 1997).

Fleming, George F., 'The Case of Ireland against the Science and Art Department', *The Irish Ecclesiastical Record*, 4th series, vol. 15 (February 1904), pp. 128–141.

Foster, John Wilson, 'Natural Science and Irish Culture', *Éire-Ireland*, vol. 26, no. 2 (1991), pp. 92–103.

Foster, John Wilson, *Recoveries: Neglected Episodes in Irish Cultural History, 1860–1912* (Dublin: University College Dublin Press, 2002).

Foster, John Wilson, and Helena C.G. Chesney (eds), *Nature in Ireland: A Scientific and Cultural History* (Dublin: The Lilliput Press, 1997).

Frederick, Sister Mary, *Religion and Evolution since 1859: Some Effects of the Theory of Evolution on the Philosophy of Religion* (Chicago: Loyola University Press, 1935).

Friedman, Richard Elliott, *The Disappearance of God: A Divine Mystery* (Boston: Little, Brown & Co., 1995).

Fuller, Louise, *Irish Catholicism since 1950: The Undoing of a Culture* (Dublin: Gill & Macmillan, 2002).

Fullerton, R., 'The Evolution of Mind', parts I and II, *The Irish Ecclesiastical Record*, 4th series, vol. 26 (1909), pp. 261–275, 383–396.

Fullerton, R., 'Basis of Monism – Evolution', *The Irish Ecclesiastical Record*, 4th series, vol. 28 (1910), pp. 161–174.

Gallagher, Michael Paul, 'Secularization and New Forms of Faith', *Studies*, vol. 74 (Spring 1985), pp. 12–25.

Gannon, Patrick J., 'The Conflict between Religion and Science', *Studies*, vol. 15 (September 1926), pp. 464–479

Gannon, Patrick J., 'Evolution and Catholic Doctrine', *Studies*, vol. 17 (June 1928), pp. 271–281.

Garvin, Tom, 'Priests and Patriots: Irish Separatism and Fear of the Modern, 1890–1914', *Irish Historical Studies*, vol. 25, no. 97 (May 1986), pp. 67–81.

Garvin, Tom, *Preventing the Future: Why Was Ireland So Poor for So Long?* (Dublin: Gill & Macmillan, 2004).

Gaynor, E., 'Sir Robert S. Ball on Evolution', *The Irish Ecclesiastical Record*, 4th series, vol. 1 (1897), pp. 243–260.

Gaynor, E., 'Modern Scientific Materialism: A Necessity of Thought', *The Irish Ecclesiastical Record*, 4th series, vol. 3 (March 1898), pp. 193–215.

Gaynor, E., 'Darwinism: Sensation', *The Irish Ecclesiastical Record*, 4th series, vol. 6 (1899), pp. 147–166.

Gaughan, J. Anthony, *Alfred O'Rahilly I: Academic* (Dublin: Kingdom Books, 1986).

Gaughan, J. Anthony, *Alfred O'Rahilly III: Controversialist, Part II: Catholic Apologist* (Dublin: Kingdom Books, 1993).

Gelderd, Charles, 'The Regeneration of Lost Parts in Animals and the Theory of Matter and Form', *The Irish Ecclesiastical Record*, 4th series, vol. 25 (1909), pp. 50–64.

Gelderd, Charles, 'Modern Ideas on Darwinism', *The Irish Ecclesiastical Record*, 4th series, vol. 32 (July 1912), pp. 1–9.

Gerard, John, 'The Mainspring of the Universe', *The Irish Monthly*, vol. 16 (June 1888), pp. 325–331.

Gill, H.V., 'On the Frontier of Physical Science', *The Irish Ecclesiastical Record*, 4th series, vol. 26 (November 1909), pp. 449–460.

Gill, H.V., 'Is the "Ether" an Hypothesis', *The Irish Ecclesiastical Record*, 4th series, vol. 28 (December 1910), pp. 561–572.

Gill, H.V., 'The Need of Scientific Training in Ireland', *The Irish Ecclesiastical Record*, 5th series, vol. 14 (1919), pp. 115–123.

Gill, H.V., 'The Atom in Recent Science', *The Irish Ecclesiastical Record*, 5th series, vol. 17 (May 1921), pp. 485–495.

Gill, H.V., 'A Puzzle of Modern Science', *The Irish Ecclesiastical Record*, 5th series, vol. 18 (December 1921), pp. 593–601.

Gill, H.V., 'Catholics and Evolution Theories', *The Irish Ecclesiastical Record*, 5th series, vol. 19 (June 1922), pp. 614–624.

Gill, H.V., 'Physics and Free Will', *The Irish Ecclesiastical Record*, 5th series, vol. 40 (August 1932), pp. 144–155.

Gill, H.V., 'Science in our Schools', *Studies*, vol. 21 (September 1932), pp. 461–470.

Gill, H.V., 'Logic and Modern Science', *The Irish Ecclesiastical Record*, 5th series, vol. 44 (August 1934), pp. 113–122.

Gill, H.V., 'The Popes and Natural Science', *The Irish Ecclesiastical Record*, 5th series, vol. 50 (July 1937), pp. 15–24.

Gill, H.V., 'The Constitution of Matter', I. *The Irish Ecclesiastical Record*, 5th series, vol. 48 (July 1936), pp. 12–22.

Gill, H.V., 'The Constitution of Matter', II. *The Irish Ecclesiastical Record*, 5th series, vol. 48 (August 1936), pp. 161–169.

Gill, Henry V., 'The Space We Live In', *Studies*, vol. 20 (March 1931), pp. 67–79.

Gill, Henry V., 'Entropy, Life and Evolution', *Studies*, vol. 22 (March 1933), pp. 129–138.

Gill, Henry V., 'Facts and Fancies: Physics and Philosophy', *Studies*, vol. 32 (March 1943), pp. 91–100.

Gill, Henry V., *Fact and Fiction in Modern Science*, 2nd ed. (Dublin: M.H. Gill & Son, 1943).

Gleeson, Frances, 'Did the Tiger's roar silence the Church's voice?' *Irish Examiner* (20 March 2008), 'Religion and Ireland' supplement, p. 3.

Gliboff, Sander, 'Evolution, Revolution, and Reform in Vienna: Franz Unger's Ideas on Descent and Their Post-1848 Reception', *Journal of the History of Biology*, vol. 31 (1998), pp. 179–209.

Glick, Thomas F. (ed.), *The Comparative Reception of Darwinism* (Chicago: The University of Chicago Press, 1988).

Gordin, Michael D., 'Points Critical: Russia, Ireland, and Science at the Boundary', *Osiris*, vol. 24 (2009), pp. 99–119.

Greeley, Andrew M., 'Are the Irish Really Losing the Faith?' *Doctrine and Life*, vol. 44, no. 3 (March 1994), pp. 132–142.

Gregersen, Niels Henrik, and Ulf Görman (eds), *Design and Disorder: Perspectives from Science and Theology* (London: T&T Clark, 2002).

Grenz, Stanley J., and Roger E. Olson, *20th-Century Theology: God and the World in a Transitional Age* (Milton Keynes, UK: Paternoster Press, 1992).

Gruber, Jacob W., *A Conscience in Conflict: The Life of St. George Jackson Mivart* (Westport, Connecticut: Greenwood Press, 1960).

H., J.F., review of Leonard Huxley (ed.), *The Life and Letters of Thomas Henry Huxley*, in *The Irish Ecclesiastical Record*, 4th series, vol. 8 (July–December 1900), pp. 570–572.

H., M.F., 'Is Our Earth Alone Inhabited?' *The Irish Ecclesiastical Record*, 4th series, vol. 13 (1903), pp. 167–169.

H., W., 'What the Jesuits Have Done for Science and Literature', *The Irish Ecclesiastical Record*, vol. 7 (August 1871), pp. 511–518.

Haffner, Paul (ed.), *Discourses of the Popes from Pius XI to John Paul II to the Pontifical Academy of Sciences, 1936–1986* (Vatican City: Pontificia Academia Scientiarum, 1986).

Hamell, Patrick J., '"Humani Generis": Its Significance and Teaching', *The Irish Ecclesiastical Record*, 5th series, vol. 75 (April 1951), pp. 289–303.

Hamilton, Malcolm B., *The Sociology of Religion: Theoretical and Comparative Perspectives* (London: Routledge, 1995).

Hardiman, T.P., and E.P. O'Neill, 'The Role of Science and Innovation', in Fionán Ó Muircheartaigh (ed.), *Ireland in the Coming Times: Essays to Celebrate T.K. Whitaker's 80 Years* (Dublin: Institute of Public Administration, 1997), pp. 253–284.

Harrison, Peter (ed.), *The Cambridge Companion to Science and Religion* (Cambridge: Cambridge University Press, 2010).

Hart, John, *What Are They Saying About Environmental Theology?* (New York: Paulist Press, 2004).

Harty, John M., 'The Church and Science', *The Irish Ecclesiastical Record*, 4th series, vol. 7 (1900), pp. 158–171.

Harty, John M., 'Galileo and the Roman Congregations', *The Irish Ecclesiastical Record*, 4th series, vol. 7 (1900), pp. 289–311.

Hauber, W.A., 'Evolution and Catholic Thought', *The Ecclesiastical Review*, vol. 106, no. 3 (March 1942), pp. 161–177.

Hawking, Stephen, *A Brief History of Time: From the Big Bang to Black Holes* (Toronto: Bantam Books, 1995).

Healy, Yvonne, 'Colleges could lose cutting edge if institutes approved', *The Irish Times* (15 February 2000), Education & Living supplement, p. 3.

Heelan, Patrick A., 'The Closed View of Classical Physics: Laplacian Determinism', *Studies*, vol. 51 (Autumn 1962), pp. 376–387.

Heelan, Patrick A., 'The Way of Modern Physics', *Studies*, vol. 51 (Winter 1962), pp. 494–507.

Hegarty, Kevin, 'Is Irish Catholicism Dying?' *The Furrow*, vol. 36, no. 1 (January 1985), pp. 44–47.

Helmstadter, Richard J., and Bernard Lightman (eds), *Victorian Faith in Crisis: Essays on Continuity and Change in Nineteenth-Century Religious Belief* (Stanford, California: Stanford University Press, 1990).

Heseltine, G.C., 'Science and Pseudo-Science', *The Irish Monthly*, vol. 60 (December 1932), pp. 756–766.

Hickey, M.P., 'The Old Order Changeth', *Record of the Maynooth Union* (1897–1898), pp. 15–24.

Higgins, Michael D., 'Science and Society – Principles of Error?' *Technology Ireland* (April 1990), p. 21.

Hoare, F.R., 'Physical Determinism and Free Will', *The Irish Ecclesiastical Record*, 5th series, vol. 43 (January 1934), pp. 27–35.

Holmes, Andrew R., 'Presbyterians and Science in the North of Ireland before 1874', *The British Journal for the History of Science*, vol. 41, no. 151 (December 2008), pp. 541–565.

Holmes, J. Derek, 'Newman and Mivart – Two Attitudes to a Nineteenth-Century Problem', *Clergy Review*, new series, vol. 50, no. 11 (November 1965), pp. 852–867.

Houghton, John, *The Search for God: Can Science Help?* (Oxford: Lion Publishing, 1995).

Howard, Michael, and W. Roger Louis (eds), *The Oxford History of the Twentieth Century* (Oxford: Oxford University Press, 1998).

Inglis, Tom, *Moral Monopoly: The Rise and Fall of the Catholic Church in Modern Ireland*, 2nd ed. (Dublin: University College Dublin Press, 1998).

Inglis, Tom, 'A Religious Frenzy?' in Michael Peillon and Eamonn Slater (eds), *Encounters with Modern Ireland: A Sociological Chronicle, 1995–1996* (Dublin: Institute of Public Administration, 1998), pp. 73–79.

Inglis, Tom, 'Religion, Identity, State and Society', in Joe Cleary and Claire Connolly (eds), *The Cambridge Companion to Modern Irish Culture* (Cambridge: Cambridge University Press, 2005), pp. 59–77.

Ingram, Richard E., 'A New Cosmology', *Studies*, vol. 39 (December 1950), pp. 445–452.

Ingram, Richard E., review of E.L. Mascall, *Christian Theology and Natural Science, Some Questions on Their Relations*, in *Studies*, vol. 45 (Winter 1956), pp. 473–475.

J., S., 'State and Technical Education in France', *The Irish Monthly*, vol. 56 (May 1928), pp. 233–237.

Jarrell, Richard A., 'The Department of Science and Art and Control of Irish Science, 1853–1905', *Irish Historical Studies*, vol. 23, no. 92 (November 1983), pp. 330–347.

Jedin, Hubert, and John Dolan (eds), *History of the Church: The Church in the Age of Liberalism* (London: Burns & Oates, 1981), vol. 8.

Jensen, J. Vernon, 'The X Club: Fraternity of Victorian Scientists', *The British Journal for the History of Science*, vol. 5, no. 17 (1970), pp. 63–72.

Jesuit Centre for Faith and Justice, 'Unemployment and Technology', *Doctrine and Life*, vol. 36, no. 4 (April 1986), pp. 188–194.

Johnson, H.J.T., 'Leo XIII, Cardinal Newman and the Inerrancy of Scripture', *The Downside Review*, vol. 69 (1951), pp. 411–427.

Johnston, George Sim, 'The Galileo Affair', *Position Paper 250* (October 1994), pp. 315–326.

Joll, James, *Europe Since 1870: An International History*, 4th ed. (London: Penguin Books, 1990).

Jones, Greta, 'Eugenics in Ireland: the Belfast Eugenics Society, 1911–15', *Irish Historical Studies*, vol. 28, no. 109 (May 1992), pp. 81–95.

Jones, Greta, 'Catholicism, Nationalism and Science', *The Irish Review*, no. 20 (Spring 1997), pp. 47–61.

Jones, Greta, 'Contested Territories: Alfred Cort Haddon, Progressive Evolutionism and Ireland', *History of European Ideas*, vol. 24, no. 3 (1998), pp. 195–211.

Jones, Greta, 'Scientists against Home Rule', in D. George Boyce and Alan O'Day (eds), *Defenders of the Union: A Survey of British and Irish Unionism since 1801* (London: Routledge, 2001), pp. 188–208.

Jones, Roisin, and Martin Steer (eds), *Darwin, Praeger and the Clare Island Surveys* (Dublin: Royal Irish Academy, 2009).

Joy, John C., 'Notes on Current Educational Topics', *The Irish Monthly*, vol. 58 (November 1930), pp. 547–552.

Judge, T.E., 'The Spirit of Modern Science', *The Irish Ecclesiastical Record*, 3rd series, vol. 13 (1892), pp. 1081–1095.

Kearney, Richard, *Postnationalist Ireland: Politics, Culture, Philosophy* (London: Routledge, 1997).

Kelham, Brian B., 'The Royal College of Science for Ireland (1867–1926)', *Studies*, vol. 56 (Autumn 1967), pp. 297–309.

Kelly, Aodhán, 'The Darwin Debate in Dublin, 1859–1908' (M. Litt. thesis, National University of Ireland, Maynooth, 2009).

Kelly, James, 'The Idea of Life: Aristotle's Theory v. Modern Science', *The Irish Ecclesiastical Record*, 4th series, vol. 14 (October 1903), pp. 317–324.

Kennedy, David, 'Dr. D.B. Reid and the Teaching of Chemistry', *Studies*, vol. 31 (September 1942), pp. 341–350.

Kennedy, Henry, 'The Winter Dairying Problem', *Studies*, vol. 19 (December 1930), pp. 537–548.

Kennedy, Henry, 'Winter Fodder and a New Discovery', *Studies*, vol. 20 (September 1931), pp. 389–394.

Kennedy, Henry, 'Some Problems of Our Agriculture', *Studies*, vol. 27 (June 1938), pp. 240–246.

Kenny, Robert, 'From the Curse of Ham to the Curse of Nature: The Influence of Natural Selection on the Debate on Human Unity before the Publication of *The Descent of Man*', *The British Journal for the History of Science*, vol. 40, part 3 (September 2007), pp. 367–388.

Keogh, Dermot, *Twentieth-Century Ireland: Nation and State* (Dublin: Gill & Macmillan, 1994).

Keogh, Ann, and Dermot Keogh, *Bertram Windle: The Honan Bequest and the Modernisation of University College Cork, 1904–1919* (Cork: Cork University Press, 2010).

Kevles, Daniel J., 'From Eugenics to Patents: Genetics, Law, and Human Rights', *Annals of Human Genetics*, vol. 75 (2011), pp. 326–333.

Kilcoyne, Colm, 'Church to blame for the shift from religion', *Sunday Tribune* (22 February 1998), p. 19

Kilmister, C.W., *Schrödinger: Centenary Celebration of a Polymath* (Cambridge: Cambridge University Press, 1987).

King, Ursula, *Spirit of Fire: The Life and Vision of Teilhard de Chardin* (Maryknoll, New York: Orbis Books, 1996).

Kuhn, Thomas S., *The Structure of Scientific Revolutions*, 2nd ed. (Chicago: The University of Chicago Press, 1970).

Lanczos, Cornelius, 'Modern Physics in Perspective', *Studies*, vol. 52 (Autumn 1963), pp. 283–293.

Lanczos, Cornelius, 'The Inspired Guess in the History of Physics', *Studies*, vol. 53 (Winter 1964), pp. 398–412.

Lane, Dermot, 'Theology and Science in Dialogue', *The Irish Theological Quarterly*, new series, 52 (1986), pp. 31–53.

Lane, Dermot A. (ed.), *Religion and Culture in Dialogue: A Challenge for the Next Millennium* (Dublin: The Columba Press, 1993).

Lane, Dermot A., 'The Future of Creation', *Milltown Studies*, vol. 34 (Autumn 1994), pp. 94–122.

Lane, Dermot A. (ed.), *New Century, New Society: Christian Perspectives* (Dublin: The Columba Press, 1999).

Langford, Jerome J., *Galileo, Science and the Church*, 3rd ed. (N.p.: Ann Arbor Paperbacks: The University of Michigan Press, 1992).

Lanigan, Stephen M., 'Mr. Stephen M. Lanigan's "Science and Scepticism": A Few Words of Explanation by the Author', *The Irish Monthly*, vol. 8 (September 1880), pp. 506–509.

Larkin, Emmet, *The Historical Dimensions of Irish Catholicism* (Washington, DC: The Catholic University of America Press; Dublin: Four Courts Press, 1984).

Latourette, Kenneth Scott, *Christianity in a Revolutionary Age: A History of Christianity in the Nineteenth and Twentieth Centuries*. Vol. 1 of *The Nineteenth Century in Europe: Background and the Roman Catholic Phase* (London: Eyre & Spottiswoode, 1959).

Leaney, Enda, 'Missionaries of Science: provincial lectures in nineteenth-century Ireland', *Irish Historical Studies*, vol. 34, no. 135 (May 2005), pp. 266–288.

Leaney, Enda, 'Science and Conflict in Nineteenth-Century Ireland', in Neil Garnham and Keith Jeffery (eds), *Culture, Place and Identity* (Dublin: University College Dublin Press, 2005), pp. 66–67.

Leaney, Enda, 'Phrenology in Nineteenth-Century Ireland', *New Hibernia Review*, vol. 10, no. 3 (Autumn 2006), pp. 24–42.

Lee, J.J., *Ireland, 1912–1985: Politics and Society* (Cambridge: Cambridge University Press, 1989).

Lee, Joseph, *The Modernisation of Irish Society, 1848–1918* (Dublin: Gill & Macmillan, 1989).

Lee, Stephen J., *The European Dictatorships, 1918–1945* (London: Methuen, 1987).

Lennon, F., 'The Future of the Earth (Viewed from a Physicist's Standpoint)', *The Irish Ecclesiastical Record*, 3rd series, vol. 9 (April 1888), pp. 308–318.

Lennon, F., review of Gerald Molloy's *Gleanings in Science* (London: Macmillan, 1888), in *The Irish Ecclesiastical Record*, 3rd series, vol. 10 (June 1889), pp. 61–69.

Lightman, Bernard, *The Origins of Agnosticism: Victorian Unbelief and the Limits of Knowledge* (Baltimore: The Johns Hopkins University Press, 1987).

Lightman, Bernard, 'Huxley and Scientific Agnosticism: The Strange History of a Failed Rhetorical Strategy', *The British Journal for the History of Science*, vol. 35 (2002), pp. 271–289.

Lindberg, David C., and Ronald L. Numbers (eds), *God and Nature: Historical Essays on the Encounter between Christianity and Science* (Berkeley: University of California Press, 1986).

Lindberg, David C., and Ronald L. Numbers (eds), *When Science and Christianity Meet* (Chicago: The University of Chicago Press, 2003).

Little, Arthur, 'The Differential of Humpty Dumpty or Alice and the Scientists', *Studies*, vol. 34 (September 1945), pp. 369–376.

Livingstone, David N., *Darwin's Forgotten Defenders: The Encounter between Evangelical Theology and Evolutionary Thought* (Grand Rapids, Michigan: William B. Eerdmans; Edinburgh: Scottish Academic Press, 1987).

Livingstone, David N., *Adam's Ancestors: Race, Religion and the Politics of Human Origins* (Baltimore: The Johns Hopkins University Press, 2008).

Lloyd, J.A., 'Is There Life on Other Worlds?' *Studies*, vol. 16 (December 1927), pp. 653–670.

Lockwood, Robert P., 'The Galileo Affair', *Position Paper 324* (December 2000), pp. 339–342; republished with minor amendments in *Position Paper 329* (May 2001), pp. 159–162.

Lynch, Tim, 'Secularisation in Ireland', *The Furrow*, vol. 36, no. 8 (August 1985), pp. 506–510.

Lyons, F.S.L., *Ireland since the Famine* (London: Fontana Press, 1985).

Lysaght, John Gerard, 'Robert Lloyd Praeger and the Culture of Science in Ireland, 1865–1953' (PhD thesis, St Patrick's College, Maynooth, 1996).

Lysaght, Sean, 'Themes in the Irish History of Science', *The Irish Review*, vol. 19 (Spring-Summer 1996), pp. 87–97.

MacCaffrey, James, 'The Papal Encyclical on Modernism', *The Irish Ecclesiastical Record*, 4th series, vol. 22 (December 1907), pp. 561–575.

MacConaill, M.A., review of Anthony Standen, *Science Is a Sacred Cow*, in *Studies*, vol. 42 (March 1953), pp. 105–106

MacConaill, M.A., 'The Evolutionary Dilemma', *The Irish Theological Quarterly*, vol. 20, no. 4 (October 1953), pp. 410–415.

MacConaill, M.A., 'Piltdown and Peking: An Essay on Evidence', *The Irish Ecclesiastical Record*, 5th series, vol. 102 (1964), pp. 367–374.

MacConaill, Michael A., 'Evolution and Enthusiasm', *Studies*, vol. 41 (September-December 1952), pp. 355–361.

MacKenzie, Norman, and Jeanne MacKenzie, *The Time Traveller: The Life of H.G. Wells* (London: Weidenfeld & Nicolson, 1973).

Mackey, J.P., 'Original Sin and Polygenism: The State of the Question', *The Irish Theological Quarterly*, vol. 34, no. 2 (April 1967), pp. 99–114.

Mackey, James P., 'Theology, Science and the Imagination: Exploring the Issues', *The Irish Theological Quarterly*, new series, vol. 52 (1986), pp. 1–18.

MacLaughlin, P.J., 'Centenary of the Discovery of Quaternions', *Studies*, vol. 32 (December 1943), pp. 441–456.

MacLaughlin, P.J., 'Philosophy and Science: The Place of Science in Human Affairs', *Studies*, vol. 39 (March 1950), pp. 100–102.

MacLeod, Roy M., 'The X-Club: A Social Network of Science in Late-Victorian England', *Notes and Records of the Royal Society of London*, vol. 24, no. 2 (April 1970), pp. 305–322.

Maguire, E., 'Anglicanism versus Modernism', *The Irish Theological Quarterly*, vol. 12 (April 1917), pp. 124–145.

Maguire, E., 'Facts and Theories of Life I: Facts Historical and Biological', *The Irish Theological Quarterly*, vol. 12 (October 1917), pp. 330–341.

Maguire, E., 'Facts and Theories of Life II: The Development Hypothesis', *The Irish Theological Quarterly*, vol. 13 (1918), pp. 201–214.

Maguire, E., 'Facts and Theories of Life III: Vitalism', *The Irish Theological Quarterly*, vol. 14 (1919), pp. 110–125.

Malcolm, Elizabeth, and Greta Jones (eds), *Medicine, Disease and the State in Ireland, 1650–1940* (Cork: Cork University Press, 1999).

Mangan, Céline, 'Creation Theology in the Bible', *Doctrine and Life*, vol. 45, no. 2 (February 1995), pp. 164–170.

Marini-Bettòlo, G.B., *Outlines of the Activity of the Pontifical Academy of Sciences, 1936–1986* (Vatican City: Pontificia Academia Scientiarum, 1986).

Mathew, David, *Lord Acton and His Times* (London: Eyre & Spottiswoode, 1968).

McBride, Lawrence W. (ed.), *Reading Irish Histories: Texts, Contexts, and Memory in Modern Ireland* (Dublin: Four Courts Press, 2003).

McBrien, Richard P., *Lives of the Popes: The Pontiffs from St. Peter to John Paul II* (New York: Harper Collins, 2000).

McCaffrey, Lawrence J., *The Irish Catholic Diaspora in America* (Washington, DC: The Catholic University of America Press, 1997).

McCann, Joseph (ed.), *Religion and Science: Education, Ethics and Public Policy* (Drumcondra, Dublin: St Patrick's College, 2003).

McCarthy, Fachtna, and Joseph McCann, *Religion and Science* (Dublin: Veritas, 2003).

McCarthy, Michael J.F., *Priests and People in Ireland* (Dublin: Hodges and Figgis & Co.; London: Simpkin, Marshall, Hamilton, Kent & Co., 1903).

McCartney, Donal, *The Dawning of Democracy: Ireland, 1800–1870* (Dublin: Helicon, 1987).

McCloskey, C. John, '12 Step TV Recovery Program', *Position Paper 255* (March 1995), pp. 97–99.

McConnell, David, 'Science and Post-Christian Ireland', *The Irish Review*, vol. 27 (Summer 2001), pp. 40–47.

McDonagh, Enda, 'A Post-Christian Ireland? An Introduction', *The Irish Review*, vol. 27 (Summer 2001), pp. 1–6.

McDonald, W., 'God: Known or Unknown?' *The Irish Ecclesiastical Record*, 4th series, vol.11 (January–June 1902), pp. 328–339.

McDonald, W., 'Some Tendencies of Modern Apologetics: Proof of Theism', *The Irish Theological Quarterly*, vol. 1 (January 1907), pp. 1–14.

McDonald, Walter, 'The Kinetic Theory of Activity', *The Irish Ecclesiastical Record*, 4th series, vol. 2 (October 1897), pp. 289–308.

McDonald, Walter, 'A Maynooth Union, as a Social and Academic Memorial of the Centenary', *Record of the Maynooth Union* (1895–1896), pp. 11–21.

McDonald, Walter, *Some Ethical Questions of Peace and War with Special Reference to Ireland*, introduction by Tom Garvin (London: Burns, Oates & Washbourne, 1920; republished, Dublin: University College Dublin Press, 1998).

McDonald, Walter, *Reminiscences of a Maynooth Professor*, edited with a memoir by Denis Gwynn (London: Jonathan Cape, 1925; republished, Cork: Mercier, 1967).

McDowell, R.B., and D.A. Webb, *Trinity College Dublin, 1592–1952: An Academic History* (Dublin: Trinity College Dublin Press in association with Environmental Publications, 2004).

McGarrigle, Francis J., 'Could the World Have Had No Beginning?' *The Irish Ecclesiastical Record*, 5th series, vol. 41 (January 1933), pp. 1–12.

McGrath, Alister E., *Christian Theology: An Introduction*, 2nd ed. (Cambridge, Massachusetts: Blackwell Publishers, 1997).

McGrath, Alister E., *Science and Religion: An Introduction* (Oxford: Blackwell Publishers, 1999).

McGrath, Fergal, *Newman's University: Idea and Reality* (Dublin: Browne & Nolan, 1951).

McGrath, P.J., 'Believing in God', *The Irish Theological Quarterly*, vol. 42, no. 2 (April 1975), pp. 87–96.

McGuinness, Philip, 'The Hue and Cry of Heresy: John Toland, Isaac Newton & the Social Context of Scientists', *History Ireland*, vol. 4, no. 4 (Winter 1996), pp. 22–27.

McLaughlin, P.J., 'Fundamentals of Physical Science', *Studies*, vol. 27 (1938), pp. 656–666.

McLaughlin, P.J., 'Science, Philosophy and Religion', *The Irish Ecclesiastical Record*, 5th series, vol. 63 (January 1944), pp. 1–6.

McLaughlin, P.J., 'Modern Science and the Five Ways', *The Irish Ecclesiastical Record*, 5th series, vol. 69 (April 1947), pp. 273–289.

McLaughlin, P.J., *The Church and Modern Science* (Dublin: Clonmore & Reynolds; London: Burns, Oates & Washbourne, 1957).

McLaughlin, Patrick J., 'A Century of Science in the IER: Monsignor Molloy and Father Gill', *The Irish Ecclesiastical Record*, 5th series, vol. 102 (1964), pp. 251–261.

McLeod, Hugh, *Religion and the People of Western Europe, 1789–1970* (Oxford: Oxford University Press, 1981).

McLeod, Hugh, *Secularisation in Western Europe, 1848–1914* (Basingstoke, UK: Macmillan Press; New York: St Martin's Press, 2000).

McMillan, Norman (ed.), *Prometheus's Fire: A History of Scientific and Technological Education in Ireland* (n.p.: Tyndall Publications, 2000).

McMullin, Ernan, 'Natural Science and Christian Thought', *The Irish Theological Quarterly*, vol. 26, no. 1 (January 1959), pp. 1–22.

McMullin, Ernan, review of W.J. Ong (ed.), *Darwin's Vision and Christian Perspectives* in *The Irish Theological Quarterly*, vol. 28 (April 1961), pp. 161–164.

McMullin, Ernan (ed.), *The Church and Galileo* (Notre Dame, Indiana: University of Notre Dame Press, 2005).

McOuat, Gordon, and Mary P. Winsor, 'J.B.S. Haldane's Darwinism in its religious context', *The British Journal for the History of Science*, vol. 28, no. 97 (June 1995), pp. 227–231.

McRedmond, Louis, 'A Brawling Church: The Malaise of Irish Catholicism', *Doctrine and Life*, vol. 34, no. 7 (September 1985), pp. 377–383

McRedmond, Louis, *Thrown among Strangers: John Henry Newman in Ireland* (Dublin: Veritas, 1990).

McRedmond, Louis, 'Could Newman Have Succeeded in Ireland?' in *Proceedings of the John Henry Newman Centenary Symposium* (Cork: Department of Education, University College Cork, November 1990), pp. 1–17.

McRedmond, Louis, *To the Greater Glory: A History of the Irish Jesuits* (Dublin: Gill & Macmillan, 1991).

McSweeney, Bill, *Roman Catholicism: The Search for Relevance* (Oxford: Basil Blackwell, 1980).

Meehan, John, 'Haeckel and the Existence of God', *The Irish Ecclesiastical Record*, 4th series, vol. 14 (July–December 1903), pp. 134–158.

Messenger, Ernest C., *Evolution and Theology: The Problem of Man's Origin* (London: Burns, Oates & Washbourne, 1931).

Miller, David M., 'Religious History', in Laurence M. Geary and Margaret Kelleher (eds), *Nineteenth-Century Ireland: A Guide to Recent Research* (Dublin: University College Dublin Press, 2005), pp. 61–76.

Mitchell, Gerard, '"Humani Generis" and Theology', *The Irish Theological Quarterly*, vol. 19, no. 1 (January 1952), pp. 1–16.

Mitchell, Gerard, 'Evolution and Polygenism', *The Irish Theological Quarterly*, vol. 19, no. 3 (July 1952), pp. 279–285.

Mivart, St George, *The Genesis of Species*, 2nd ed. (London: Macmillan, 1871).

Mivart, St George, 'Modern Catholics and Scientific Freedom', *The Nineteenth Century*, vol. 18 (July 1885), pp. 30–47.

Mivart, St. George, 'The Catholic Church and Biblical Criticism', *The Nineteenth Century*, vol. 22 (July 1887), pp. 31–51.

Mivart, St George, 'Letter from Dr. Mivart on the Bishop of Newport's Article in Our Last Number', *The Dublin Review*, 3rd series, vol. 19 (January–April 1888), pp. 180–187.

Mivart, St George, 'Roman Congregations and Modern Thought', *The North American Review*, vol. 170 (1900), pp. 562–574.

Mivart, St. George, 'Some Recent Catholic Apologists', *Fortnightly Review*, vol. 67 (1900), pp. 24–44.

Mollan, Charles, William Davis and Brendan Finucane (eds), *Irish Innovators in Science and Technology* (Dublin: Royal Irish Academy, 2002).

Mollan, Charles (ed.), *Science and Ireland – Value for Society* (Dublin: The Royal Dublin Society, 2005).

Molloy, G., 'On the Teaching of Experimental and Practical Science in the Secondary Schools of Ireland', *The Irish Ecclesiastical Record*, 4th series, vol. 16 (October 1904), pp. 289–297.

Molloy, Gerald, 'Geology and Revelation', parts 1–9, *The Irish Ecclesiastical Record*, vol. 3 (1867), pp. 121–134, 241–261, 358–374, 448–467; vol. 4 (1868), pp. 49–66, 169–187, 326–341, 373–385; vol. 5 (1869), pp. 49–73, 193–223.

Molloy, Gerald, *Geology and Revelation: or, The Ancient History of the Earth Considered in the Light of Geological Facts and Revealed Religion* (London: Longmans, Green, Reader & Dyer; Dublin: McGlashan & Gill, and W.B. Kelly, 1870).

Molloy, Gerald, 'On the Philosophy of a Candle', *The Irish Monthly*, vol. 4 (1876), pp. 529–538.

Molony, Jeremiah, 'The Catholic Education Question', *The Irish Ecclesiastical Record*, new series, vol. 8 (August 1872), pp. 489–497.

Monod, Jacques, *Chance and Necessity: An Essay on the Natural Philosophy of Modern Biology* (New York: Vintage Books, 1972).

Moody, T.W., 'The Irish University Question of the Nineteenth Century', *History*, vol. 43, no. 148 (June 1958), pp. 90–109.

Mooney, Canice, 'The Dublin Institute for Advanced Studies', *The Irish Ecclesiastical Record*, 5th series, vol. 64 (1944), pp. 187–190.

Moore, James R., *The Post-Darwinian Controversies: A Study of the Protestant Struggle to Come to Terms with Darwin in Great Britain and America, 1870–1900* (Cambridge: Cambridge University Press, 1979).

Moore, John J., review of William H. Kane, John D. Corcoran, Benedict M. Ashley and Raymond J. Nogar, *Science in Synthesis: A Dialectical Approach to the Integration of the Physical and Natural Sciences*, in *Studies*, vol. 44 (Summer 1955), pp. 247–249.

Moore, John J., 'The Darwin Centenary and the Theologian: A Survey of Modern Approaches to Evolution', *The Irish Theological Quarterly*, vol. 26, no. 2 (April 1959), pp. 117–130.

Moore, W. Leo, 'Insect Life and the Argument from Design', *The Irish Theological Quarterly*, vol. 9 (1914), pp. 133–144.

Moore, Walter, *Shrödinger: Life and Thought* (Cambridge: Cambridge University Press, 1992).

Moran, W., 'An Echo of the Modernist Crisis', *The Irish Ecclesiastical Record*, 5th series, vol. 37 (1931), pp. 249–263.

Morgan, Gilbert T., 'Chemistry, the War, and Ireland', *Studies*, vol. 5 (March 1916), pp. 32–43.

Morrison, John L., 'William Seton – a Catholic Darwinist', *The Review of Politics*, vol. 21, no. 3 (1959), pp. 566–584.

Morrissey, Thomas J., *William J. Walsh, Archbishop of Dublin, 1841–1921: No Uncertain Voice* (Dublin: Four Courts Press, 2000).

Mulvihill, Mary, *Ingenious Ireland: A County-by-County Exploration of Irish Mysteries and Marvels* (Dublin: Townhouse, 2002).

Muir, Hazel (ed.), *Larousse Dictionary of Scientists* (New York: Larousse, 1994).

Murphy, Francis Xavier, *The Papacy Today* (London: Weidenfeld & Nicolson, 1981).

Murphy, J., 'Darwinism', *The Irish Ecclesiastical Record*, 3rd series, vol. 5 (1884), pp. 584–594.

Murphy, J., 'Evolution and Faith', *The Irish Ecclesiastical Record*, 3rd series, vol. 5 (1884), pp. 756–767.

Murphy, J., 'Faith and Evolution', *The Irish Ecclesiastical Record*, 3rd series, vol. 6 (1885), pp. 481–496, 723–736.

Murphy, J., 'The Case of Galileo', *The Nineteenth Century*, vol. 19 (May 1886), pp. 722–739.

Murphy, James (ed.), *Evangelicals and Catholics in Nineteenth-Century Ireland* (Dublin: Four Courts Press, 2005).

Murphy, John A., *The College: A History of Queen's/University College Cork* (Cork: Cork University Press, 1995).

Neswald, Elizabeth, 'Science, Sociability and the Improvement of Ireland: The

Galway Mechanics' Institute, 1826–51', *The British Journal for the History of Science*, vol. 39, no. 143 (December 2006), pp. 503–534.

Neuhaus, Richard John (ed.), *Biblical Interpretation in Crisis: The Ratzinger Conference on Bible and Church* (Grand Rapids, Michigan: William B. Eerdmans, 1989).

Newman, John Henry, *The Idea of a University*, edited with introduction and notes by I.T. Ker (London: Oxford University Press, 1976).

Nolan, Thomas J., 'Science and Manufacture', *Studies*, vol. 15 (June 1926), pp. 255–273

Norman, E.R., *Anti-Catholicism in Victorian England* (London: George Allen & Unwin, 1968).

Norman, Edward, *The English Catholic Church in the Nineteenth Century* (Oxford: Clarendon Press, 1984).

Numbers, Ronald L., and John Stenhouse (eds), *Disseminating Darwinism: The Role of Place, Race, Religion and Gender* (Cambridge: Cambridge University Press, 1999).

O'Brien, Jennifer, 'Irish Public Opinion and the Risorgimento, 1859–60', *Irish Historical Studies*, vol. 34, no. 135 (May 2005), pp. 289–305.

O'Brien, John A., *Evolution and Religion: A Study of the Bearing of Evolution upon the Philosophy of Religion* (New York: The Century Co., 1932).

O'Connell, D.J.K., 'Pius XII: Recollections and Impressions', *Studies*, vol. 47 (Winter 1958), pp. 361–368.

O'Connor, Robert, 'A Living from the Land', *Studies*, vol. 44 (Winter 1955), pp. 401–418.

O'Connor, Sean, 'Post Primary Education: Now and in the Future', *Studies*, vol. 57 (Autumn 1968), pp. 233–251.

O'Doherty, Caroline, 'Losing our religion', *Irish Examiner* (20 March 2008), p. 1.

O'Doherty, Caroline, 'Your opinions, your views', *Irish Examiner* (20 March 2008), 'Religion and Ireland' supplement, pp. 6–7.

O'Doherty, Caroline, 'A life of mistrust . . . and sacrifice', *Irish Examiner* (24 June 2011), pp. 10–11.

O'Doherty, E.F., 'Inspired Guess or Prepared Insight', *Studies*, vol. 53 (Winter 1964), pp. 413–419.

O'Donovan, James L., 'Experimental Research in University College, Dublin', *Studies*, vol. 10 (March 1921), pp. 109–122

Ó Drisceoil, Donal, *Censorship in Ireland, 1939–1945: Neutrality, Politics and Society* (Cork: Cork University Press, 1996).

O'Flynn, John A., '"Divino Afflante Spiritu": The New Encyclical on the Scriptures', *The Irish Ecclesiastical Record*, 5th series, vol. 63 (May 1944), pp. 289–300.

O'Flynn, John A., '"Humani Generis" and Sacred Scripture', *The Irish Theological Quarterly*, vol. 19, no. 1 (January 1952), pp. 17–24.

O'Flynn, John A., '"Humani Generis" and Sacred Scripture', *The Irish Theological Quarterly*, vol. 19, no. 2 (April 1952), pp. 163–174.

O'Hea, Leo, 'The Days of Genesis', *The Irish Ecclesiastical Record*, 5th series, vol. 9 (March 1917), pp. 196–205.

Oldroyd, David, and Ian Langham (eds), *The Wider Domain of Evolutionary Thought* (Dordrecht, Holland: D. Reidel Publishing Company, 1983).

O'Leary, Don, *Vocationalism and Social Catholicism in Twentieth-Century Ireland: The Search for a Christian Social Order* (Dublin: Irish Academic Press, 2000).

O'Leary, Don, *Roman Catholicism and Modern Science: A History* (New York: Continuum, 2006).

O'Leary, Don, 'From the *Origin* to *Humani Generis*: Ireland as a Case Study', in Louis Caruana (ed.), *Darwin and Catholicism: The Past and Present Dynamics of a Cultural Encounter* (London: T&T Clark International, 2009), pp. 13–26.

O'Mahony, J., 'On Some Difficulties Recently Raised Against the Argument from Design for the Existence of God', *The Irish Theological Quarterly*, vol. 3 (1908), pp. 293–306.

O'Mahony, T.P. 'Reform needed if Church is to survive', *Irish Examiner* (20 March 2008), 'Religion and Ireland' supplement, p. 8.

Ong, Walter J. (ed.), *Darwin's Vision and Christian Perspectives* (New York: Macmillan, 1960).

O'Rahilly, Alfred, *Electromagnetics: A Discussion of Fundamentals* (London: Longmans, Green & Co.; Cork: Cork University Press, 1938).

O'Rahilly, Alfred, *Religion and Science: Broadcast Talks* (Dublin: The Standard, 1948).

O'Reilly, J.M., 'The Threatening Metempsychosis of a Nation', *Record of the Maynooth Union* (1899–1900), pp. 48–59.

O'Riordan, M., 'Scientific Dogma v. Dogmatic Science', *The New Ireland Review*, vol. 9, no. 6 (August 1898), pp. 321–328.

O'Riordan, M., 'A Catholic Truth Society for Ireland', *Record of the Maynooth Union* (1898–1899), pp. 38–44.

O'Riordan, M., *Catholicity and Progress in Ireland*, 2nd ed. (London: Kegan Paul, Trench, Trübner & Co.; St Louis: B. Herder, 1906).

O'Sullivan, Kevin, 'Attendance at Mass has fallen from 77% to 60% in past four years, survey on Catholic attitudes finds', *The Irish Times* (4 February 1998), p. 3.

Outram, Dorinda, 'Heavenly Bodies and Logical Minds', *Graph: Irish Literary Review*, no. 4 (Spring 1988), pp. 9–11.

Parry, J.P., *Democracy and Religion: Gladstone and the Liberal Party, 1867–1875* (Cambridge: Cambridge University Press, 1986).

Pašeta, Senia, *Before the Revolution: Nationalism, Social Change and Ireland's Catholic Élite, 1879–1922* (Cork: Cork University Press, 1999).

Pašeta, Senia, 'The Catholic Hierarchy and the Irish University Question, 1880–1908', *History*, vol. 85, no. 278 (April 2000), pp. 268–284.

Patten, Eve, 'Ireland's "Two Cultures" Debate: Victorian Science and the Literary Revival', *Irish University Review*, vol. 33, no. 1 (Spring/Summer 2003), pp. 1–13.

Paul, Harry W., 'Science and the Catholic Institutes in Nineteenth-Century France', *Societas – a Review of Social History*, vol. 1, no. 4 (1971), pp. 271–285.

Paul, Harry W., *The Edge of Contingency: French Catholic Reaction to Scientific Change from Darwin to Duhem* (Gainesville: University Presses of Florida, 1979).

Paul-Dubois, L., *Contemporary Ireland* (Dublin: Maunsel, 1911).

Peillon, Michael, and Eamonn Slater (eds), *Encounters with Modern Ireland: A Sociological Chronicle, 1995–1996* (Dublin: Institute of Public Administration, 1998).

Penet, Jean-Christophe, 'Closer to Brussels Than to Rome? The EU as the New External Referent for a Secularised Irish Society and a Redefined Catholic Identity', *Études Irlandaises*, vol. 34, no. 1 (2009), pp. 53–66.

Philbin, William J., 'New Directions for the Maynooth Union', *The Irish Theological Quarterly*, vol. 22, no. 4 (October 1955), pp. 281–292.

Pierse, Garrett, 'The Apostacy of "Science"', *The Catholic Bulletin*, vol. 2 (February 1912), pp. 55–58.

Pierse, Garrett, 'Evolution and Creation: A New Argument for the Latter', *The Irish Theological Quarterly*, vol. 15 (July 1920), pp. 227–238.

Pierse, Garrett, 'The Ideal as Furnishing a Proof for the Existence of God', *The Irish Theological Quarterly*, vol. 16 (1921), pp. 156–166.

Plunkett, Horace, *Ireland in the New Century: With an Epilogue in Answer to Some Critics*, 3rd ed. (New York: E.P. Dutton & Co., 1908).

Pollak, Andy, '78% of Catholics follow own consciences in making moral decisions, survey shows', *The Irish Times* (16 December 1996), p. 1.

Pollak, Andy, 'Poll shows church's moral authority in decline', *The Irish Times* (16 December 1996), p. 5.

Porter, George, 'What Science Is For', *New Scientist*, vol. 112, no. 1535 (20 November 1986), pp. 32–34.

Porter, Neil, 'Galileo and the Inquisition', *Doctrine and Life*, vol. 43, no. 6 (July–August 1993), pp. 349–357.

Poupard, Paul, 'Creation, Culture and Faith', *The Furrow*, vol. 46, no. 5 (May 1995), pp. 271–281.

Power, Leonora, 'Catholics Who Gave Their Names to Science', *The Irish Monthly*, vol. 75 (April 1947), pp. 168–173.

Praeger, Robert Lloyd, *The Way That I Went* (Cork: The Collins Press, 1997).

Privilege, John, *Michael Logue and the Catholic Church in Ireland, 1879–1925* (Manchester: Manchester University Press, 2009).

Pyenson, Lewis, and Susan Sheets-Pyenson, *Servants of Nature: A History of Scientific Institutions, Enterprises and Sensibilities* (London: Fontana Press, 1999).

Quigley, Michael, 'Review Article: Natural History and Irish History', *Irish Historical Studies*, vol. 31, no. 121 (May 1998), pp. 115–123.

Rahilly, Alfred J., 'The Meaning of Evolution', *Studies*, vol. 1 (March 1912), pp. 32–51.

Rahilly, Alfred J., 'The Scientific Standpoint', *Studies*, vol. 2 (June 1913), pp. 52–62.

Regan, David, 'Is Irish Catholicism Dying?' *Doctrine and Life*, vol. 34, no. 8 (October 1984), pp. 472–474.

Regan, David, 'Ireland, a Church in Need of Conversion', parts 1 and 2, *Doctrine and Life*, vol. 34, no. 13 and no. 14 (April and May–June 1985), pp. 201–209, 265–270.

Reilly, Conor, 'Adam and Primitive Man', *The Irish Theological Quarterly*, vol. 26 (1959), pp. 331–345.

Reilly, Joseph, 'Essential Oils and Medicinal Herbs: Suggested Industries for Ireland', *Studies*, vol. 22 (September 1933), pp. 373–388.

Reston, James, *Galileo: A Life* (London: Cassell, 1994).

Reville, William, 'Trying to reconcile Darwin and doctrine', *The Irish Times* (18 March 1996), p. 2.

Reville, William, 'Faith in God can co-exist with theory of evolution', *The Irish Times* (13 October 1997).

Reville, William, 'Is Science Replacing Religion?' http://understandingscience. ucc.ie/naturalworld/science_replacing_religion.pdf (accessed on 9 November 2011); article first published in *The Irish Times* (7 December 1998).

Reville, William, 'Is religion the people's opium?' *The Irish Times* (7 November 2002), p. 10.

Reville, William, 'God knows, Richard Dawkins is wrong', *The Irish Times* (13 March 2003), p. 15.

Reville, William, 'A little knowledge leads away from God, much . . . leads towards Him', *The Irish Times* (3 March 2005), p. 15.

Reville, William, 'Conflict between science and religion over our origins not necessary', *The Irish Times* (11 August 2005), p. 13.

Reville, William, 'Looking for signs of the hand of God in Intelligent Design', *The Irish Times* (22 September 2005), p. 13.

Reville, William, 'Prof Dawkins should target PC rather than religion', *The Irish Times* (4 January 2007), p. 13.

Richardson, W. Mark and Wesley J. Wildman (eds), *Religion and Science: History, Method, Dialogue* (New York: Routledge, 1996).

Rickaby, J., 'Faith versus Freethinking', *The Irish Theological Quarterly*, vol. 16 (1921), pp. 20–33.

Root, John D., 'English Catholic Modernism and Science: The Case of George Tyrrell', *Heythrop Journal*, vol. 18 (July 1977), pp. 271–288.

Root, John D., 'The Final Apostasy of St. George Jackson Mivart', *The Catholic Historical Review*, vol. 71, no. 1 (January 1995), pp. 1–25.

Russell, Bertrand, 'What I Believe: The Faith of a Rationalist', *The Listener* (29 May 1947), pp. 826, 836.

Russell, Bertrand, *The Scientific Outlook*, 2nd ed. (London: George Allen & Unwin, 1949).

Russell, Robert John, William R. Stoeger and Francisco J. Ayala (eds), *Evolutionary and Molecular Biology: Scientific Perspectives on Divine Action* (Vatican City State: Vatican Observatory Publications; Berkeley, California: Center for Theology and the Natural Sciences, 1998).

Ryan, Conor, 'The struggle to win back the faithful's hearts and minds', *Irish Examiner* (20 March 2008), 'Religion and Ireland' supplement, p. 2.

Ryan, Wilfrid, 'The Charter of Science', *The Irish Ecclesiastical Record*, 5th series, vol. 1 (1913), pp. 251–263.

Ryan, W.P., *The Pope's Green Island* (London: James Nisbet & Co., 1912).

Sasse, Hermann, 'Rome and the Inspiration of Scripture', *The Reformed Theological Review*, vol. 22, no. 2 (June 1963), pp. 33–45.

Schoenl, William J., *The Intellectual Crisis in English Catholicism: Liberal*

Catholics, Modernists, and the Vatican in the Late Nineteenth and Early Twentieth Centuries (New York: Garland Publishing, 1982).

Schoof, Mark, *A Survey of Catholic Theology, 1800–1970* (Paramus, New Jersey: Paulist Newman Press, 1970).

Schrödinger, Erwin, *What is Life?: With Mind and Matter and Autobiographical Sketches*, Canto ed. (Cambridge: Cambridge University Press, 1992).

Scotti, Paschal, 'Wilfrid Ward: A Religious Fabius Maximus', *The Catholic Historical Review*, vol. 88, no. 1 (January 2002), pp. 42–64.

Scully, John J., 'Comments on Foregoing Article: (1) Education for Agriculture', *Studies*, vol. 57 (Autumn 1968), pp. 252–260.

Segre, Michael, 'Critiques and Contentions: Light on the Galileo Case?' *Isis*, vol. 88 (1997), pp. 484–504.

Selley, E.A., 'Is Our Earth Alone Inhabited?' *The Irish Ecclesiastical Record*, 4th series, vol. 12 (1902), pp. 416–441.

Selley, E.A., 'The Nebular Theory and Divine Revelation', parts 1 and 2, *The Irish Ecclesiastical Record*, 4th series, vol. 13 (1903), pp. 335–349, 418–429.

Sexton, P., 'Science and Religion', *The Capuchin Annual* (1933), pp. 189–198.

Sharratt, Michael, *Galileo: Decisive Innovator* (Cambridge: Cambridge University Press, 1996).

Shearer, Andy, 'What's Cultural about Science & Technology?' *Technology Ireland* (March 1991), p. 17.

Sheehan, Canon, *Early Essays and Lectures* (London: Longmans, Green & Co., 1917).

Sheehan, P.A., *Literary Life, Essays, Poems* (Dublin: The Phoenix Publishing Company, n.d.).

Shine, John, 'The Place of Modernism as a Philosophy of Religion', *The Irish Theological Quarterly*, vol. 3 (January 1908), pp. 22–31.

Sigerson, George, 'Genesis and Evolution I', *The New Ireland Review*, vol. 1, no. 1 (March 1894), pp. 18–26.

Sigerson, George, 'Genesis and Evolution II', *The New Ireland Review*, vol. 1, no. 2 (April 1894), pp. 87–95.

Simonsson, Tord, *Logical and Semantic Structures in Christian Discourses* (Oslo: Universitetsforlaget, 1971).

Slater, T., 'Evolution in Doctrine and Progress in Theology', *The Irish Ecclesiastical Record*, 4th series, vol. 14 (1903), pp. 506–519.

Slater, T., 'The Evolution of Religion', *The Irish Ecclesiastical Record*, 5th series, vol. 17 (June 1921), pp. 561–570.

Smart, J.J.C., and J.J. Haldane, *Atheism and Theism*. 2nd ed. (Malden, Massachusetts: Blackwell Publishing, 2003).

Smith, William L., '*Euntes Docete Omnes Gentes*: Emigrant Irish Secular Priests in America', *History Ireland*, vol. 8, no. 3 (Autumn 2000), pp. 39–43.

Smyth, Kevin, review of C.A. Coulson, *Science and Christian Belief*, in *Studies*, vol. 44 (Winter 1955), pp. 483–484.

Spurway, Neil, 'The Erosion of Faith and Its Consequences', *Studies*, vol. 86, no. 344 (Winter 1997), pp. 336–345.

Stark, Rodney, and Roger Finke, *Acts of Faith: Explaining the Human Side of Religion* (Berkeley: University of California Press, 2000).

Stenhouse, John, 'Catholicism, Science, and Modernity: The Case of William Miles Maskell', *The Journal of Religious History*, vol. 22, no. 1 (February 1998), pp. 59–82.

Stourton, Edward, *Absolute Truth: The Catholic Church in the World Today* (London: Viking, 1998).

Stuhlmueller, Carroll, 'Catholic Biblical Scholarship and College Theology', *The Thomist*, vol. 23, no. 4 (October 1960), pp. 533–563.

Swann, Brenda, and Francis Aprahamian (eds), *J.D. Bernal: A Life in Science and Politics* (London: Verso, 1999).

Swinburne, Richard, 'Arguments for the Existence of God', *Milltown Studies*, vol. 33 (Spring 1994), pp. 22–36.

Taylor, Geoffrey, 'Evidence and Evolution', parts 1–5, *The Irish Monthly*, vol. 76 (March–October 1948), pp. 117–123, 157–164, 221–227, 407–413, 464–471.

Taylor, Monica, *Sir Bertram Windle: A Memoir* (London: Longmans, Green & Co., 1932).

Teegan, J.A., 'Thomism and Modern Science', *Studies*, vol. 36 (June 1947), pp. 187–193.

Teegan, James A., 'Science and Reality', *Studies*, vol. 37 (June 1948), pp. 203–211.

Thomson, David, *Europe since Napoleon*, Revised ed. (London: Penguin Books, 1966).

Tobin, Fergal, *The Best of Decades: Ireland in the Nineteen Sixties* (Dublin: Gill & Macmillan, 1984).

Toner, P.J., 'The Encyclical on Modernism', *The Irish Theological Quarterly*, vol. 3 (January 1908), pp. 1–21.

Tracey, Alice, 'Professor John Tyndall', *Carloviana*, vol. 1, no. 3 (January 1949), pp. 127–143.

Trench, Brian, 'Science, Culture and Public Affairs', *The Republic*, no. 3 (July 2003), pp. 53–63.

Trench, Brian, 'Paradoxes of Irish Scientific Culture', *The Irish Review*, no. 43 (Summer 2011), pp. 1–13.

Turner, Frank Miller, *Between Science and Religion: The Reaction to Scientific Naturalism in Late Victorian England* (New Haven: Yale University Press, 1974).

Turner, Frank M., *Contesting Cultural Authority: Essays in Victorian Intellectual Life* (Cambridge: Cambridge University Press, 1993).

Tyndall, John, *Fragments of Science: A Series of Detached Essays, Addresses, and Reviews*, 6th ed. (London: Longmans, Green & Co., 1879), vol. 1.

Tyndall, John, *Fragments of Science: A Series of Detached Essays, Addresses, and Reviews* (New York: D. Appleton & Co., 1896), vol. 2.

Tyndall, John, *Professor Tyndall's Belfast Speech (28th January, 1890) and Correspondence with Mr. Gladstone* (Dublin: The Irish Loyal and Patriotic Union, 1890).

Vaughan, John S., 'Bishop Clifford's Theory of the Days of Creation', *The Dublin Review*, 3rd series, vol. 9 (January 1883), pp. 32–47.

Vaughan, John S., 'Faith and Evolution: A Further Consideration on the Question', *The Irish Ecclesiastical Record*, 3rd series, vol. 6 (1885), pp. 413–424.

Vaughan, John S., 'Faith and Evolution: A Reply', *The Irish Ecclesiastical Record*, 3rd series, vol. 6 (1885), pp. 651–664.

Vaughan, John S., 'Man or Monkey?' *The Irish Ecclesiastical Record*, 3rd series, vol. 10 (1889), pp. 1–11.

Vaughan, J.S. 'Is Our Earth Alone Inhabited? A Friendly Comment upon Rev. E.A. Selley's Essay', *The Irish Ecclesiastical Record*, 4th series, vol. 13 (1903), pp. 132–143.

Vidler, Alec R., *The Modernist Movement in the Roman Church: Its Origins & Outcome* (London: Cambridge University Press, 1934).

Vidler, A.R., *A Century of Social Catholicism, 1820–1920* (London: S.P.C.K., 1964).

Vitoria, Mary A., 'The Mystery of Life: Evolution Is Not Enough', *Position Paper 301* (January 1999), pp. 30–34.

Vollert, Cyril, '*Humani Generis* and the Limits of Theology', *Theological Studies*, vol. 12 (March 1951), pp. 3–23.

Von Aretin, Karl Otmar, *The Papacy and the Modern World* (London: Weidenfeld & Nicolson, 1970).

Von Arx, Jeffrey Paul, *Progress and Pessimism: Religion, Politics and History in Late-Nineteenth-Century Britain* (Cambridge, Massachusetts: Harvard University Press, 1985).

Vox Clamantis in Deserto, 'Science in Secondary Schools', *The Irish Monthly*, vol. 58, no. 679 (January 1930), pp. 23–27.

Walsh, Pius, 'Waves and the New Physics', *The Irish Ecclesiastical Record*, 5th series, vol. 69 (September 1947), pp. 798–806.

Walsh, Pius, 'Origins of Quantum Physics', *The Irish Ecclesiastical Record*, 5th series, vol. 70 (September 1948), pp. 610–617.

Walsh, Pius, 'The Meson: Ultimate Bond', *The Irish Ecclesiastical Record*, 5th series, vol. 75 (February 1951), pp. 140–148.

Walsh, Pius, 'Synthesis in Science', *The Irish Ecclesiastical Record*, 5th series, vol. 77 (April 1952), pp. 274–281.

Walshe, T.J., 'Botanical Evolution in Theory and in Fact', *The Irish Theological Quarterly*, vol. 4 (January 1909), pp. 81–91.

Ward, Wilfrid, *Problems and Persons* (London: Longmans, Green & Co., 1903).

Waters, John, *An Intelligent Person's Guide to Modern Ireland* (London: Duckworth, 1998).

Weigel, Gustave, 'Current Theology: Gleanings from the Commentaries on *Humani Generis*', *Theological Studies*, vol. 12 (1951), pp. 520–549.

Weigel, George, *Witness to Hope: The Biography of John Paul II* (New York: Cliff Street Books, 2001).

Weinberg, Steven, *The First Three Minutes: A Modern View of the Origin of the Universe* (London: Andre Deutsch, 1977).

Wells, H.G., *The Fate of Homo Sapiens: An Unemotional Statement of the Things That Are Happening to Him Now, and of the Immediate Possibilities Confronting Him* (London: Secker & Warburg, 1939).

Wells, H.G., Julian Huxley and G.P. Wells, *Evolution – Fact and Theory* (London: Cassell, 1934).

Wheeler, T.S., 'From Atom to Atomic Bomb: The Chemist through the Ages', *Studies*, vol. 39 (March 1950), pp. 1–14.

Wheeler, T.S., 'Newman and Science', *Studies*, vol. 42 (Summer 1953), pp. 179–196.

Whelan, Christopher T. (ed.), *Values and Social Change in Ireland* (Dublin: Gill & Macmillan, 1994).

Whyte, J.H., *Church and State in Modern Ireland, 1923–1979*. 2nd ed (Dublin: Gill & Macmillan, 1984).

Whyte, Nicholas, 'Lords of Ether and of Light: The Irish Astronomical Tradition of the Nineteenth Century', *The Irish Review*, nos 17–18 (Winter 1995), pp. 127–141.

Whyte, Nicholas, *Science, Colonialism and Ireland* (Cork: Cork University Press, 1999).

Wibberley, T., 'Agricultural Education', *Studies*, vol. 8 (September 1919), pp. 424–433.

Wibberley, T., 'The Irish Climate and Tillage Farming', *Studies*, vol. 8 (December 1919), pp. 590–597.

Wibberley, T., 'The Irish Climate and Tillage Farming', *Studies*, vol. 9 (June 1920), pp. 281–290.

Williams, W.J., 'The Shannon Scheme and the Teaching of Science: A Plea for Realism in Education', with comments by Edward Leen, John J. Nolan and Hugh Ryan, *Studies*, vol. 15 (June 1926), pp. 177–192.

Windle, Bertram C.A., *What Is Life? A Study of Vitalism and Neo-Vitalism* (London: Sands & Co.; St Louis: B. Herder, 1908).

Windle, Bertram C.A., *A Century of Scientific Thought & Other Essays* (London: Burns & Oates, 1915).

Windle, Bertram C.A., *The Church and Science* (London: Catholic Truth Society, 1920).

Windle, Bertram C.A., *The Evolutionary Problem As It Is Today* (New York: Joseph F. Wagner; London: B. Herder, 1927).

Windle, Bertram C.A., *The Catholic Church and Its Reactions with Science* (London: Burns, Oates & Washbourne, 1927).

Withers, Charles, Rebekah Higgitt and Diarmid Finnegan, 'Historical Geographies of Provincial Science: Themes in the Setting and Reception of the British Association for the Advancement of Science in Britain and Ireland, 1831– c. 1939', *The British Journal for the History of Science*, vol. 41, no. 150 (September 2008), pp. 385–415.

Woodlock, Barth., 'University Education in Ireland', *The Irish Ecclesiastical Record*, vol. 4 (1868), pp. 432–447.

Yarce, Jorge, 'Television and Family Life', *Position Paper 170* (January 1988), pp. 58–65.

Yearley, Steven, 'Colonial Science and Dependent Development: The Case of the Irish Experience', *Sociological Review*, vol. 37 (1989), pp. 308–331.

Yorke, Peter C., 'Concerning Certain Aspects of Clerical Education', *Record of the Maynooth Union* (1898–1899), pp. 47–58.

Young, David, *The Discovery of Evolution* (Cambridge: Cambridge University Press, 1992).

Young, Filson, *Ireland at the Cross Roads: An Essay in Explanation* (London: Grant Richards, 1903).

Young, John, 'Original Sin – a Controverted Teaching', *Position Papers 320/321* (August–September 2000), pp. 245–252.

Zahm, John Augustine, *Evolution and Dogma*, introduction by Thomas J. Schlereth (Chicago: D.H. McBride, 1896; republished, New York: Arno Press, 1978).

Index